TOKYO GHOUL

SUI ISHIDA

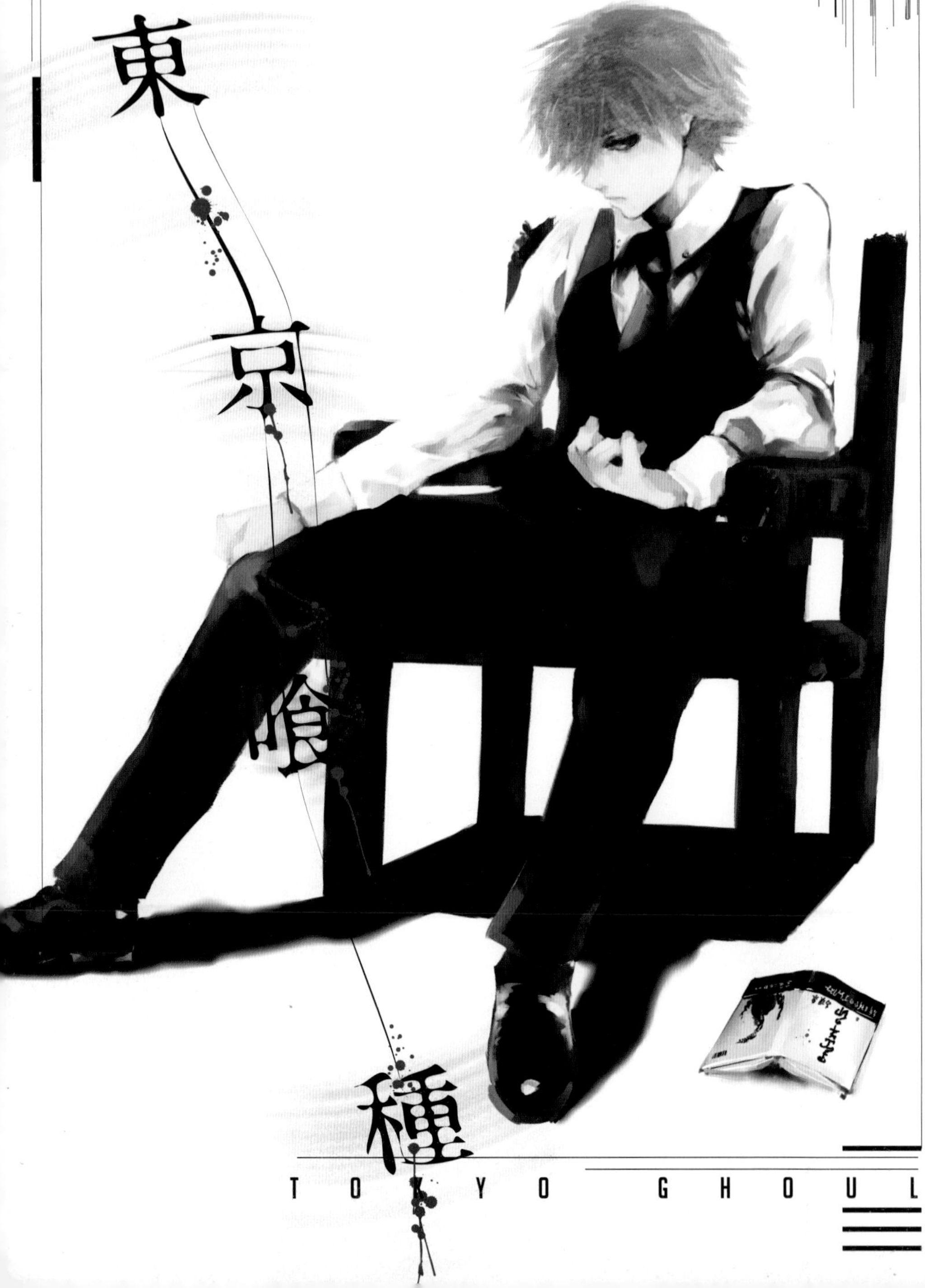
TOKYO GHOUL
東京喰種
T O K Y O G H O U L

YAMORI/ YAKUMO OMORI

ヤモリ／大守八雲 （ヤ ク モ　オ オ モ リ）

BORN March 15th Pisces

From the 13th Ward An Executive Member of the Aogiri Tree

BLOOD-TYPE: B

Size: 186 cm 101 kg FEET 28.9 CM

Likes: Torture, screams, expressions of agony
Hobbies: Collecting torture instruments, finding durable victims
Rc Type: Rinkaku
Unique States: Kakuja (incomplete)

NICO

ニ コ

BORN November 2nd Scorpio

Queer in Love

BLOOD-TYPE: A

Size: 175 cm 52 kg FEET 25.5 cm

Likes: Handsome men, beautiful things, fun things, accessories
Hobbies: Being a better woman, finding handsome men, fashion, singing
Hot: Yamori (top pick), Ayato, Tatara, etc...
Rc Type: ?

SUI ISHIDA was born in Fukuoka, Japan. He is the author of *Tokyo Ghoul* and several *Tokyo Ghoul* one-shots, including one that won him second place in the *Weekly Young Jump* 113th Grand Prix award in 2010. *Tokyo Ghoul* began serialization in *Weekly Young Jump* in 2011 and was adapted into an anime series in 2014.

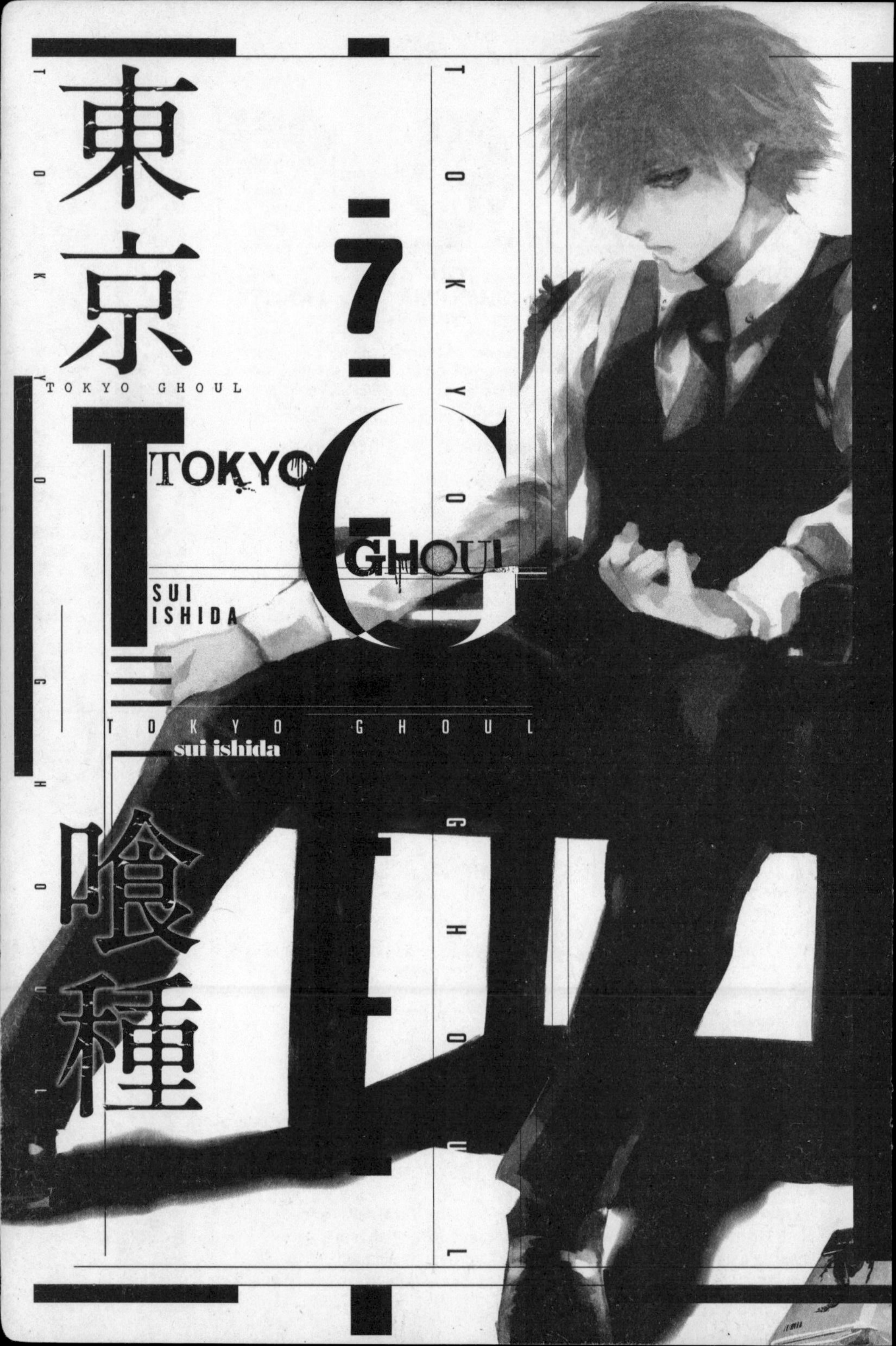
東京喰種
TOKYO GHOUL
7
TOKYO GHOUL
SUI ISHIDA
TOKYO GHOUL
sui ishida

TOKYO GHOUL SO FAR

VS

ANTEIKU

The café where Ghouls gather. Known for their slow-brewed coffee. Has many human fans as well. Helping each other is the Ghouls' motto.

20TH WARD

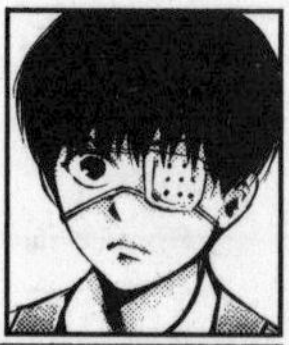

KEN KANEKI (KANEKI)

An ordinary young man with a fondness for literature who meets with an accident, has Rize's organs transplanted and becomes a half-Ghoul. Struggling to find his place in the world. Abducted by the Aogiri Tree and currently held captive in the 11th Ward.

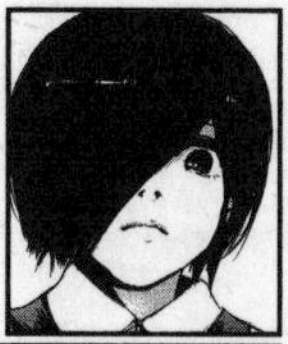

TOUKA KIRISHIMA (TOUKA)

A conflicted heroine with two sides, rage and kindness. Longs to become human. Seems to hate investigators…?

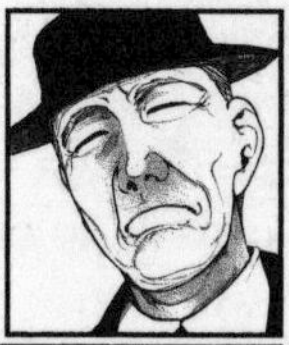

YOSHIMURA (MANAGER)

The owner of Anteiku. Guides Kaneki so he can live as a Ghoul. Often works with Yomo. Shrouded by mystery.

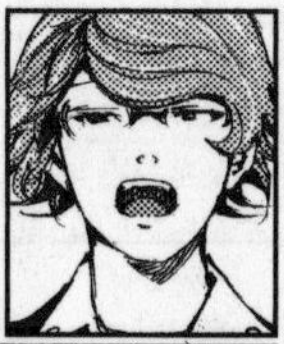

NISHIKI NISHIO (NISHIKI)

A 2nd year at Kaneki's university. Adept at blending into human society. Eats *taiyaki* with no difficulty.

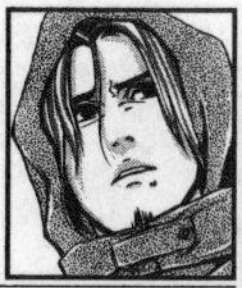

RENJI YOMO (YOMO)

Does not appear out in the open that often. Frequently works with Yoshimura. Concerned about Kaneki's condition.

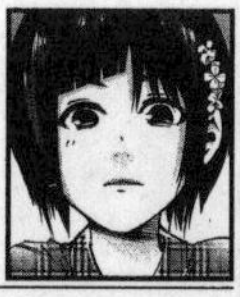

HINAMI FUEGUCHI (HINAMI)

An orphan whose parents were killed by the CCG. Displays tremendous power when she is awakened. Living with Touka.

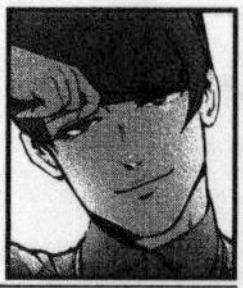

SHU TSUKIYAMA

A Gourmet who seeks the taste of the unknown. Obsessed with Kaneki, who is a half-Ghoul.

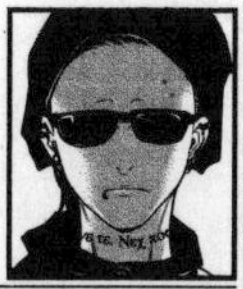

UTA

Owner of HySy Artmask Studio, a mask shop in the 4th Ward. Has a troubled history with Yomo.

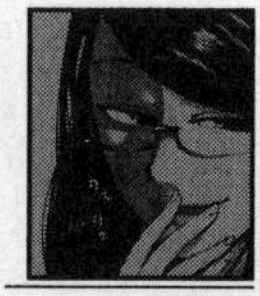

RIZE KAMISHIRO DECEASED (RIZE)

Freewheeling Binge Eater who despises boredom. Previously lived in the 11th Ward. Meets Kaneki in the 20th Ward and is caught in an accident. There are rumors she used an alias to hide her true identity.

[GHOUL]

A creature that appears human yet consumes humans. The top of the food chain. Finds anything other than humans and coffee unpleasant. Releases a highly lethal weapon unique to Ghouls known as Kagune to prey on humans. Can be cannibalistic. Only sustains damages from Kagune or Quinques that are made from Kagune.

AOGIRI TREE
11TH WARD

A group of Ghouls with the ambition of ruling Ghouls and humans with force. Appoints a Ghoul called the One-Eyed King as their leader, but much is still unknown.

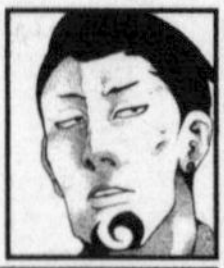

KAZUICHI BANJO

Former leader of the 11th Ward who admires Rize. Plans an escape with Kaneki after having doubts about the Aogiri Tree.

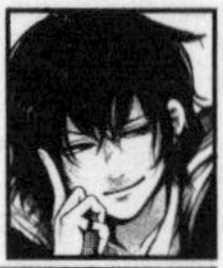

AYATO KIRISHIMA

Touka's younger brother. Even more hot-blooded than his sister. Recruited by Aogiri because of it. Has disdain for his sister and the 20th Ward.

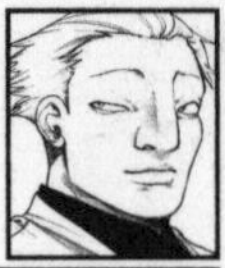

YAMORI

Possesses unrivaled combat skills. Feared as the 13th Ward's "Jason" for his brutal nature.

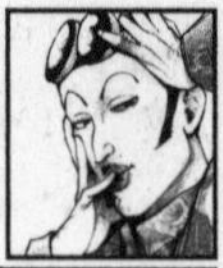

NICO

Yamori's partner. Has a keen sense of smell.

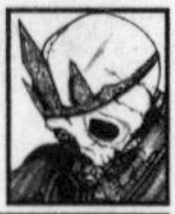

ONE-EYED KING

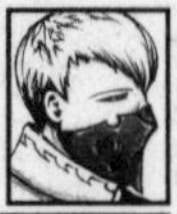

TATARA

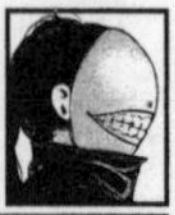

NORO

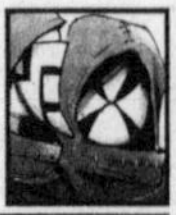

BIN BROTHERS

人 HUMANS 間

CCG
GHOUL INVESTIGATORS

11TH WARD SPECIAL TASK FORCE

A government agency founded by Tsuneyoshi Washu. Develops Ghoul extermination specialists at the Academy to maintain peace in the wards. Its principal functions are the development and improvement of Quinques.

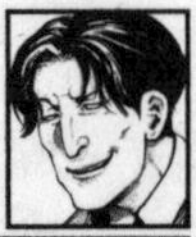

ITSUKI MARUDE
(SPECIAL INVESTIGATOR)

Commands the 11th Ward Special Task Force. Not very fond of Amon.

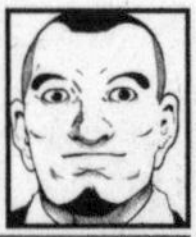

YUKINORI SHINOHARA
(SPECIAL INVESTIGATOR)

Ex-Academy instructor. A onetime colleague of Mado and Amon's drill instructor. Appears easygoing, but…

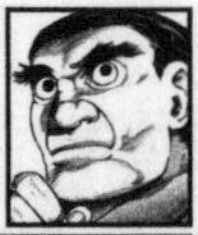

IWAO KUROIWA
(SPECIAL INVESTIGATOR)

Lieutenant Commander of the 11th Ward Special Task Force. His rough-hewn looks match his rock-solid-sounding name. Called Iwaccho by Shinohara.

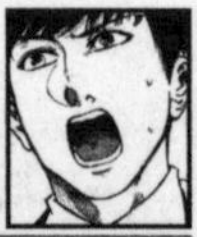

KOTARO AMON
(RANK 1 INVESTIGATOR)

An Investigator with a very strong sense of justice. Determined to eradicate Ghouls. Dedicated to avenging Mado's loss through his ongoing battle with Kaneki.

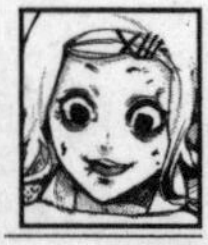

JUZO SUZUYA
(RANK 3 INVESTIGATOR)

An eccentric who joined the CCG as under special dispensation. Enjoys killing and longs for exceptionally lethal Quinques.

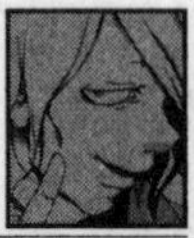

KUREO MADO
DECEASED

An investigator with an unusual obsession with Quinques. Loathed the Ghouls who killed his family. Eventually lost his life.

Summary

When he's turned into a Ghoul by fellow student Rize, Ken Kaneki struggles on a very personal level with the existence of creatures that take human lives to survive. Now, news has reached Kaneki that numerous Ghoul investigators are being dispatched to designated wards, their intentions unknown. (And in the midst of it, an old enemy with a new face resurfaces.) Kaneki is forcibly abducted by a group of Ghouls calling themselves the Aogiri Tree. He plans an escape with Banjo and other anti-Aogiri Ghouls, but it ends in failure and Kaneki is eventually captured by Yamori.

東京喰

TOKYO GHOUL

TOKYO GHOUL

TOKYO GHOUL

SUI ISHIDA

CONTENTS

7

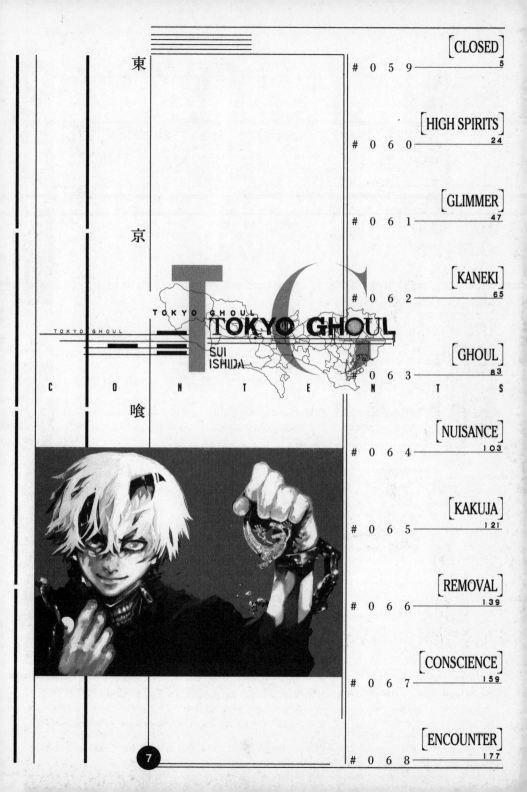

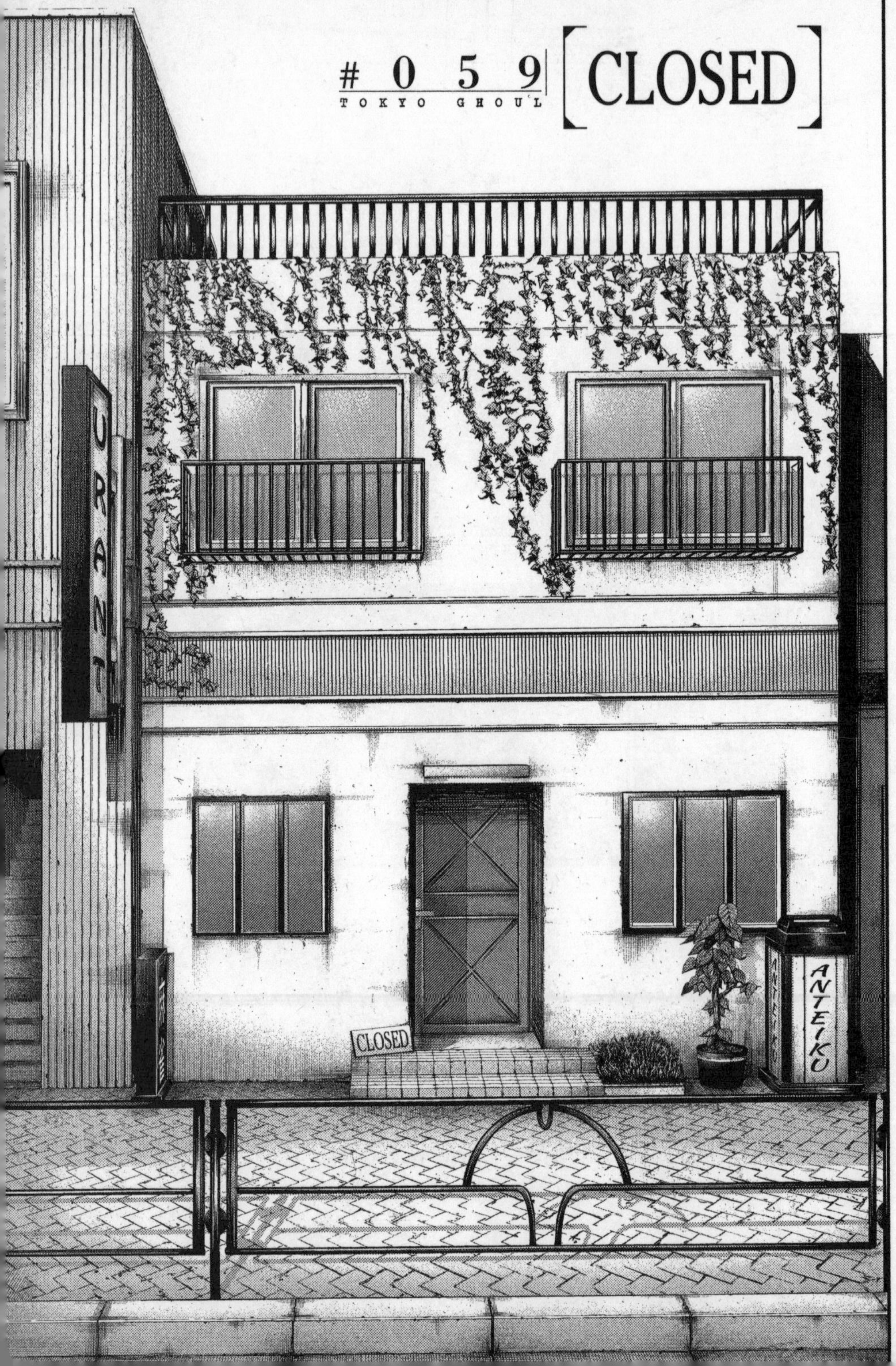
#059
TOKYO GHOUL
[CLOSED]
URANT
CLOSED
ANTEIKU

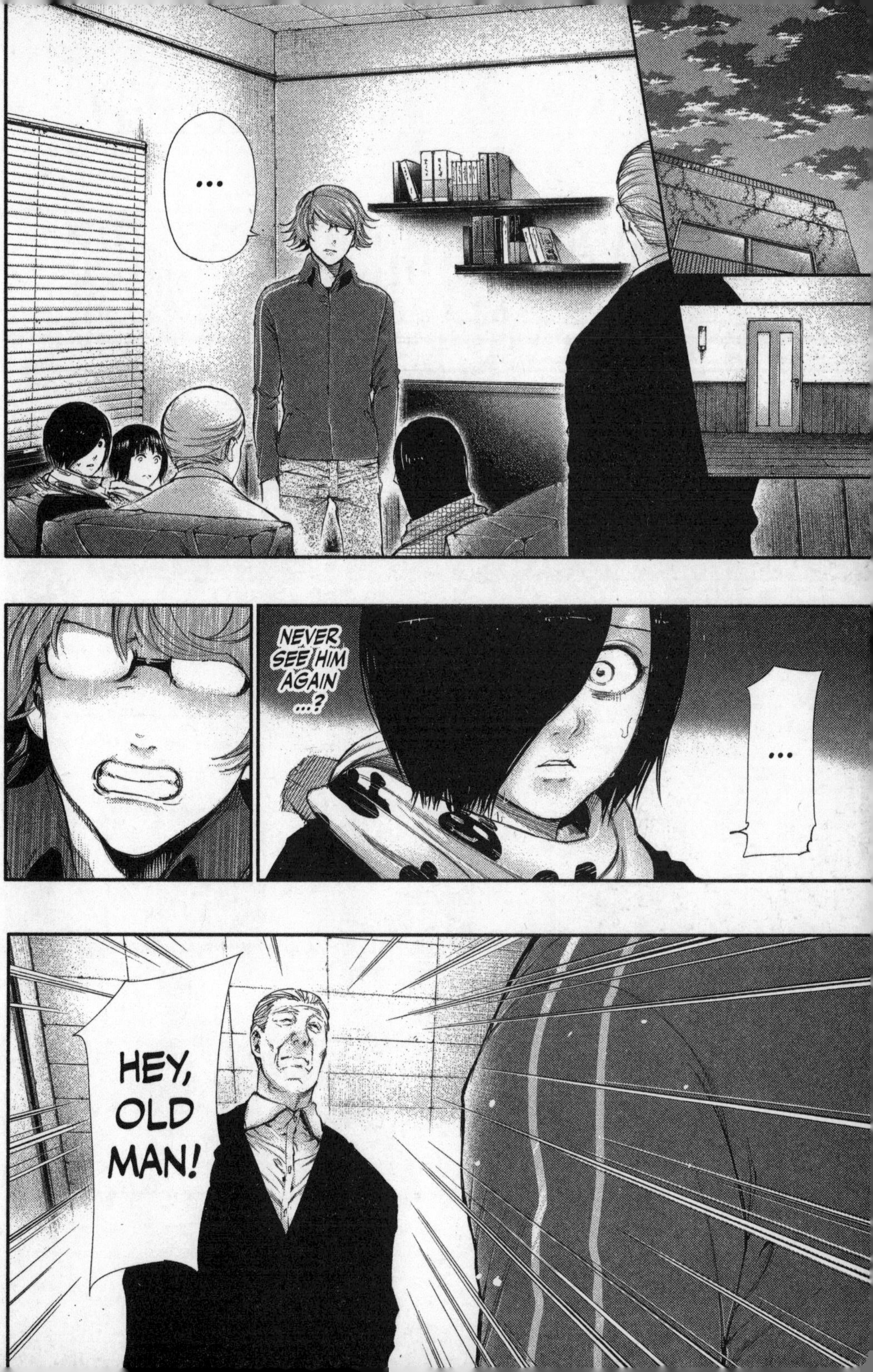
...
...
NEVER SEE HIM AGAIN ...?
HEY, OLD MAN!

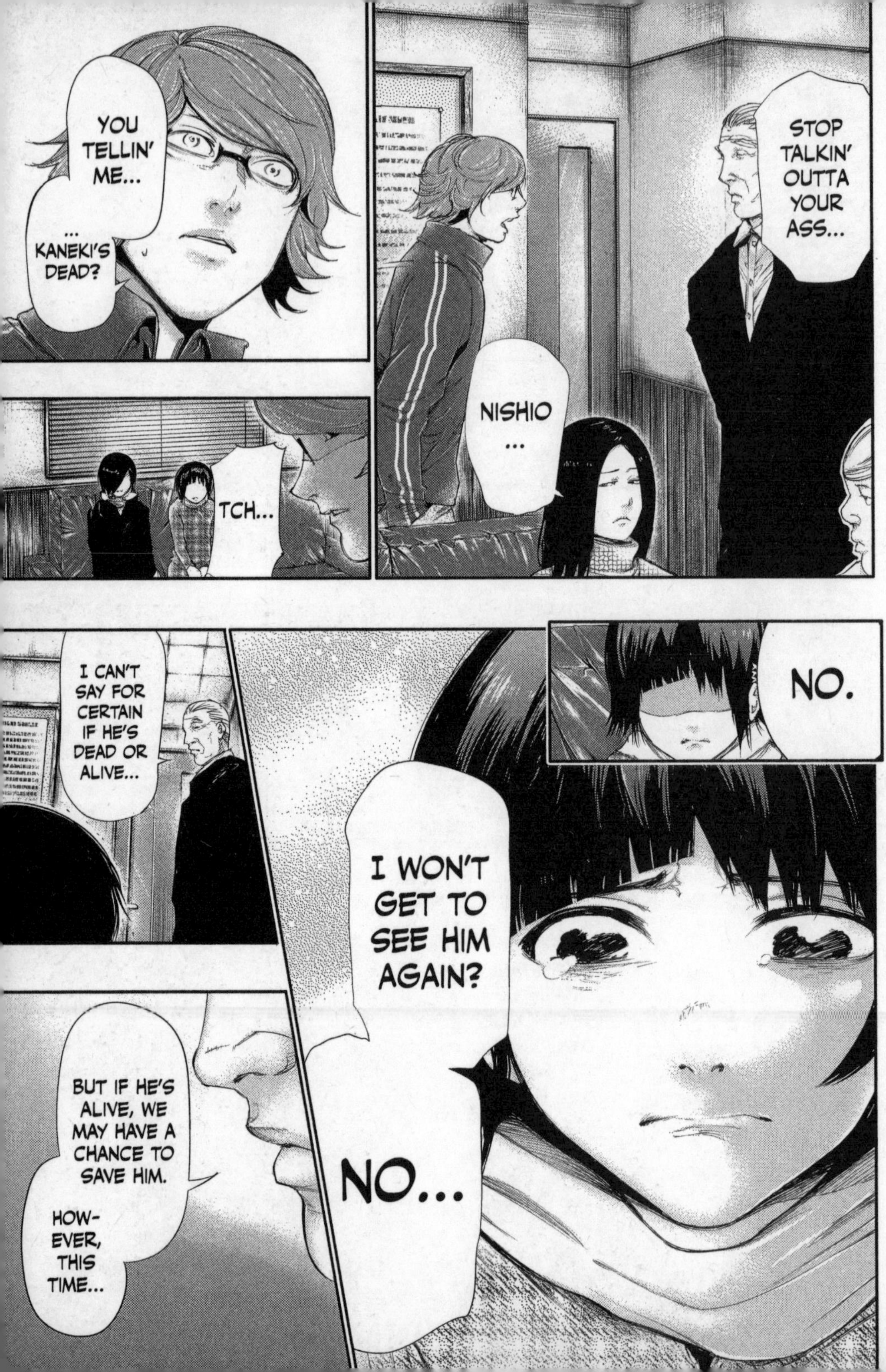
STOP TALKIN' OUTTA YOUR ASS...
NISHIO ...
YOU TELLIN' ME...
... KANEKI'S DEAD?
TCH...
NO.
I WON'T GET TO SEE HIM AGAIN?
NO...
I CAN'T SAY FOR CERTAIN IF HE'S DEAD OR ALIVE...
BUT IF HE'S ALIVE, WE MAY HAVE A CHANCE TO SAVE HIM.
HOW-EVER, THIS TIME...

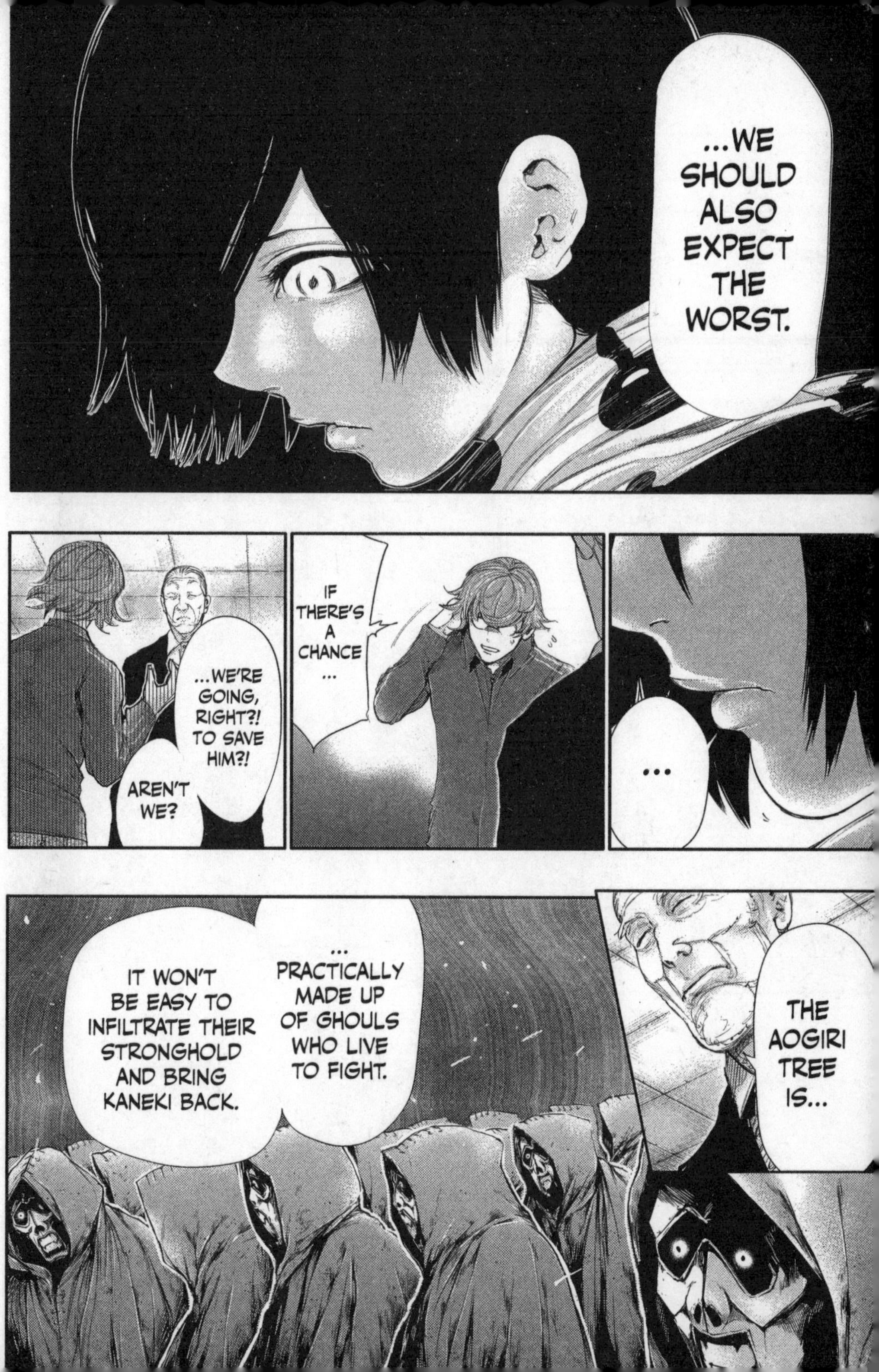
...WE SHOULD ALSO EXPECT THE WORST.
...
IF THERE'S A CHANCE...
...WE'RE GOING, RIGHT?! TO SAVE HIM?!
AREN'T WE?
THE AOGIRI TREE IS...
...PRACTICALLY MADE UP OF GHOULS WHO LIVE TO FIGHT.
IT WON'T BE EASY TO INFILTRATE THEIR STRONGHOLD AND BRING KANEKI BACK.

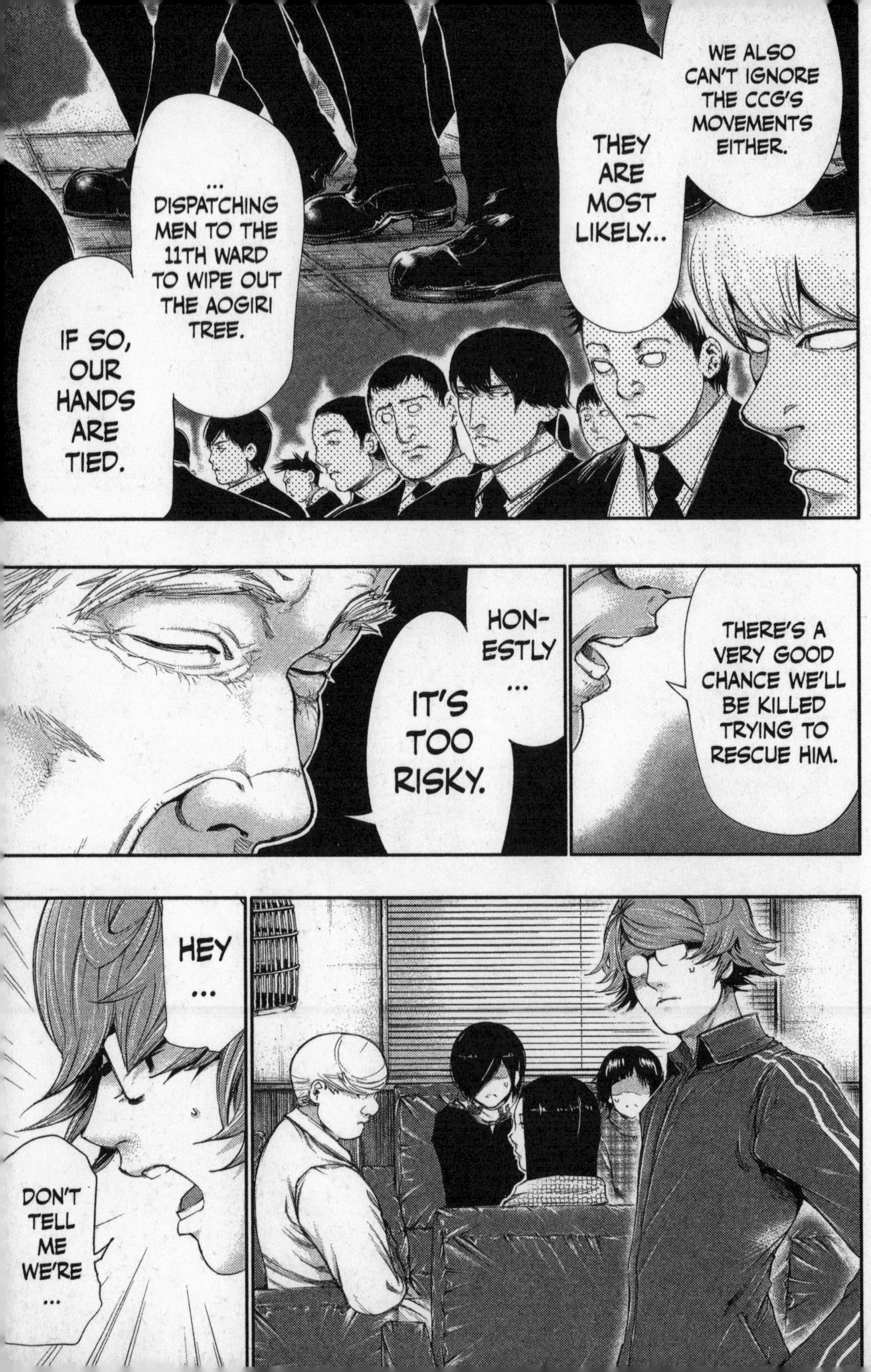
WE ALSO CAN'T IGNORE THE CCG'S MOVEMENTS EITHER.
THEY ARE MOST LIKELY...
... DISPATCHING MEN TO THE 11TH WARD TO WIPE OUT THE AOGIRI TREE.
IF SO, OUR HANDS ARE TIED.
THERE'S A VERY GOOD CHANCE WE'LL BE KILLED TRYING TO RESCUE HIM.
HON-ESTLY ...
IT'S TOO RISKY.
HEY ...
DON'T TELL ME WE'RE ...

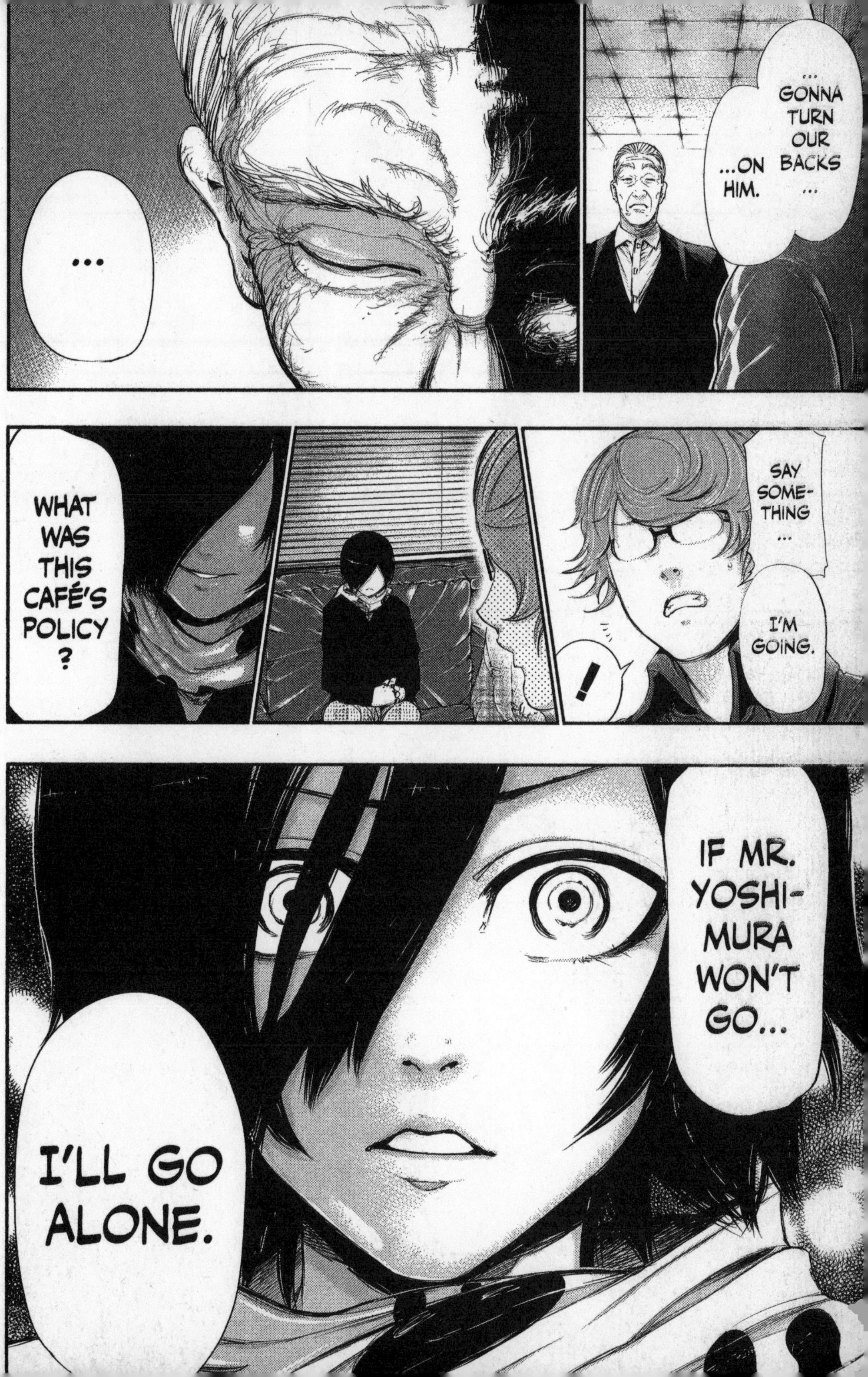
...GONNA TURN OUR BACKS...
...ON HIM.
...
SAY SOME-THING...
I'M GOING.
!
WHAT WAS THIS CAFÉ'S POLICY?
IF MR. YOSHI-MURA WON'T GO...
I'LL GO ALONE.

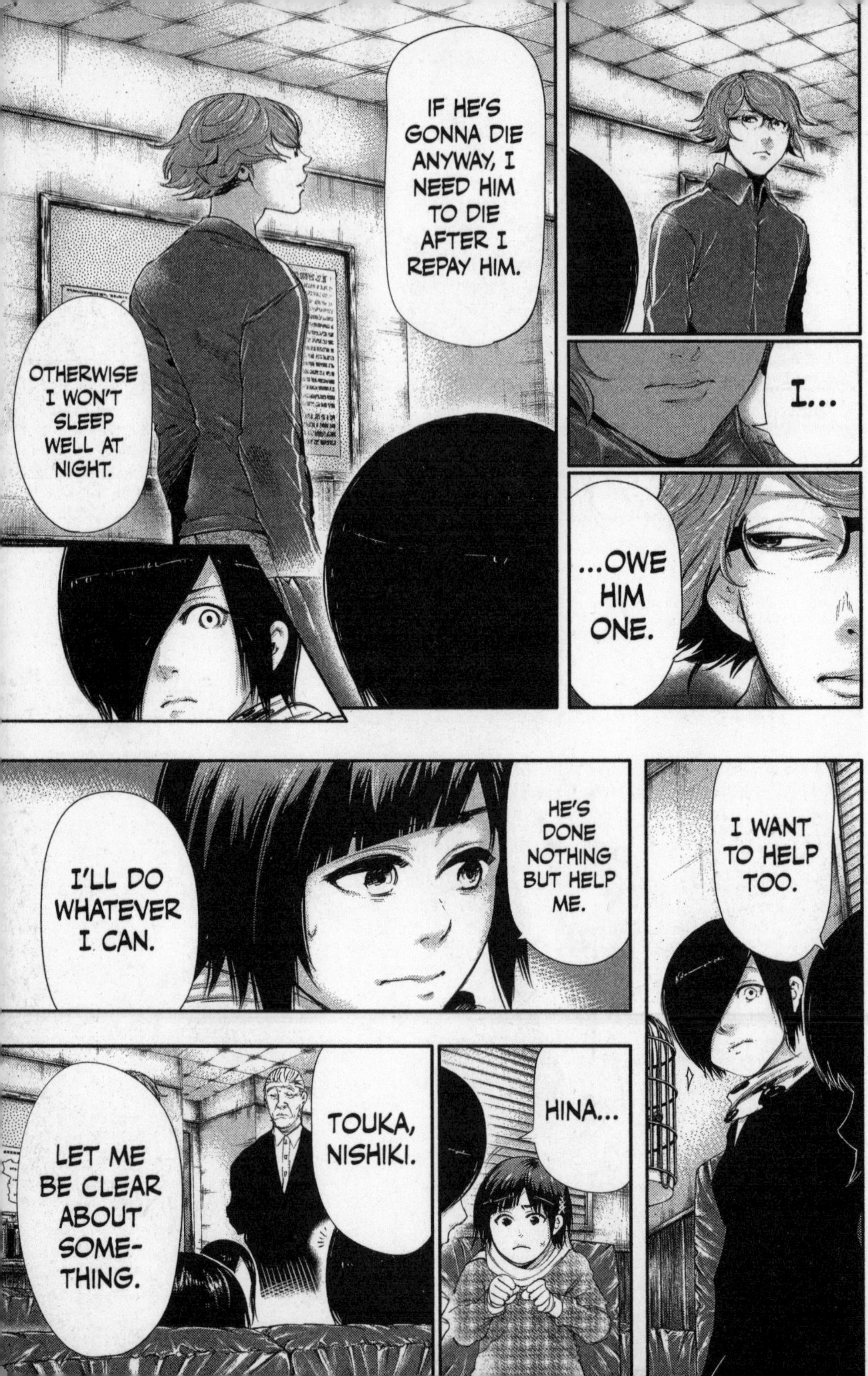
I...
...OWE HIM ONE.
IF HE'S GONNA DIE ANYWAY, I NEED HIM TO DIE AFTER I REPAY HIM.
OTHERWISE I WON'T SLEEP WELL AT NIGHT.
I WANT TO HELP TOO.
HE'S DONE NOTHING BUT HELP ME.
I'LL DO WHATEVER I CAN.
HINA...
TOUKA, NISHIKI.
LET ME BE CLEAR ABOUT SOMETHING.

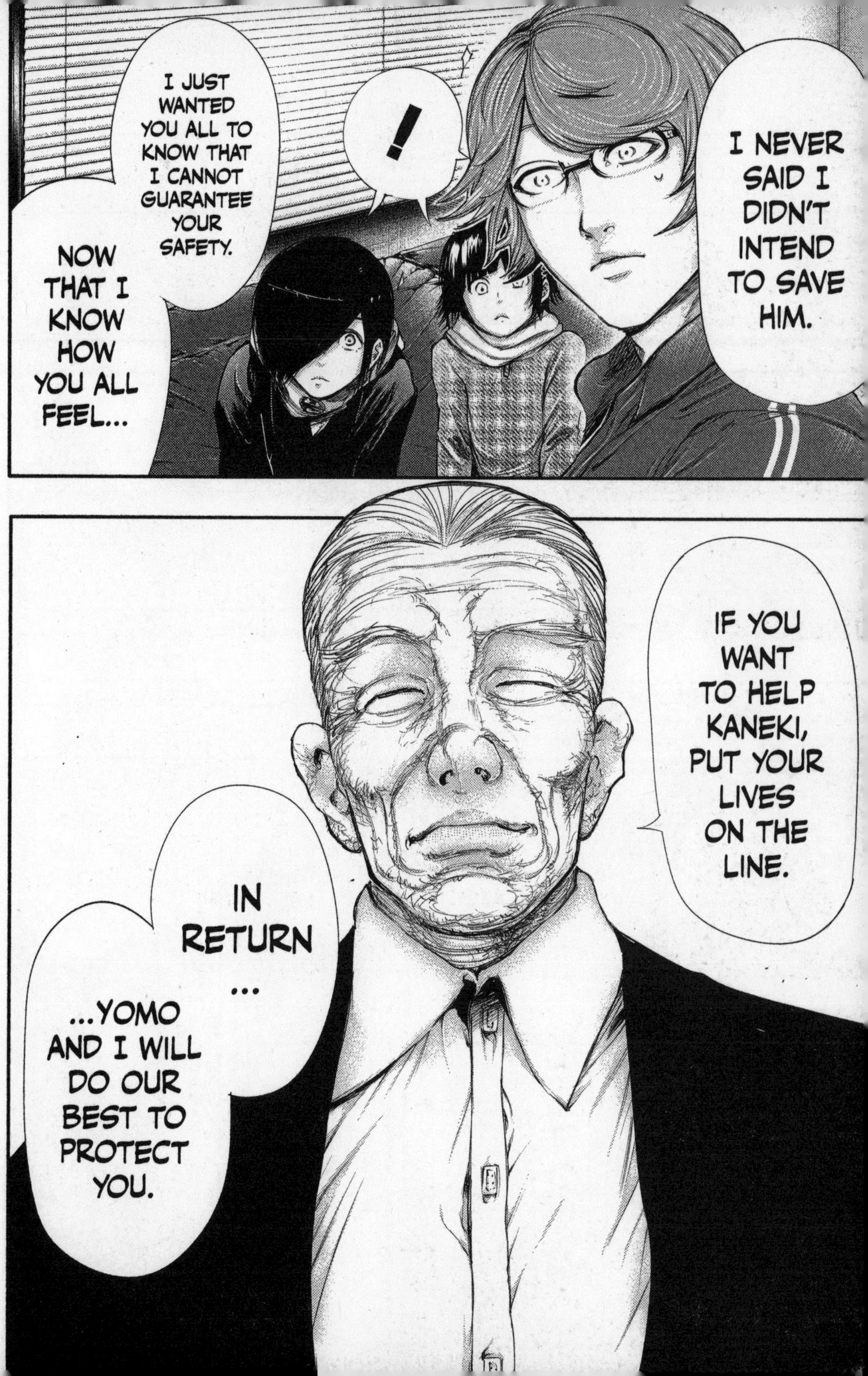
I NEVER SAID I DIDN'T INTEND TO SAVE HIM.
!
I JUST WANTED YOU ALL TO KNOW THAT I CANNOT GUARANTEE YOUR SAFETY.
NOW THAT I KNOW HOW YOU ALL FEEL...
IF YOU WANT TO HELP KANEKI, PUT YOUR LIVES ON THE LINE.
IN RETURN...
...YOMO AND I WILL DO OUR BEST TO PROTECT YOU.

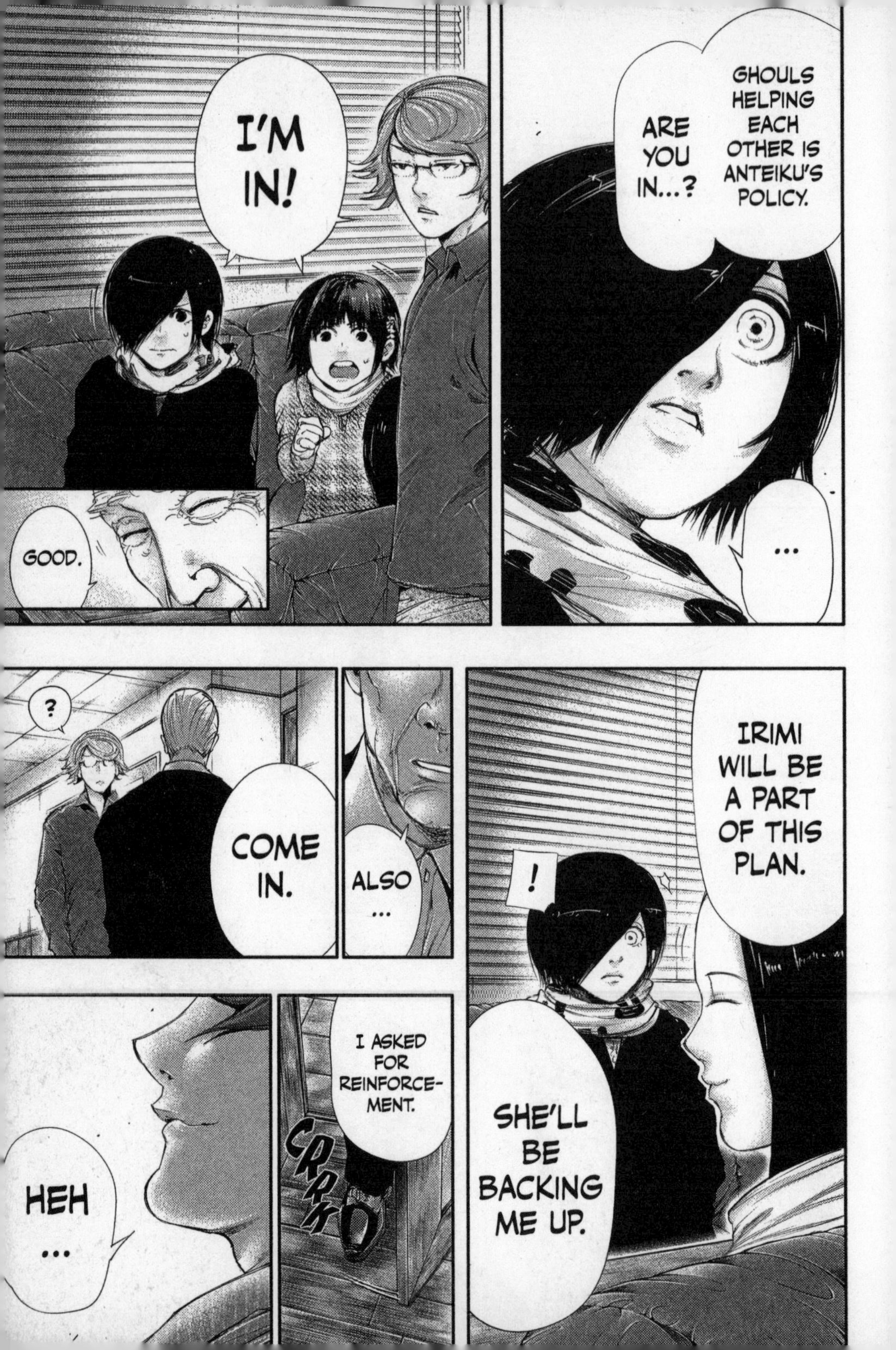
GHOULS HELPING EACH OTHER IS ANTEIKU'S POLICY.
ARE YOU IN...?
...
I'M IN!
GOOD.
IRIMI WILL BE A PART OF THIS PLAN.
!
SHE'LL BE BACKING ME UP.
ALSO ...
COME IN.
?
I ASKED FOR REINFORCE-MENT.
CRRK
HEH ...

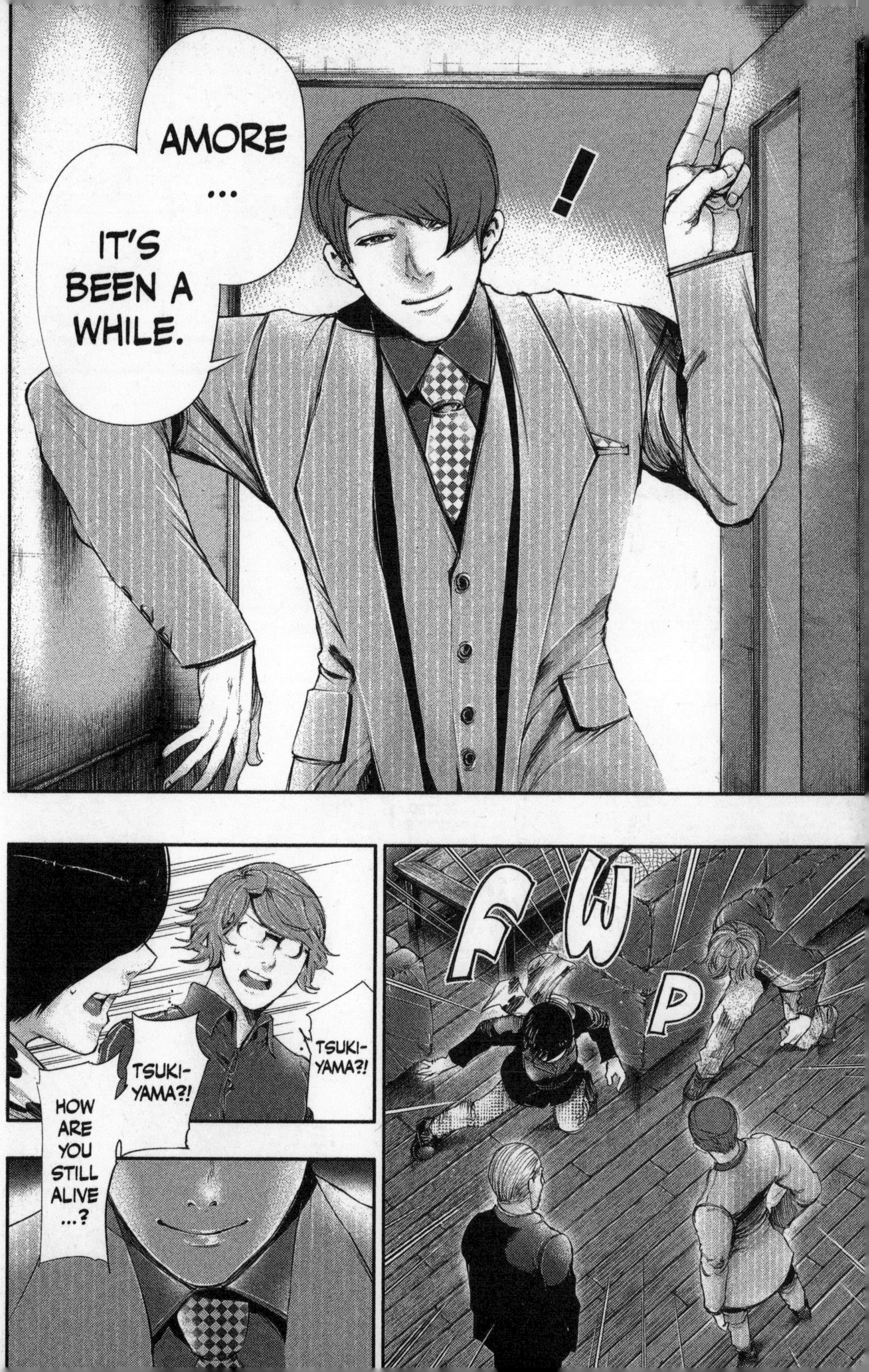
!
AMORE ...
IT'S BEEN A WHILE.
FWP
TSUKI-YAMA?!
TSUKI-YAMA?!
HOW ARE YOU STILL ALIVE ...?

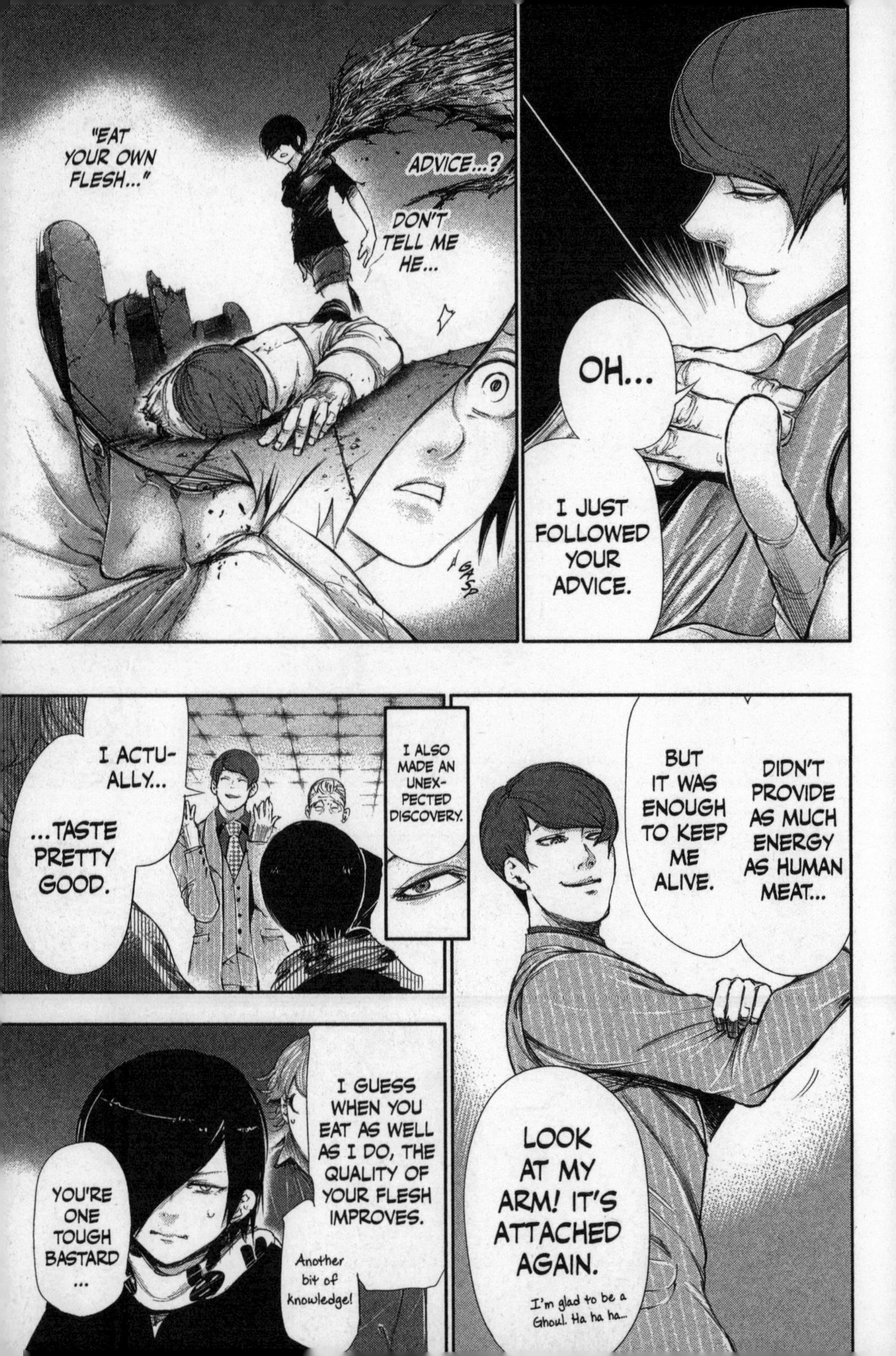
OH...
I JUST FOLLOWED YOUR ADVICE.
ADVICE...?
"EAT YOUR OWN FLESH..."
DON'T TELL ME HE...
GASA
DIDN'T PROVIDE AS MUCH ENERGY AS HUMAN MEAT...
BUT IT WAS ENOUGH TO KEEP ME ALIVE.
LOOK AT MY ARM! IT'S ATTACHED AGAIN.
I'm glad to be a Ghoul. Ha ha ha...
I ALSO MADE AN UNEXPECTED DISCOVERY.
I ACTUALLY...
...TASTE PRETTY GOOD.
I GUESS WHEN YOU EAT AS WELL AS I DO, THE QUALITY OF YOUR FLESH IMPROVES.
Another bit of knowledge!
YOU'RE ONE TOUGH BASTARD...

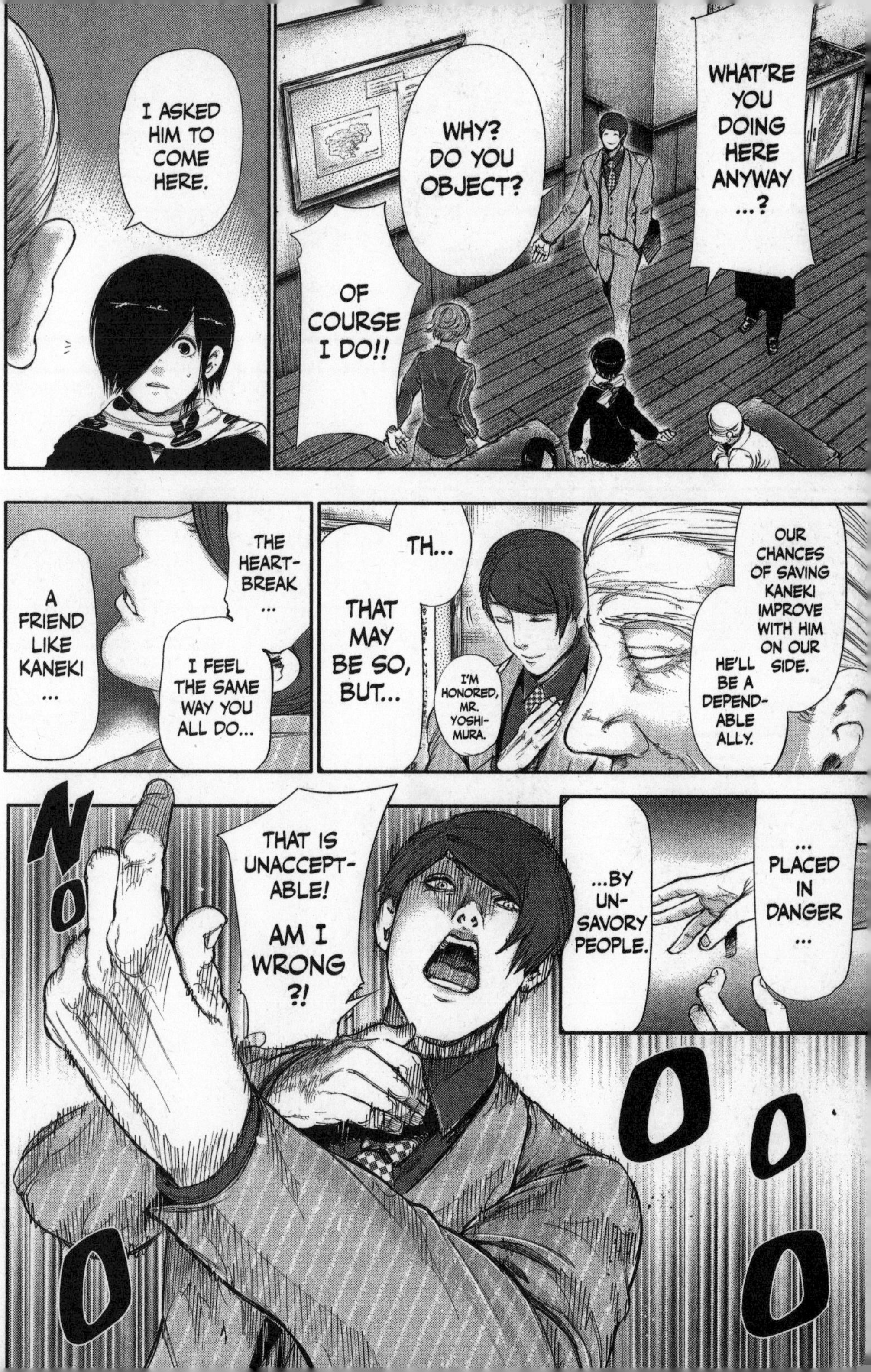
WHAT'RE YOU DOING HERE ANYWAY ...?
WHY? DO YOU OBJECT?
OF COURSE I DO!!
I ASKED HIM TO COME HERE.
OUR CHANCES OF SAVING KANEKI IMPROVE WITH HIM ON OUR SIDE.
HE'LL BE A DEPENDABLE ALLY.
I'M HONORED, MR. YOSHIMURA.
TH...
THAT MAY BE SO, BUT...
THE HEART-BREAK ...
I FEEL THE SAME WAY YOU ALL DO...
A FRIEND LIKE KANEKI ...
... PLACED IN DANGER ...
...BY UN-SAVORY PEOPLE.
THAT IS UNACCEPT-ABLE!
AM I WRONG ?!
NOOOOO

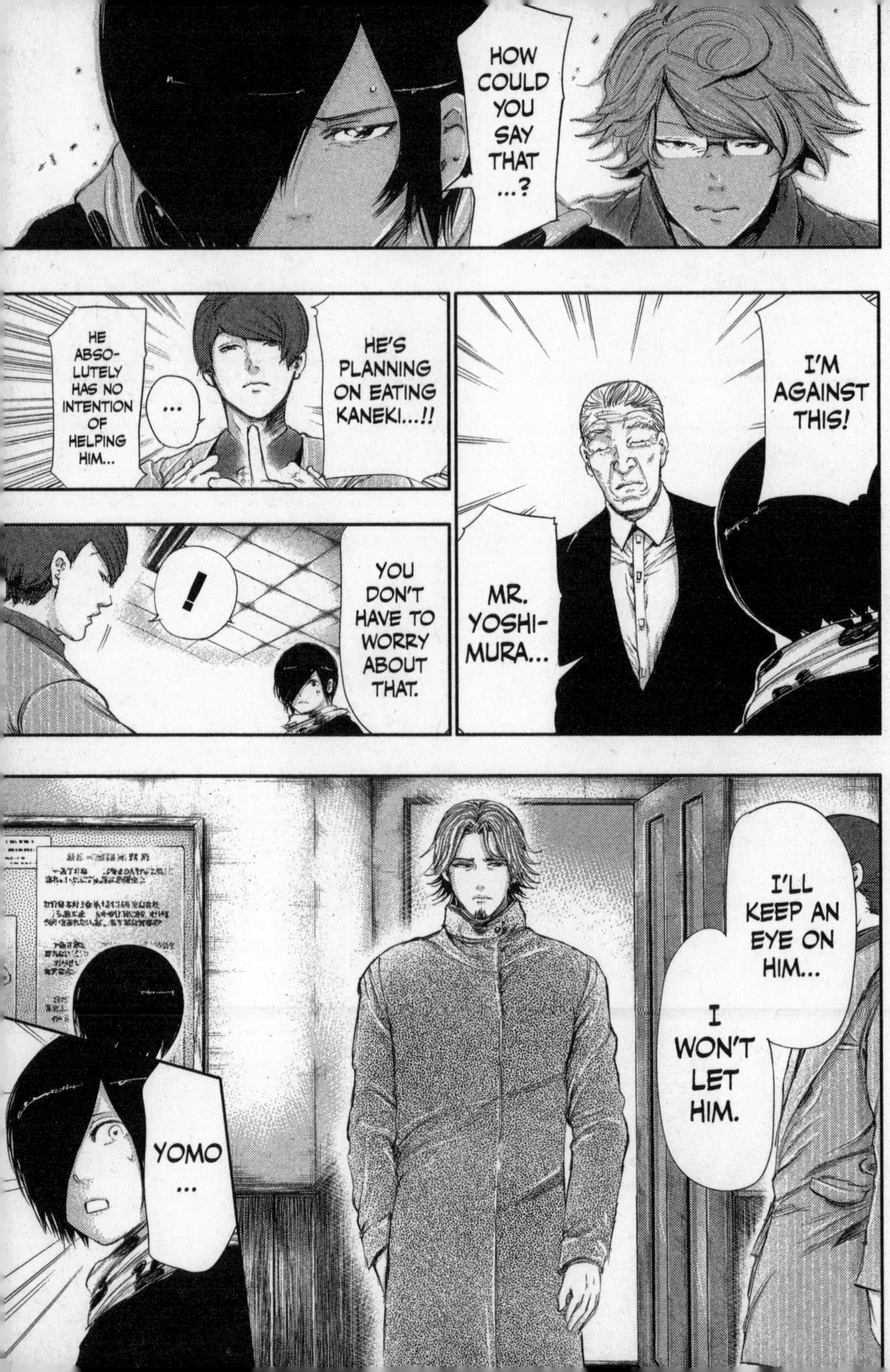
HOW COULD YOU SAY THAT ...?
I'M AGAINST THIS!
MR. YOSHIMURA...
HE'S PLANNING ON EATING KANEKI...!!
...
HE ABSOLUTELY HAS NO INTENTION OF HELPING HIM...
YOU DON'T HAVE TO WORRY ABOUT THAT.
!
I'LL KEEP AN EYE ON HIM...
I WON'T LET HIM.
YOMO ...

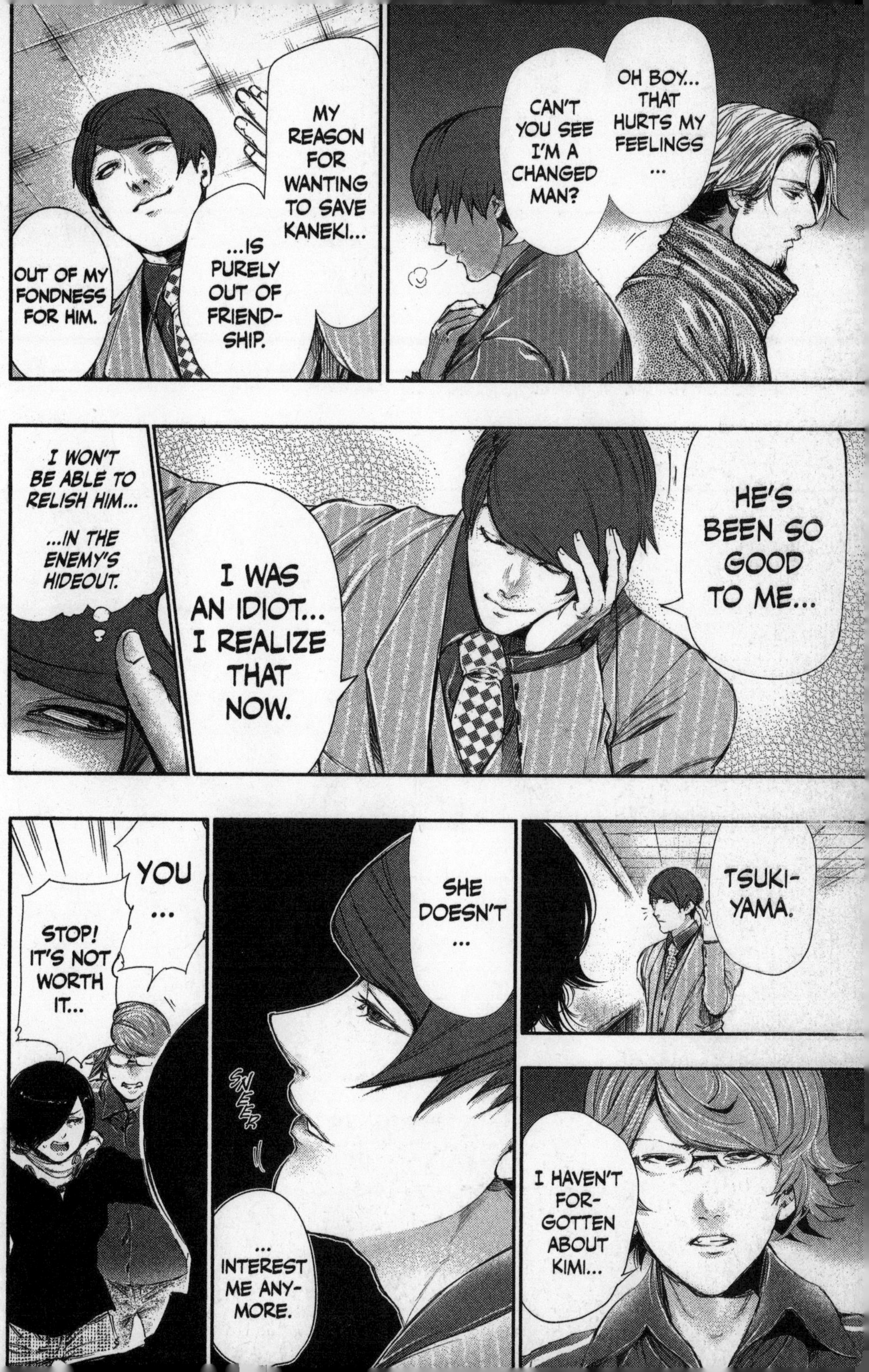
OH BOY... THAT HURTS MY FEELINGS ...
CAN'T YOU SEE I'M A CHANGED MAN?
MY REASON FOR WANTING TO SAVE KANEKI...
...IS PURELY OUT OF FRIENDSHIP.
OUT OF MY FONDNESS FOR HIM.
HE'S BEEN SO GOOD TO ME...
I WAS AN IDIOT... I REALIZE THAT NOW.
I WON'T BE ABLE TO RELISH HIM...
...IN THE ENEMY'S HIDEOUT.
TSUKI-YAMA.
I HAVEN'T FOR-GOTTEN ABOUT KIMI...
SHE DOESN'T ...
SNEER
... INTEREST ME ANY-MORE.
YOU ...
STOP! IT'S NOT WORTH IT...

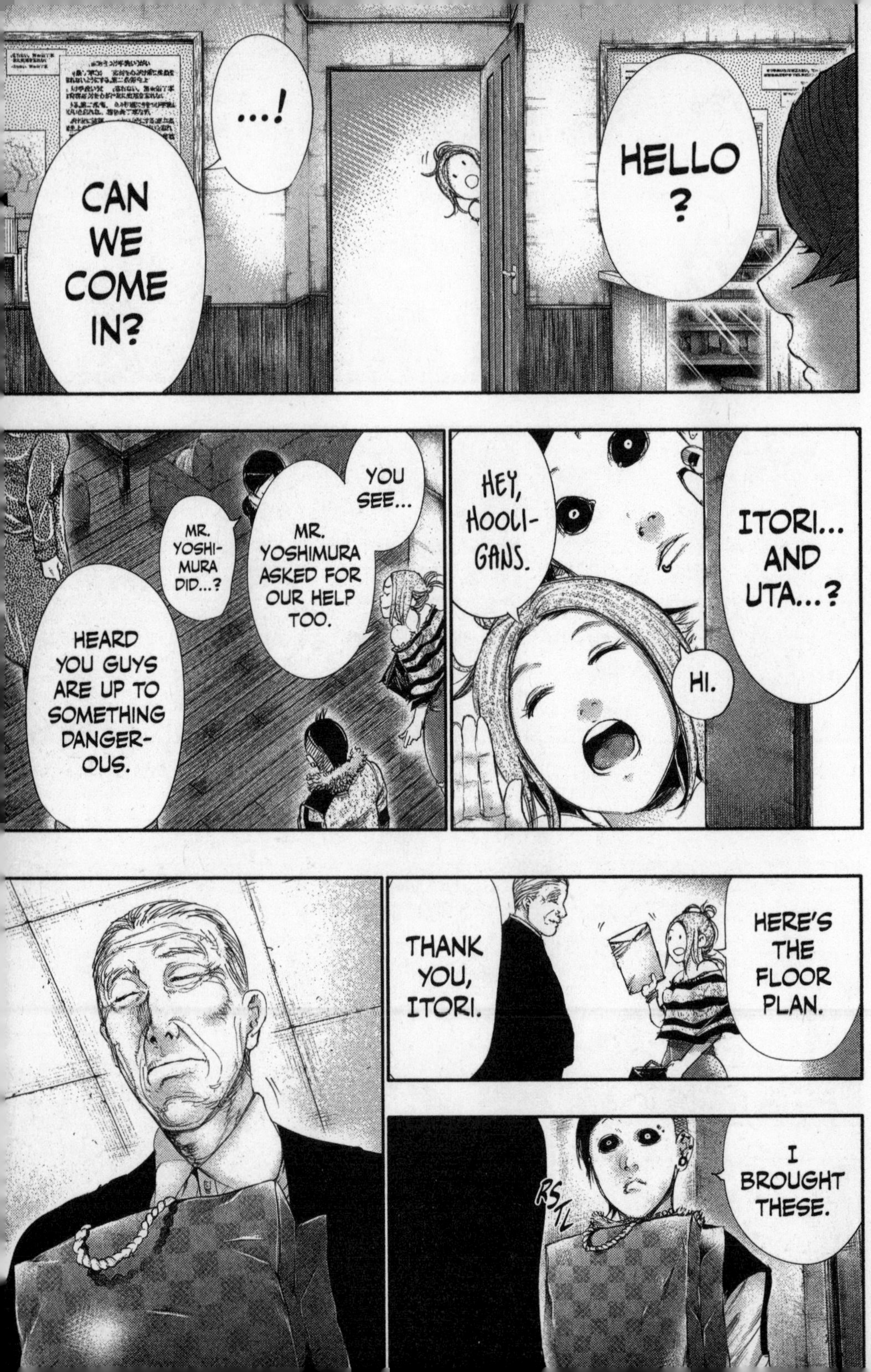
HELLO?
...!
CAN WE COME IN?
ITORI... AND UTA...?
HEY, HOOLI-GANS.
HI.
YOU SEE...
MR. YOSHIMURA ASKED FOR OUR HELP TOO.
MR. YOSHI-MURA DID...?
HEARD YOU GUYS ARE UP TO SOMETHING DANGER-OUS.
HERE'S THE FLOOR PLAN.
THANK YOU, ITORI.
I BROUGHT THESE.
RSTL

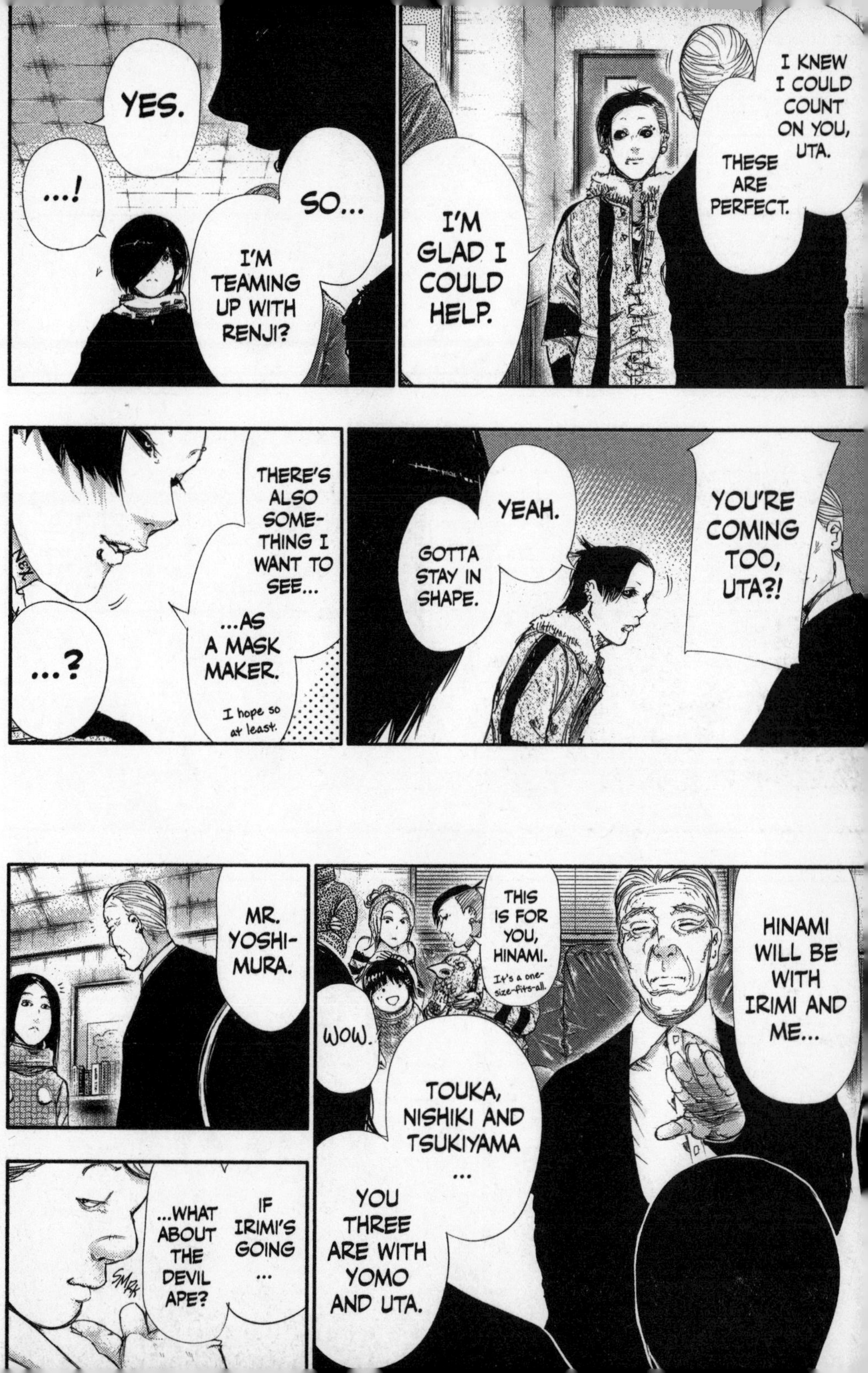
I KNEW I COULD COUNT ON YOU, UTA.
THESE ARE PERFECT.
I'M GLAD I COULD HELP.
SO...
I'M TEAMING UP WITH RENJI?
YES.
...!
YOU'RE COMING TOO, UTA?!
YEAH.
GOTTA STAY IN SHAPE.
THERE'S ALSO SOMETHING I WANT TO SEE...
...AS A MASK MAKER.
I hope so at least.
...?
HINAMI WILL BE WITH IRIMI AND ME...
THIS IS FOR YOU, HINAMI.
It's a one-size-fits-all.
WOW.
TOUKA, NISHIKI AND TSUKIYAMA...
YOU THREE ARE WITH YOMO AND UTA.
MR. YOSHIMURA.
IF IRIMI'S GOING...
...WHAT ABOUT THE DEVIL APE?
SMRK

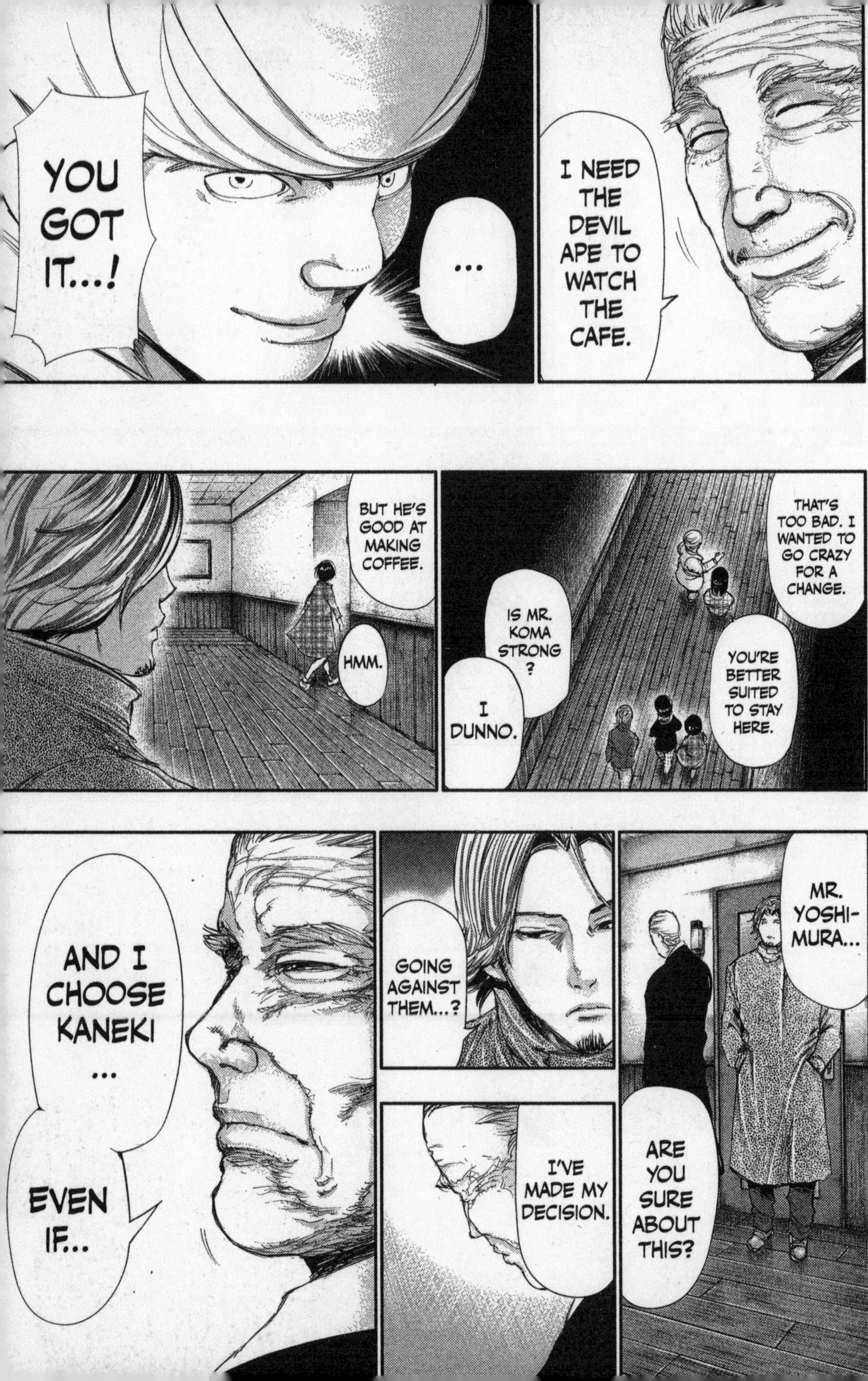

I NEED THE DEVIL APE TO WATCH THE CAFE.
...
YOU GOT IT...!
THAT'S TOO BAD. I WANTED TO GO CRAZY FOR A CHANGE.
YOU'RE BETTER SUITED TO STAY HERE.
IS MR. KOMA STRONG?
I DUNNO.
BUT HE'S GOOD AT MAKING COFFEE.
HMM.
MR. YOSHIMURA...
ARE YOU SURE ABOUT THIS?
GOING AGAINST THEM...?
I'VE MADE MY DECISION.
AND I CHOOSE KANEKI...
EVEN IF...

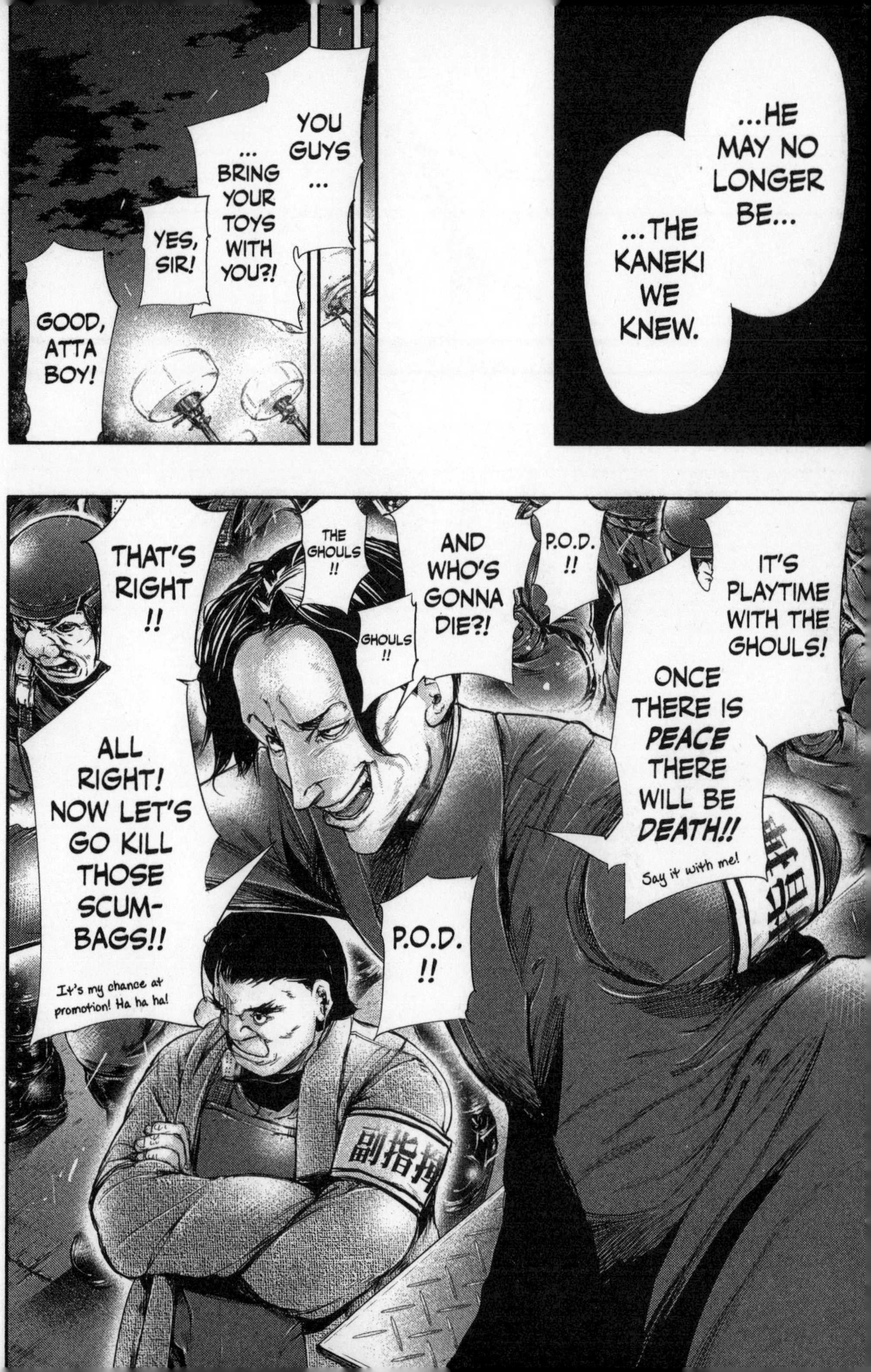
...HE MAY NO LONGER BE...
...THE KANEKI WE KNEW.
YOU GUYS...
...BRING YOUR TOYS WITH YOU?!
YES, SIR!
GOOD, ATTA BOY!
IT'S PLAYTIME WITH THE GHOULS!
ONCE THERE IS *PEACE* THERE WILL BE *DEATH!!*
Say it with me!
P.O.D. !!
AND WHO'S GONNA DIE?!
GHOULS !!
THE GHOULS !!
THAT'S RIGHT !!
P.O.D. !!
副指揮
ALL RIGHT! NOW LET'S GO KILL THOSE SCUM-BAGS!!
It's my chance at promotion! Ha ha ha!

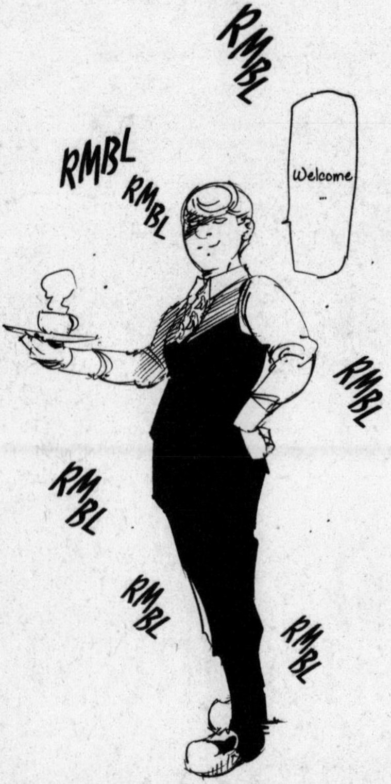
RMBL
Welcome ...
RMBL
RMBL
RMBL
RMBL
RMBL
RMBL
RMBL

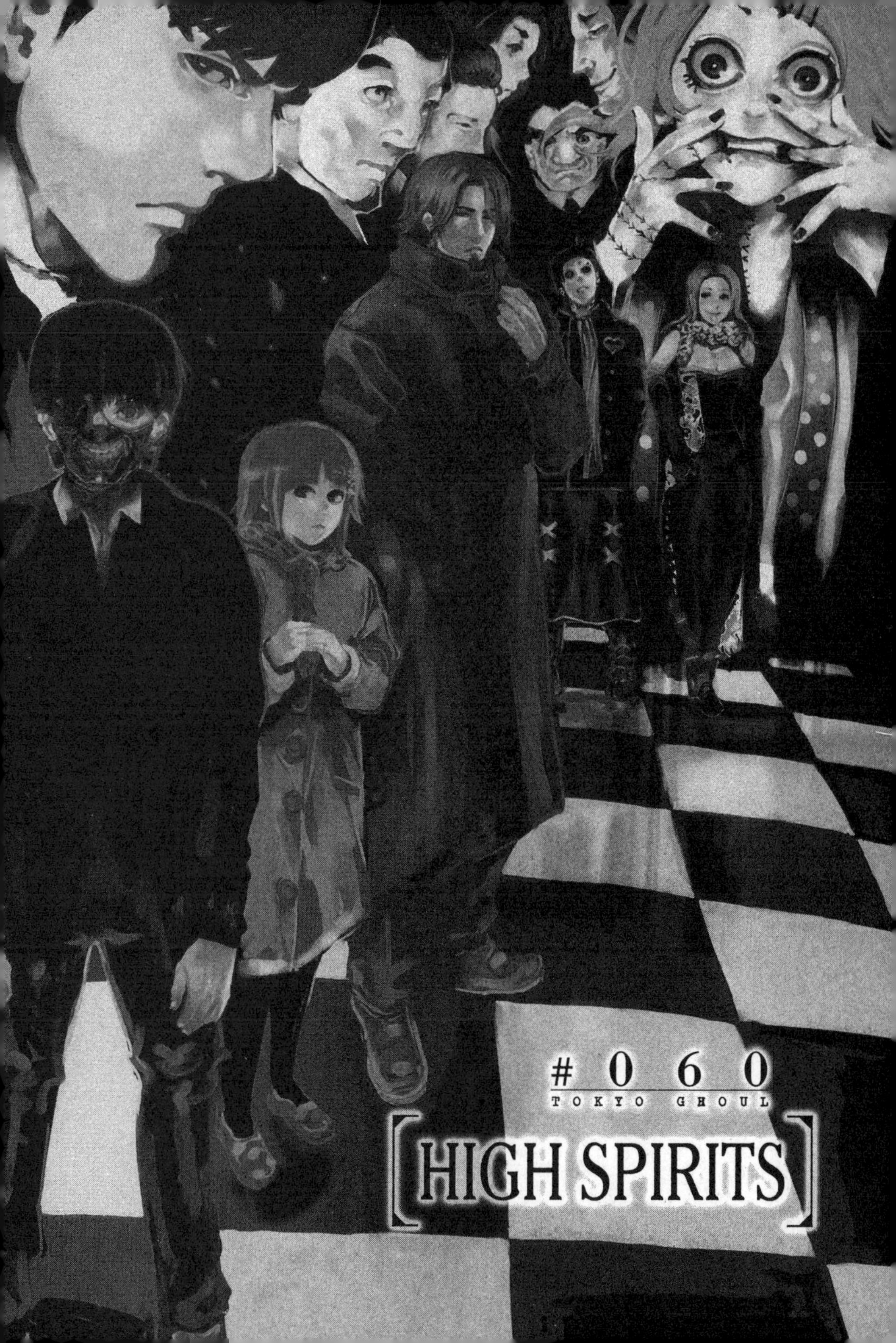
#060
TOKYO GHOUL
[HIGH SPIRITS]

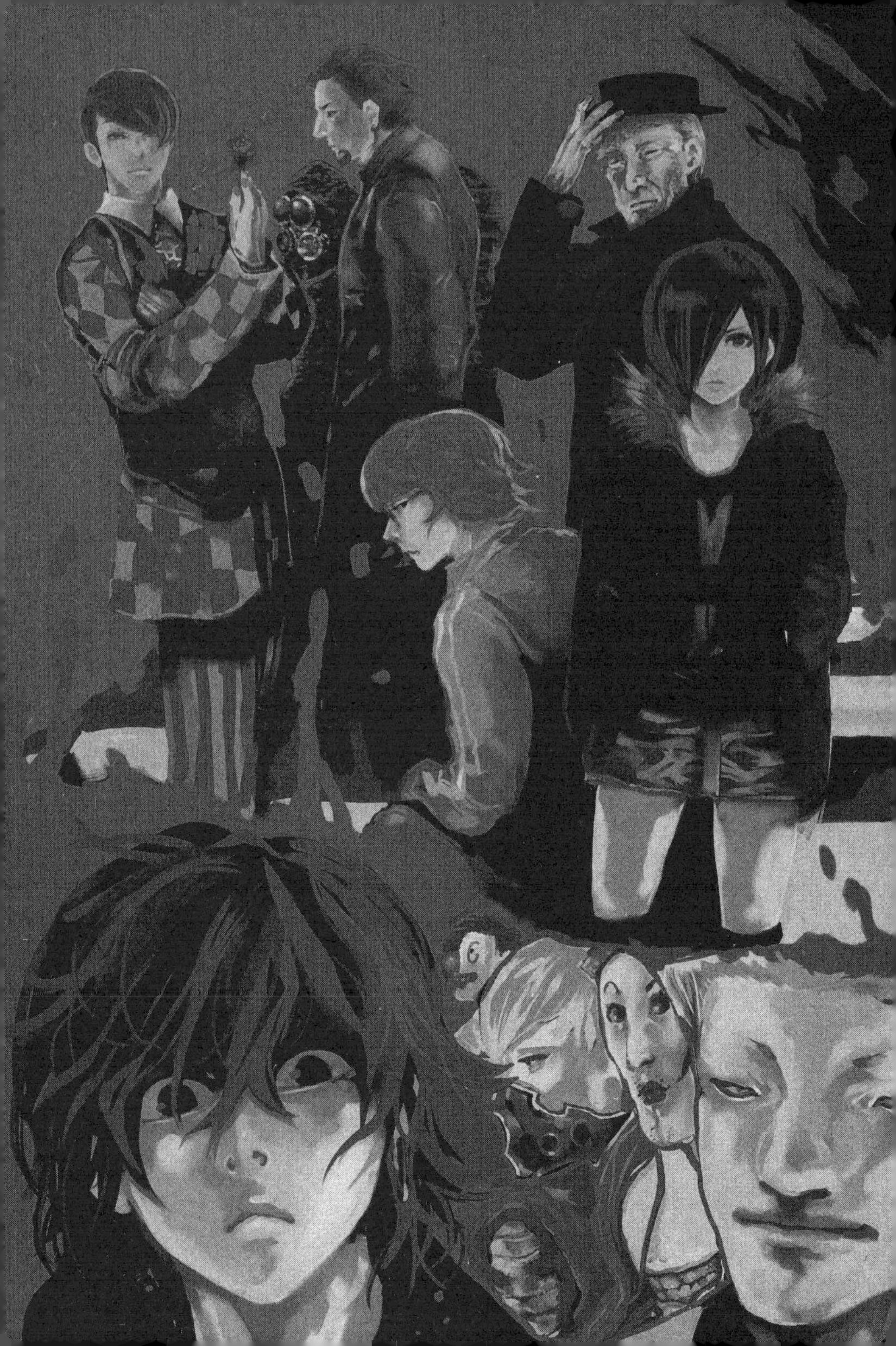

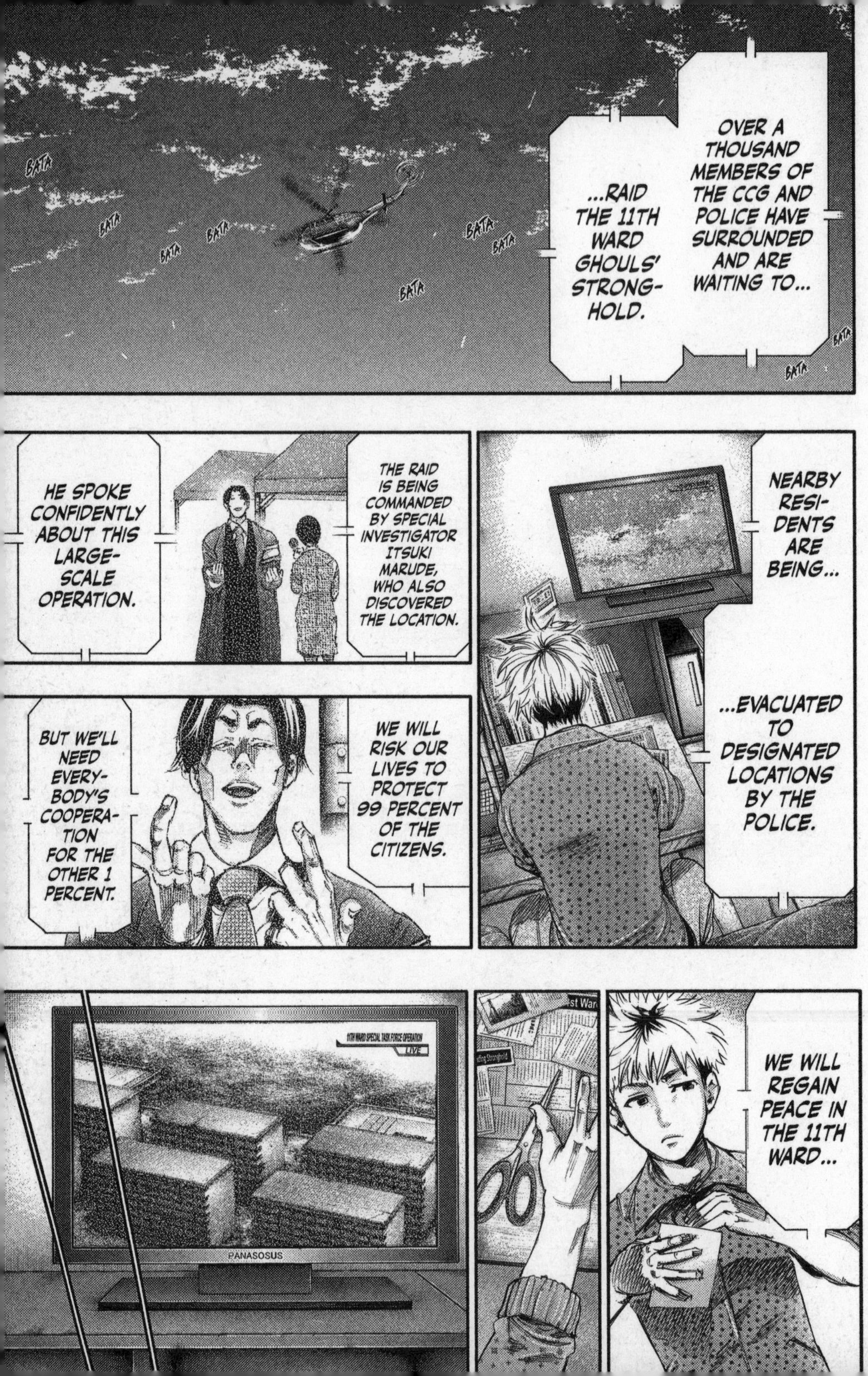

OVER A THOUSAND MEMBERS OF THE CCG AND POLICE HAVE SURROUNDED AND ARE WAITING TO...
...RAID THE 11TH WARD GHOULS' STRONGHOLD.
BATA BATA BATA BATA BATA BATA BATA BATA BATA
NEARBY RESIDENTS ARE BEING...
...EVACUATED TO DESIGNATED LOCATIONS BY THE POLICE.
THE RAID IS BEING COMMANDED BY SPECIAL INVESTIGATOR ITSUKI MARUDE, WHO ALSO DISCOVERED THE LOCATION.
HE SPOKE CONFIDENTLY ABOUT THIS LARGE-SCALE OPERATION.
WE WILL RISK OUR LIVES TO PROTECT 99 PERCENT OF THE CITIZENS.
BUT WE'LL NEED EVERYBODY'S COOPERATION FOR THE OTHER 1 PERCENT.
WE WILL REGAIN PEACE IN THE 11TH WARD...
11TH WARD SPECIAL TASK FORCE OPERATION
LIVE
PANASOSUS

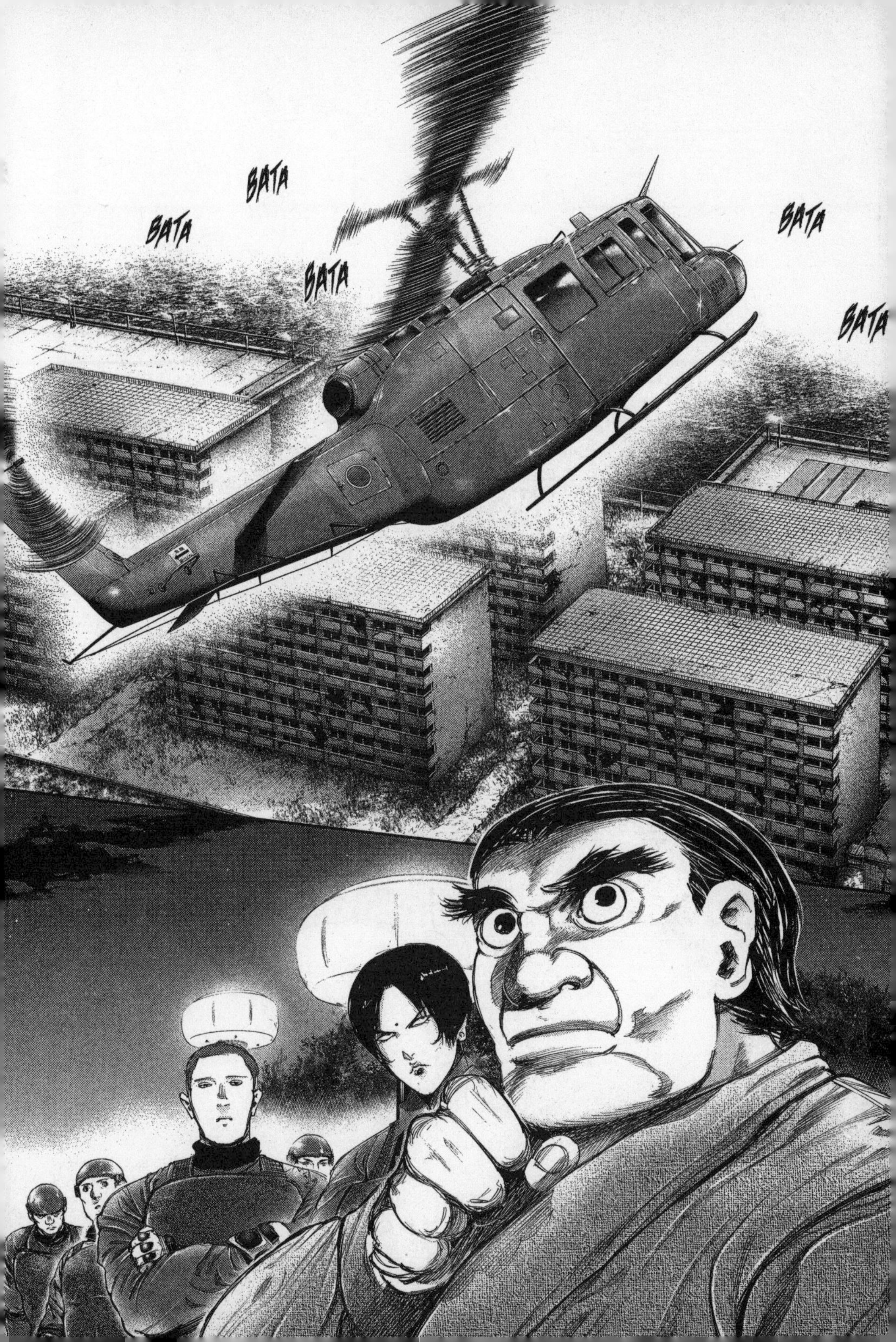
BATA
BATA
BATA
BATA
BATA

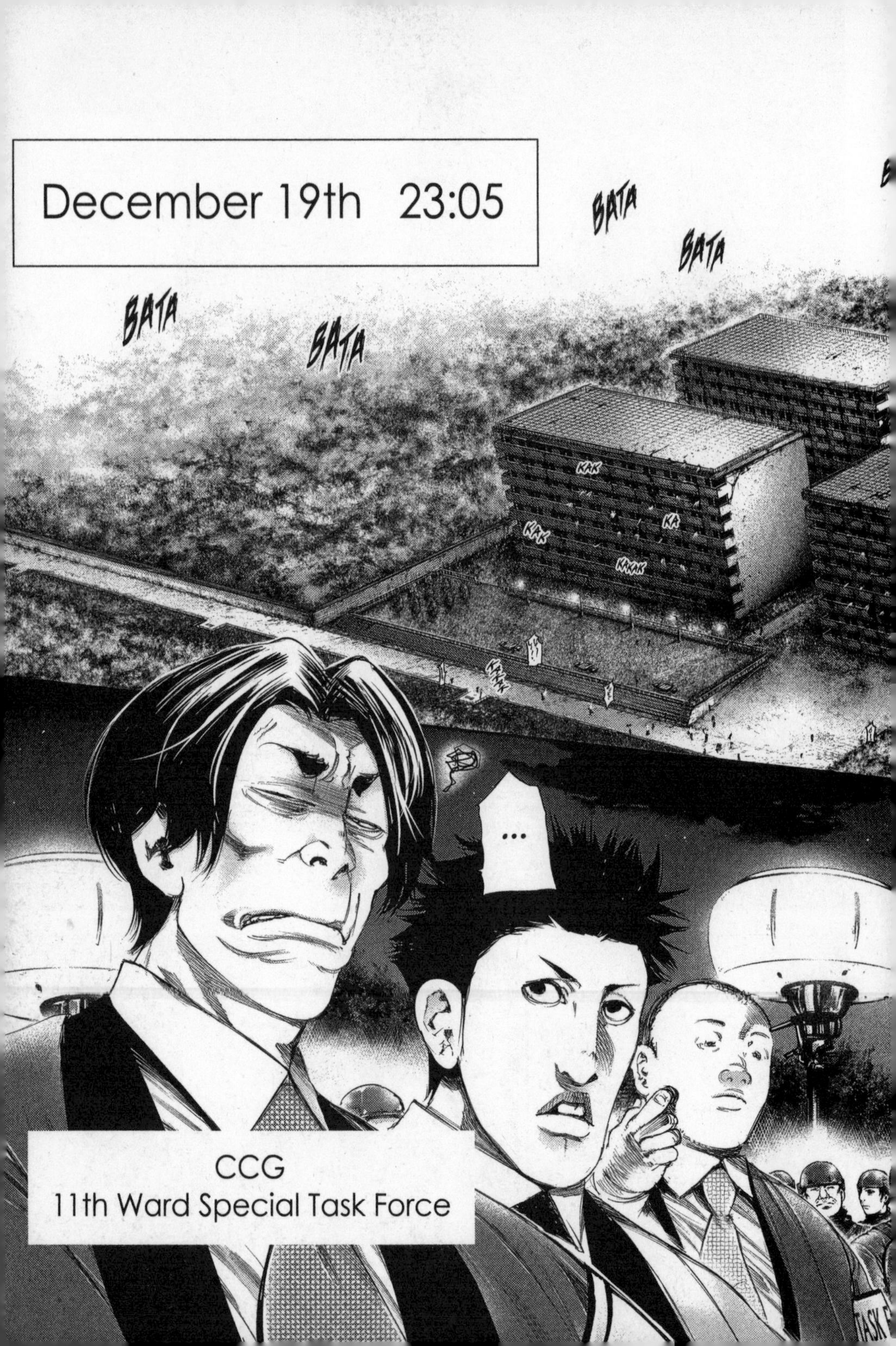

December 19th 23:05
BATA
BATA
BATA
BATA
KAK
KA
KAK
KAKAK
...
CCG
11th Ward Special Task Force

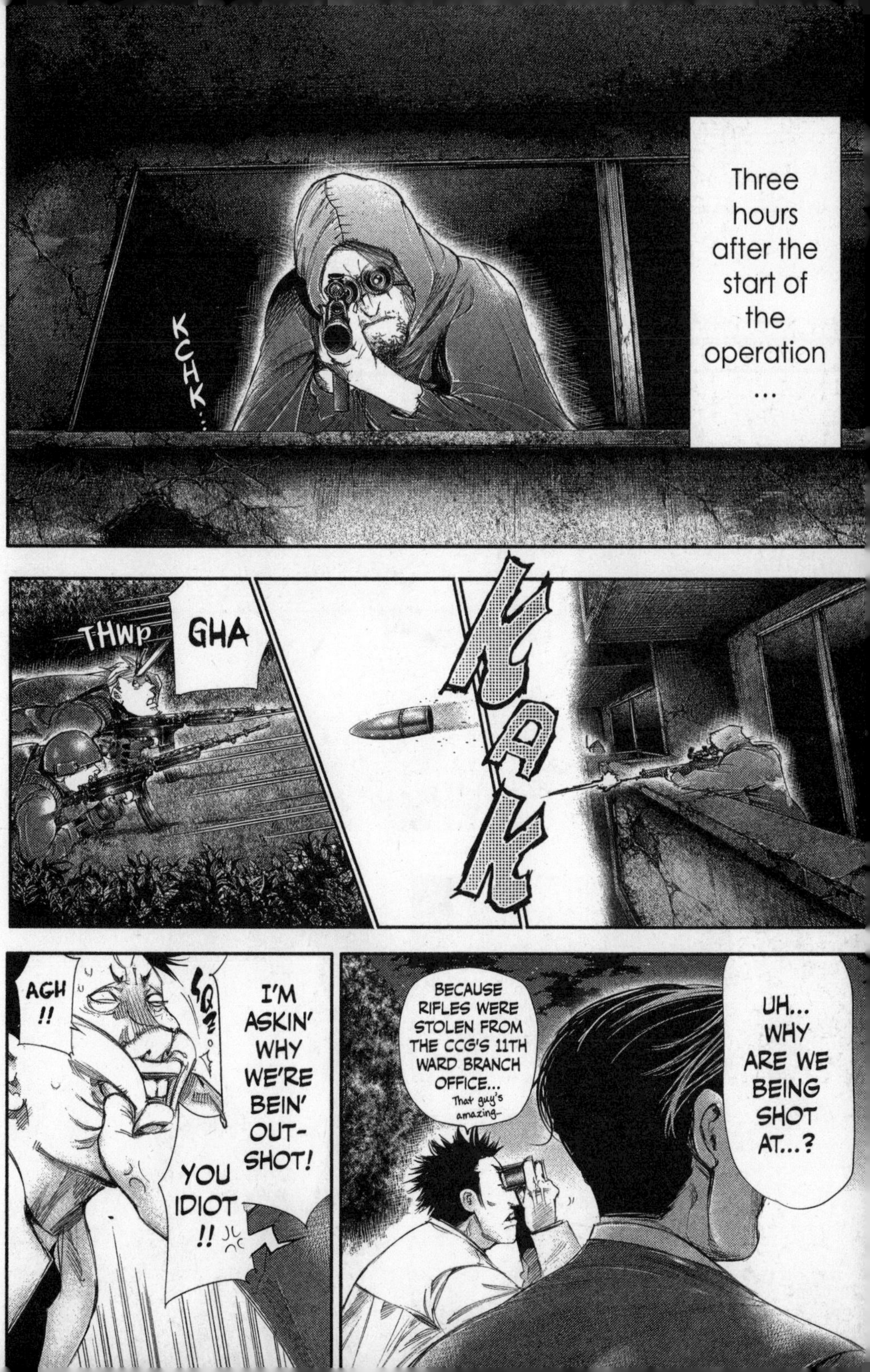
Three hours after the start of the operation ...
KCHK...
KRAK
GHA
THWp
UH... WHY ARE WE BEING SHOT AT...?
BECAUSE RIFLES WERE STOLEN FROM THE CCG'S 11TH WARD BRANCH OFFICE...
That guy's amazing...
I'M ASKIN' WHY WE'RE BEIN' OUT-SHOT!
YOU IDIOT!!
AGH!!

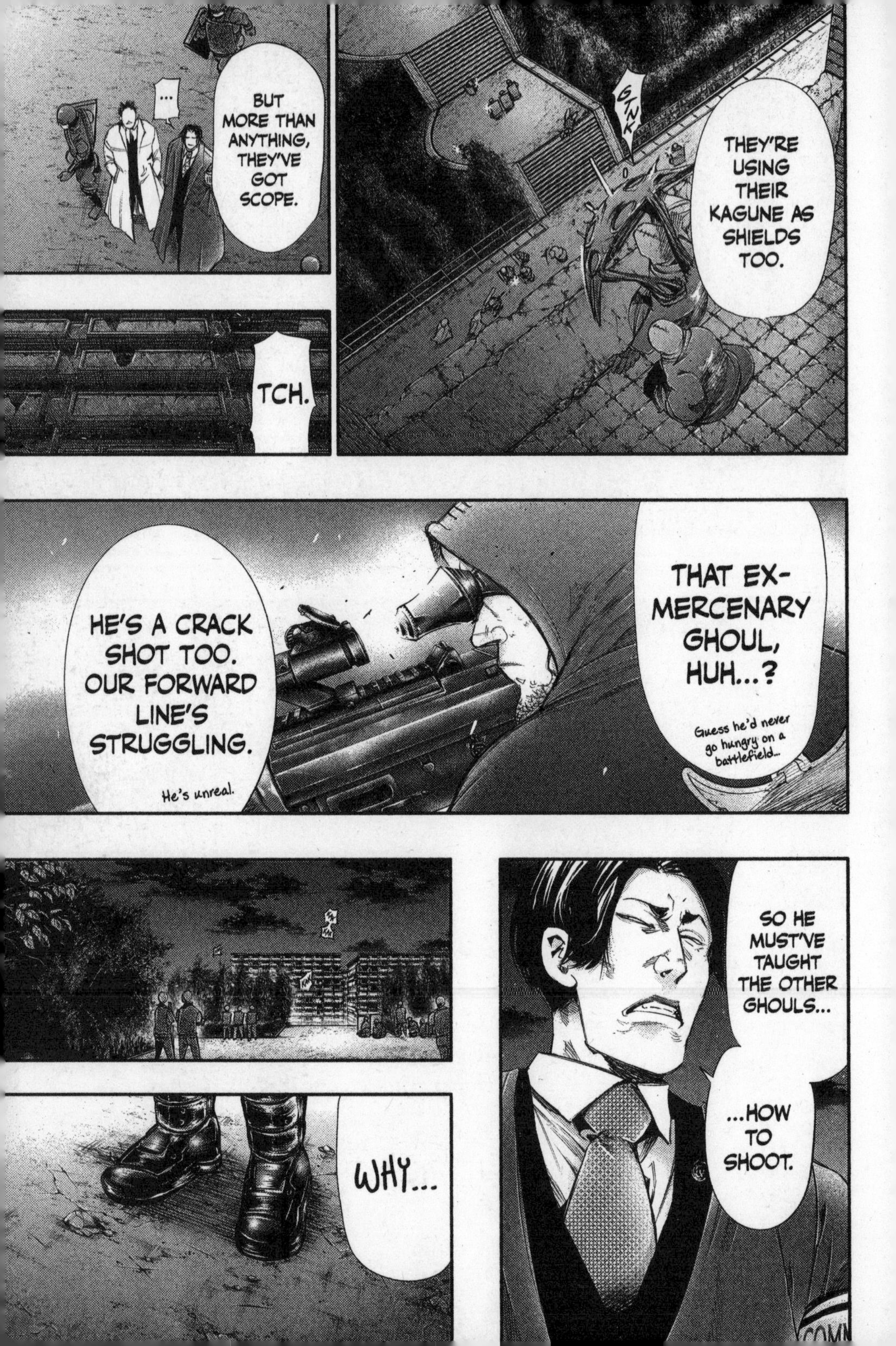
THEY'RE USING THEIR KAGUNE AS SHIELDS TOO.
...
BUT MORE THAN ANYTHING, THEY'VE GOT SCOPE.
TCH.
THAT EX-MERCENARY GHOUL, HUH...?
Guess he'd never go hungry on a battlefield...
HE'S A CRACK SHOT TOO. OUR FORWARD LINE'S STRUGGLING.
He's unreal.
SO HE MUST'VE TAUGHT THE OTHER GHOULS...
...HOW TO SHOOT.
WHY...

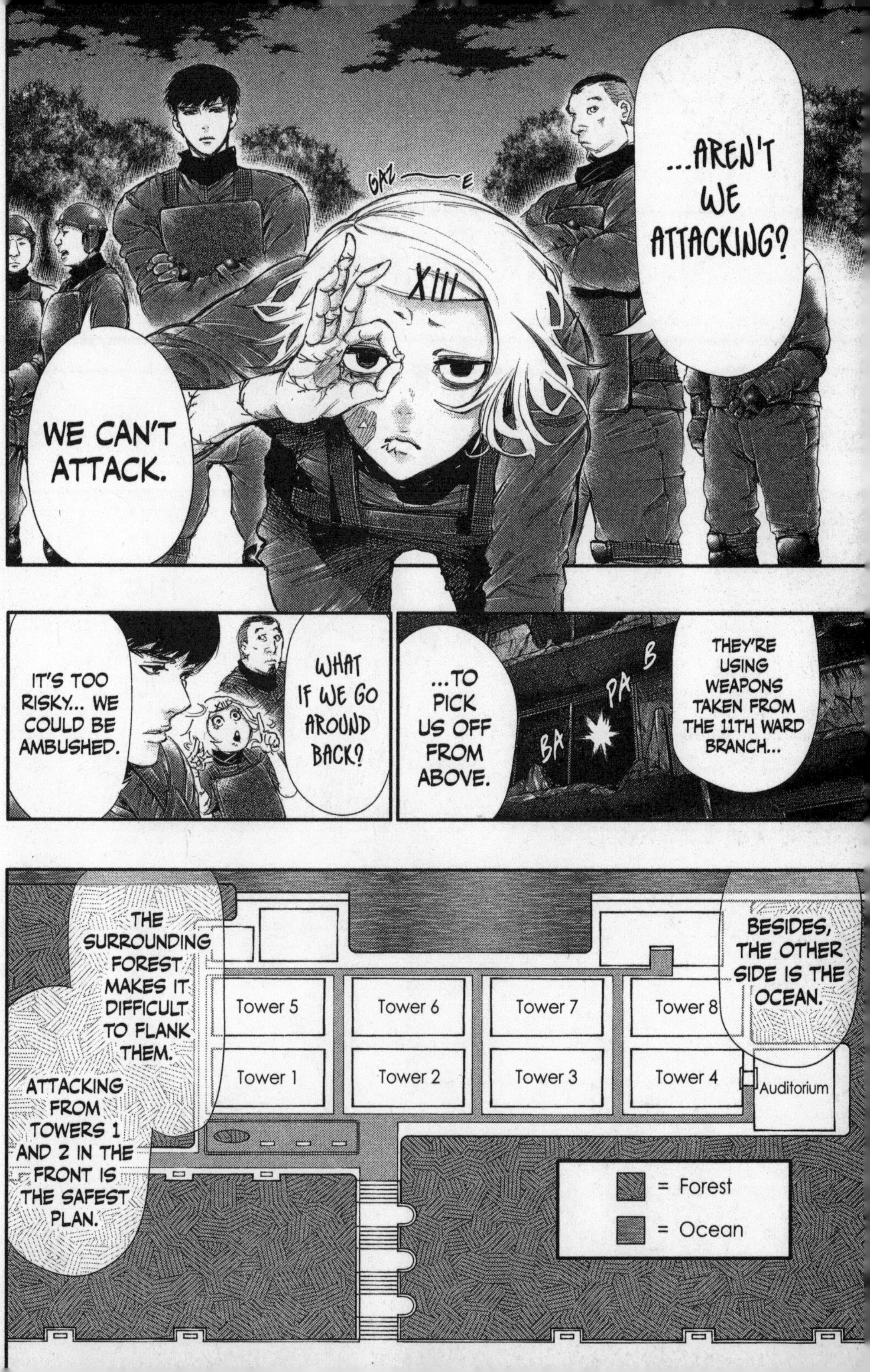
...AREN'T WE ATTACKING?
GAZ——E
WE CAN'T ATTACK.
THEY'RE USING WEAPONS TAKEN FROM THE 11TH WARD BRANCH...
BA PA B
...TO PICK US OFF FROM ABOVE.
WHAT IF WE GO AROUND BACK?
IT'S TOO RISKY... WE COULD BE AMBUSHED.
THE SURROUNDING FOREST MAKES IT DIFFICULT TO FLANK THEM.
ATTACKING FROM TOWERS 1 AND 2 IN THE FRONT IS THE SAFEST PLAN.
BESIDES, THE OTHER SIDE IS THE OCEAN.
Tower 5
Tower 6
Tower 7
Tower 8
Tower 1
Tower 2
Tower 3
Tower 4
Auditorium
= Forest
= Ocean

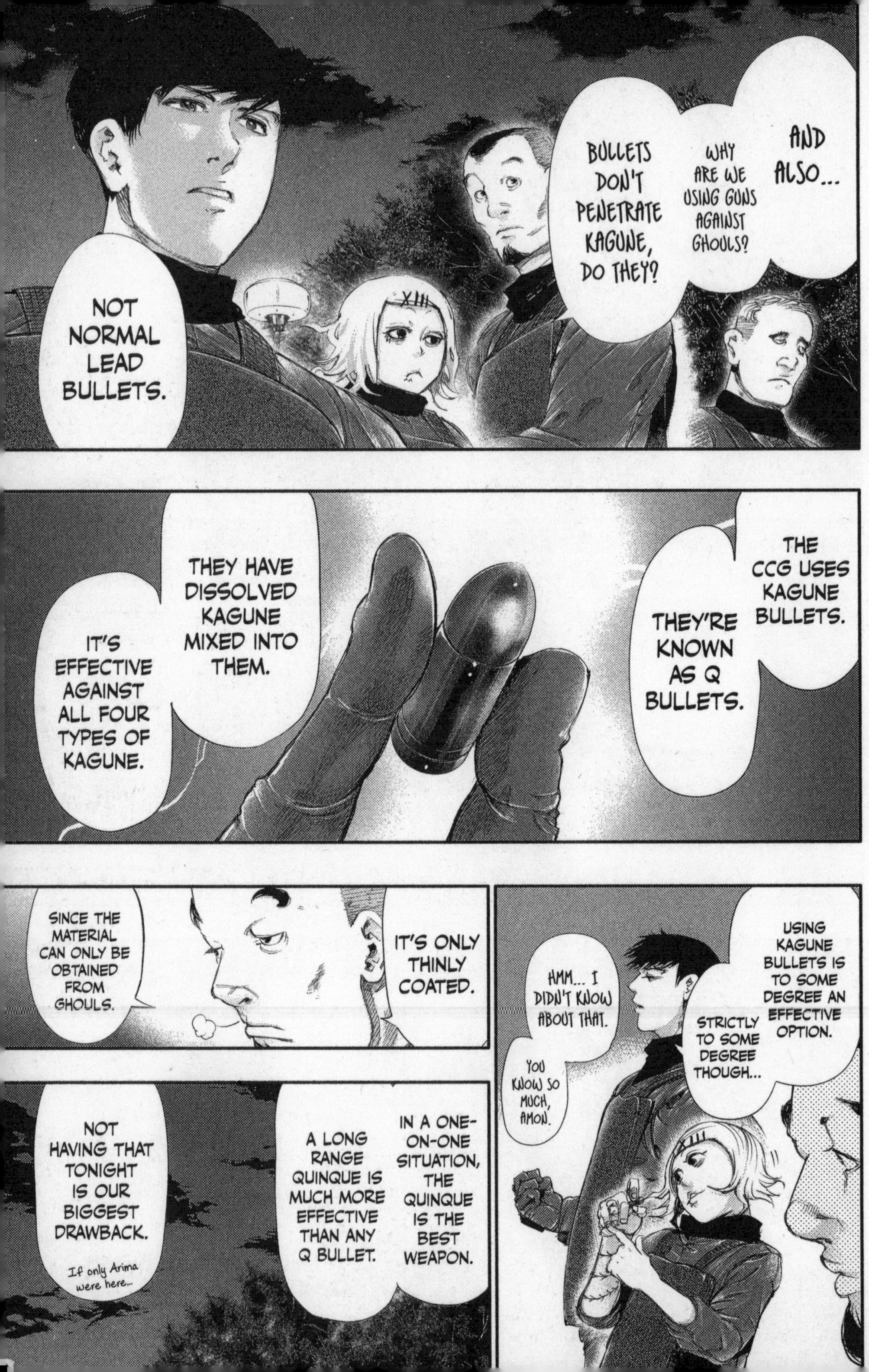
AND ALSO...
WHY ARE WE USING GUNS AGAINST GHOULS?
BULLETS DON'T PENETRATE KAGUNE, DO THEY?
NOT NORMAL LEAD BULLETS.
THE CCG USES KAGUNE BULLETS.
THEY'RE KNOWN AS Q BULLETS.
THEY HAVE DISSOLVED KAGUNE MIXED INTO THEM.
IT'S EFFECTIVE AGAINST ALL FOUR TYPES OF KAGUNE.
USING KAGUNE BULLETS IS TO SOME DEGREE AN EFFECTIVE OPTION.
STRICTLY TO SOME DEGREE THOUGH...
HMM... I DIDN'T KNOW ABOUT THAT.
YOU KNOW SO MUCH, AMON.
IT'S ONLY THINLY COATED.
SINCE THE MATERIAL CAN ONLY BE OBTAINED FROM GHOULS.
IN A ONE-ON-ONE SITUATION, THE QUINQUE IS THE BEST WEAPON.
A LONG RANGE QUINQUE IS MUCH MORE EFFECTIVE THAN ANY Q BULLET.
NOT HAVING THAT TONIGHT IS OUR BIGGEST DRAWBACK.
If only Arima were here...

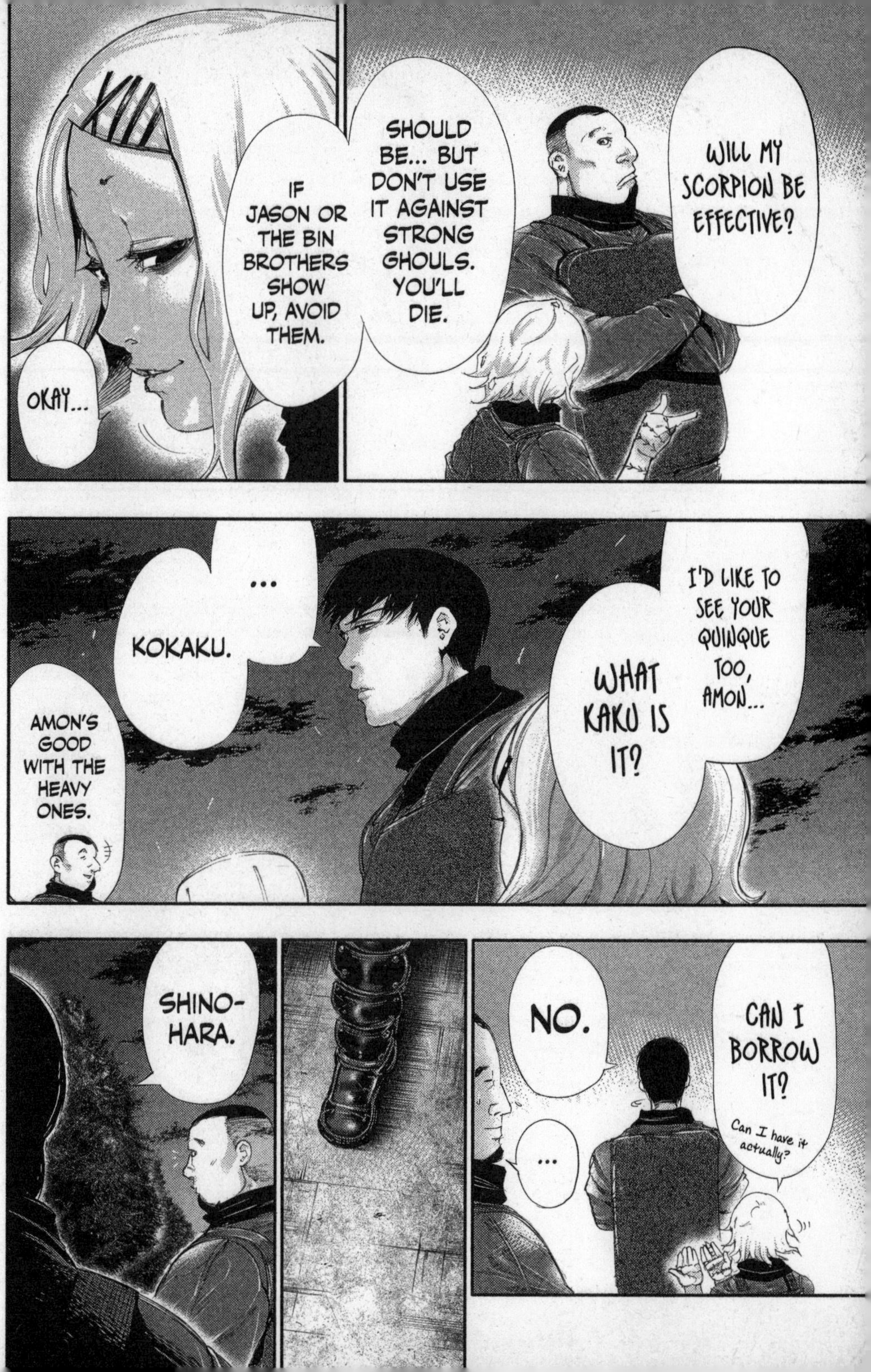
WILL MY SCORPION BE EFFECTIVE?
SHOULD BE... BUT DON'T USE IT AGAINST STRONG GHOULS. YOU'LL DIE.
IF JASON OR THE BIN BROTHERS SHOW UP, AVOID THEM.
OKAY...
I'D LIKE TO SEE YOUR QUINQUE TOO, AMON...
WHAT KAKU IS IT?
...
KOKAKU.
AMON'S GOOD WITH THE HEAVY ONES.
CAN I BORROW IT?
Can I have it actually?
NO.
...
SHINO-HARA.

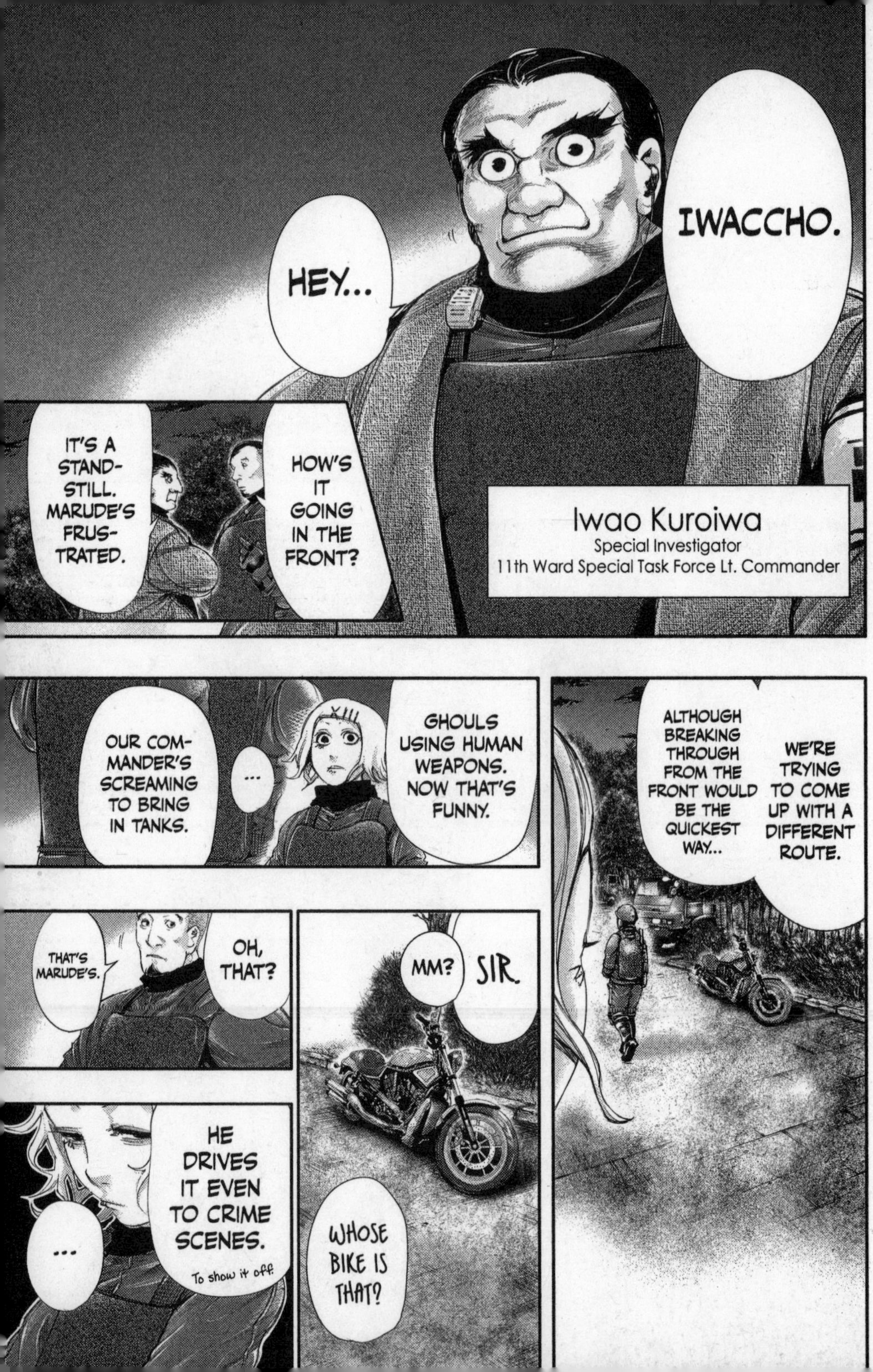
IWACCHO.
HEY...
Iwao Kuroiwa
Special Investigator
11th Ward Special Task Force Lt. Commander
HOW'S IT GOING IN THE FRONT?
IT'S A STAND-STILL. MARUDE'S FRUS-TRATED.
WE'RE TRYING TO COME UP WITH A DIFFERENT ROUTE.
ALTHOUGH BREAKING THROUGH FROM THE FRONT WOULD BE THE QUICKEST WAY...
GHOULS USING HUMAN WEAPONS. NOW THAT'S FUNNY.
...
OUR COM-MANDER'S SCREAMING TO BRING IN TANKS.
SIR.
MM?
WHOSE BIKE IS THAT?
OH, THAT?
THAT'S MARUDE'S.
HE DRIVES IT EVEN TO CRIME SCENES.
To show it off.
...

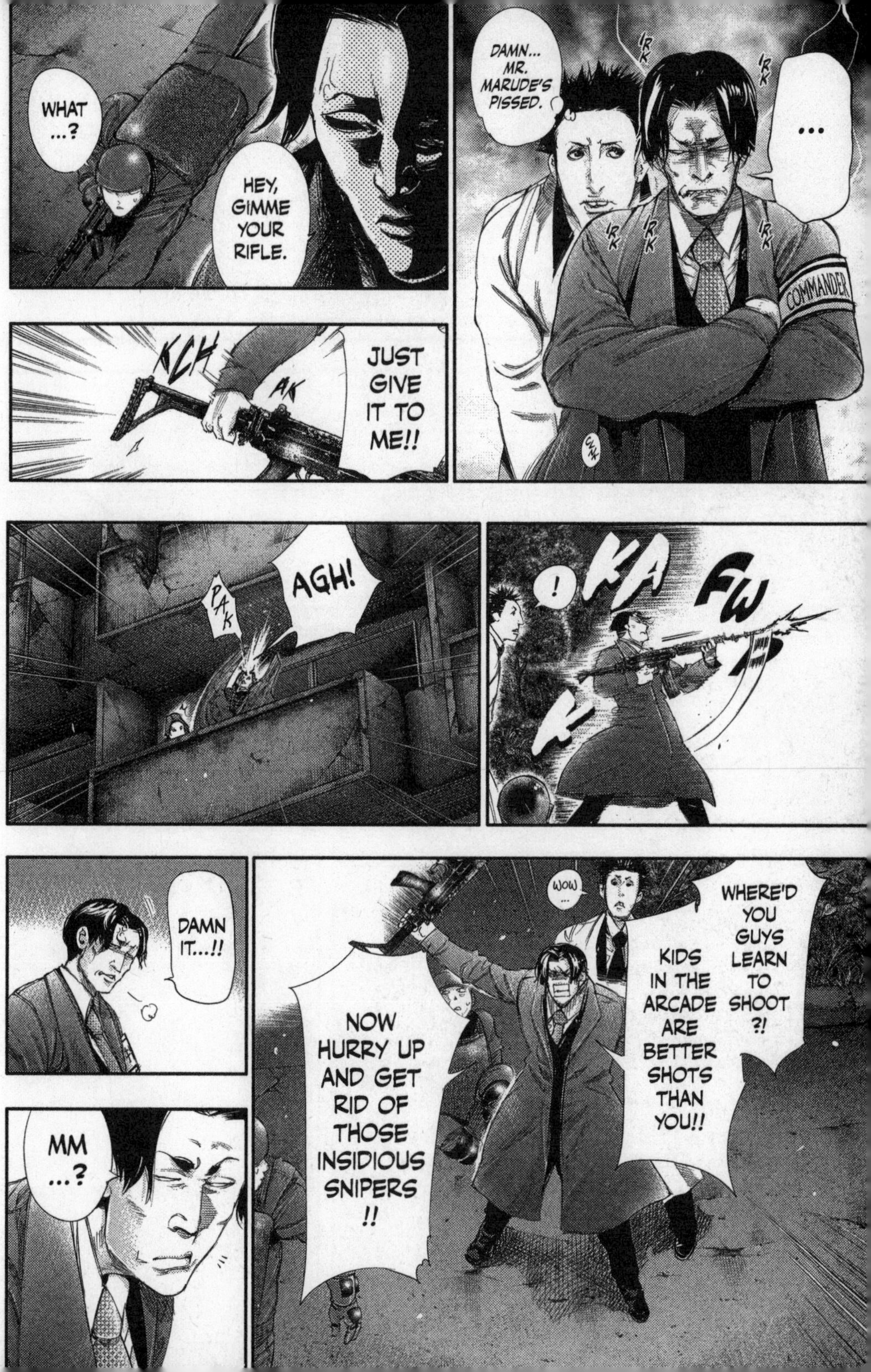
IRK
IRK
...
DAMN... MR. MARUDE'S PISSED.
IRK
IRK
IRK
COMMANDER
WHAT ...?
HEY, GIMME YOUR RIFLE.
KCK
AK
JUST GIVE IT TO ME!!
!
KA
FW
K
AGH!
PAK
WHERE'D YOU GUYS LEARN TO SHOOT ?!
KIDS IN THE ARCADE ARE BETTER SHOTS THAN YOU!!
WOW ...
NOW HURRY UP AND GET RID OF THOSE INSIDIOUS SNIPERS !!
DAMN IT...!!
MM ...?

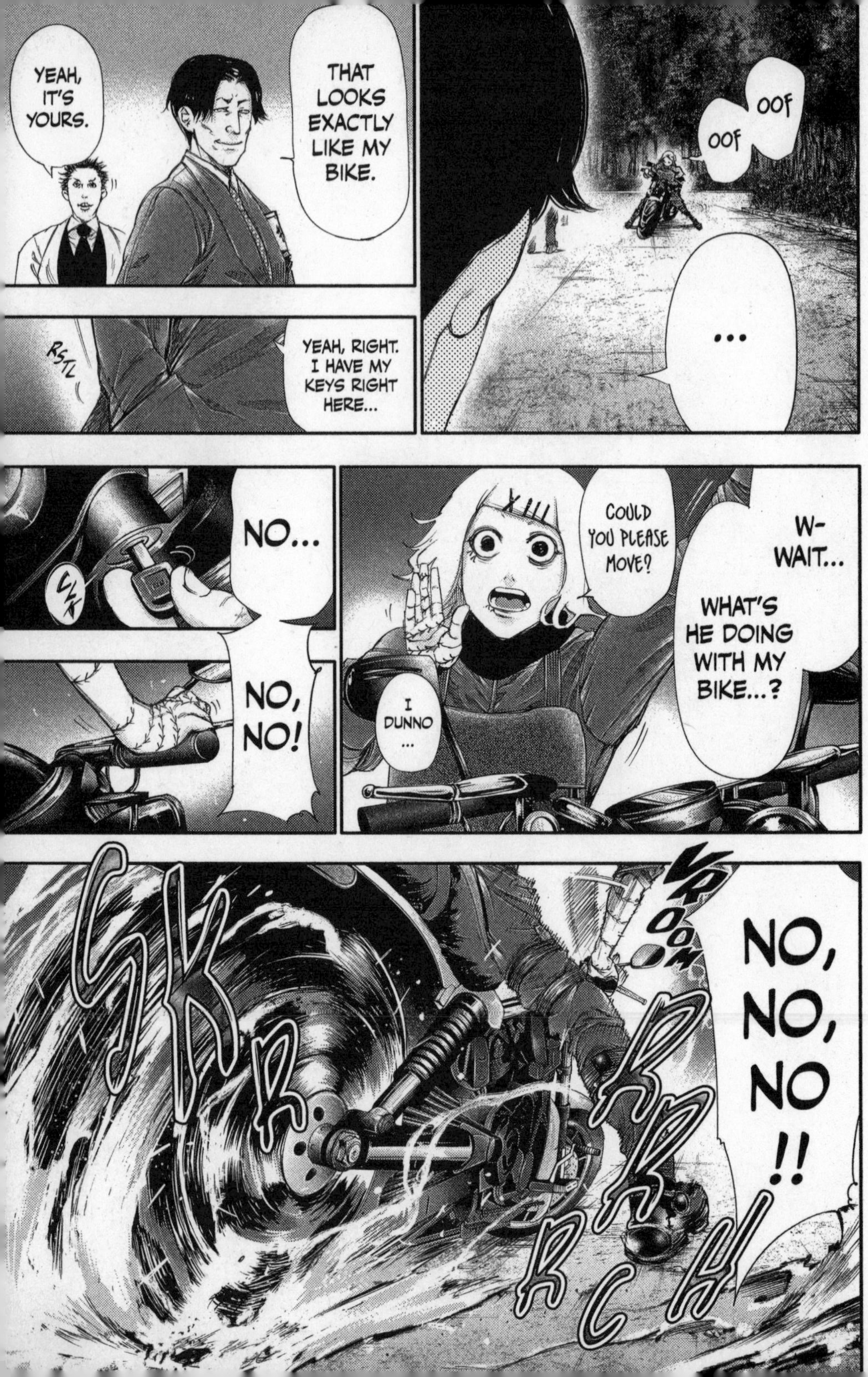
OOF
OOF
...
THAT LOOKS EXACTLY LIKE MY BIKE.
YEAH, IT'S YOURS.
RSTL
YEAH, RIGHT. I HAVE MY KEYS RIGHT HERE...
W- WAIT...
WHAT'S HE DOING WITH MY BIKE...?
COULD YOU PLEASE MOVE?
I DUNNO ...
NO...
NO, NO!
NO, NO, NO!!
VROOOM

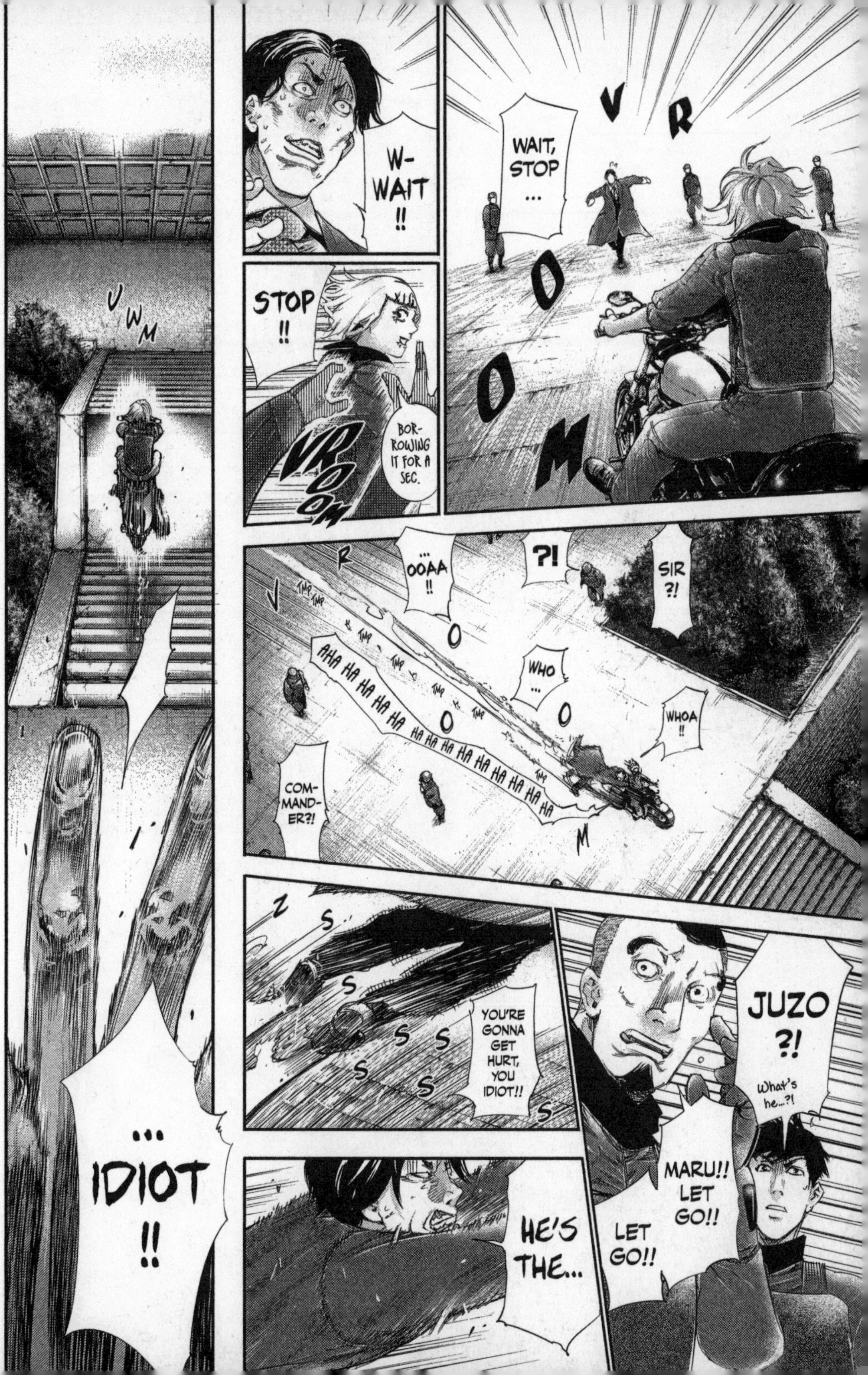
VROOM
WAIT, STOP ...
W-WAIT !!
STOP !!
BOR-ROWING IT FOR A SEC.
VROOOM
?!
SIR ?!
... OOAA !!
WHO ...
WHOA !!
AHA HA HA HA HA HA HA HA HA HA HA HA HA HA HA HA HA
COM-MANDER?!
VROOOM
JUZO ?!
What's he...?!
YOU'RE GONNA GET HURT, YOU IDIOT!!
MARU!! LET GO!!
LET GO!!
HE'S THE...
VWM
... IDIOT !!

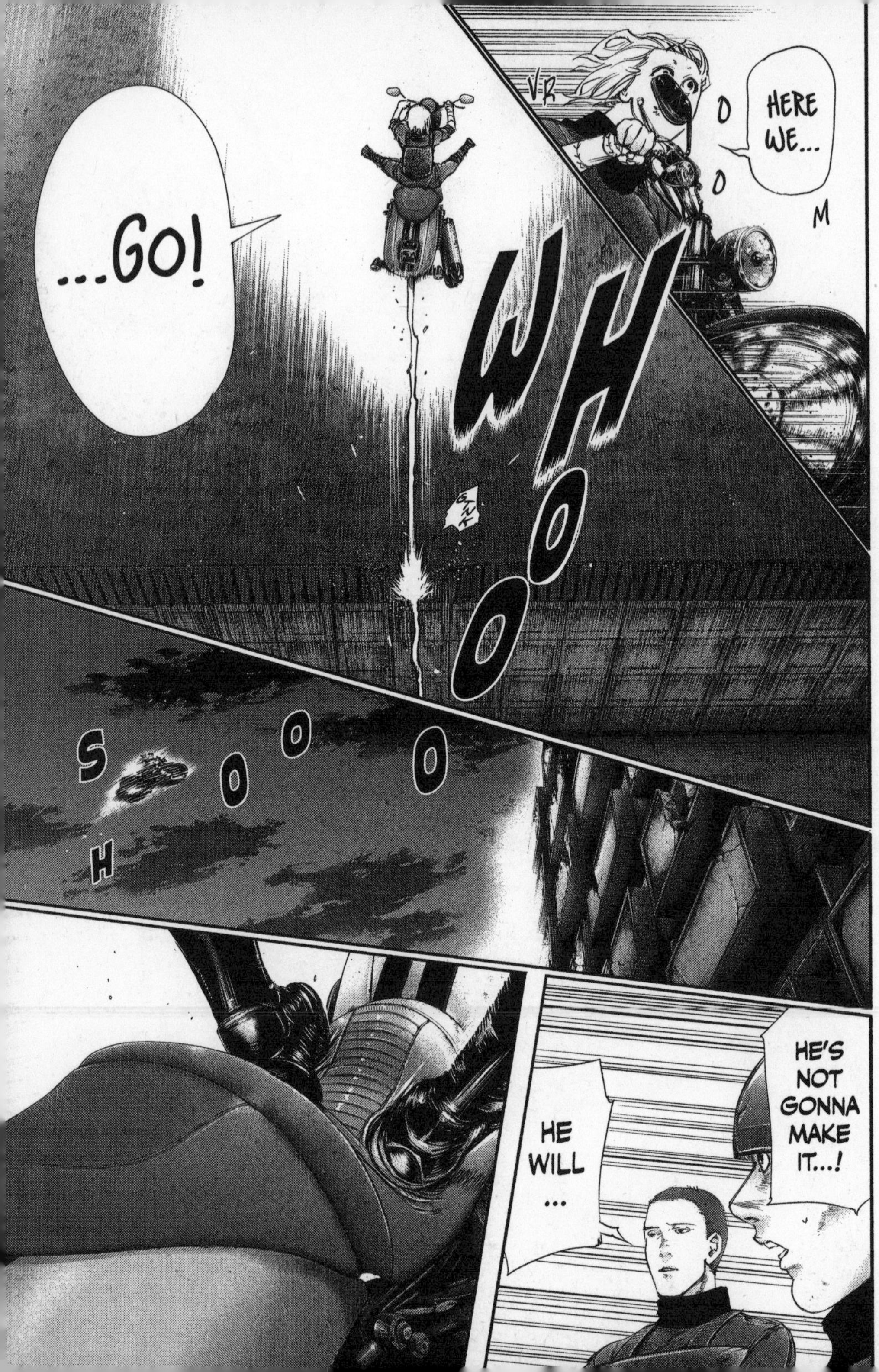

HERE WE...
VROOOM
...GO!
WHOOOO
SHOOOO
HE'S NOT GONNA MAKE IT...!
HE WILL...

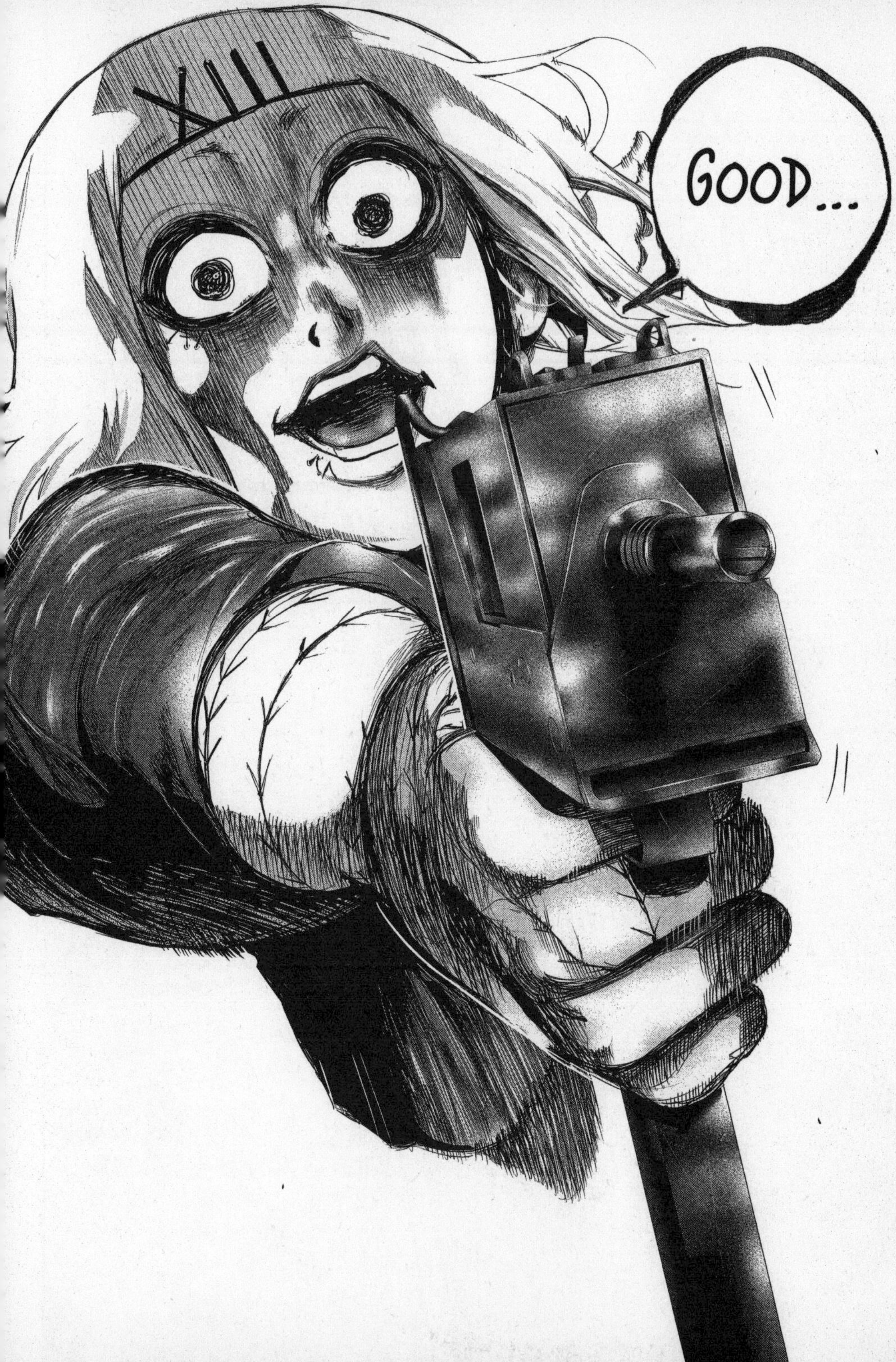
GOOD...

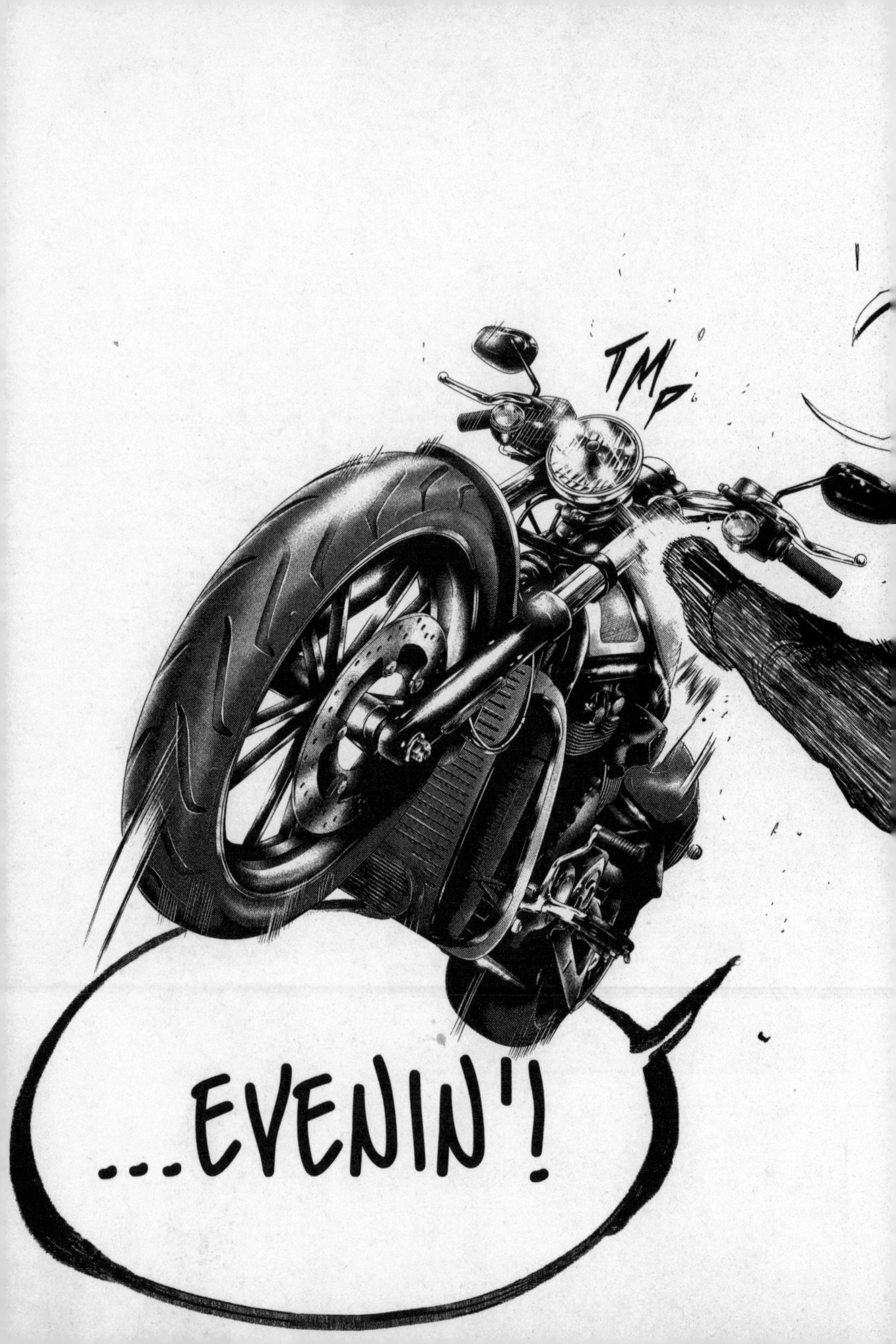
TMP
...EVENIN'!

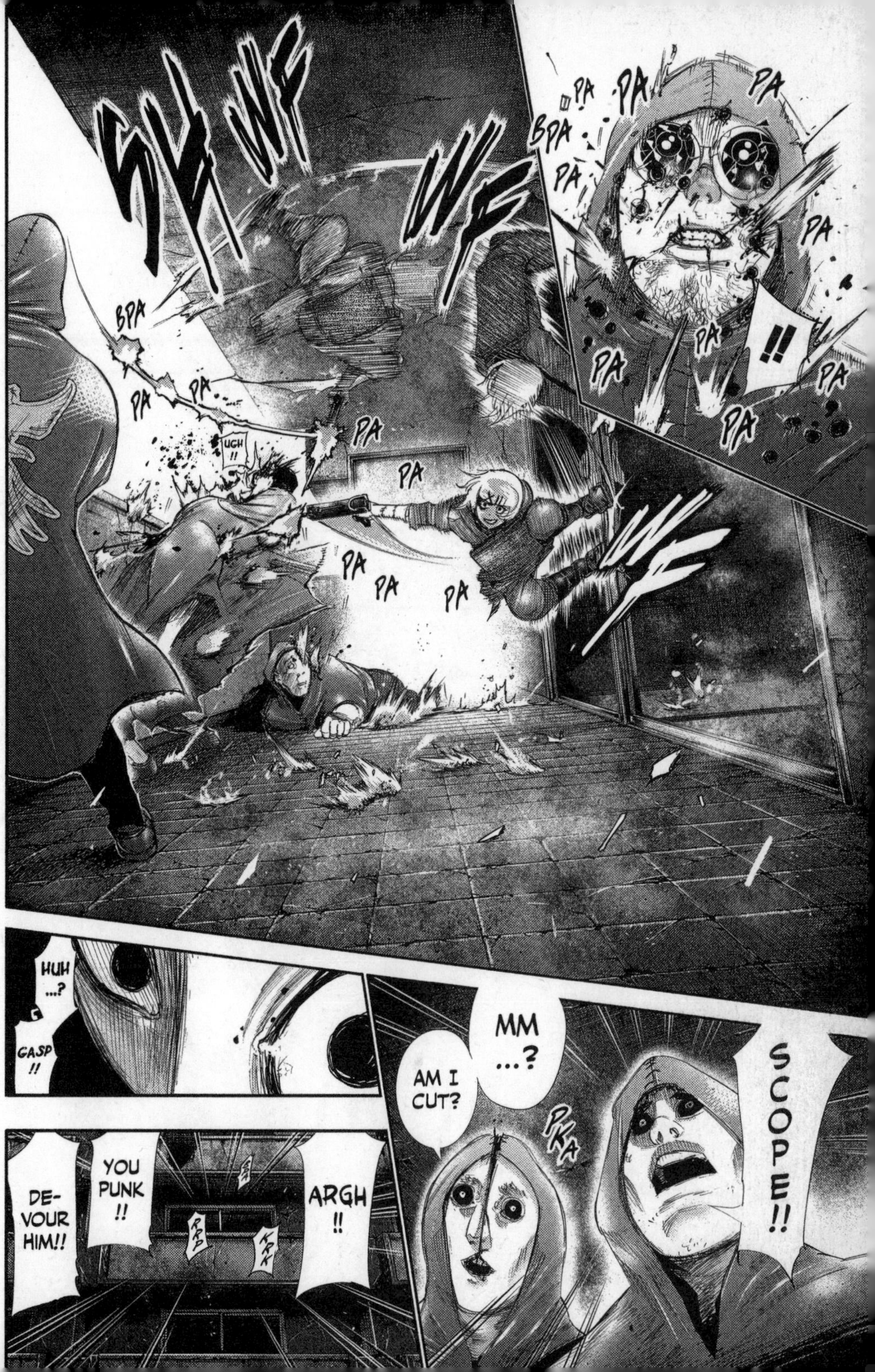
PA
PA
PA
BPA
PA
PA
PA
!!
PA
PA
PA
PA
SHWF
WF
BPA
PA
PA
UGH!!
PA
PA
PA
PA
PA
WF
MM ...?
AM I CUT?
PKA
SCOPE!!
HUH ...?
GASP!!
ARGH!!
YOU PUNK!!
DE-VOUR HIM!!

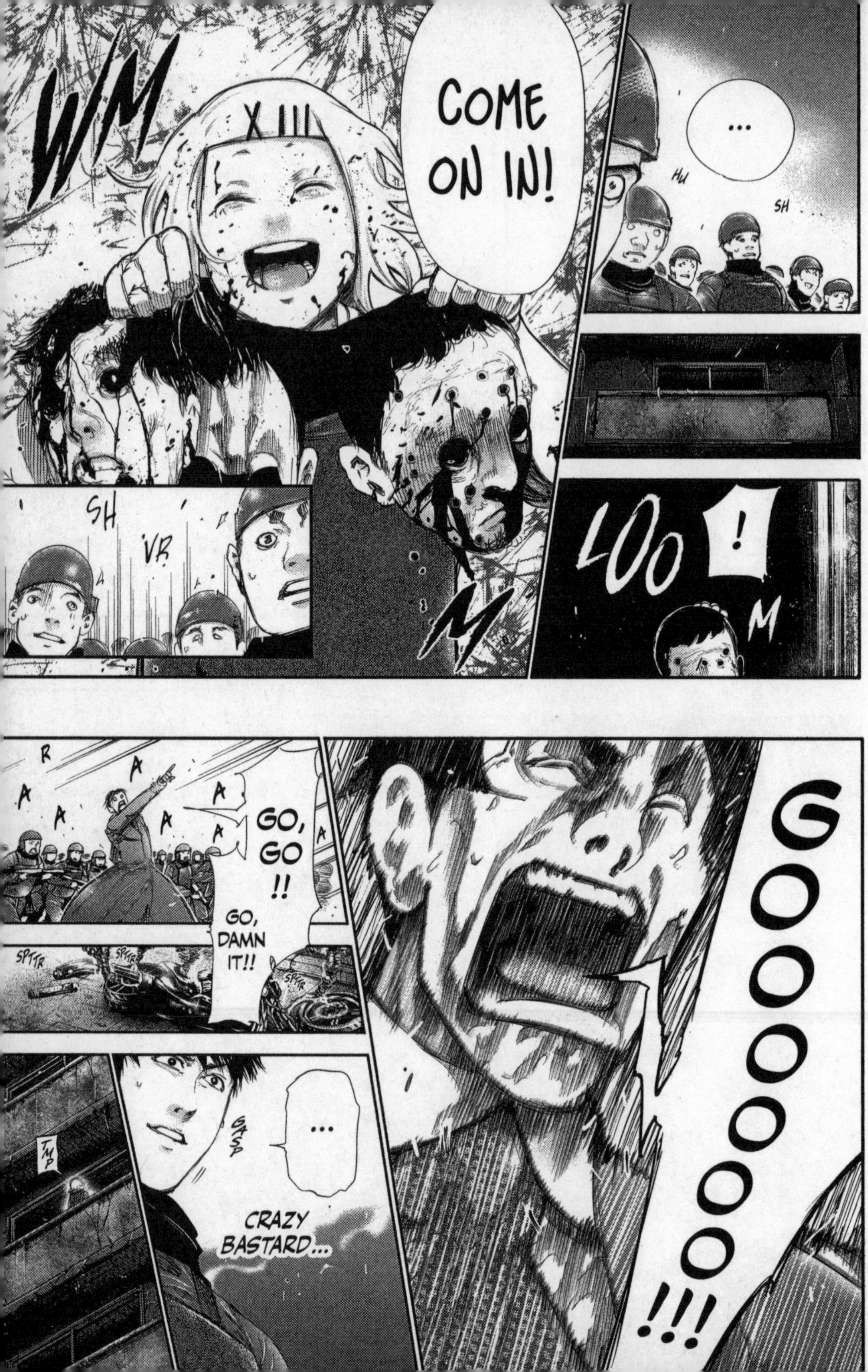
...
HU
SH
LOO
!
M
COME ON IN!
WM
M
SH
VR
GOOOOOOOOO!!!
RAAAAAAAA
GO, GO!!
GO, DAMN IT!!
SPTTR
SPTTR
SPTTR
...
GASP
TMP
CRAZY BASTARD...

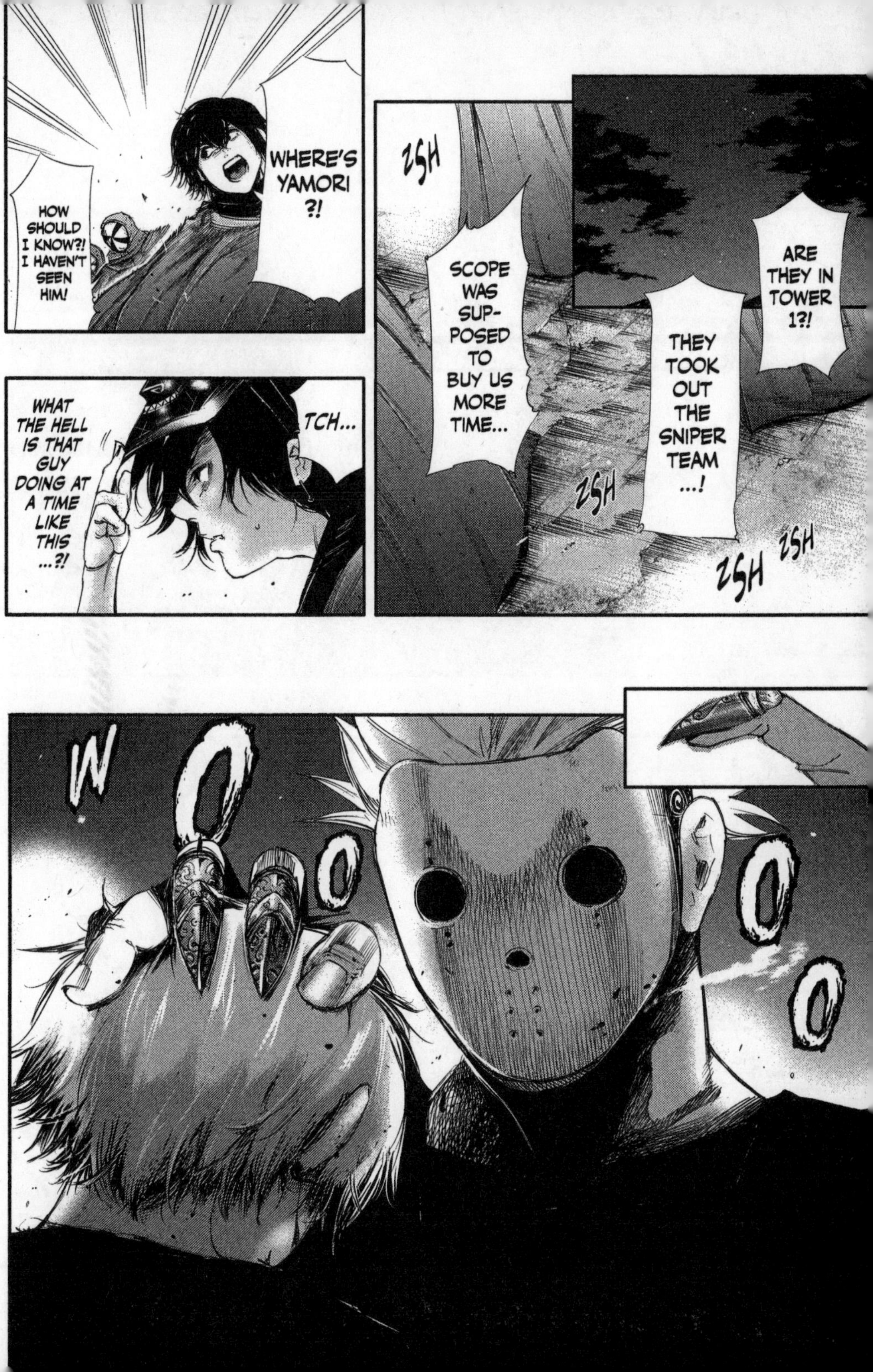
ARE THEY IN TOWER 1?!
THEY TOOK OUT THE SNIPER TEAM ...!
ZSH
SCOPE WAS SUP-POSED TO BUY US MORE TIME...
ZSH
ZSH
ZSH
WHERE'S YAMORI ?!
HOW SHOULD I KNOW?! I HAVEN'T SEEN HIM!
TCH...
WHAT THE HELL IS THAT GUY DOING AT A TIME LIKE THIS ...?!
WOOOOO

東京
トーキョーグール
喰種
Tokyo
Ghoul

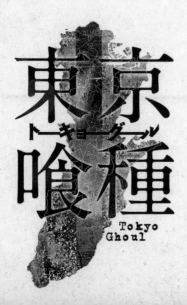

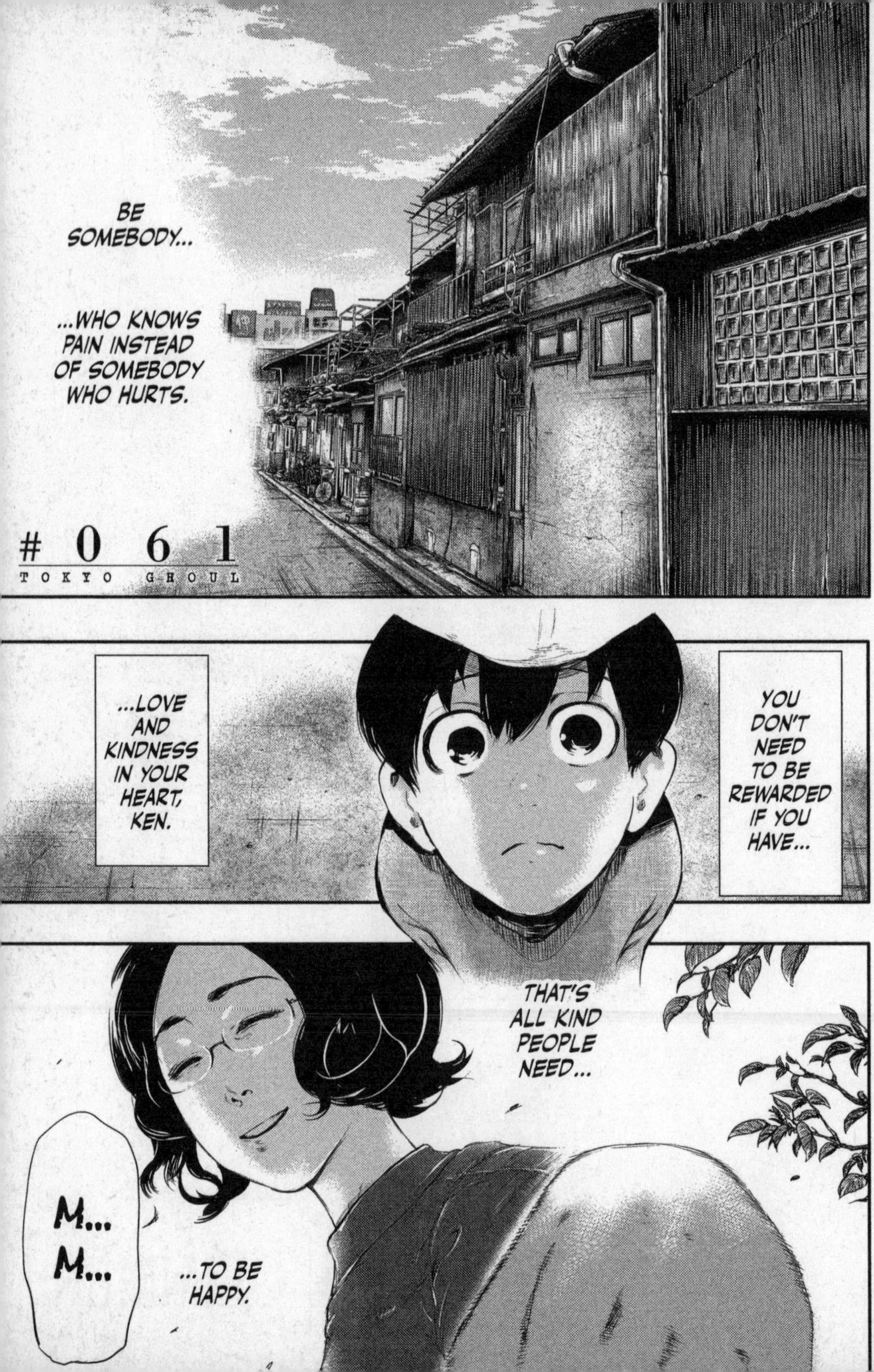
BE SOMEBODY...
...WHO KNOWS PAIN INSTEAD OF SOMEBODY WHO HURTS.
#061
TOKYO GHOUL
YOU DON'T NEED TO BE REWARDED IF YOU HAVE...
...LOVE AND KINDNESS IN YOUR HEART, KEN.
THAT'S ALL KIND PEOPLE NEED...
...TO BE HAPPY.
M... M...

SOMEBODY
WHO
KNOWS PAIN
INSTEAD OF
SOMEBODY
WHO
HURTS...

MOM...

#061
TOKYO GHOUL

[GLIMMER]

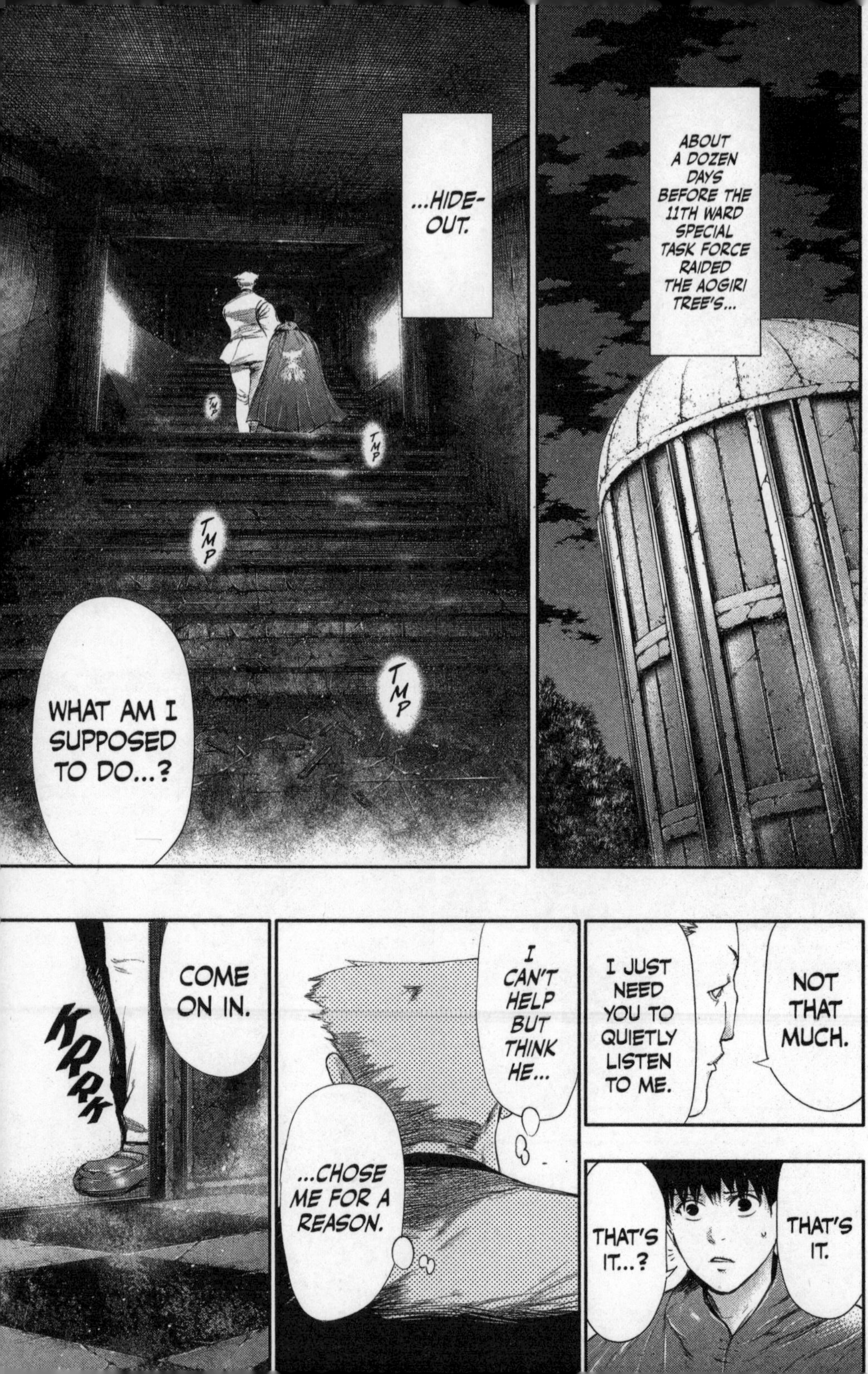
ABOUT A DOZEN DAYS BEFORE THE 11TH WARD SPECIAL TASK FORCE RAIDED THE AOGIRI TREE'S...
...HIDE-OUT.
TMP
TMP
TMP
TMP
WHAT AM I SUPPOSED TO DO...?
NOT THAT MUCH.
I JUST NEED YOU TO QUIETLY LISTEN TO ME.
THAT'S IT.
THAT'S IT...?
I CAN'T HELP BUT THINK HE...
...CHOSE ME FOR A REASON.
COME ON IN.
KRRK

IS HE DEAD...?

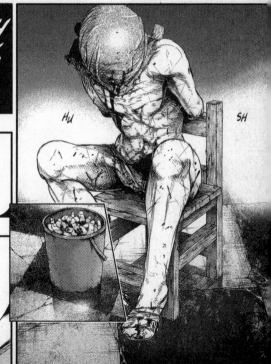

HE'S ONE OF MY MEN.

PUNISH-MENT FOR SCREWING UP.

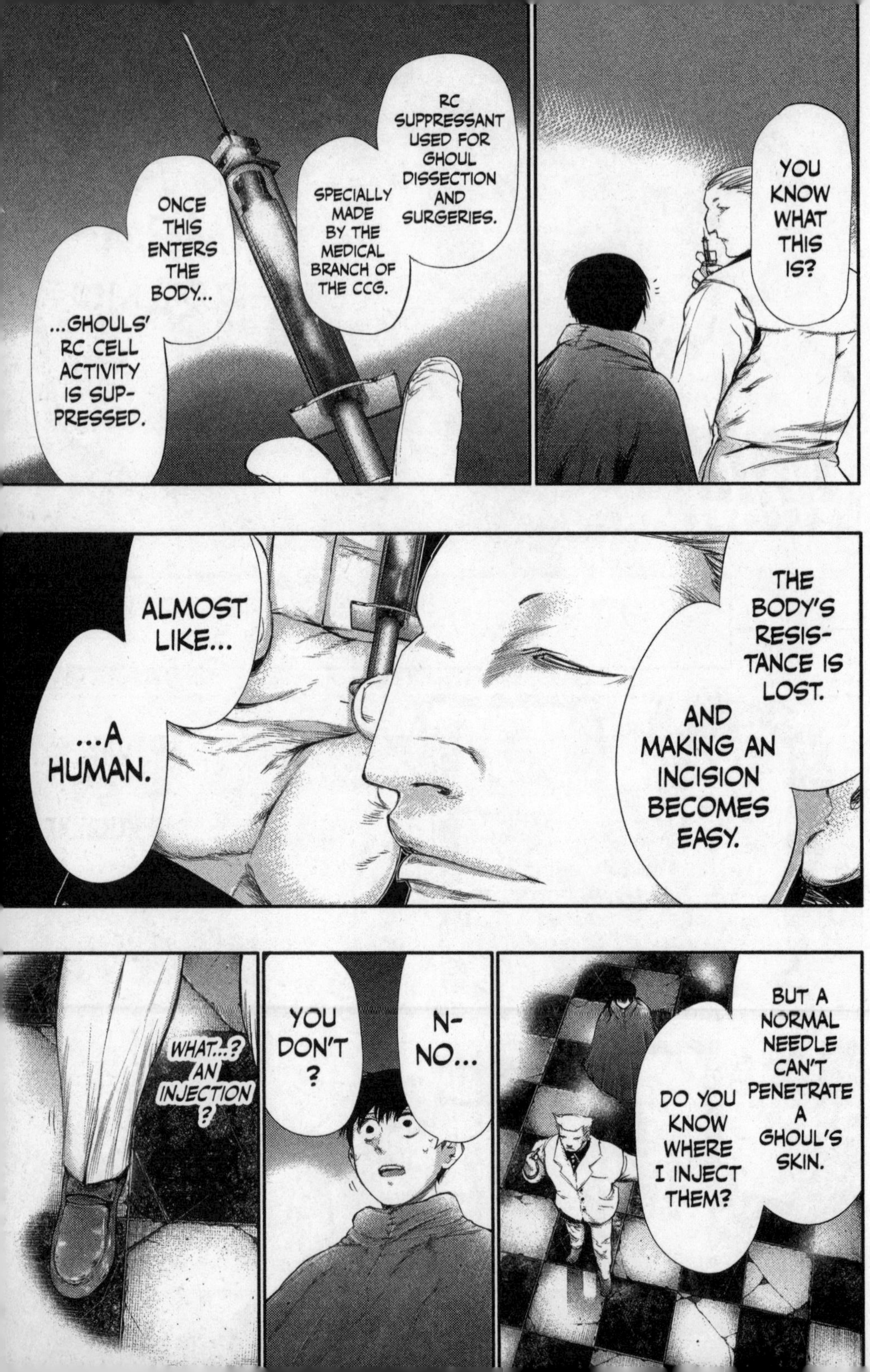
YOU KNOW WHAT THIS IS?
RC SUPPRESSANT USED FOR GHOUL DISSECTION AND SURGERIES.
SPECIALLY MADE BY THE MEDICAL BRANCH OF THE CCG.
ONCE THIS ENTERS THE BODY...
...GHOULS' RC CELL ACTIVITY IS SUP-PRESSED.
THE BODY'S RESIS-TANCE IS LOST.
AND MAKING AN INCISION BECOMES EASY.
ALMOST LIKE...
...A HUMAN.
BUT A NORMAL NEEDLE CAN'T PENETRATE A GHOUL'S SKIN.
DO YOU KNOW WHERE I INJECT THEM?
N-NO...
YOU DON'T?
WHAT...? AN INJECTION?

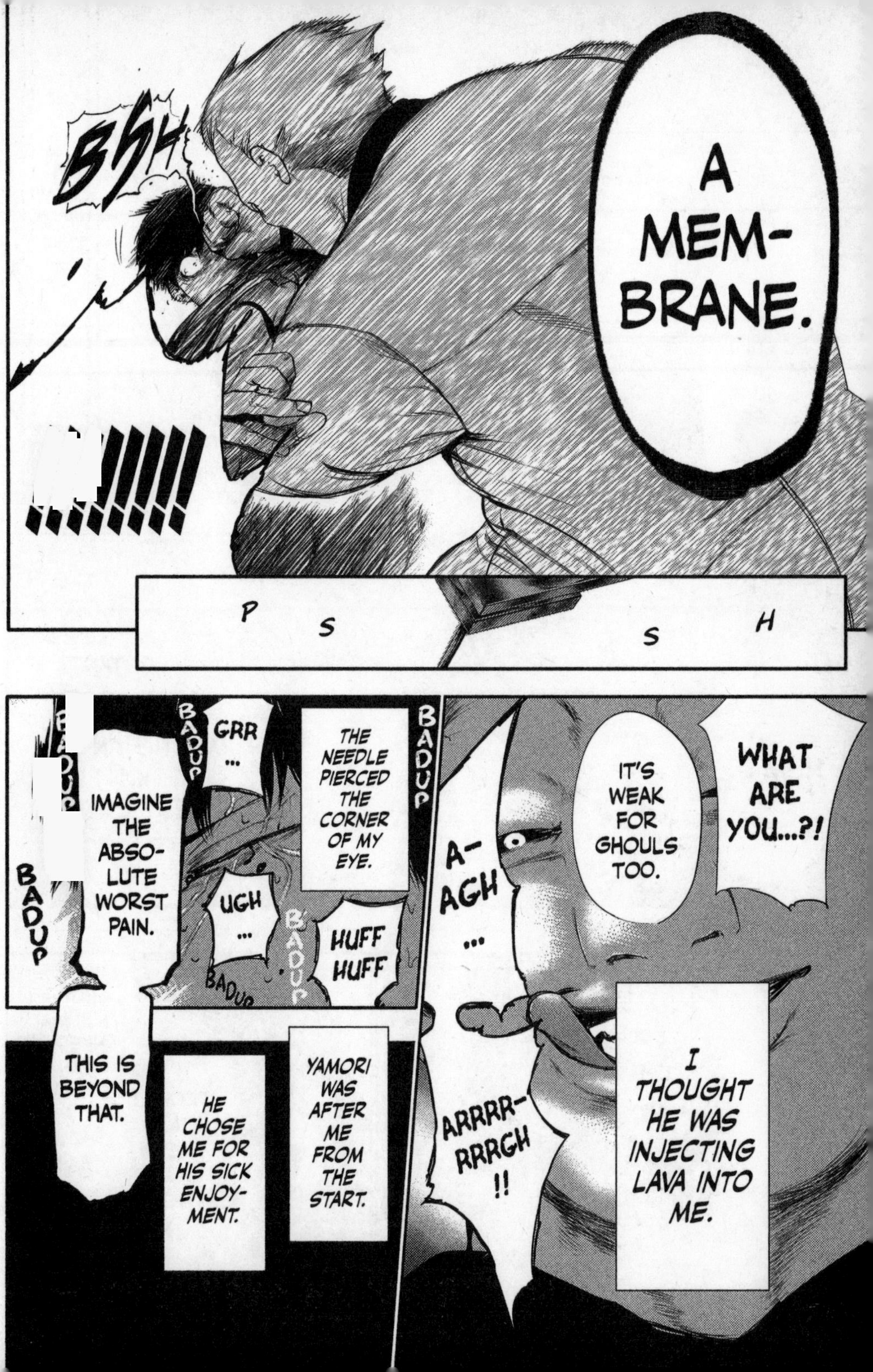
A MEM-BRANE.
BSH
!!!!!!!!!
PSSH
WHAT ARE YOU...?!
IT'S WEAK FOR GHOULS TOO.
A-AGH...
I THOUGHT HE WAS INJECTING LAVA INTO ME.
ARRRR-RRRGH!!
BADUP
THE NEEDLE PIERCED THE CORNER OF MY EYE.
BADUP
GRR...
HUFF HUFF
BADUP
UGH...
BADUP
IMAGINE THE ABSOLUTE WORST PAIN.
BADUP
YAMORI WAS AFTER ME FROM THE START.
HE CHOSE ME FOR HIS SICK ENJOYMENT.
THIS IS BEYOND THAT.

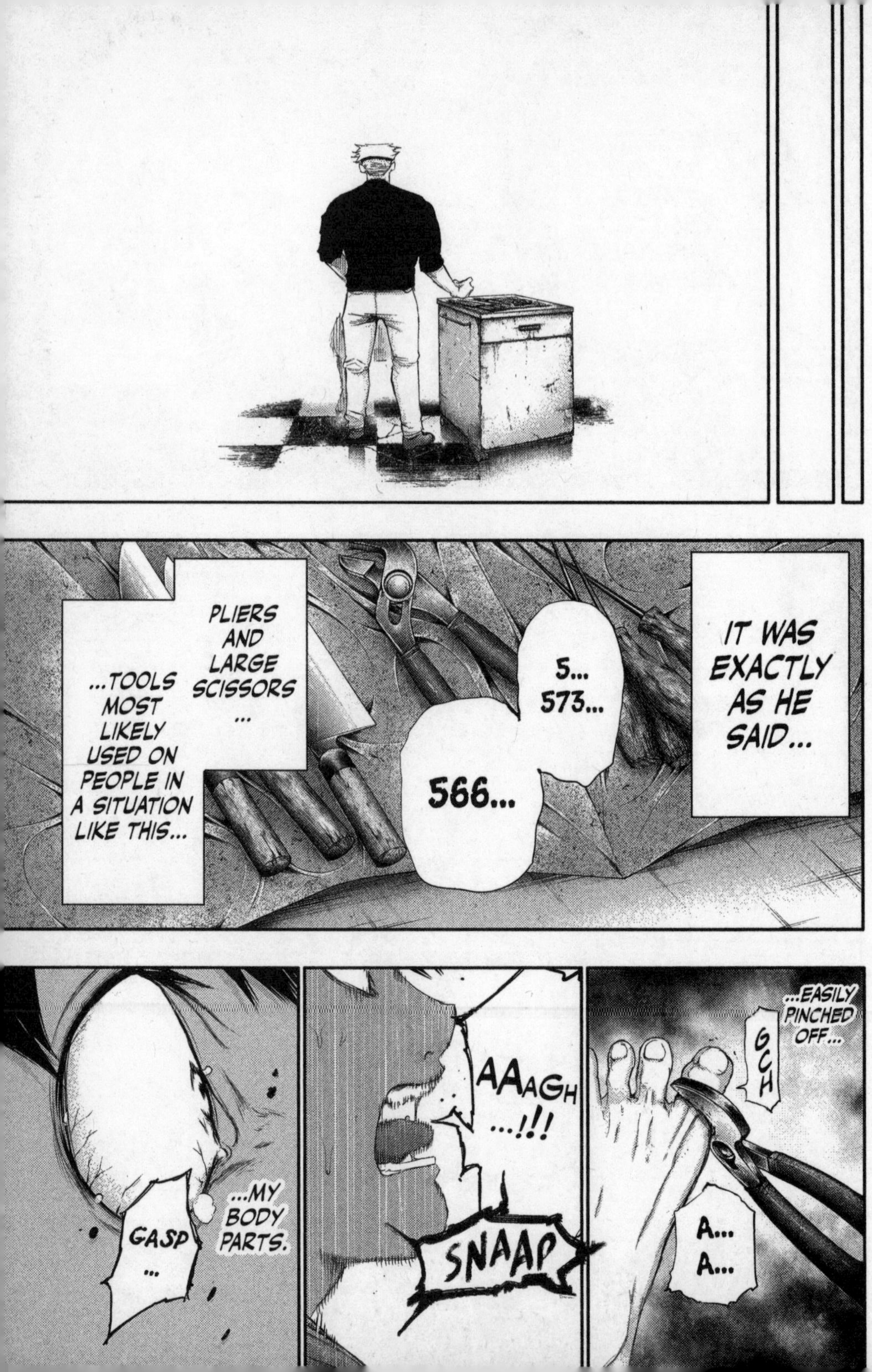
IT WAS EXACTLY AS HE SAID...
5... 573...
566...
PLIERS AND LARGE SCISSORS ...
...TOOLS MOST LIKELY USED ON PEOPLE IN A SITUATION LIKE THIS...
...EASILY PINCHED OFF...
GCH
A... A...
AAAGH ...!!!
SNAAP
...MY BODY PARTS.
GASP ...

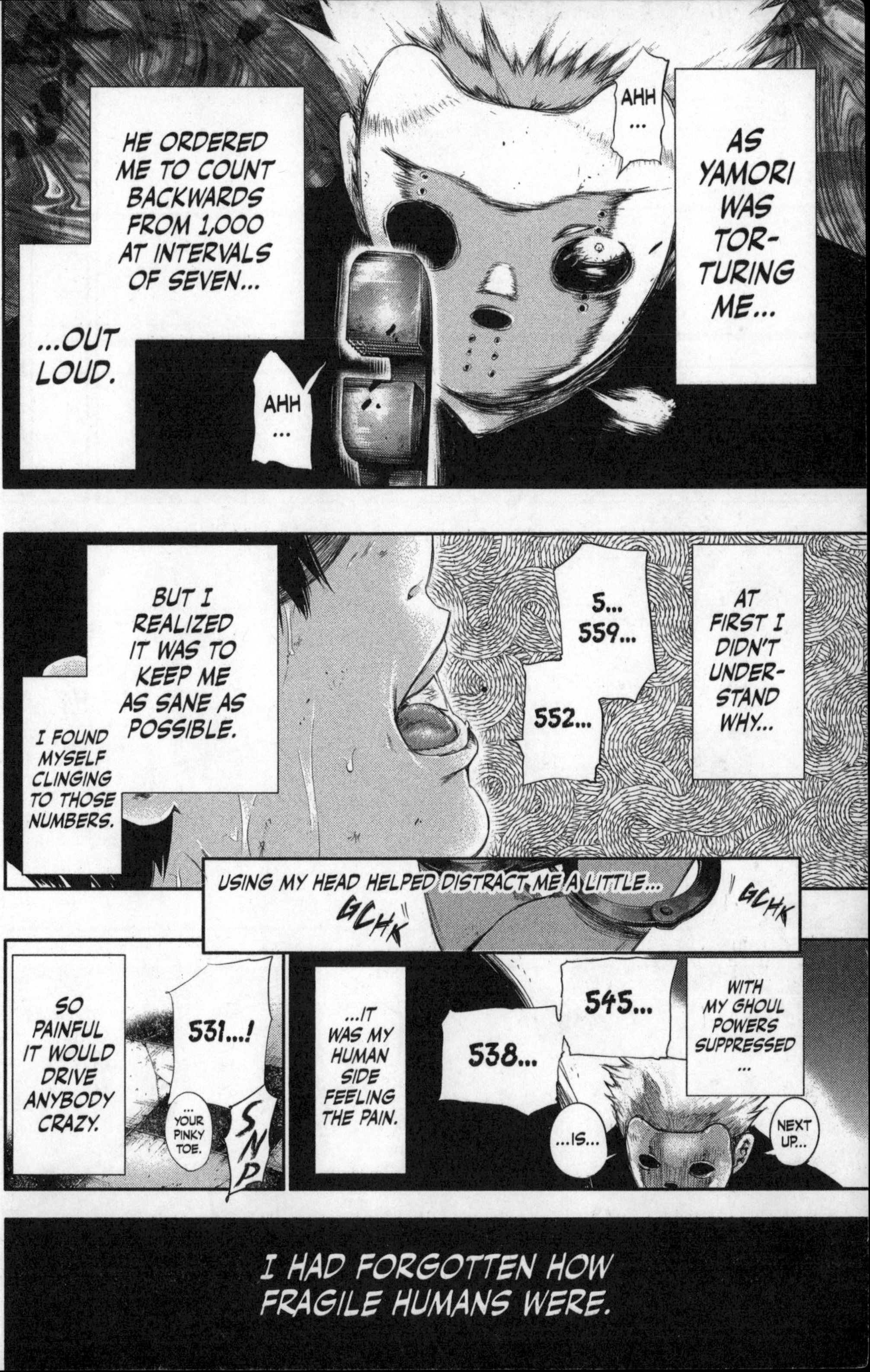
AS YAMORI WAS TOR-TURING ME...
AHH ...
HE ORDERED ME TO COUNT BACKWARDS FROM 1,000 AT INTERVALS OF SEVEN...
...OUT LOUD.
AHH ...
AT FIRST I DIDN'T UNDER-STAND WHY...
5... 559...
552...
BUT I REALIZED IT WAS TO KEEP ME AS SANE AS POSSIBLE.
I FOUND MYSELF CLINGING TO THOSE NUMBERS.
GCHK
USING MY HEAD HELPED DISTRACT ME A LITTLE...
GCHK
WITH MY GHOUL POWERS SUPPRESSED ...
545...
538...
NEXT UP...
...IS...
...IT WAS MY HUMAN SIDE FEELING THE PAIN.
531...!
... YOUR PINKY TOE.
SNP
SO PAINFUL IT WOULD DRIVE ANYBODY CRAZY.
I HAD FORGOTTEN HOW FRAGILE HUMANS WERE.

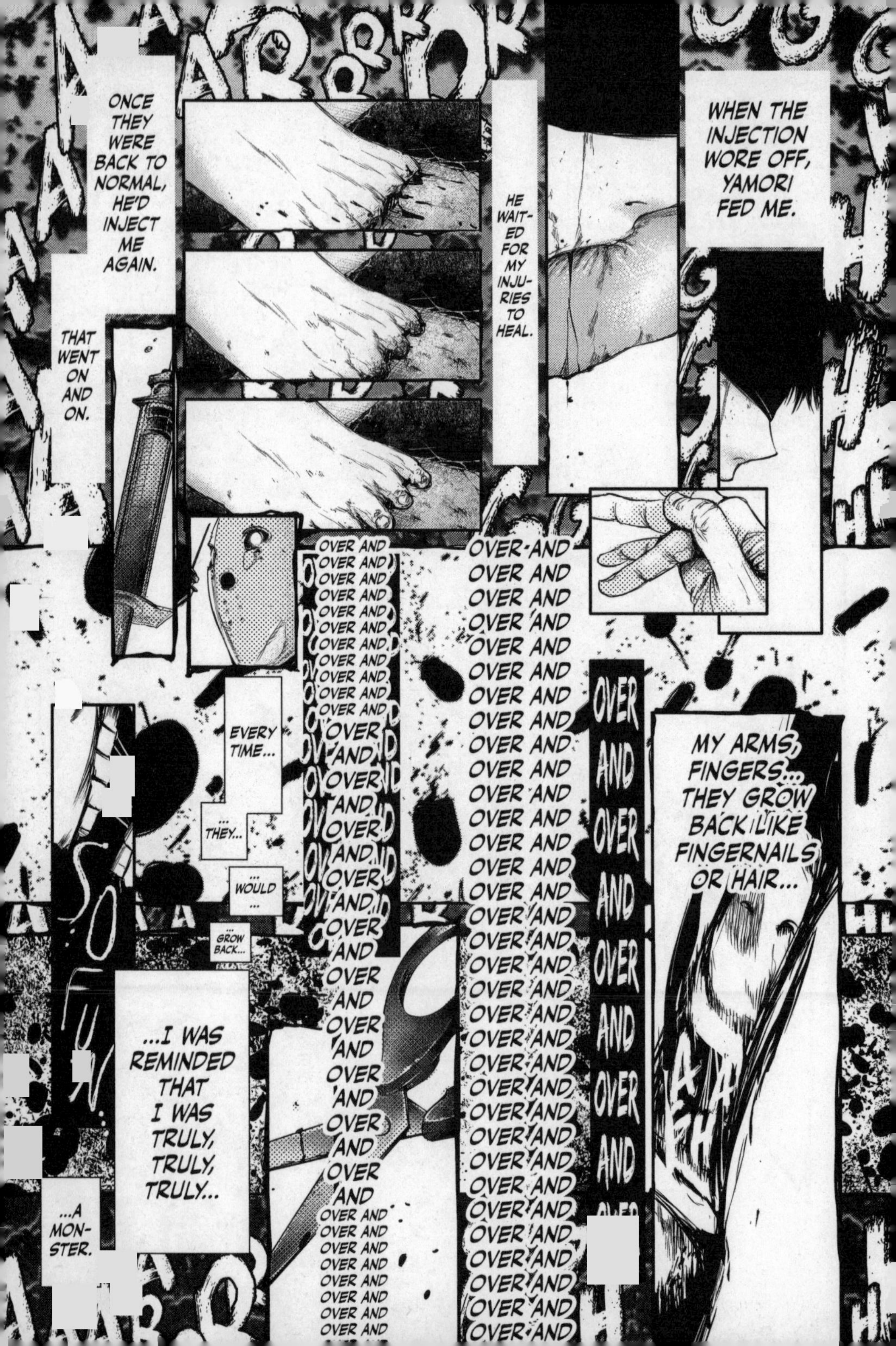
WHEN THE INJECTION WORE OFF, YAMORI FED ME.
HE WAIT-ED FOR MY INJU-RIES TO HEAL.
ONCE THEY WERE BACK TO NORMAL, HE'D INJECT ME AGAIN.
THAT WENT ON AND ON.
MY ARMS, FINGERS... THEY GROW BACK LIKE FINGERNAILS OR HAIR...
OVER AND OVER AND OVER AND OVER AND OVER AND
OVER AND OVER AND OVER AND OVER AND OVER AND OVER AND OVER AND OVER AND OVER AND OVER AND OVER AND OVER AND OVER AND OVER AND OVER AND OVER AND
OVER AND OVER AND OVER AND OVER AND OVER AND OVER AND OVER AND OVER AND OVER AND OVER AND OVER AND OVER AND OVER AND OVER AND OVER AND OVER AND
EVERY TIME...
...THEY...
...WOULD...
...GROW BACK...
...I WAS REMINDED THAT I WAS TRULY, TRULY, TRULY...
...A MON-STER.

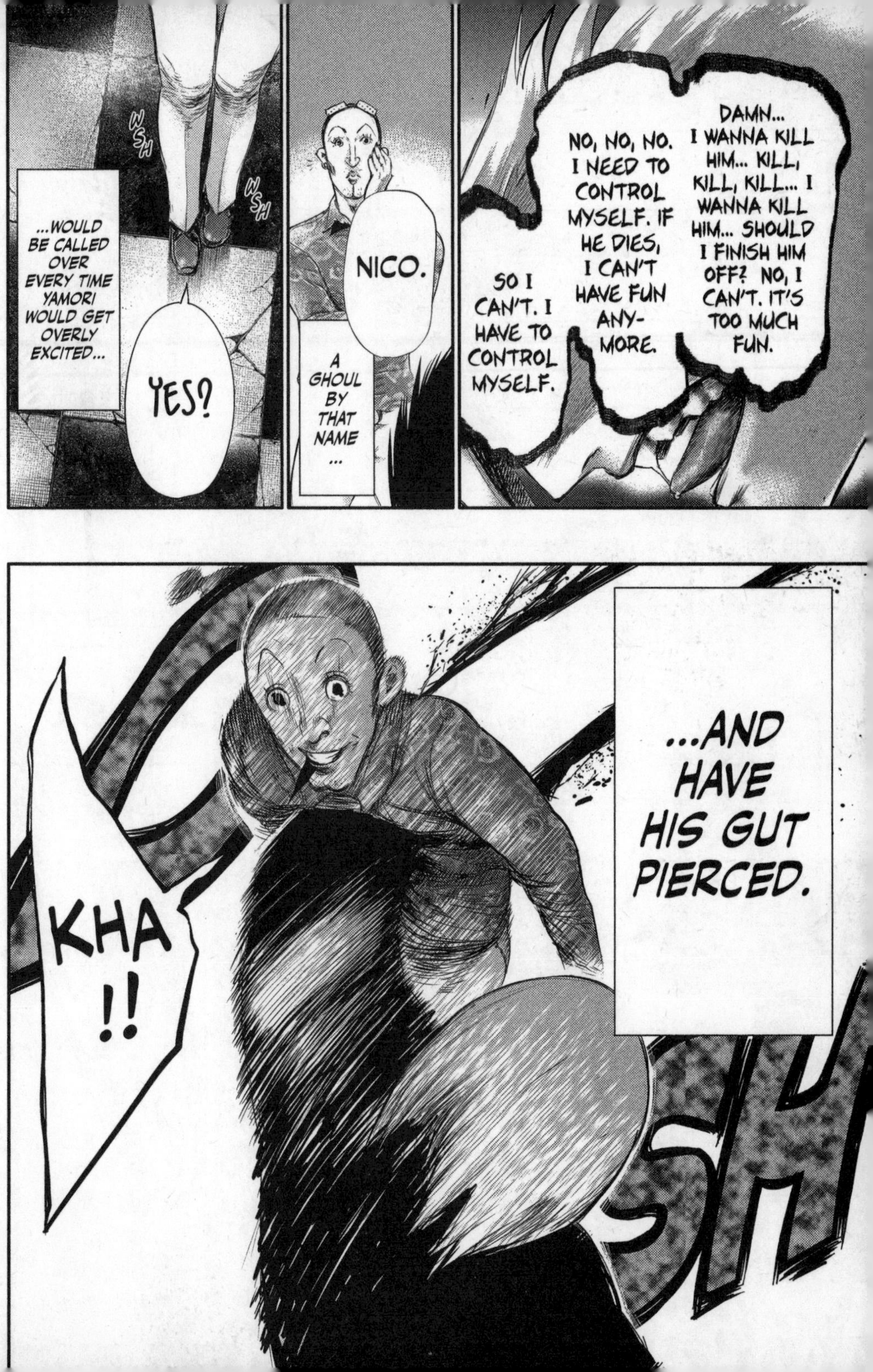
DAMN... I WANNA KILL HIM... KILL, KILL, KILL... I WANNA KILL HIM... SHOULD I FINISH HIM OFF? NO, I CAN'T. IT'S TOO MUCH FUN.
NO, NO, NO. I NEED TO CONTROL MYSELF. IF HE DIES, I CAN'T HAVE FUN ANYMORE.
SO I CAN'T. I HAVE TO CONTROL MYSELF.
NICO.
A GHOUL BY THAT NAME...
...WOULD BE CALLED OVER EVERY TIME YAMORI WOULD GET OVERLY EXCITED...
YES?
WSH
WSH
...AND HAVE HIS GUT PIERCED.
KHA!!
SH

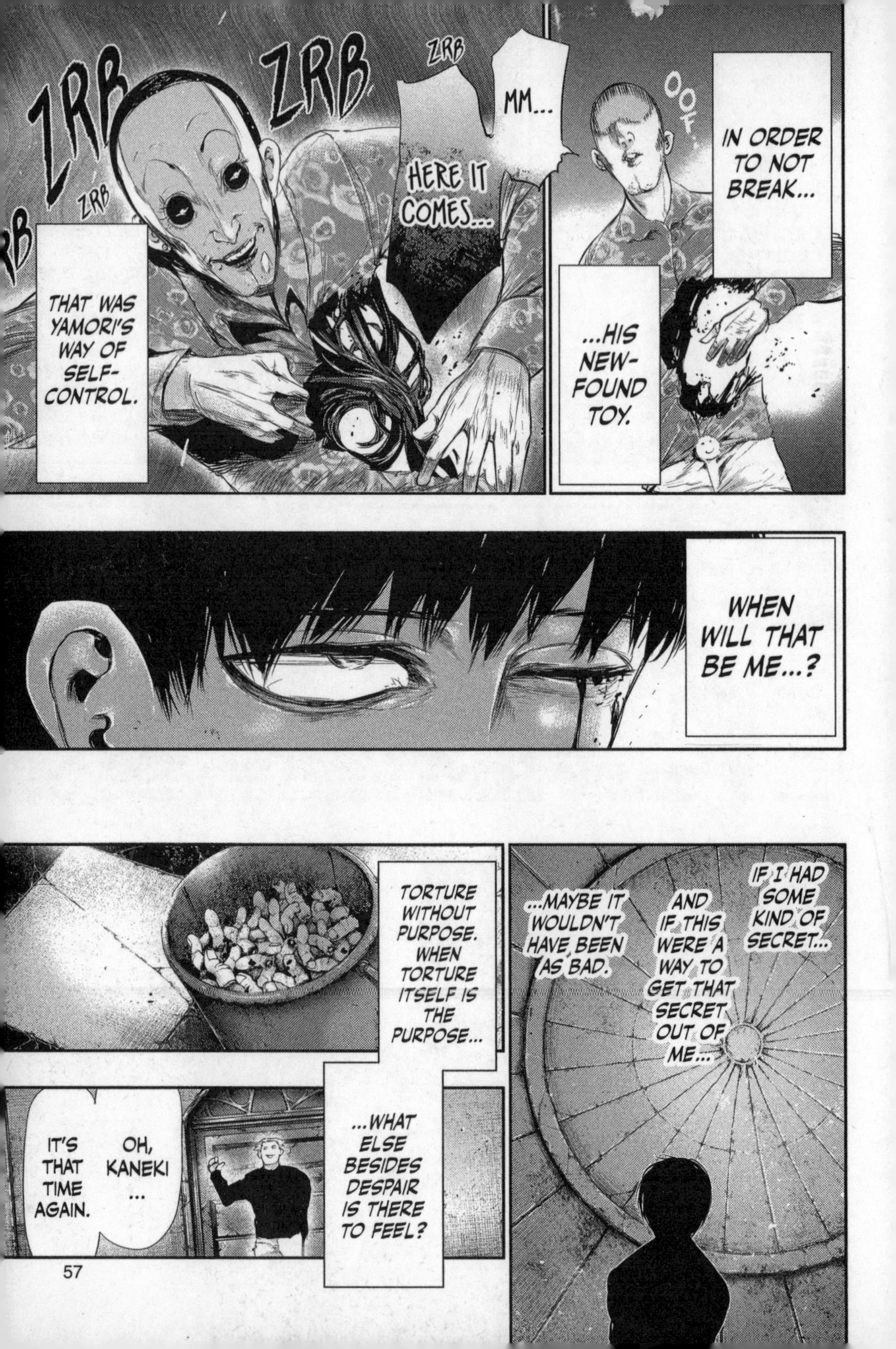
OOF
IN ORDER TO NOT BREAK...
...HIS NEW-FOUND TOY.
ZRB
MM...
ZRB
ZRB
HERE IT COMES...
ZRB
ZRB
THAT WAS YAMORI'S WAY OF SELF-CONTROL.
WHEN WILL THAT BE ME...?
IF I HAD SOME KIND OF SECRET...
AND IF THIS WERE A WAY TO GET THAT SECRET OUT OF ME...
...MAYBE IT WOULDN'T HAVE BEEN AS BAD.
TORTURE WITHOUT PURPOSE. WHEN TORTURE ITSELF IS THE PURPOSE...
...WHAT ELSE BESIDES DESPAIR IS THERE TO FEEL?
OH, KANEKI...
IT'S THAT TIME AGAIN.

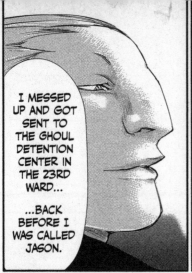

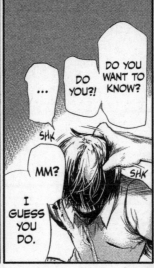

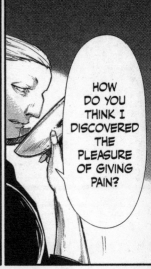

HOW DO YOU THINK I DISCOVERED THE PLEASURE OF GIVING PAIN?
DO YOU WANT TO KNOW?
DO YOU?!
...
SHK
SHK
MM?
I GUESS YOU DO.
I MESSED UP AND GOT SENT TO THE GHOUL DETENTION CENTER IN THE 23RD WARD...
...BACK BEFORE I WAS CALLED JASON.
I KNEW THE INS AND OUTS OF THE 13TH WARD...
...SO I WAS KEPT ALIVE AND AVOIDED BEING EUTHANIZED.
I THINK CLOWNS BEING IN POWER HAD SOMETHING TO DO WITH IT.
THERE WAS AN INVESTIGATOR THERE WITH A SCREW LOOSE...
HE WAS HUMAN, BUT HE WAS CRAZY.
EVERY DISADVANTAGE IN THE WORLD...
...IS FROM A LACK OF COMPETENCE.
I'M SORRY...
THE WEAK WERE TRAMPLED ON.
IMPINGED UPON, VIOLATED, ABUSED.
I'M SORRY...

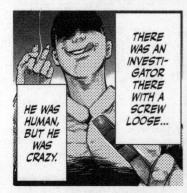

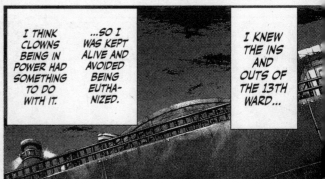

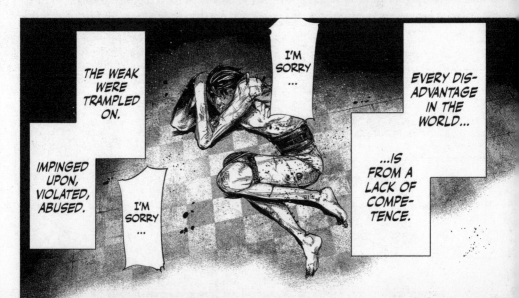

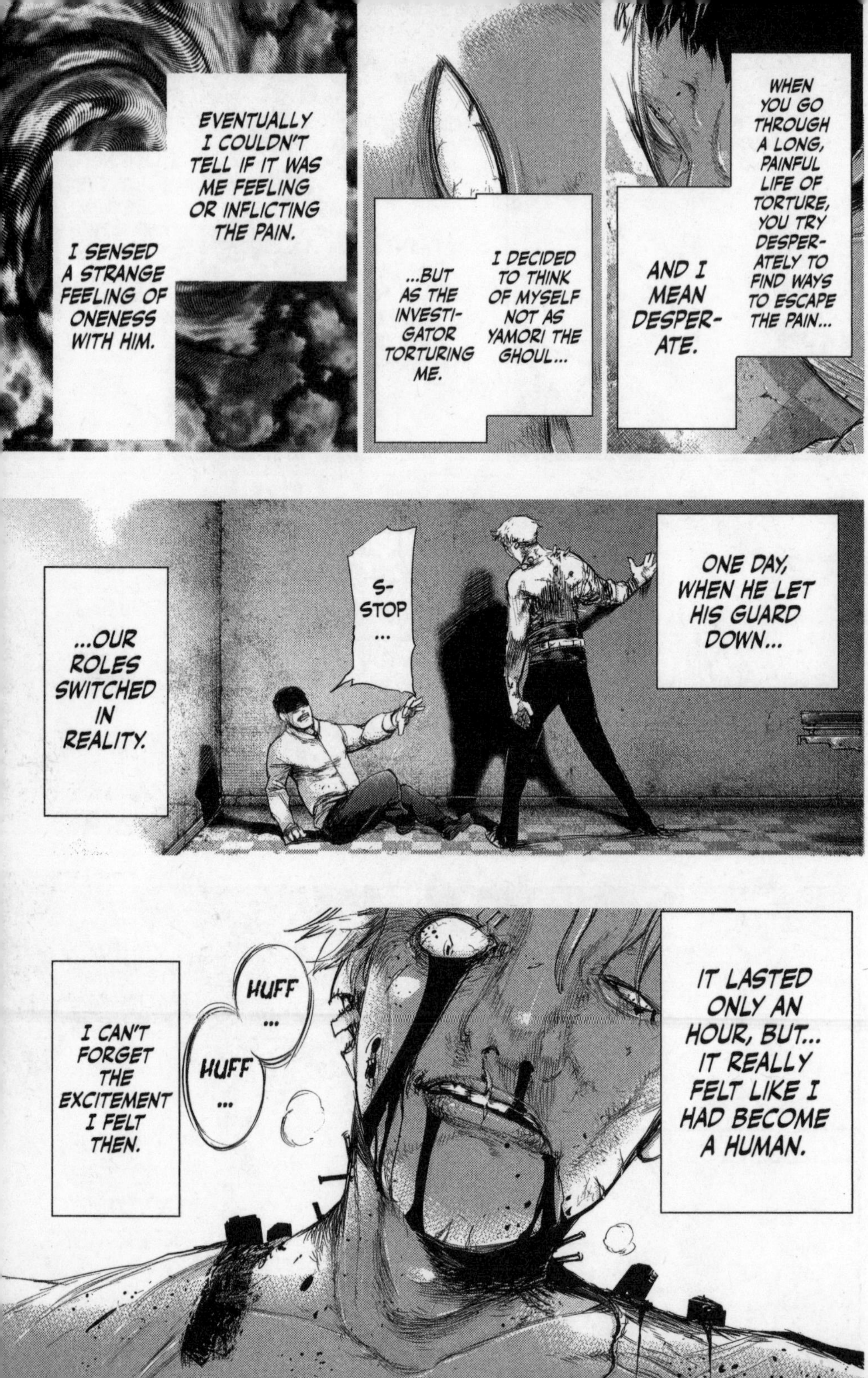
WHEN YOU GO THROUGH A LONG, PAINFUL LIFE OF TORTURE, YOU TRY DESPERATELY TO FIND WAYS TO ESCAPE THE PAIN...
AND I MEAN DESPERATE.
I DECIDED TO THINK OF MYSELF NOT AS YAMORI THE GHOUL...
...BUT AS THE INVESTIGATOR TORTURING ME.
EVENTUALLY I COULDN'T TELL IF IT WAS ME FEELING OR INFLICTING THE PAIN.
I SENSED A STRANGE FEELING OF ONENESS WITH HIM.
ONE DAY, WHEN HE LET HIS GUARD DOWN...
S-STOP...
...OUR ROLES SWITCHED IN REALITY.
IT LASTED ONLY AN HOUR, BUT... IT REALLY FELT LIKE I HAD BECOME A HUMAN.
HUFF...
HUFF...
I CAN'T FORGET THE EXCITEMENT I FELT THEN.

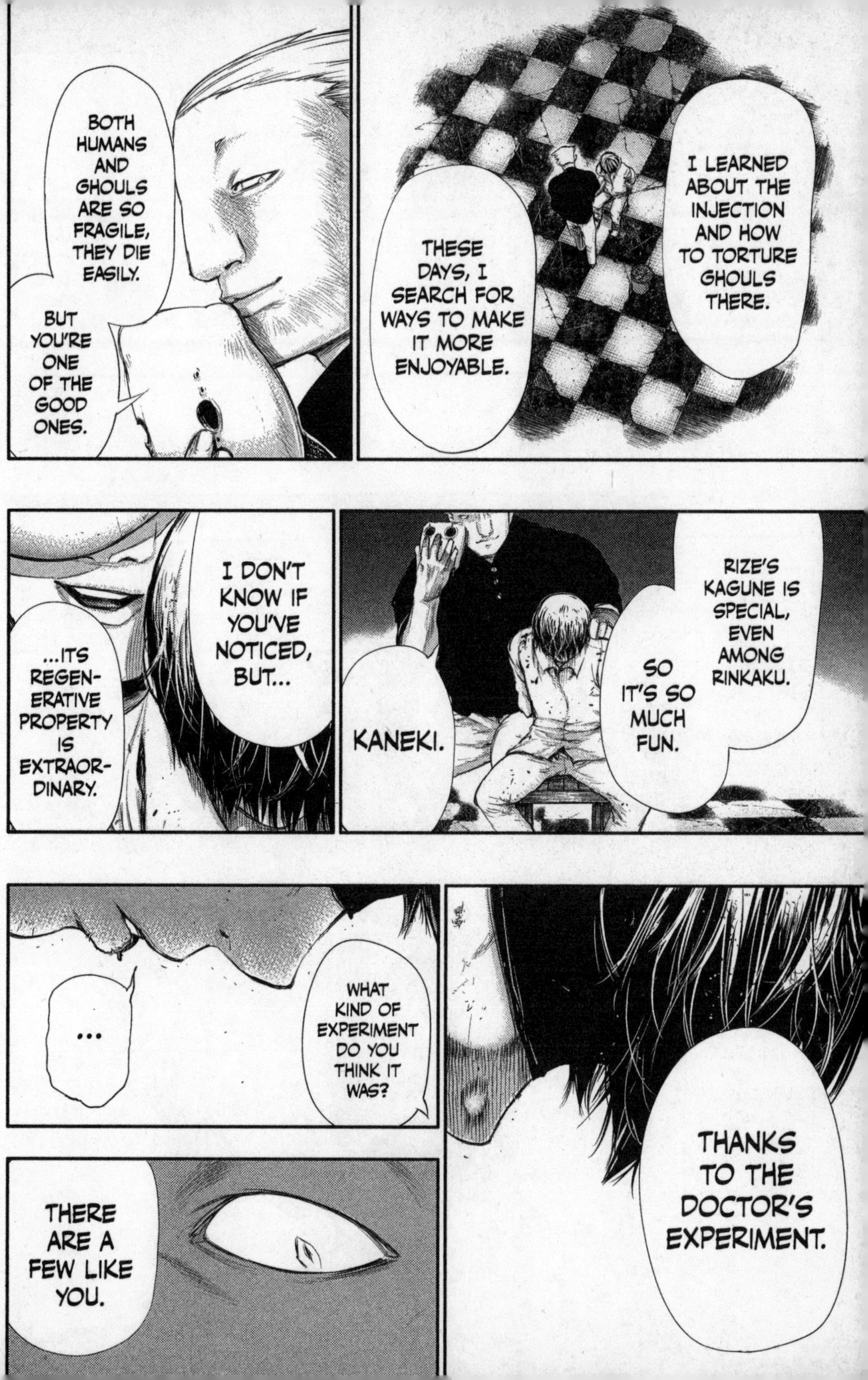
I LEARNED ABOUT THE INJECTION AND HOW TO TORTURE GHOULS THERE.
THESE DAYS, I SEARCH FOR WAYS TO MAKE IT MORE ENJOYABLE.
BOTH HUMANS AND GHOULS ARE SO FRAGILE, THEY DIE EASILY.
BUT YOU'RE ONE OF THE GOOD ONES.
RIZE'S KAGUNE IS SPECIAL, EVEN AMONG RINKAKU.
SO IT'S SO MUCH FUN.
KANEKI.
I DON'T KNOW IF YOU'VE NOTICED, BUT...
...ITS REGENERATIVE PROPERTY IS EXTRAORDINARY.
THANKS TO THE DOCTOR'S EXPERIMENT.
WHAT KIND OF EXPERIMENT DO YOU THINK IT WAS?
...
THERE ARE A FEW LIKE YOU.

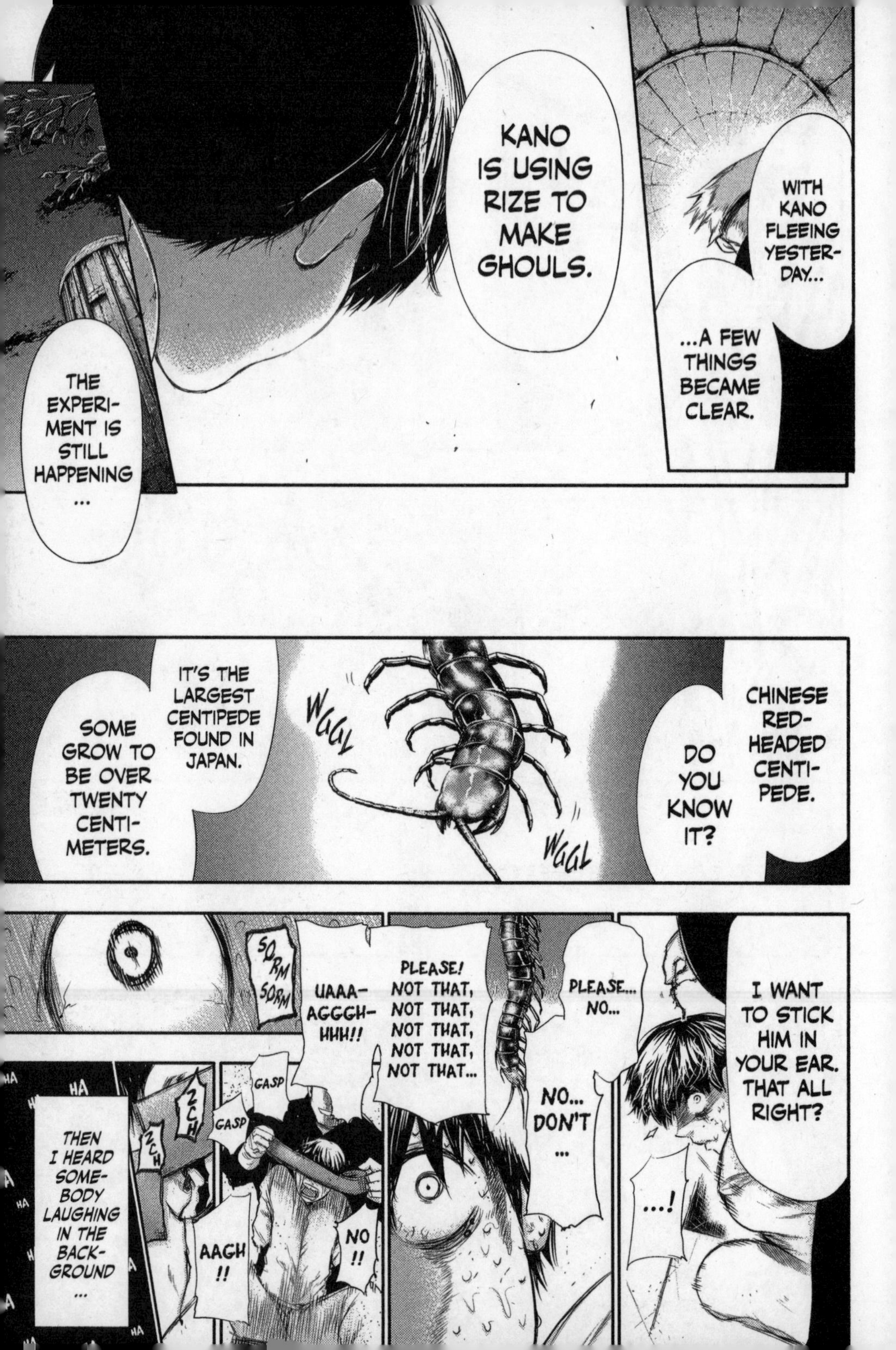
WITH KANO FLEEING YESTERDAY...
...A FEW THINGS BECAME CLEAR.
KANO IS USING RIZE TO MAKE GHOULS.
THE EXPERIMENT IS STILL HAPPENING...
CHINESE RED-HEADED CENTIPEDE.
DO YOU KNOW IT?
WGGL
WGGL
IT'S THE LARGEST CENTIPEDE FOUND IN JAPAN.
SOME GROW TO BE OVER TWENTY CENTIMETERS.
I WANT TO STICK HIM IN YOUR EAR. THAT ALL RIGHT?
...!
PLEASE... NO...
NO... DON'T...
PLEASE! NOT THAT, NOT THAT, NOT THAT, NOT THAT, NOT THAT...
UAAA-AGGGH-HHH!!
SQRM SQRM
GASP
GASP
ZCH
ZCH
NO!!
AAGH!!
HA HA
THEN I HEARD SOMEBODY LAUGHING IN THE BACKGROUND...

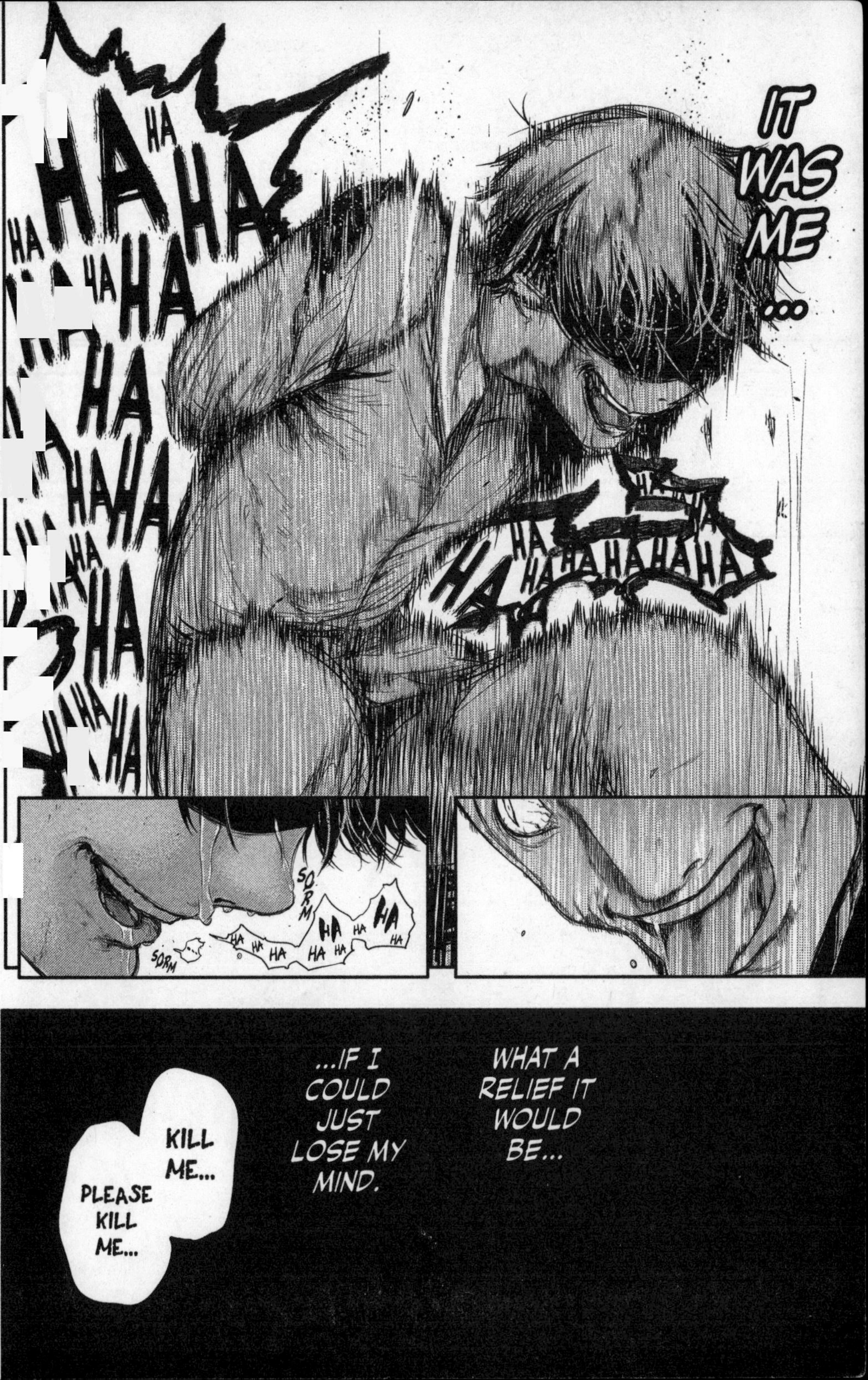
IT WAS ME...
HA HA HA HA HA HA HA HA HA HA HA HA HA HA HA HA
HA HA HA HAHAHAHAHAHA HA HA
SORM SORM
...
HA HA HA HA HA HA HA HA HA HA
WHAT A RELIEF IT WOULD BE...
...IF I COULD JUST LOSE MY MIND.
KILL ME...
PLEASE KILL ME...

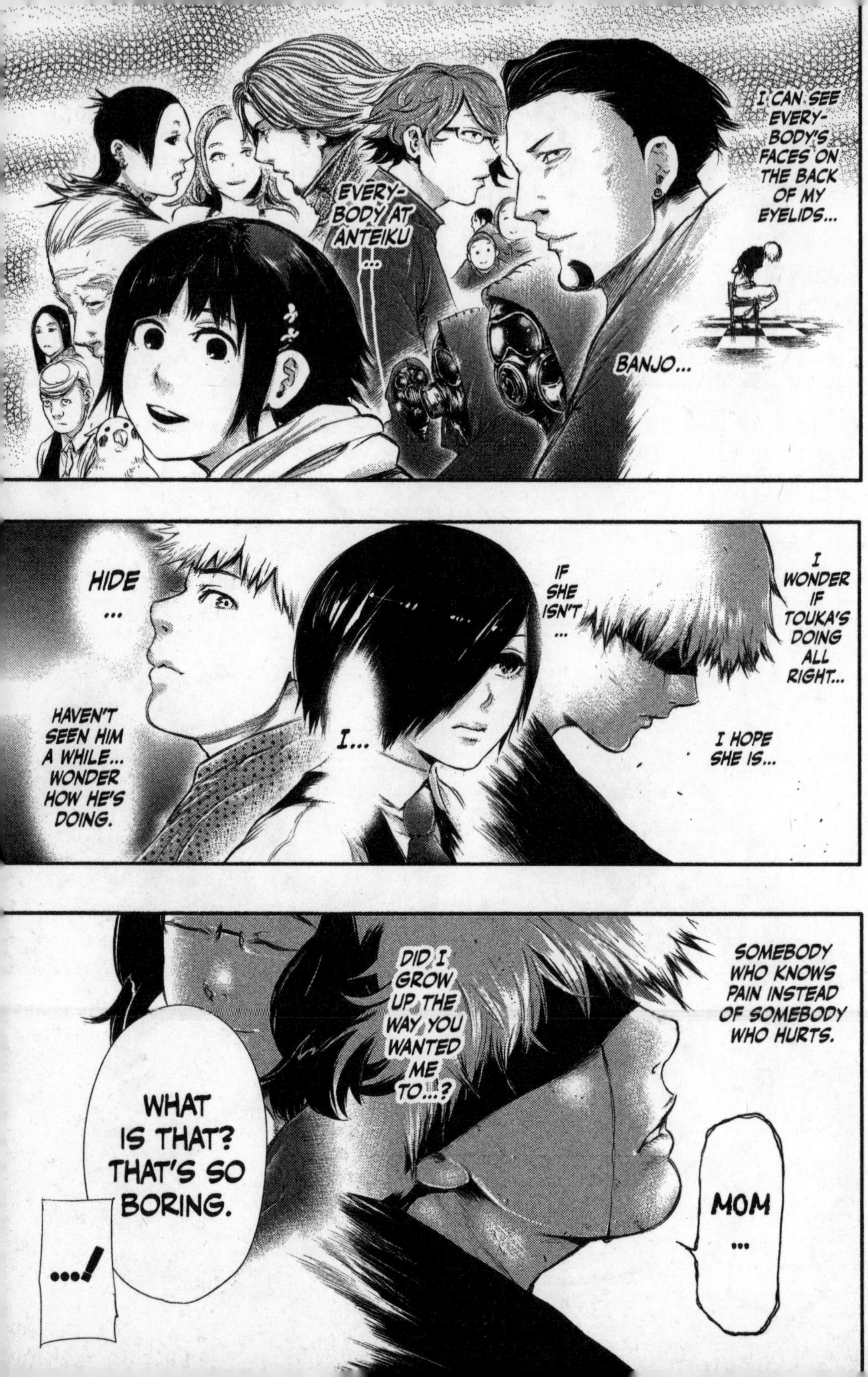
I CAN SEE EVERYBODY'S FACES ON THE BACK OF MY EYELIDS...
EVERYBODY AT ANTEIKU ...
BANJO...
I WONDER IF TOUKA'S DOING ALL RIGHT...
I HOPE SHE IS...
IF SHE ISN'T ...
I...
HIDE ...
HAVEN'T SEEN HIM A WHILE... WONDER HOW HE'S DOING.
SOMEBODY WHO KNOWS PAIN INSTEAD OF SOMEBODY WHO HURTS.
MOM ...
DID I GROW UP THE WAY YOU WANTED ME TO...?
WHAT IS THAT? THAT'S SO BORING.
...!

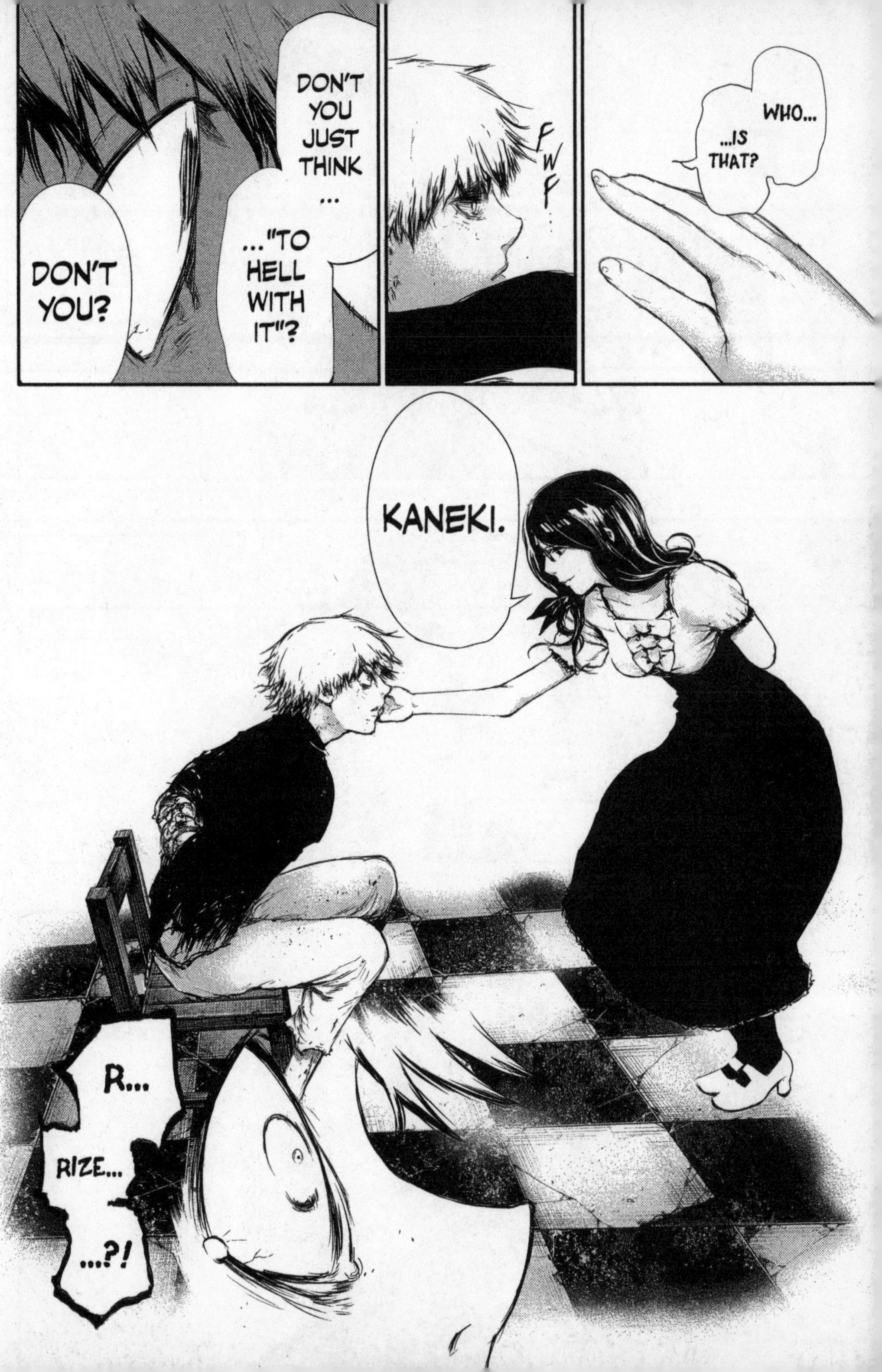
WHO...
...IS THAT?
FWF
DON'T YOU JUST THINK ...
..."TO HELL WITH IT"?
DON'T YOU?
KANEKI.
R...
RIZE...
...?!

#062
TOKYO GHOUL

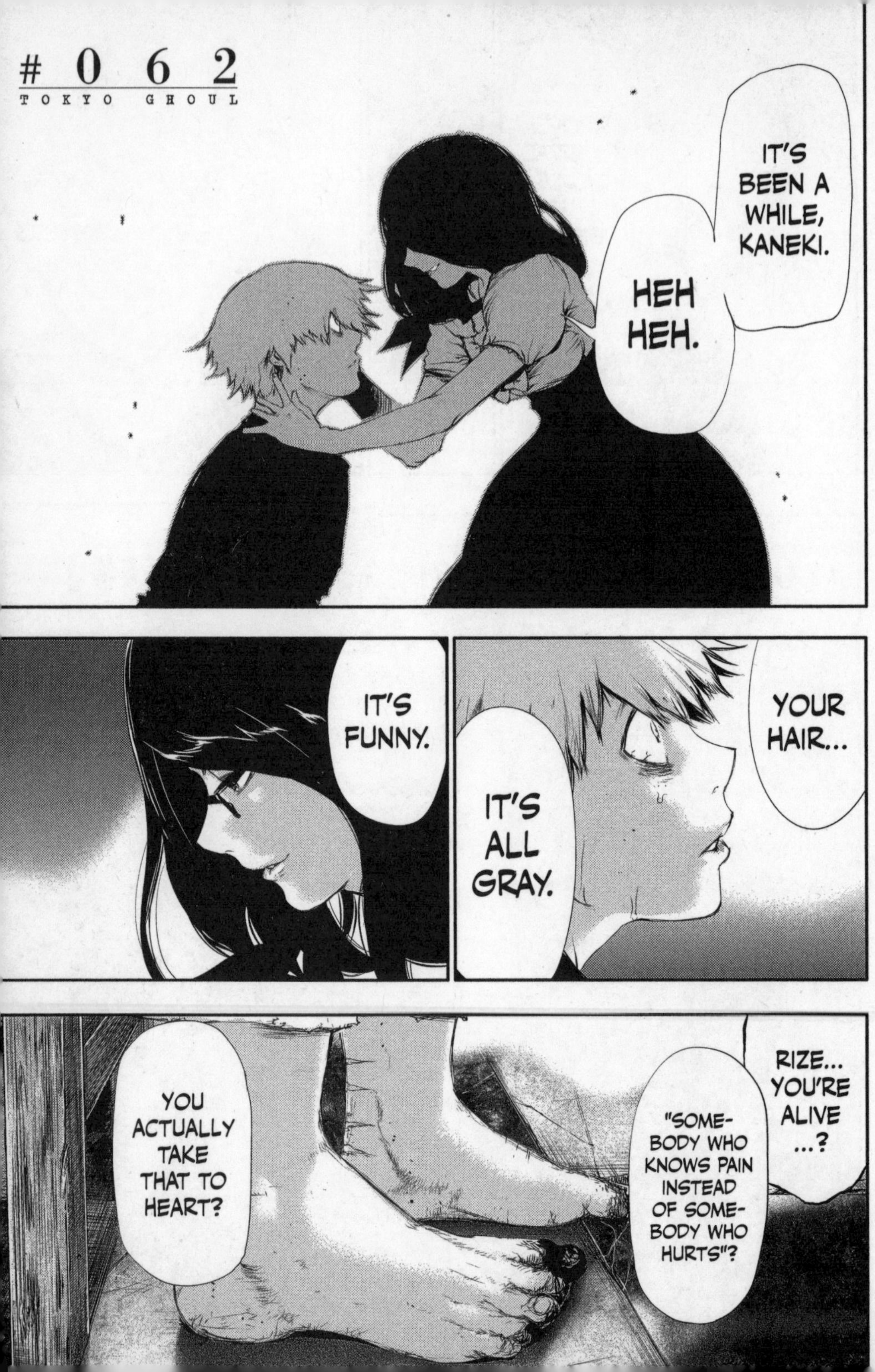
IT'S BEEN A WHILE, KANEKI.
HEH HEH.
YOUR HAIR...
IT'S ALL GRAY.
IT'S FUNNY.
RIZE... YOU'RE ALIVE ...?
"SOME-BODY WHO KNOWS PAIN INSTEAD OF SOME-BODY WHO HURTS"?
YOU ACTUALLY TAKE THAT TO HEART?

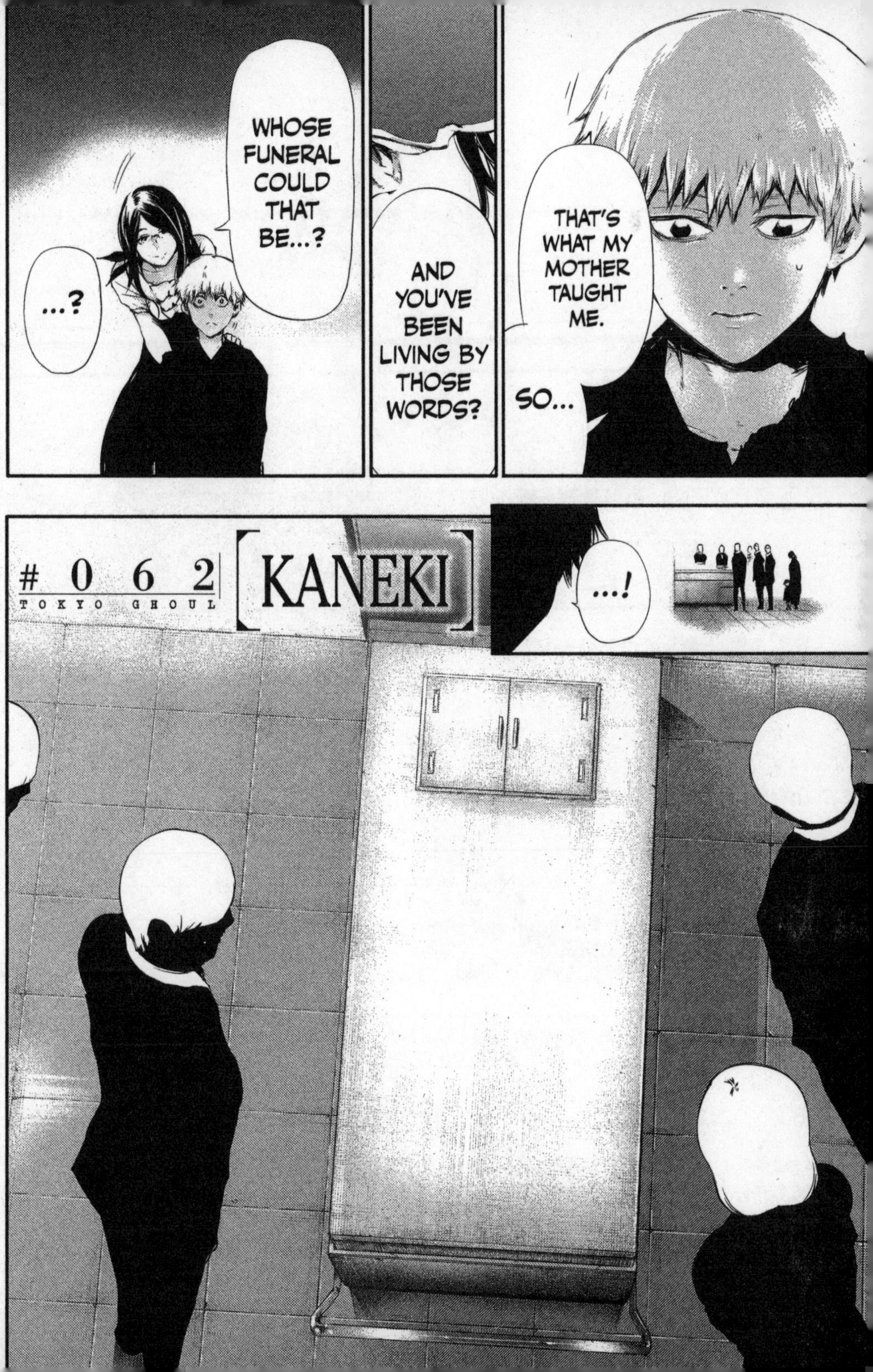
THAT'S WHAT MY MOTHER TAUGHT ME.
SO...
AND YOU'VE BEEN LIVING BY THOSE WORDS?
WHOSE FUNERAL COULD THAT BE...?
...?
...!
0 6 2
TOKYO GHOUL
KANEKI

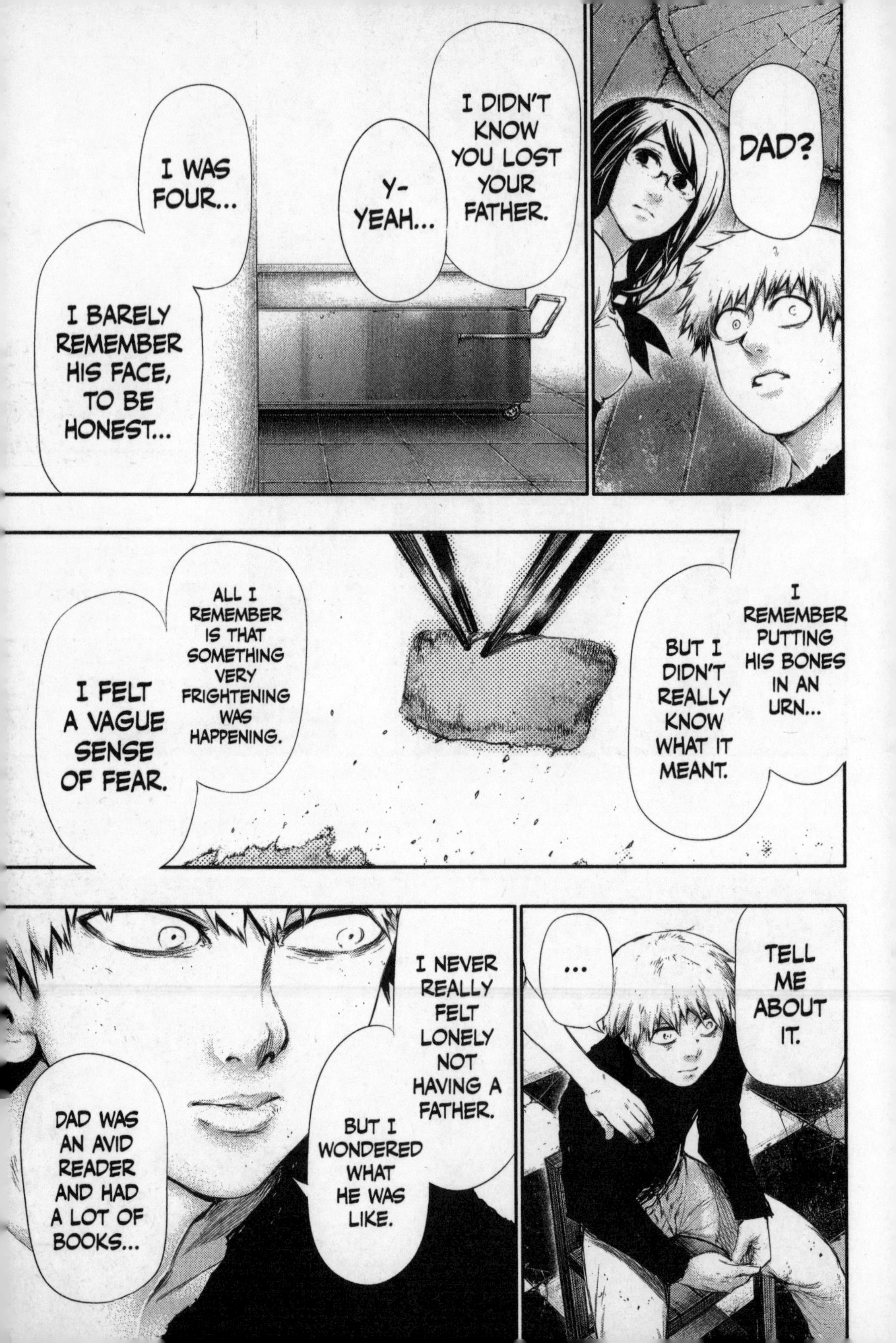
DAD?
I DIDN'T KNOW YOU LOST YOUR FATHER.
Y-YEAH...
I WAS FOUR...
I BARELY REMEMBER HIS FACE, TO BE HONEST...
I REMEMBER PUTTING HIS BONES IN AN URN...
BUT I DIDN'T REALLY KNOW WHAT IT MEANT.
ALL I REMEMBER IS THAT SOMETHING VERY FRIGHTENING WAS HAPPENING.
I FELT A VAGUE SENSE OF FEAR.
TELL ME ABOUT IT.
...
I NEVER REALLY FELT LONELY NOT HAVING A FATHER.
BUT I WONDERED WHAT HE WAS LIKE.
DAD WAS AN AVID READER AND HAD A LOT OF BOOKS...

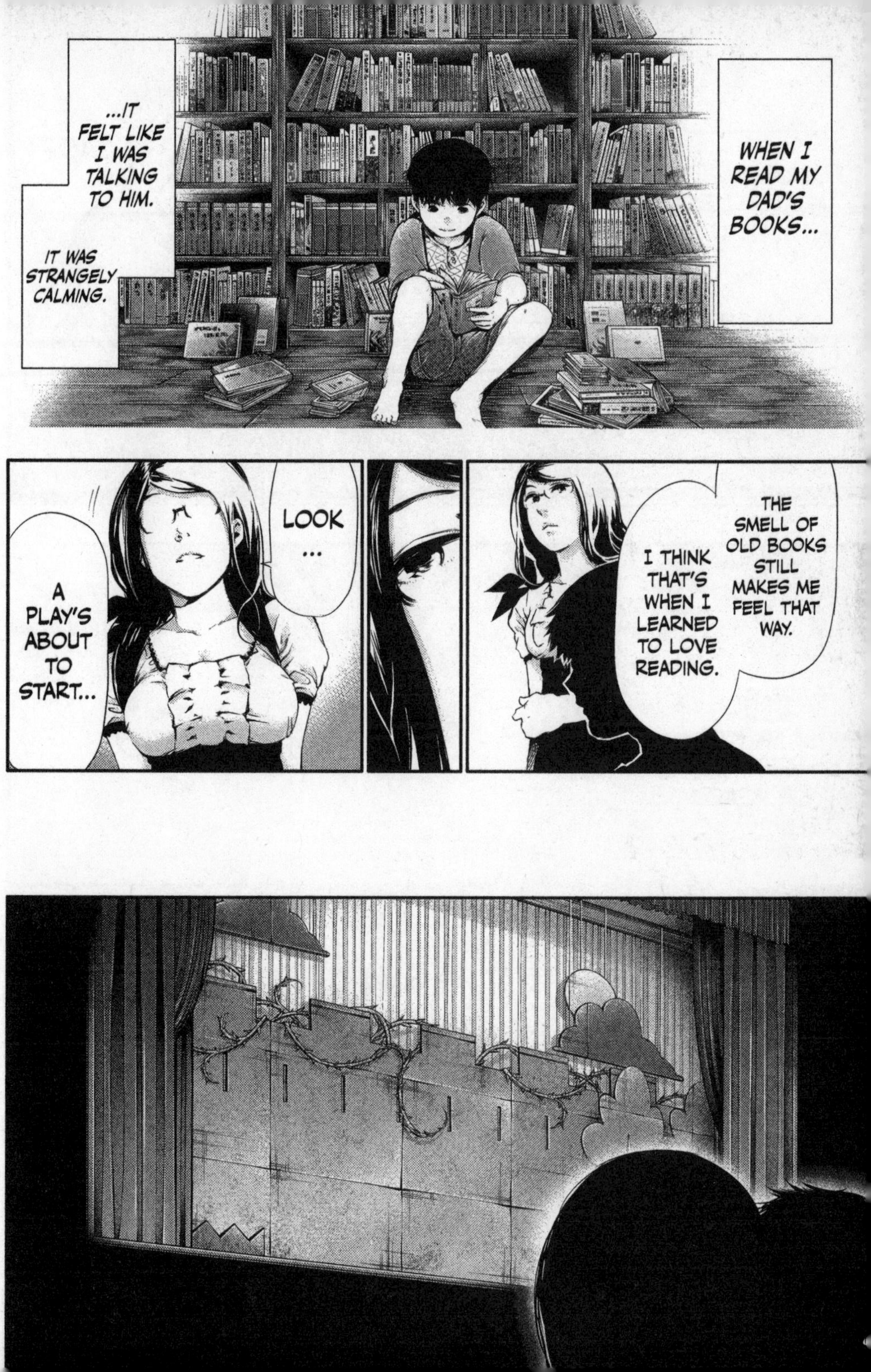
WHEN I READ MY DAD'S BOOKS...
...IT FELT LIKE I WAS TALKING TO HIM.
IT WAS STRANGELY CALMING.
THE SMELL OF OLD BOOKS STILL MAKES ME FEEL THAT WAY.
I THINK THAT'S WHEN I LEARNED TO LOVE READING.
LOOK...
A PLAY'S ABOUT TO START...

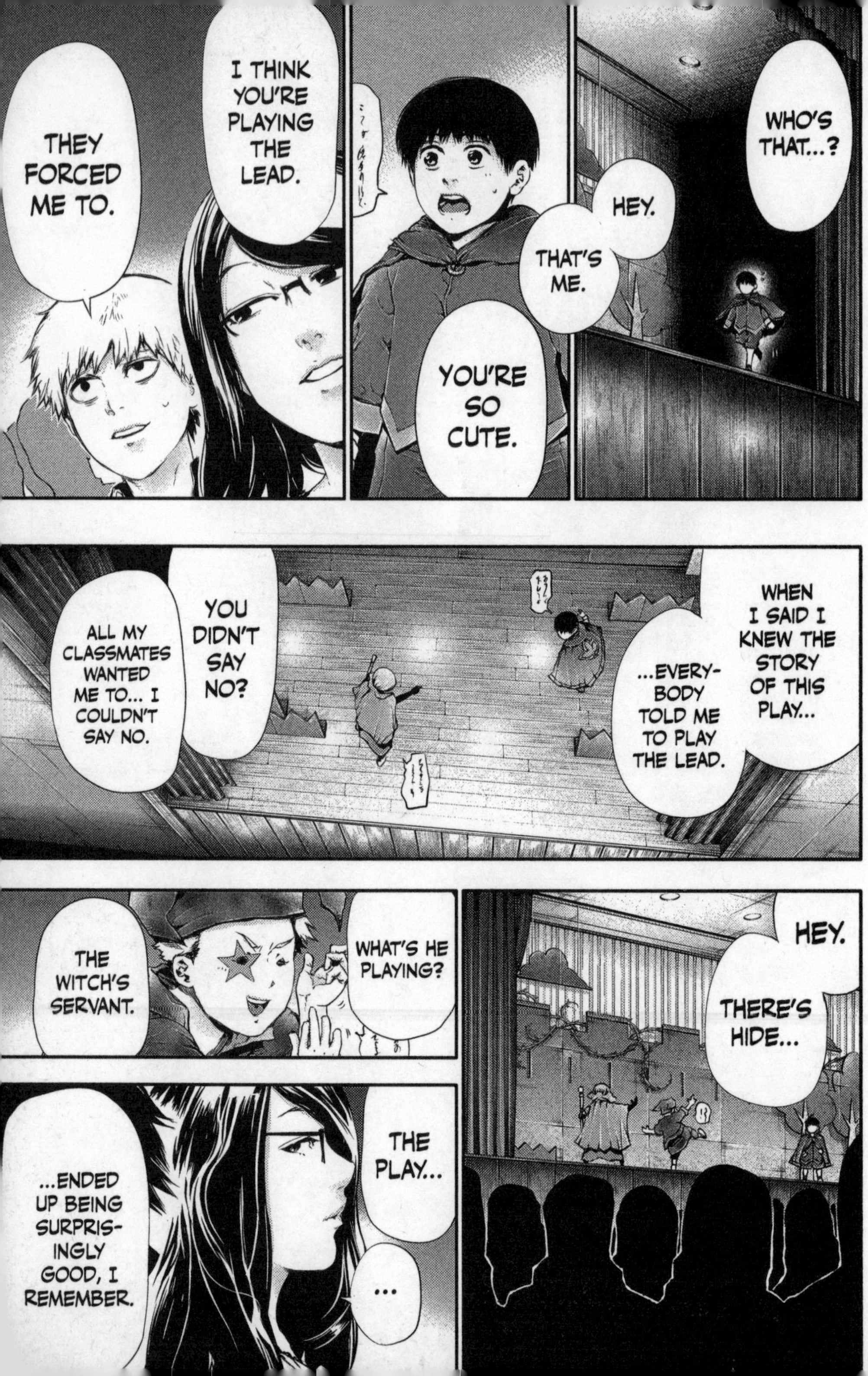
WHO'S THAT...?
HEY.
THAT'S ME.
YOU'RE SO CUTE.
I THINK YOU'RE PLAYING THE LEAD.
THEY FORCED ME TO.
WHEN I SAID I KNEW THE STORY OF THIS PLAY...
...EVERY-BODY TOLD ME TO PLAY THE LEAD.
YOU DIDN'T SAY NO?
ALL MY CLASSMATES WANTED ME TO... I COULDN'T SAY NO.
HEY.
THERE'S HIDE...
WHAT'S HE PLAYING?
THE WITCH'S SERVANT.
THE PLAY...
...
...ENDED UP BEING SURPRIS-INGLY GOOD, I REMEMBER.

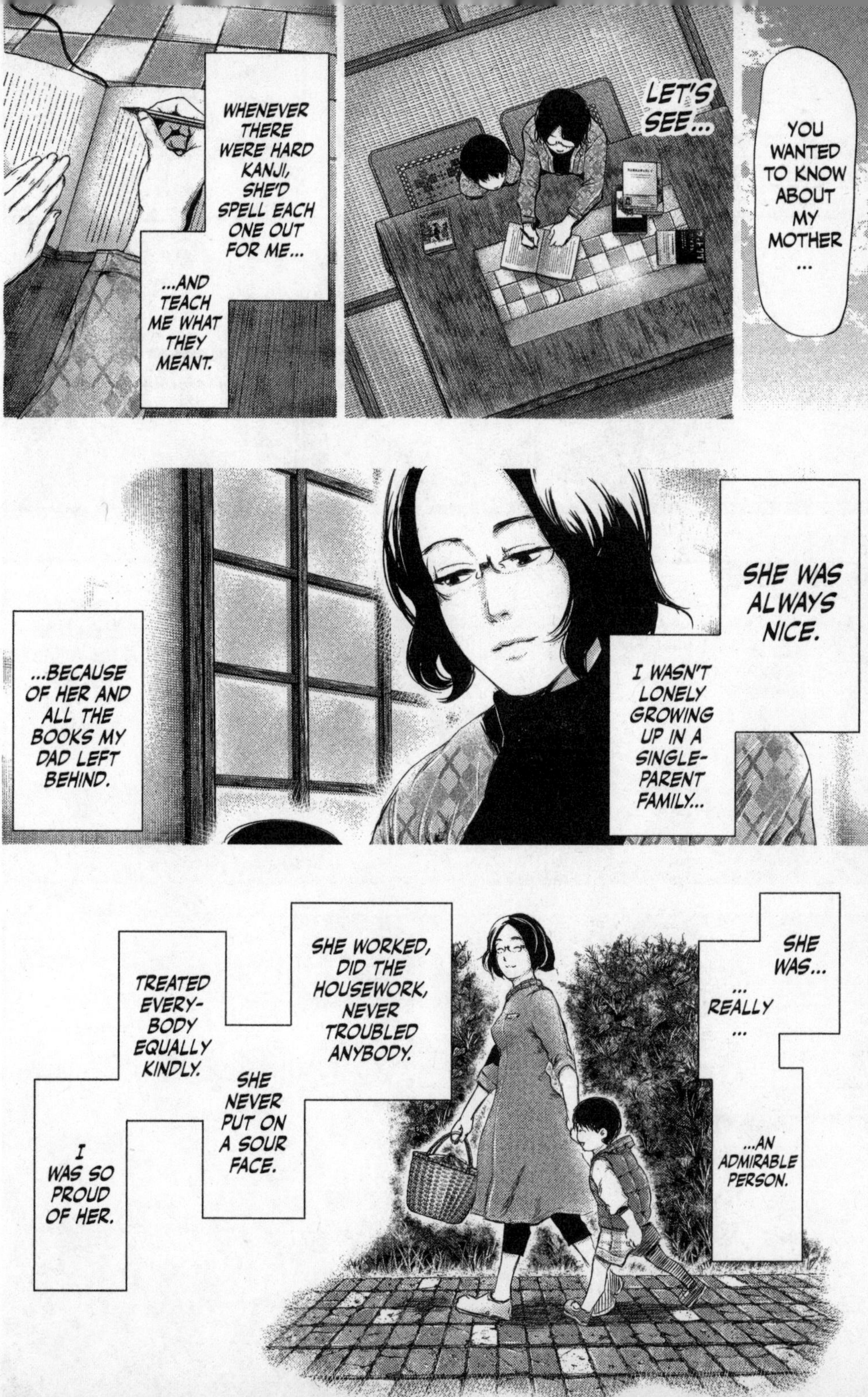
YOU WANTED TO KNOW ABOUT MY MOTHER ...
LET'S SEE...
WHENEVER THERE WERE HARD KANJI, SHE'D SPELL EACH ONE OUT FOR ME...
...AND TEACH ME WHAT THEY MEANT.
SHE WAS ALWAYS NICE.
I WASN'T LONELY GROWING UP IN A SINGLE-PARENT FAMILY...
...BECAUSE OF HER AND ALL THE BOOKS MY DAD LEFT BEHIND.
SHE WAS...
... REALLY ...
...AN ADMIRABLE PERSON.
SHE WORKED, DID THE HOUSEWORK, NEVER TROUBLED ANYBODY.
TREATED EVERY-BODY EQUALLY KINDLY.
SHE NEVER PUT ON A SOUR FACE.
I WAS SO PROUD OF HER.

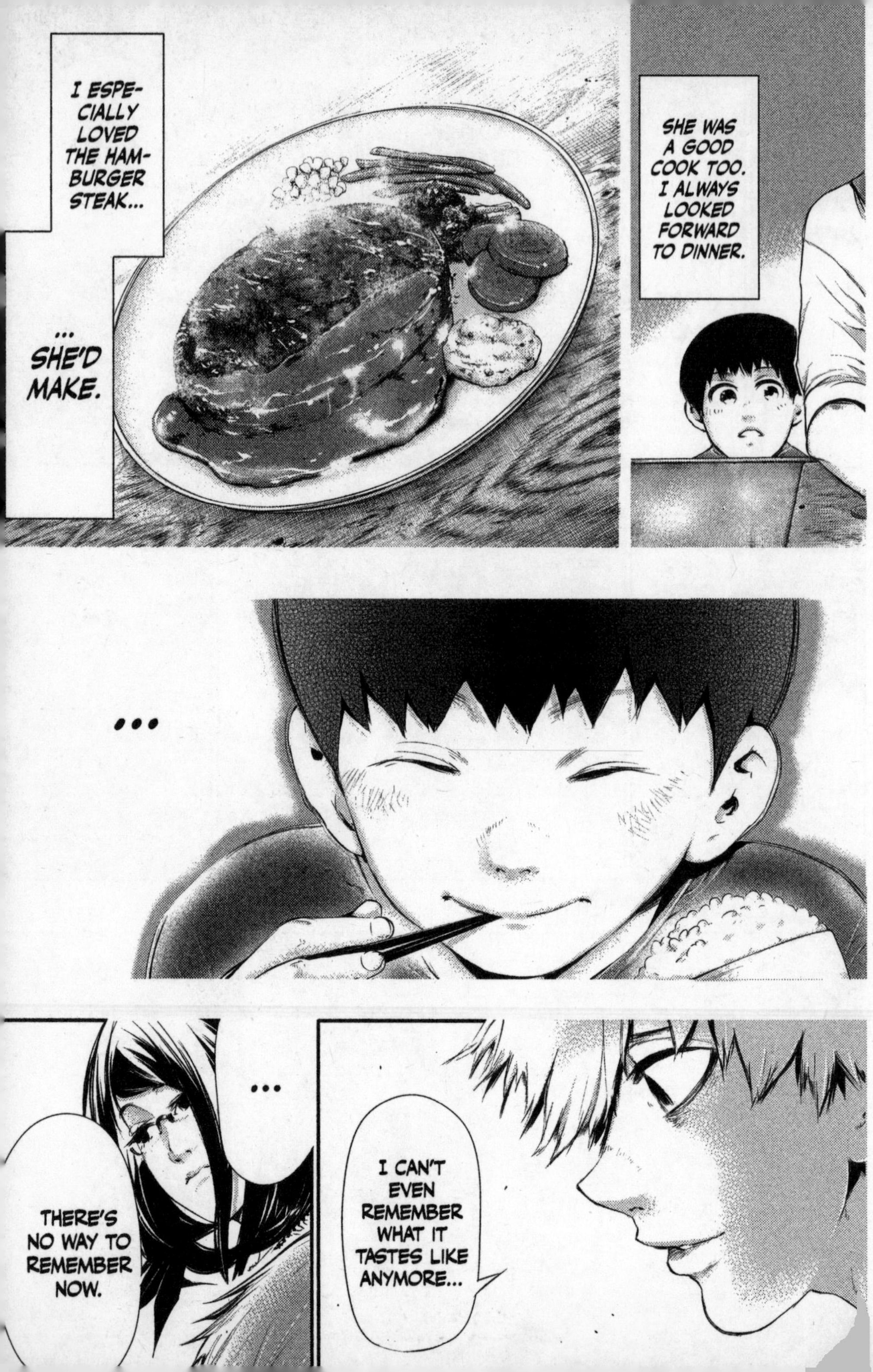
SHE WAS A GOOD COOK TOO. I ALWAYS LOOKED FORWARD TO DINNER.
I ESPECIALLY LOVED THE HAMBURGER STEAK...
...SHE'D MAKE.
...
I CAN'T EVEN REMEMBER WHAT IT TASTES LIKE ANYMORE...
...
THERE'S NO WAY TO REMEMBER NOW.

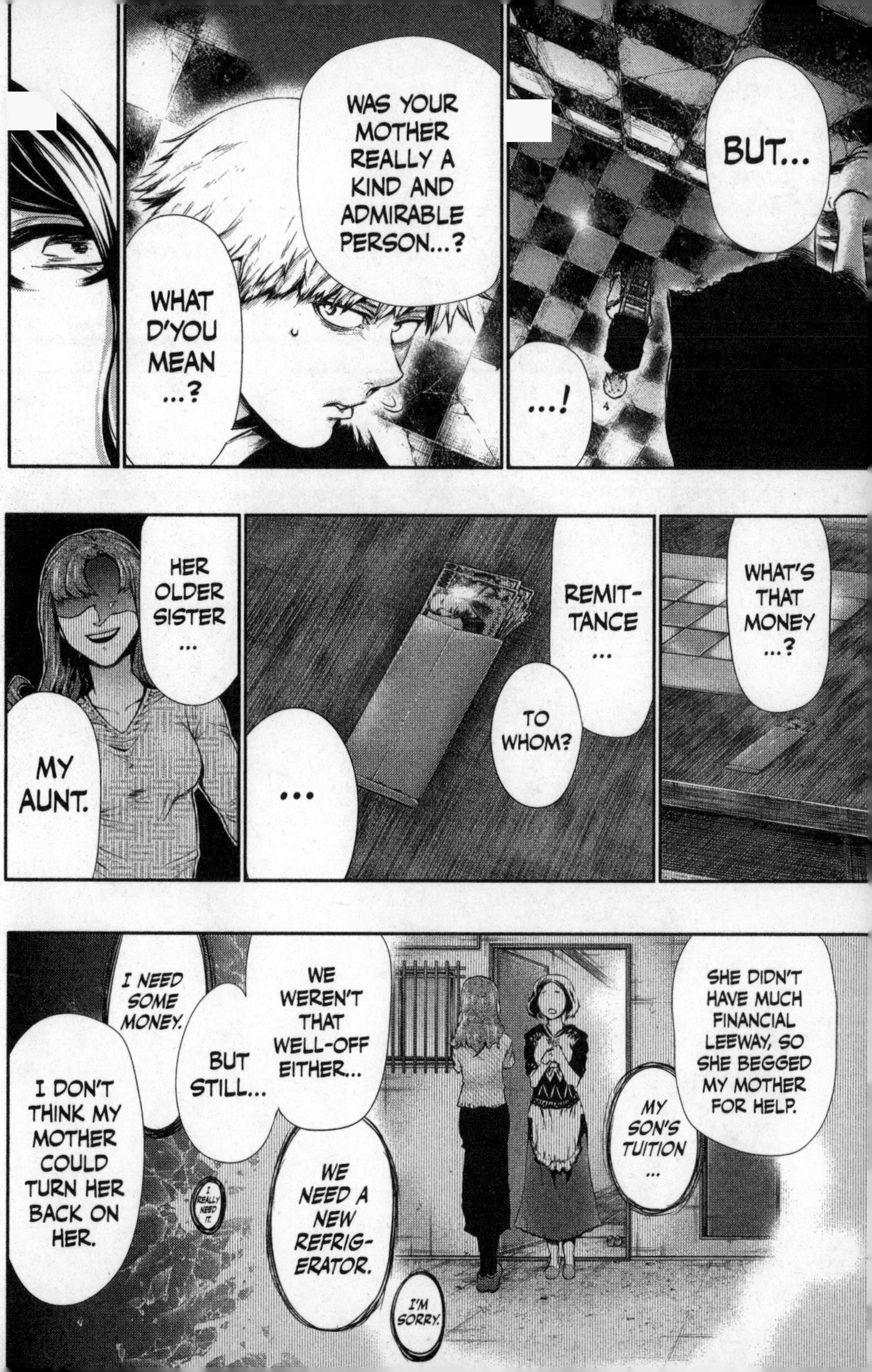
BUT...
...!
WAS YOUR MOTHER REALLY A KIND AND ADMIRABLE PERSON...?
WHAT D'YOU MEAN ...?
WHAT'S THAT MONEY ...?
REMIT-TANCE ...
TO WHOM?
...
HER OLDER SISTER ...
MY AUNT.
SHE DIDN'T HAVE MUCH FINANCIAL LEEWAY, SO SHE BEGGED MY MOTHER FOR HELP.
MY SON'S TUITION ...
WE WEREN'T THAT WELL-OFF EITHER...
I NEED SOME MONEY.
BUT STILL...
WE NEED A NEW REFRIG-ERATOR.
I REALLY NEED IT.
I'M SORRY.
I DON'T THINK MY MOTHER COULD TURN HER BACK ON HER.

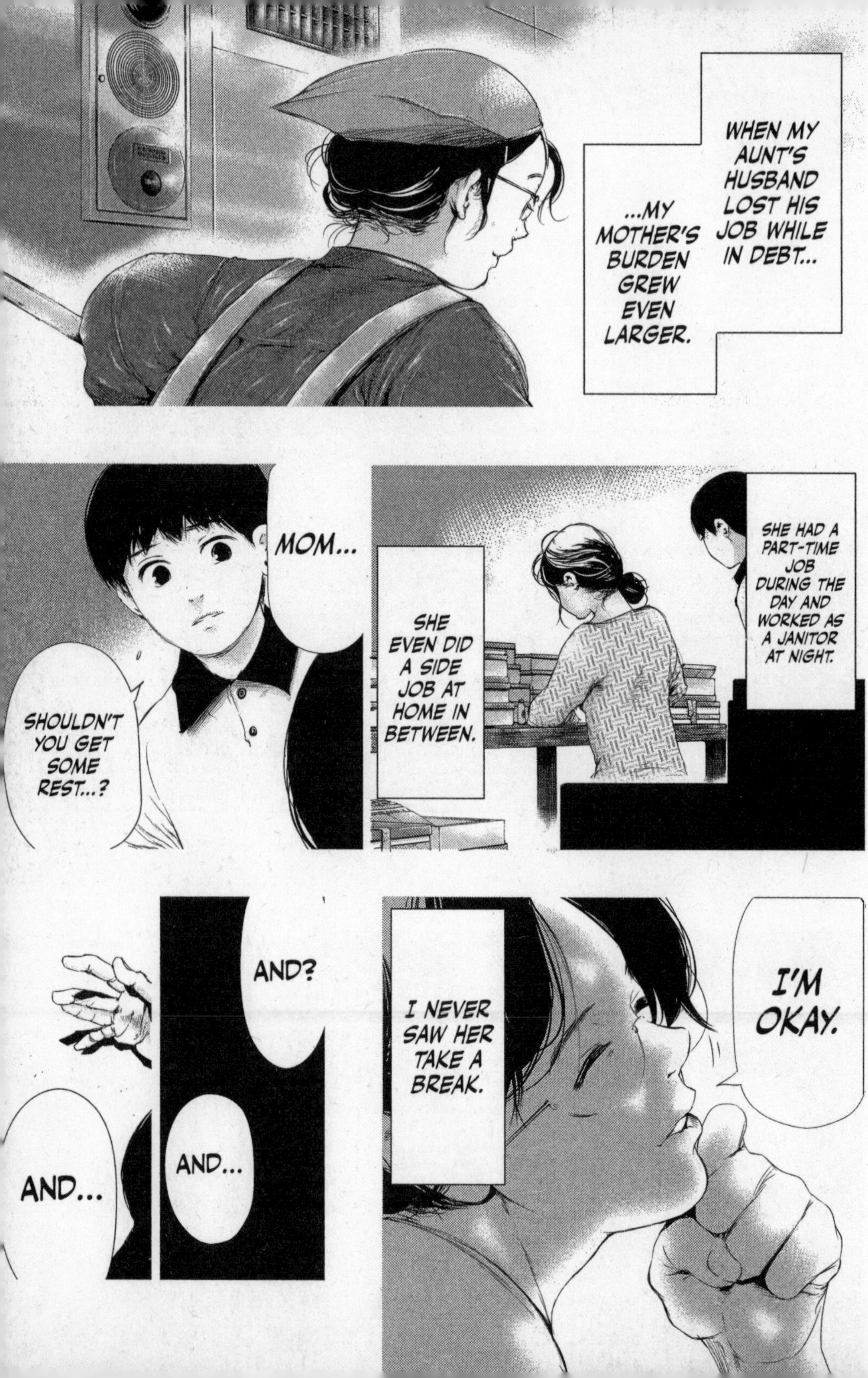
WHEN MY AUNT'S HUSBAND LOST HIS JOB WHILE IN DEBT...
...MY MOTHER'S BURDEN GREW EVEN LARGER.
SHE HAD A PART-TIME JOB DURING THE DAY AND WORKED AS A JANITOR AT NIGHT.
SHE EVEN DID A SIDE JOB AT HOME IN BETWEEN.
MOM...
SHOULDN'T YOU GET SOME REST...?
I'M OKAY.
I NEVER SAW HER TAKE A BREAK.
AND?
AND...
AND...

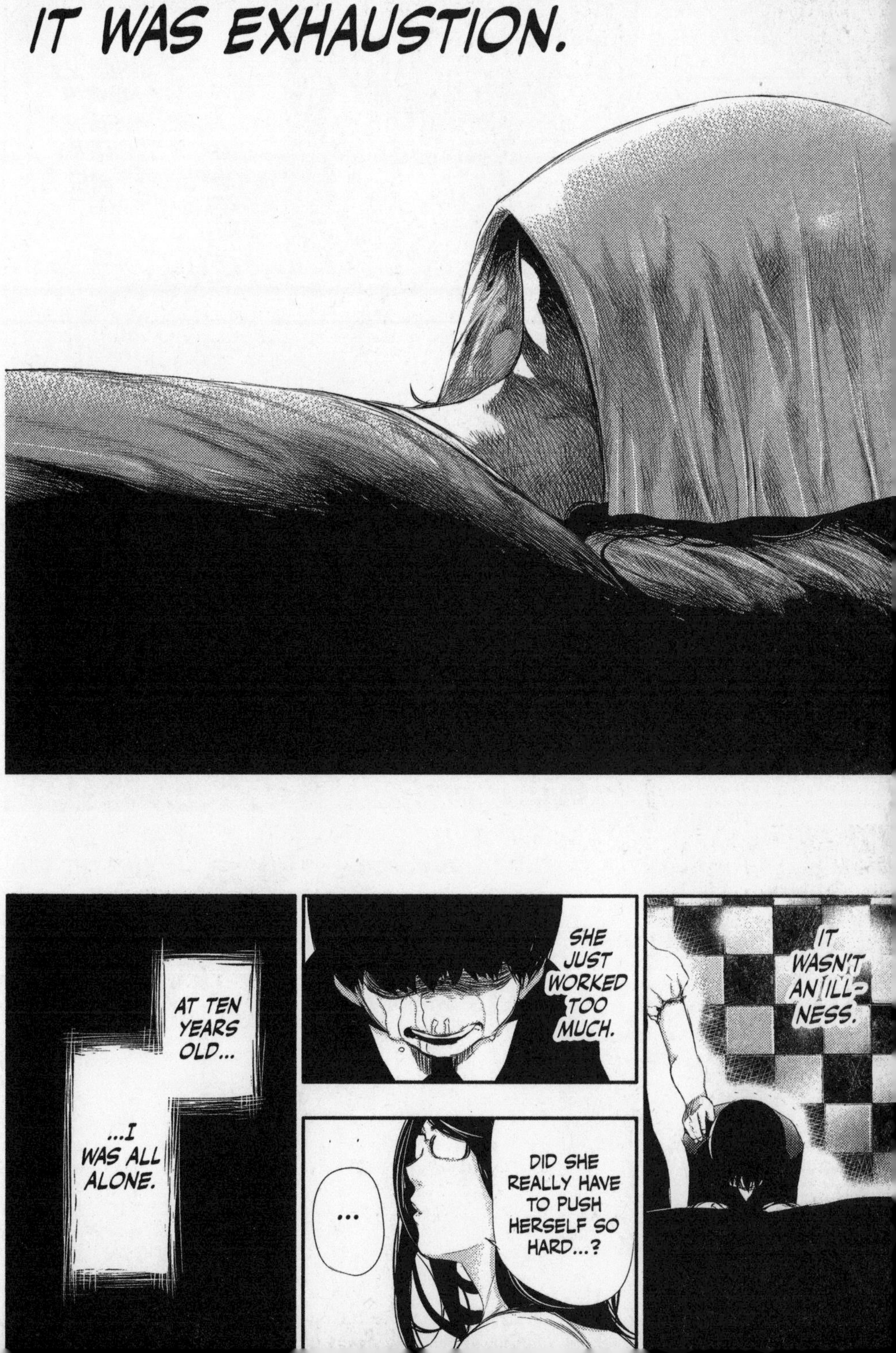
IT WAS EXHAUSTION.
IT WASN'T AN ILLNESS.
SHE JUST WORKED TOO MUCH.
DID SHE REALLY HAVE TO PUSH HERSELF SO HARD...?
...
AT TEN YEARS OLD...
...I WAS ALL ALONE.

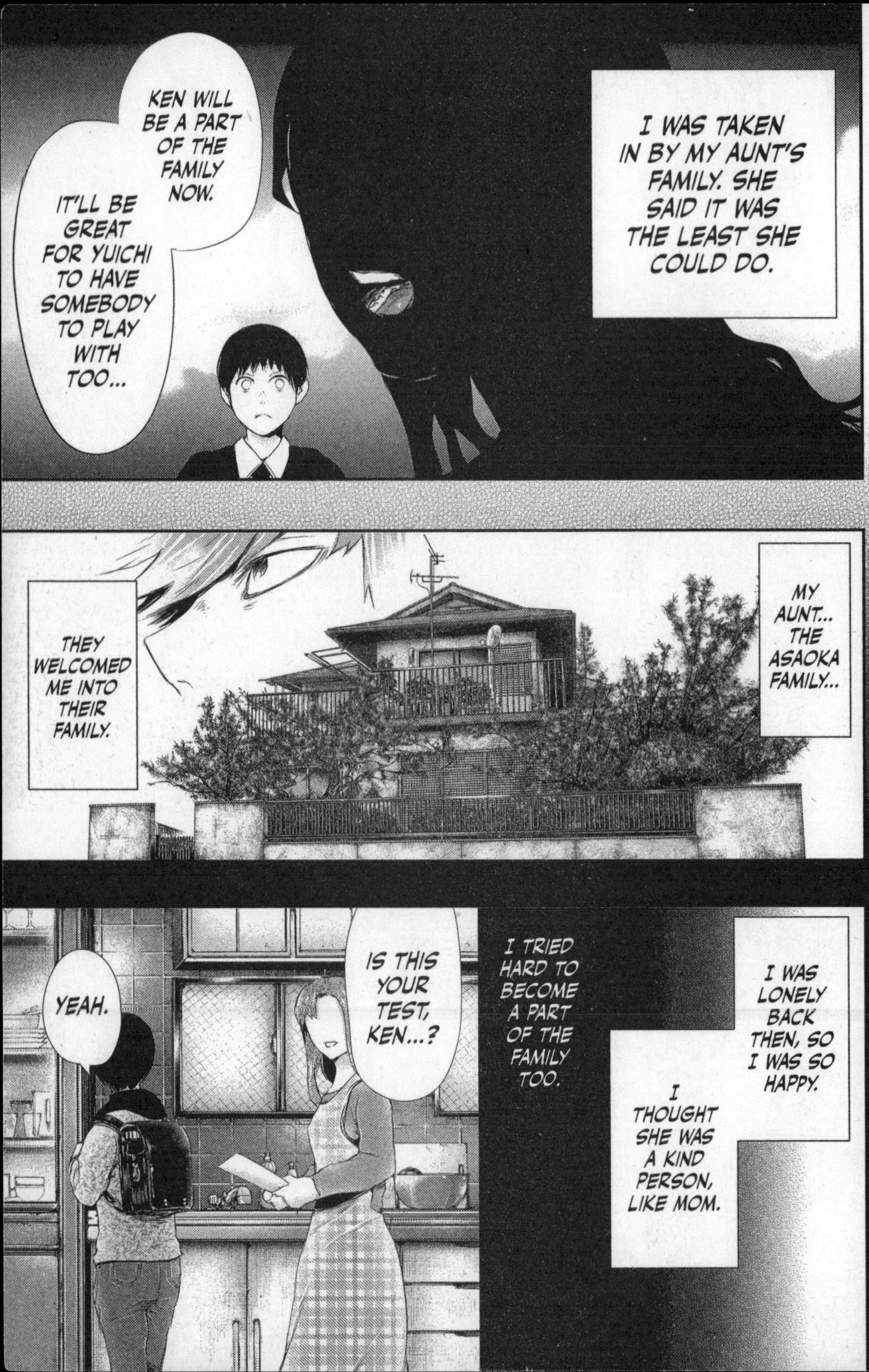
I WAS TAKEN IN BY MY AUNT'S FAMILY. SHE SAID IT WAS THE LEAST SHE COULD DO.
KEN WILL BE A PART OF THE FAMILY NOW.
IT'LL BE GREAT FOR YUICHI TO HAVE SOMEBODY TO PLAY WITH TOO...
MY AUNT... THE ASAOKA FAMILY...
THEY WELCOMED ME INTO THEIR FAMILY.
I WAS LONELY BACK THEN, SO I WAS SO HAPPY.
I THOUGHT SHE WAS A KIND PERSON, LIKE MOM.
I TRIED HARD TO BECOME A PART OF THE FAMILY TOO.
IS THIS YOUR TEST, KEN...?
YEAH.

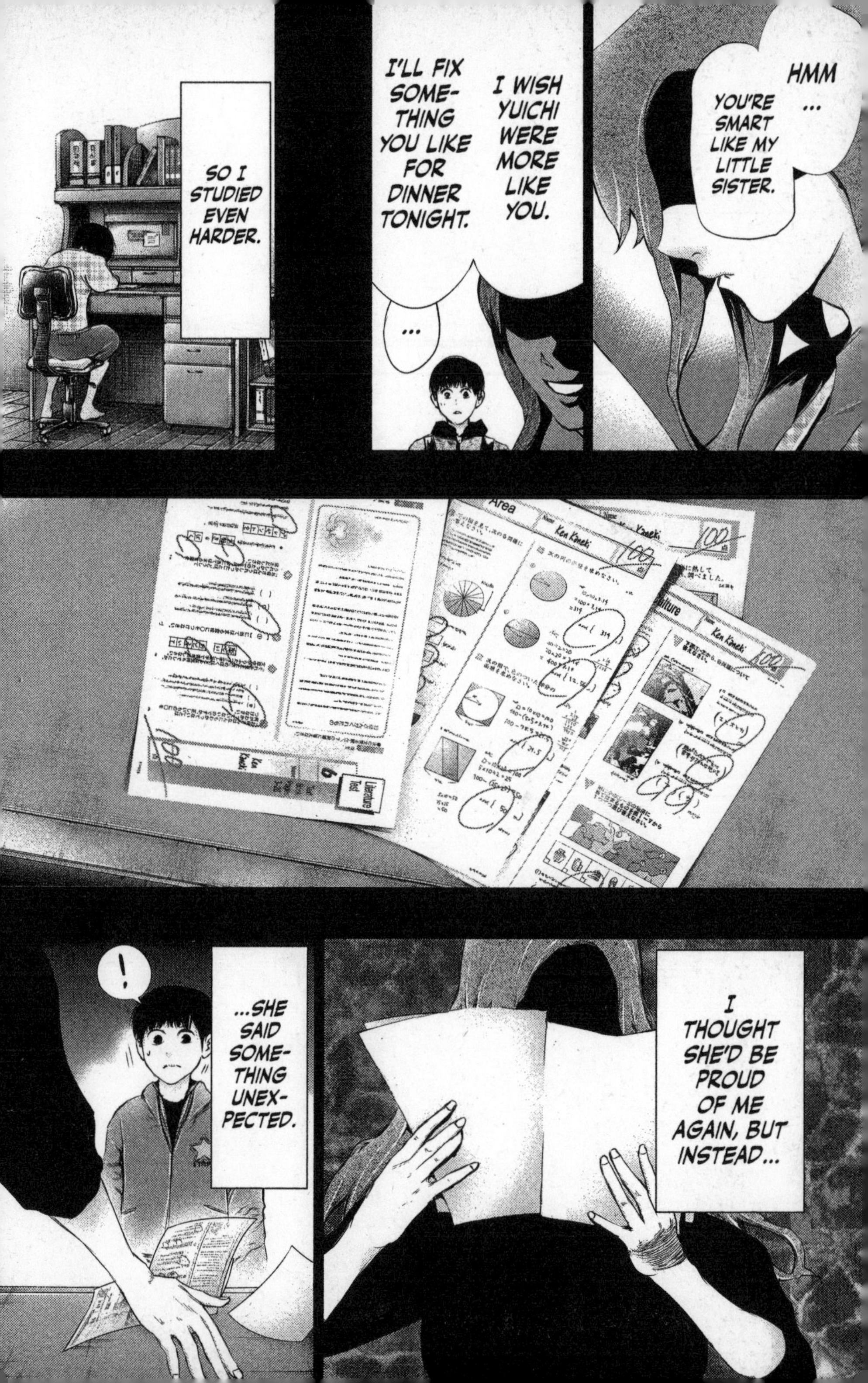
HMM ...
YOU'RE SMART LIKE MY LITTLE SISTER.
I WISH YUICHI WERE MORE LIKE YOU.
I'LL FIX SOME-THING YOU LIKE FOR DINNER TONIGHT.
...
SO I STUDIED EVEN HARDER.
I THOUGHT SHE'D BE PROUD OF ME AGAIN, BUT INSTEAD...
...SHE SAID SOME-THING UNEX-PECTED.
!

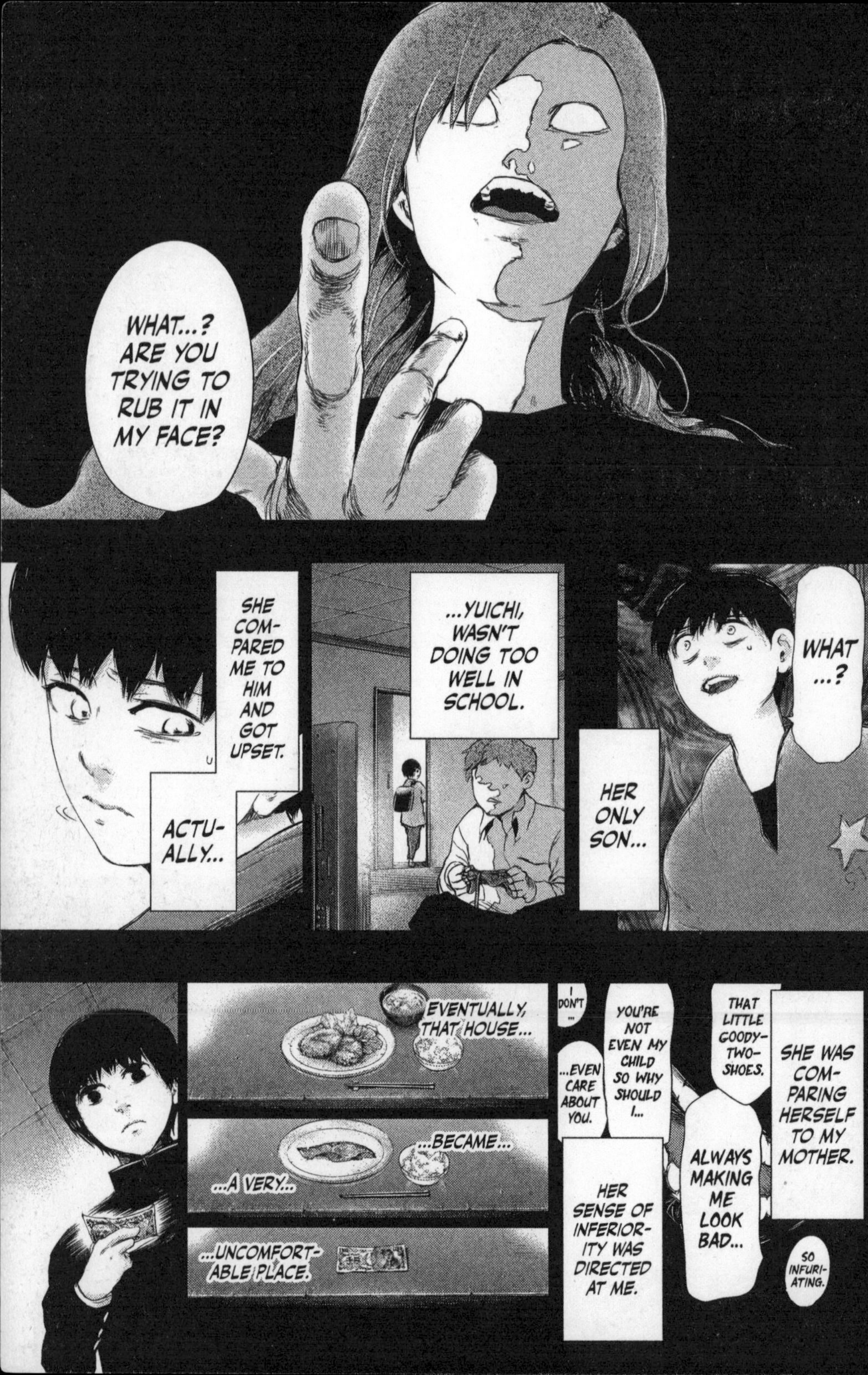
WHAT...? ARE YOU TRYING TO RUB IT IN MY FACE?
WHAT ...?
HER ONLY SON...
...YUICHI, WASN'T DOING TOO WELL IN SCHOOL.
SHE COMPARED ME TO HIM AND GOT UPSET.
ACTUALLY...
SHE WAS COMPARING HERSELF TO MY MOTHER.
THAT LITTLE GOODY-TWO-SHOES.
ALWAYS MAKING ME LOOK BAD...
SO INFURIATING.
YOU'RE NOT EVEN MY CHILD SO WHY SHOULD I...
I DON'T ...
...EVEN CARE ABOUT YOU.
HER SENSE OF INFERIORITY WAS DIRECTED AT ME.
EVENTUALLY, THAT HOUSE...
...BECAME...
...A VERY...
...UNCOMFORTABLE PLACE.

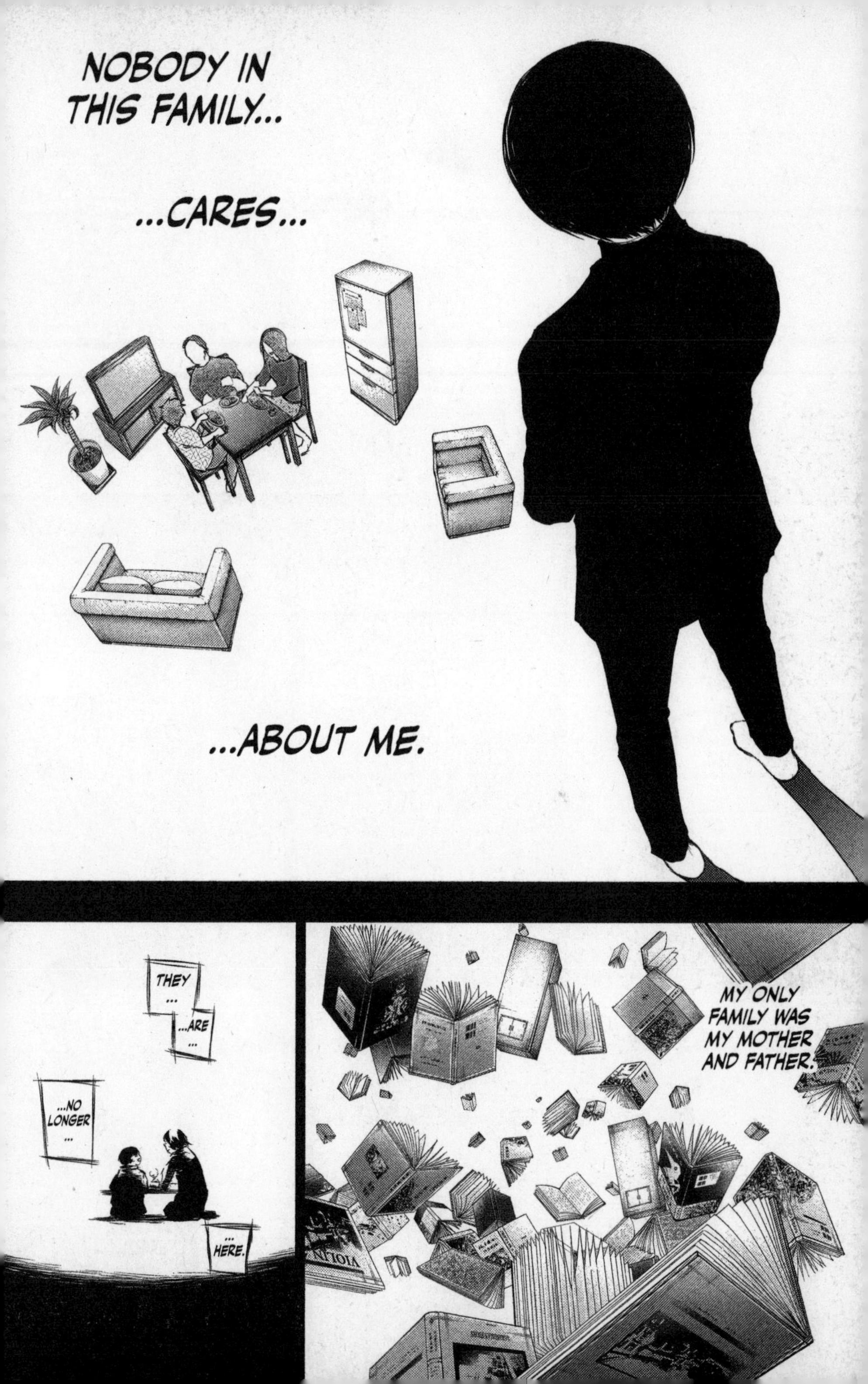
NOBODY IN THIS FAMILY...
...CARES...
...ABOUT ME.
MY ONLY FAMILY WAS MY MOTHER AND FATHER.
THEY ...
...ARE ...
...NO LONGER ...
... HERE.

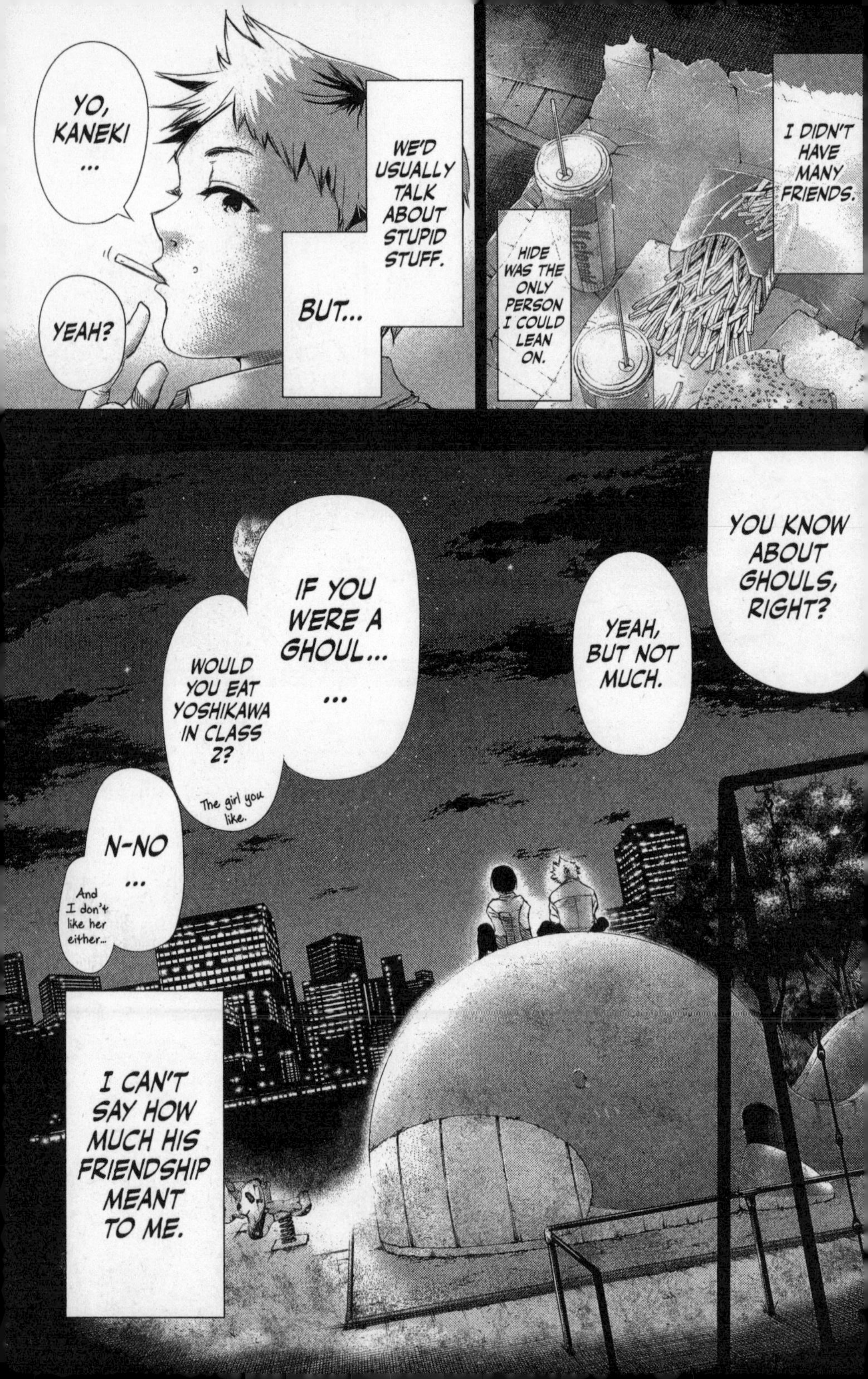
I DIDN'T HAVE MANY FRIENDS.
HIDE WAS THE ONLY PERSON I COULD LEAN ON.
WE'D USUALLY TALK ABOUT STUPID STUFF.
BUT...
YO, KANEKI ...
YEAH?
YOU KNOW ABOUT GHOULS, RIGHT?
YEAH, BUT NOT MUCH.
IF YOU WERE A GHOUL... ...
WOULD YOU EAT YOSHIKAWA IN CLASS 2?
The girl you like.
N-NO ...
And I don't like her either...
I CAN'T SAY HOW MUCH HIS FRIENDSHIP MEANT TO ME.

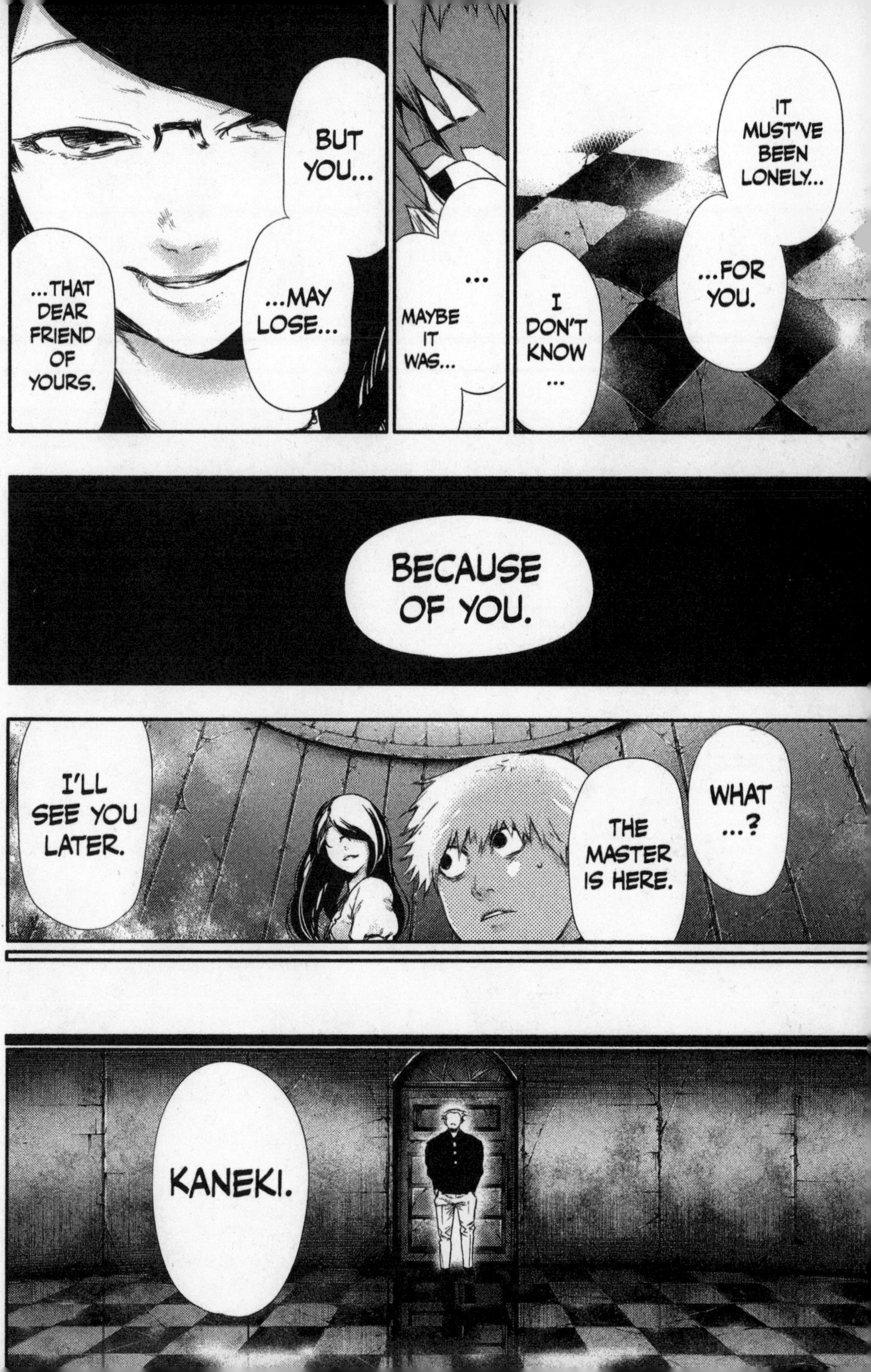
IT MUST'VE BEEN LONELY...
...FOR YOU.
I DON'T KNOW ...
...
MAYBE IT WAS...
BUT YOU...
...MAY LOSE...
...THAT DEAR FRIEND OF YOURS.
BECAUSE OF YOU.
WHAT ...?
THE MASTER IS HERE.
I'LL SEE YOU LATER.
KANEKI.

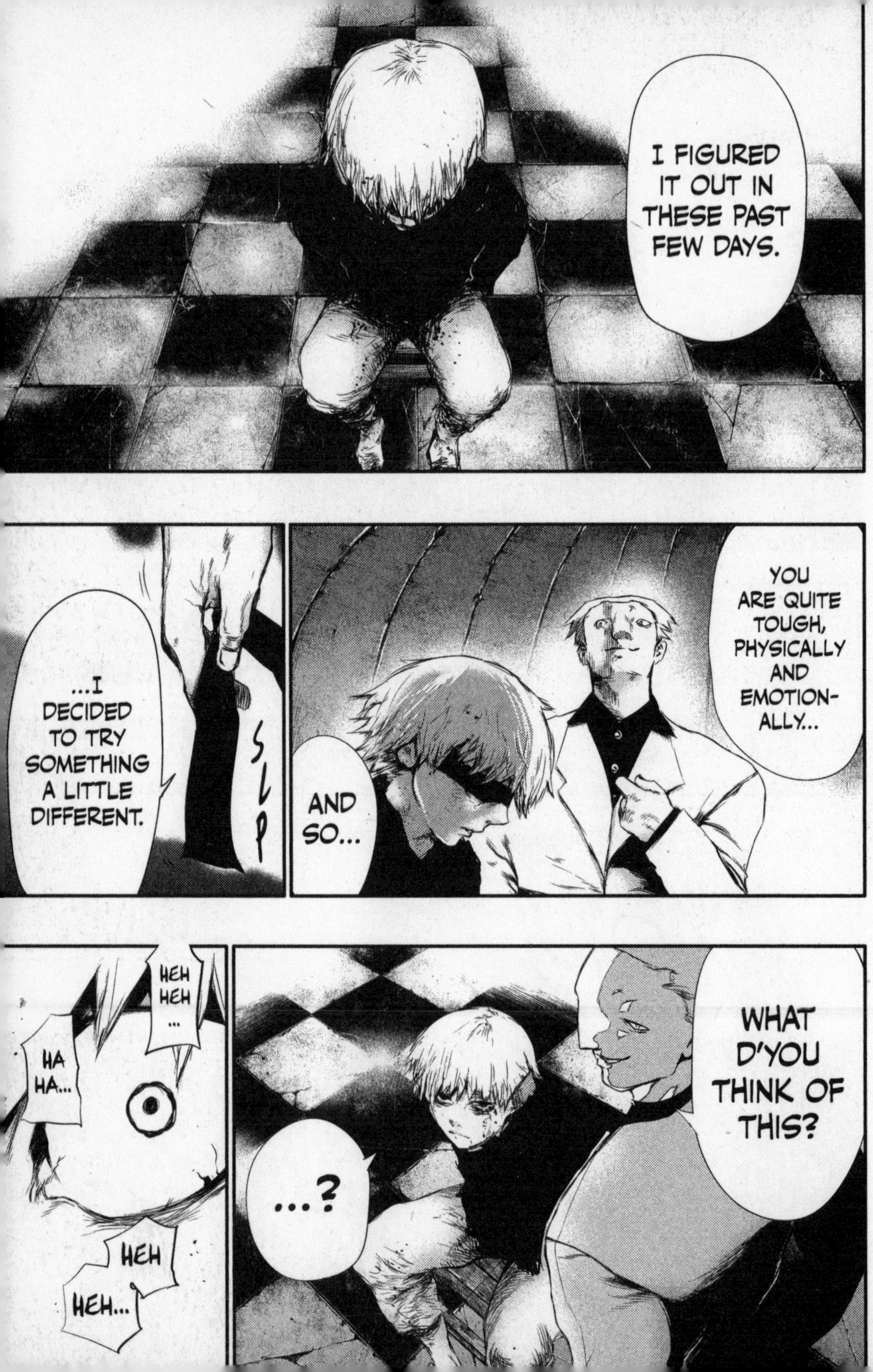
I FIGURED IT OUT IN THESE PAST FEW DAYS.
YOU ARE QUITE TOUGH, PHYSICALLY AND EMOTIONALLY...
AND SO...
...I DECIDED TO TRY SOMETHING A LITTLE DIFFERENT.
SLIP
WHAT D'YOU THINK OF THIS?
...?
HEH HEH ...
HA HA...
HEH HEH...

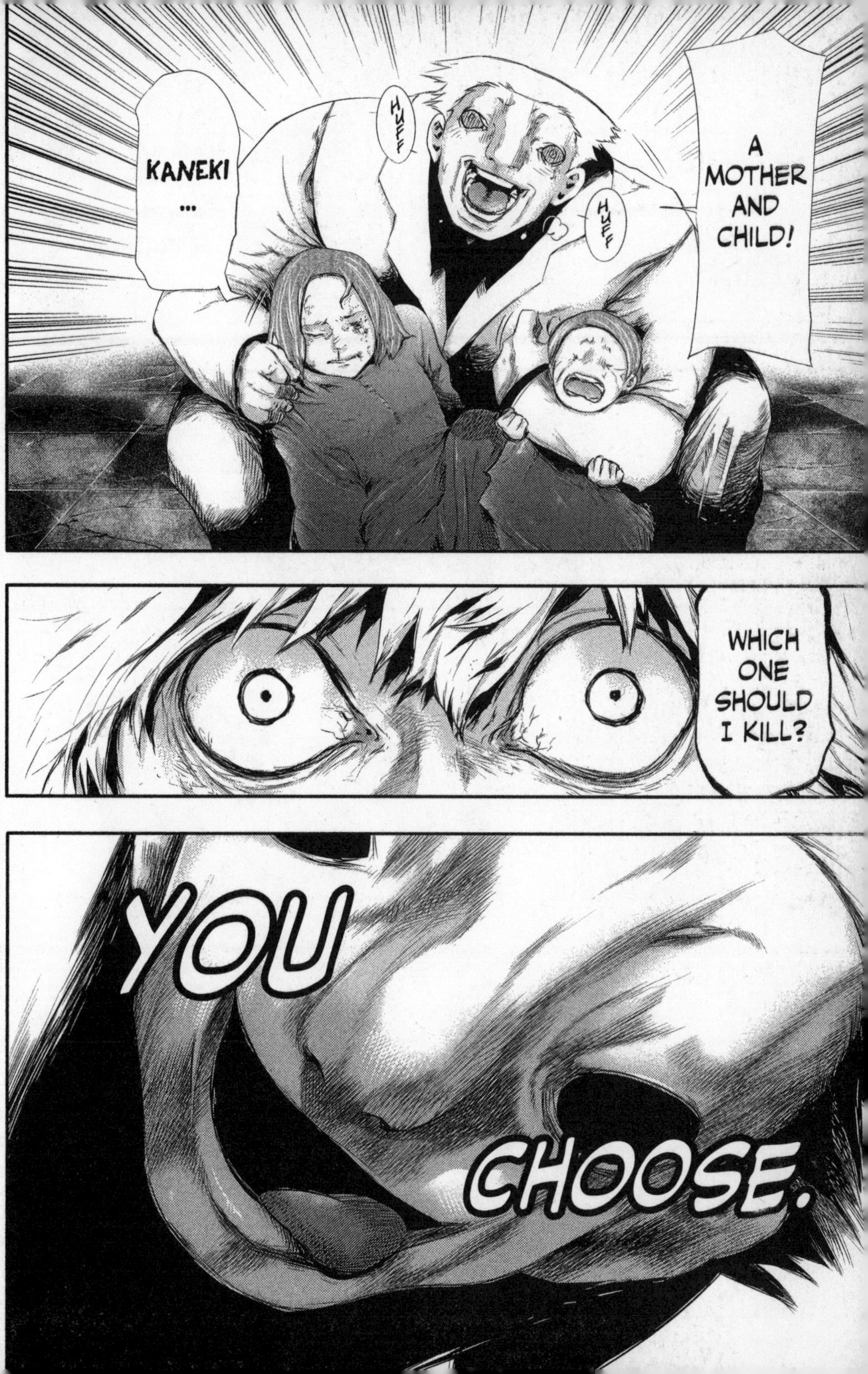
A MOTHER AND CHILD!
HUFF
HUFF
KANEKI ...
WHICH ONE SHOULD I KILL?
YOU
CHOOSE.

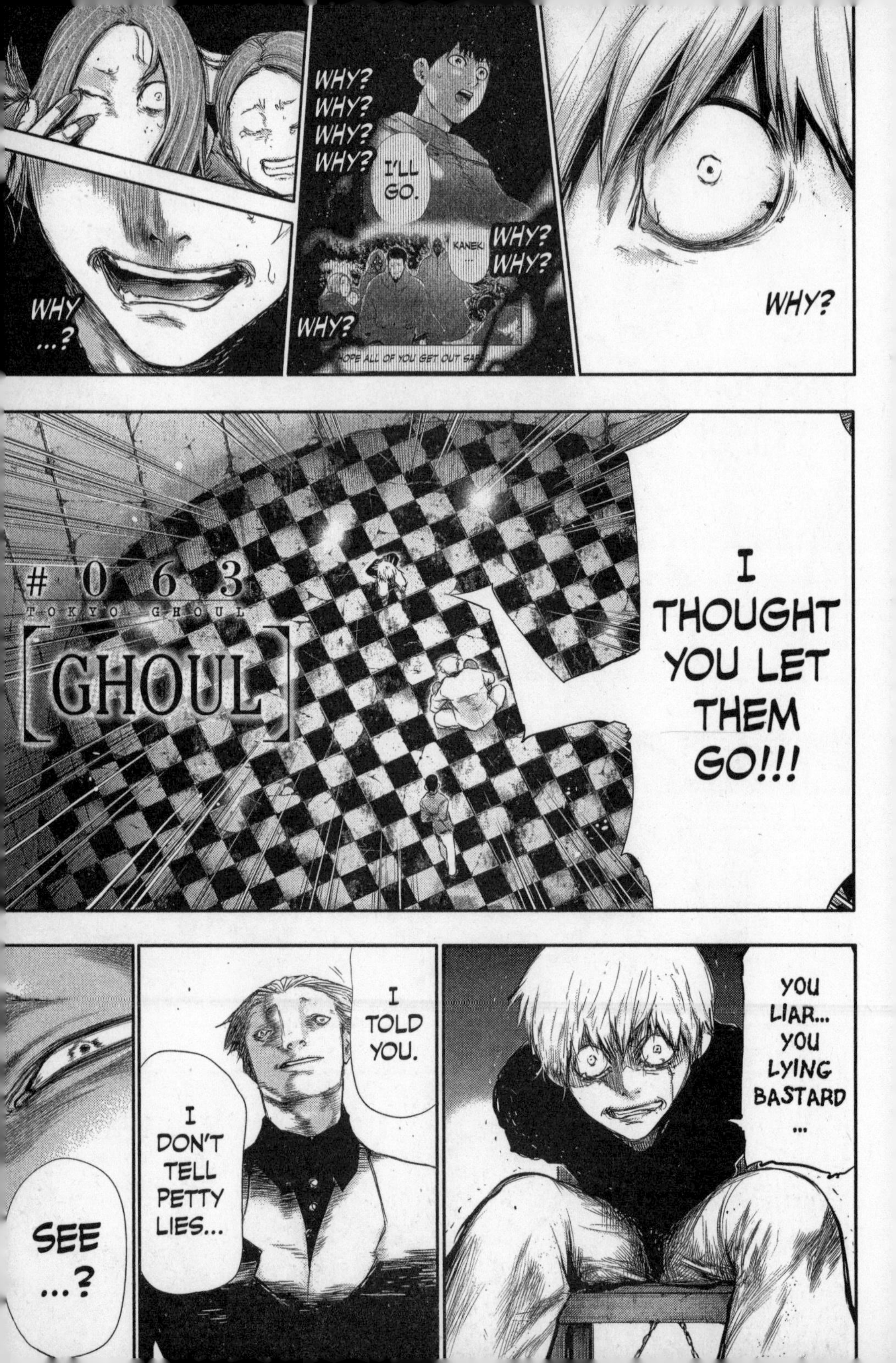
WHY?
WHY? WHY? WHY? WHY?
I'LL GO.
KANEKI ...
WHY? WHY?
WHY?
HOPE ALL OF YOU GET OUT SAF
WHY ...?
I THOUGHT YOU LET THEM GO!!!
0 6 3
TOKYO GHOUL
[GHOUL]
YOU LIAR... YOU LYING BASTARD ...
I TOLD YOU.
I DON'T TELL PETTY LIES...
SEE ...?

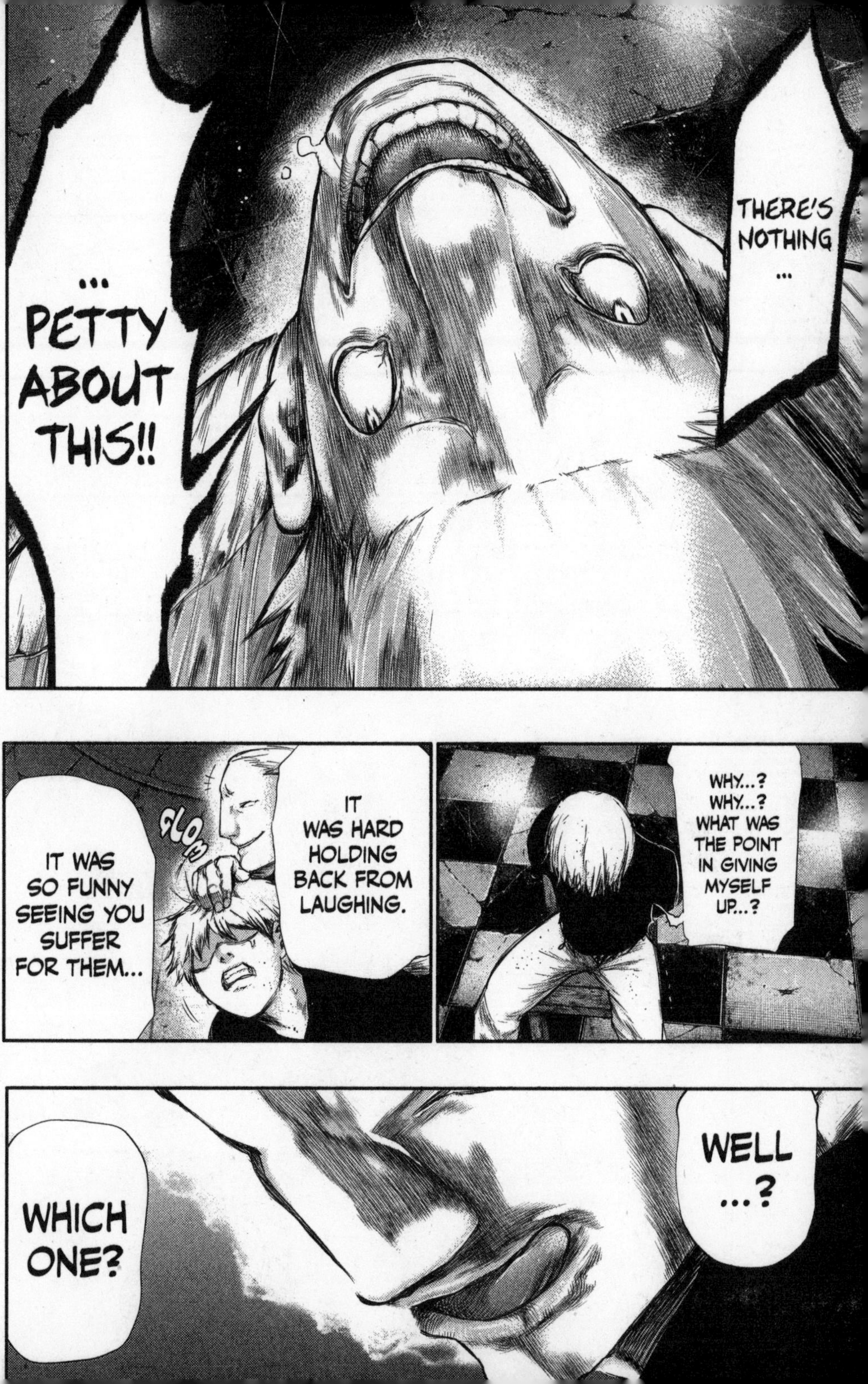
THERE'S NOTHING ...
... PETTY ABOUT THIS!!
WHY...? WHY...? WHAT WAS THE POINT IN GIVING MYSELF UP...?
IT WAS HARD HOLDING BACK FROM LAUGHING.
GLOM
IT WAS SO FUNNY SEEING YOU SUFFER FOR THEM...
WELL ...?
WHICH ONE?

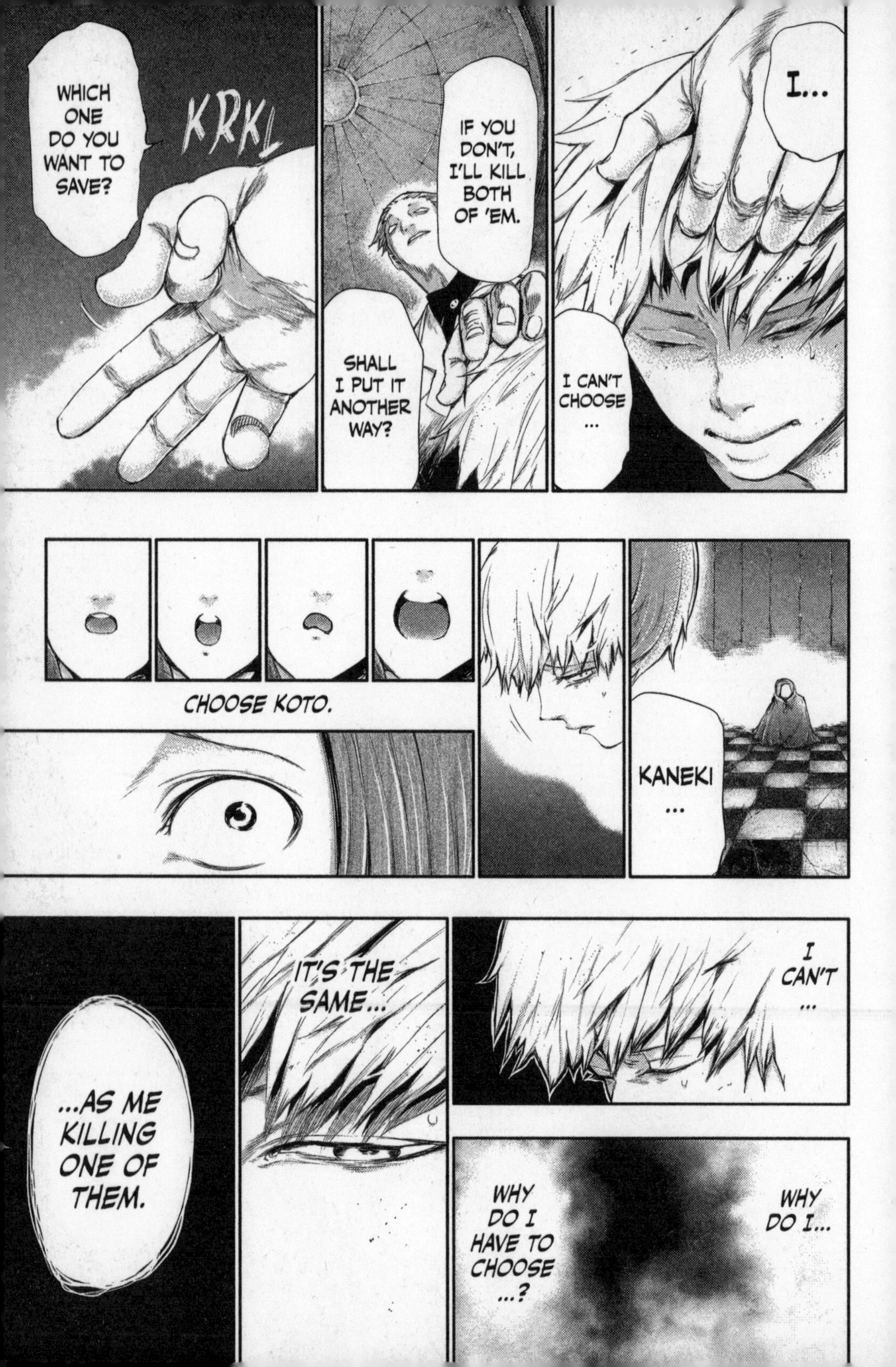
I...
I CAN'T CHOOSE ...
IF YOU DON'T, I'LL KILL BOTH OF 'EM.
SHALL I PUT IT ANOTHER WAY?
WHICH ONE DO YOU WANT TO SAVE?
KRKL
KANEKI ...
CHOOSE KOTO.
I CAN'T ...
WHY DO I...
WHY DO I HAVE TO CHOOSE ...?
IT'S THE SAME...
...AS ME KILLING ONE OF THEM.

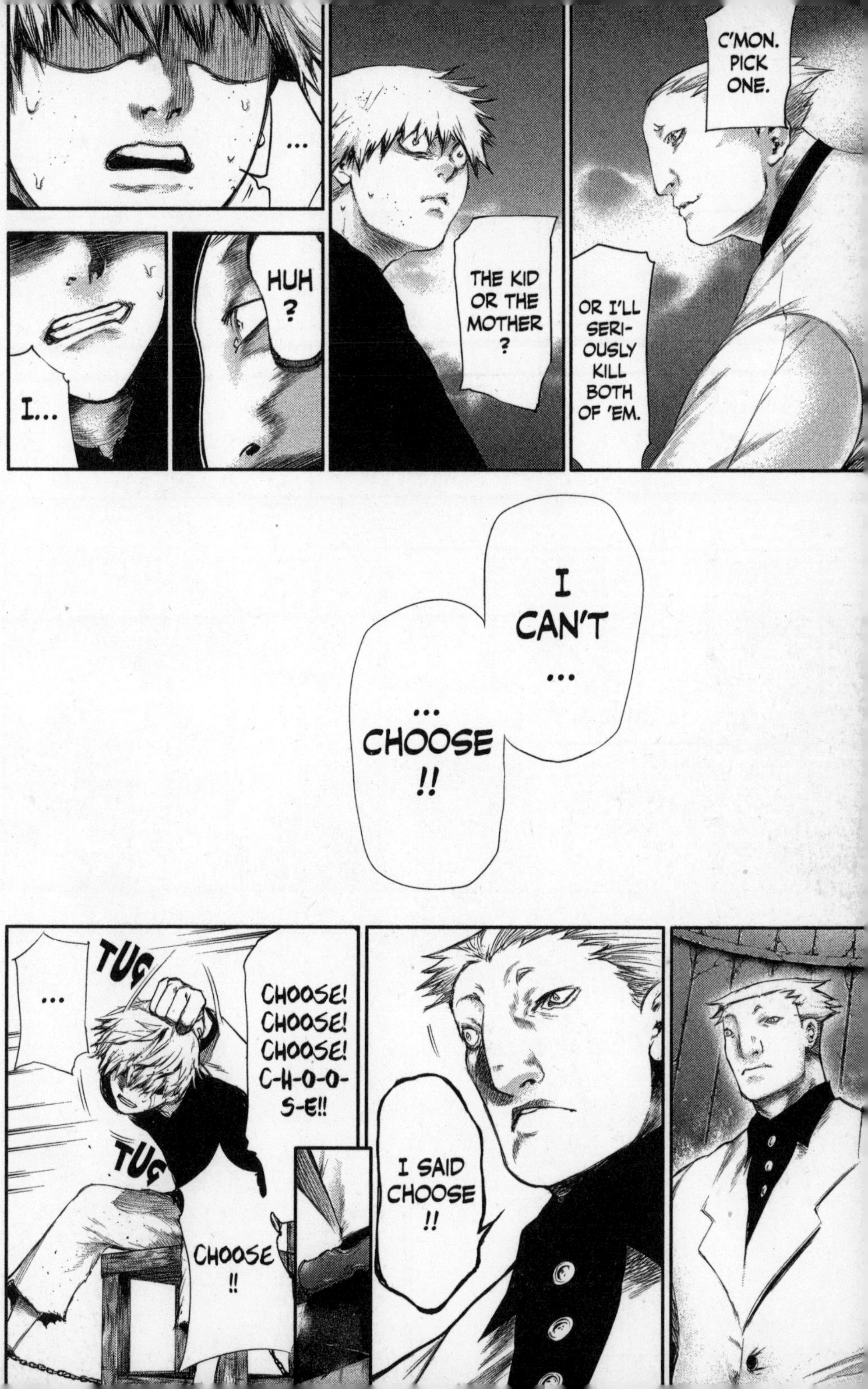
C'MON. PICK ONE.
OR I'LL SERI-OUSLY KILL BOTH OF 'EM.
THE KID OR THE MOTHER?
...
HUH?
I...
I CAN'T ...
... CHOOSE!!
I SAID CHOOSE!!
CHOOSE! CHOOSE! CHOOSE! C-H-O-O-S-E!!
TUG
...
TUG
CHOOSE!!

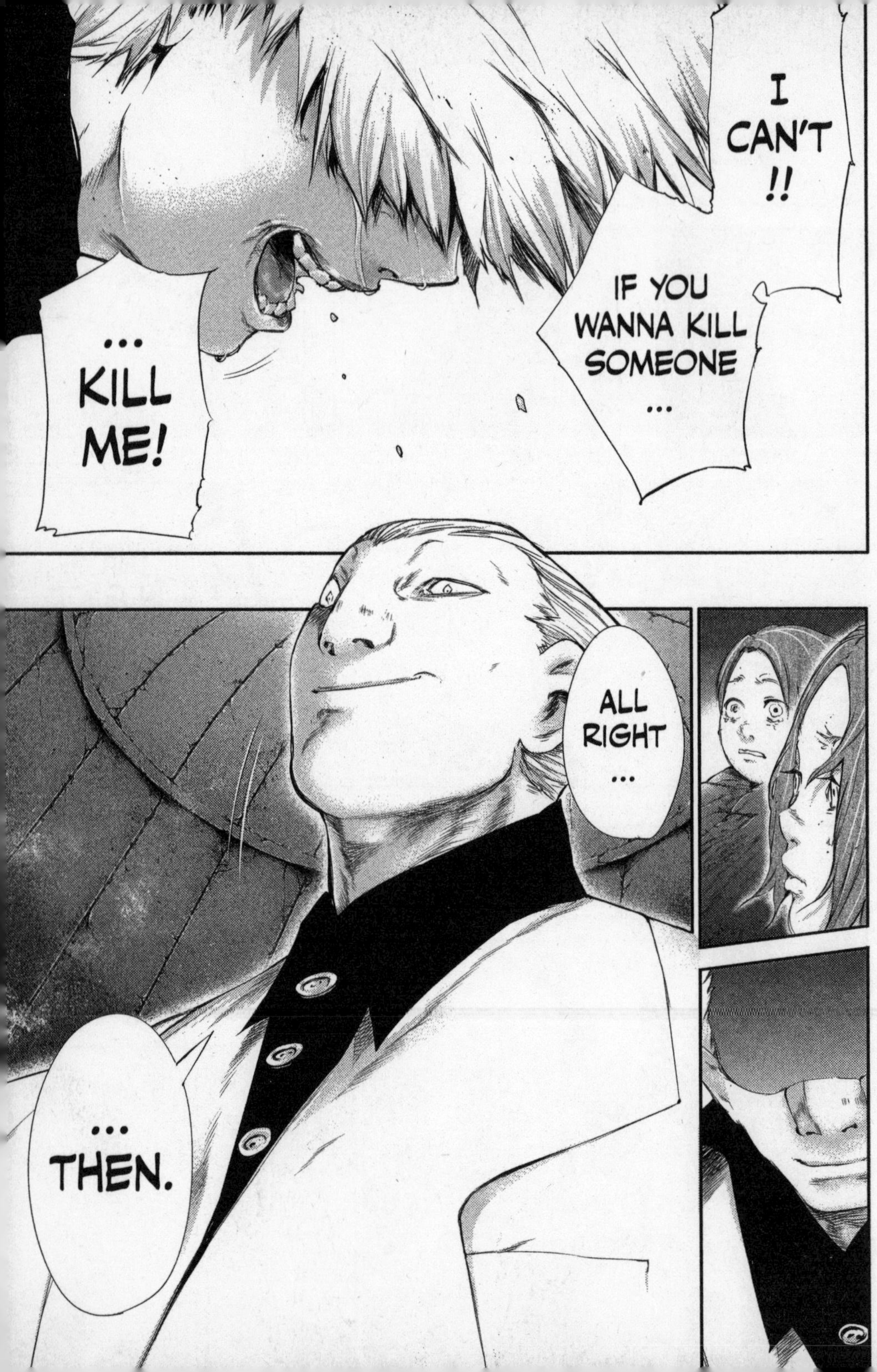
I CAN'T !!
IF YOU WANNA KILL SOMEONE ...
... KILL ME!
ALL RIGHT ...
... THEN.

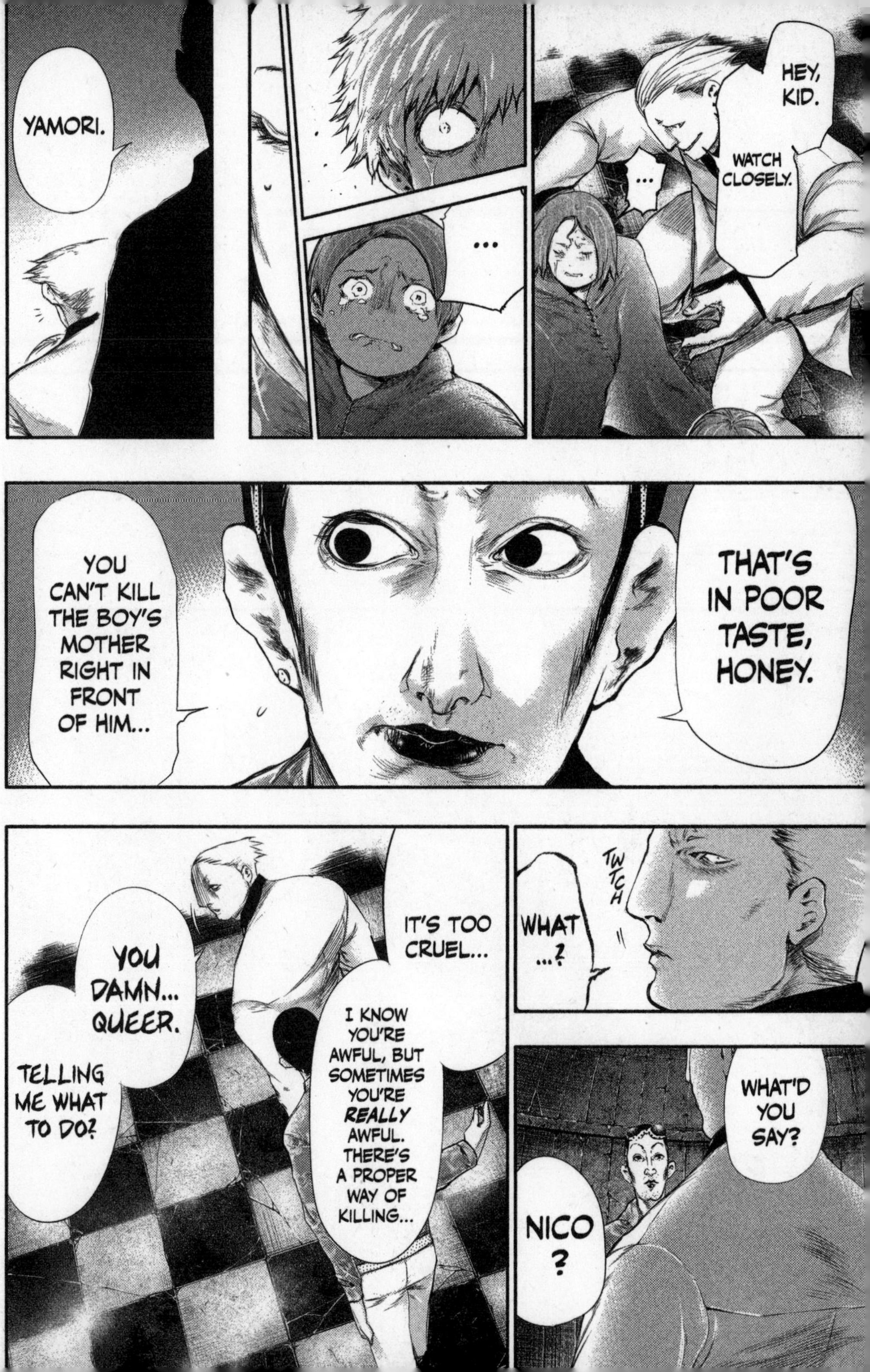
HEY, KID.
WATCH CLOSELY.
...
...
YAMORI.
THAT'S IN POOR TASTE, HONEY.
YOU CAN'T KILL THE BOY'S MOTHER RIGHT IN FRONT OF HIM...
TWTCH
WHAT ...?
WHAT'D YOU SAY?
NICO?
IT'S TOO CRUEL...
I KNOW YOU'RE AWFUL, BUT SOMETIMES YOU'RE *REALLY* AWFUL. THERE'S A PROPER WAY OF KILLING...
YOU DAMN... QUEER.
TELLING ME WHAT TO DO?

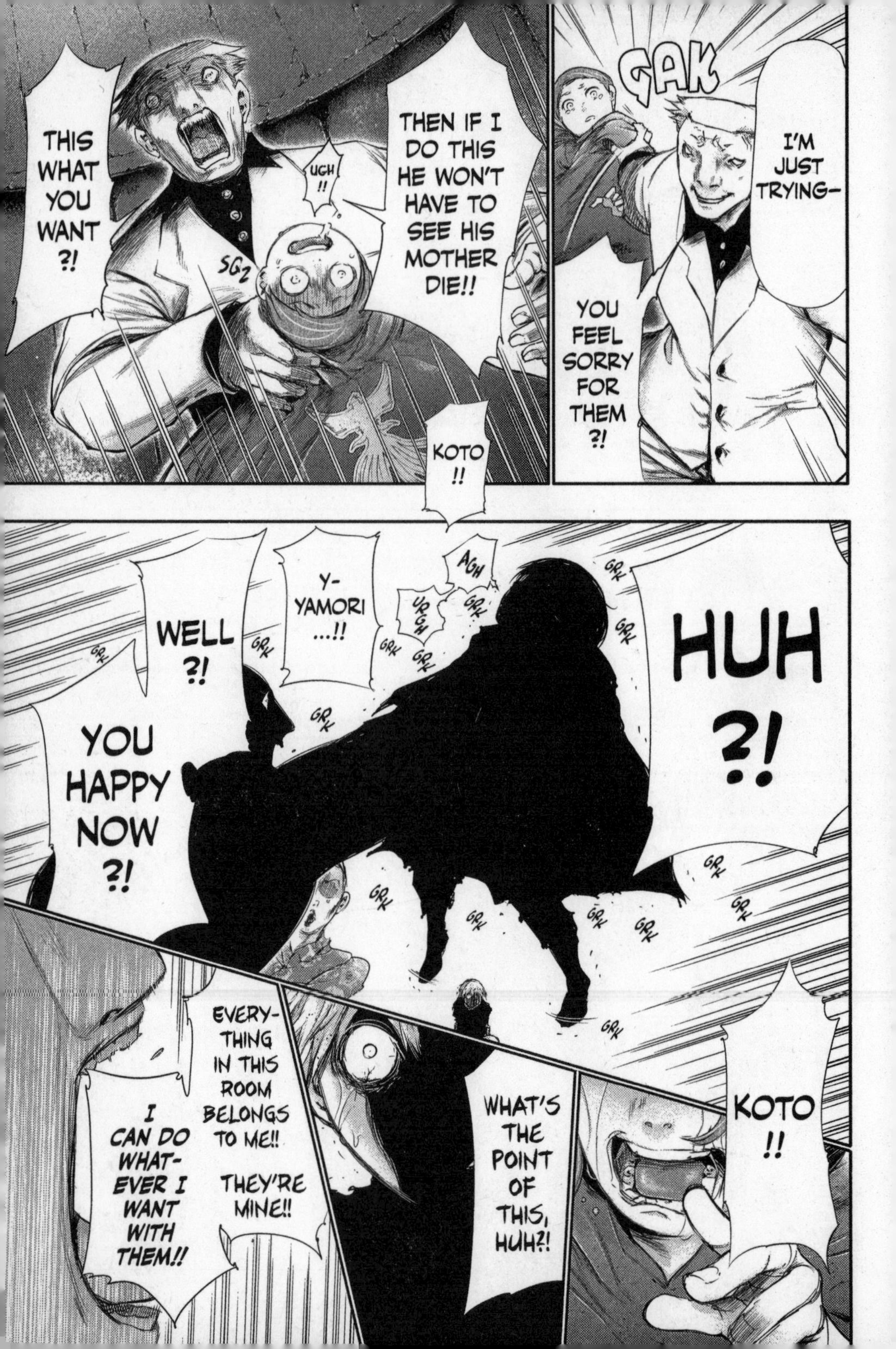
GAK
I'M JUST TRYING-
YOU FEEL SORRY FOR THEM?!
THEN IF I DO THIS HE WON'T HAVE TO SEE HIS MOTHER DIE!!
UGH!!
THIS WHAT YOU WANT?!
KOTO!!
HUH?!
GRK
AGH
URGH
Y-YAMORI...!!
WELL?!
YOU HAPPY NOW?!
KOTO!!
WHAT'S THE POINT OF THIS, HUH?!
EVERYTHING IN THIS ROOM BELONGS TO ME!!
THEY'RE MINE!!
I CAN DO WHATEVER I WANT WITH THEM!!

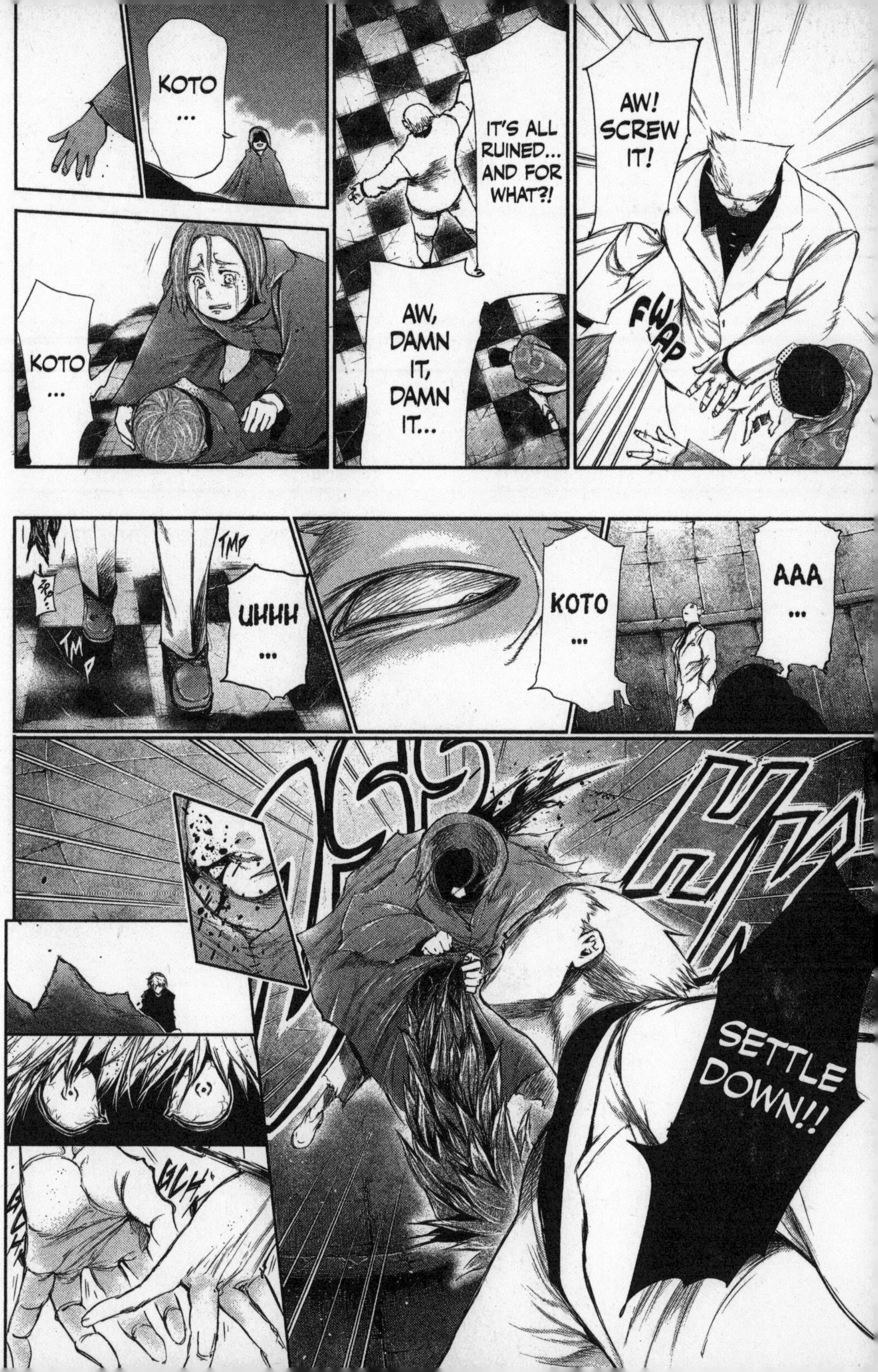
AW! SCREW IT!
FWAP
IT'S ALL RUINED... AND FOR WHAT?!
AW, DAMN IT, DAMN IT...
KOTO ...
KOTO ...
AAA ...
KOTO ...
TMP
UHHH ...
TMP
SETTLE DOWN!!
GACK

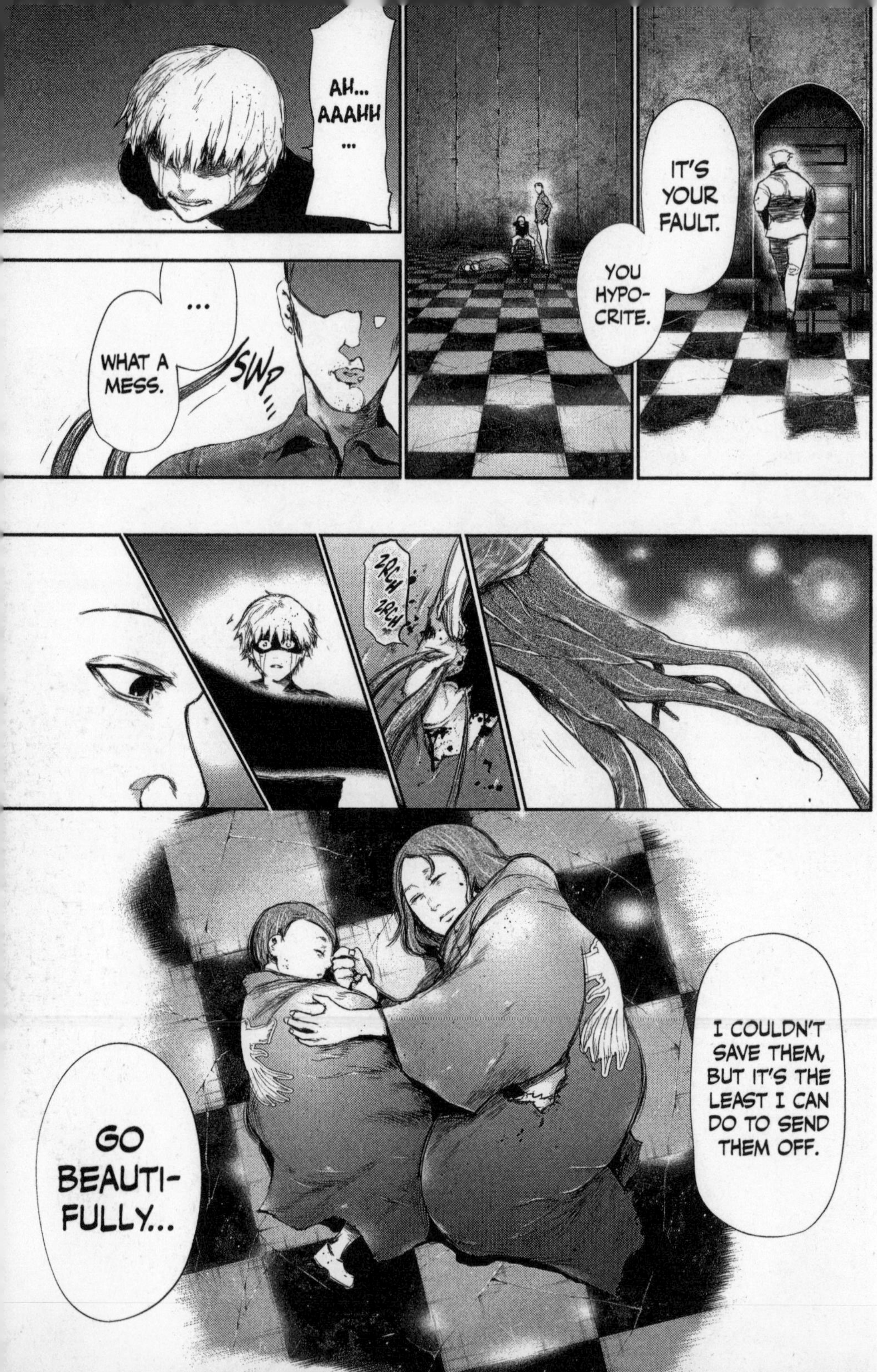
IT'S YOUR FAULT.
YOU HYPOCRITE.
AH... AAAHH ...
... WHAT A MESS.
SWP
ZRCH ZRCH
I COULDN'T SAVE THEM, BUT IT'S THE LEAST I CAN DO TO SEND THEM OFF.
GO BEAUTIFULLY...

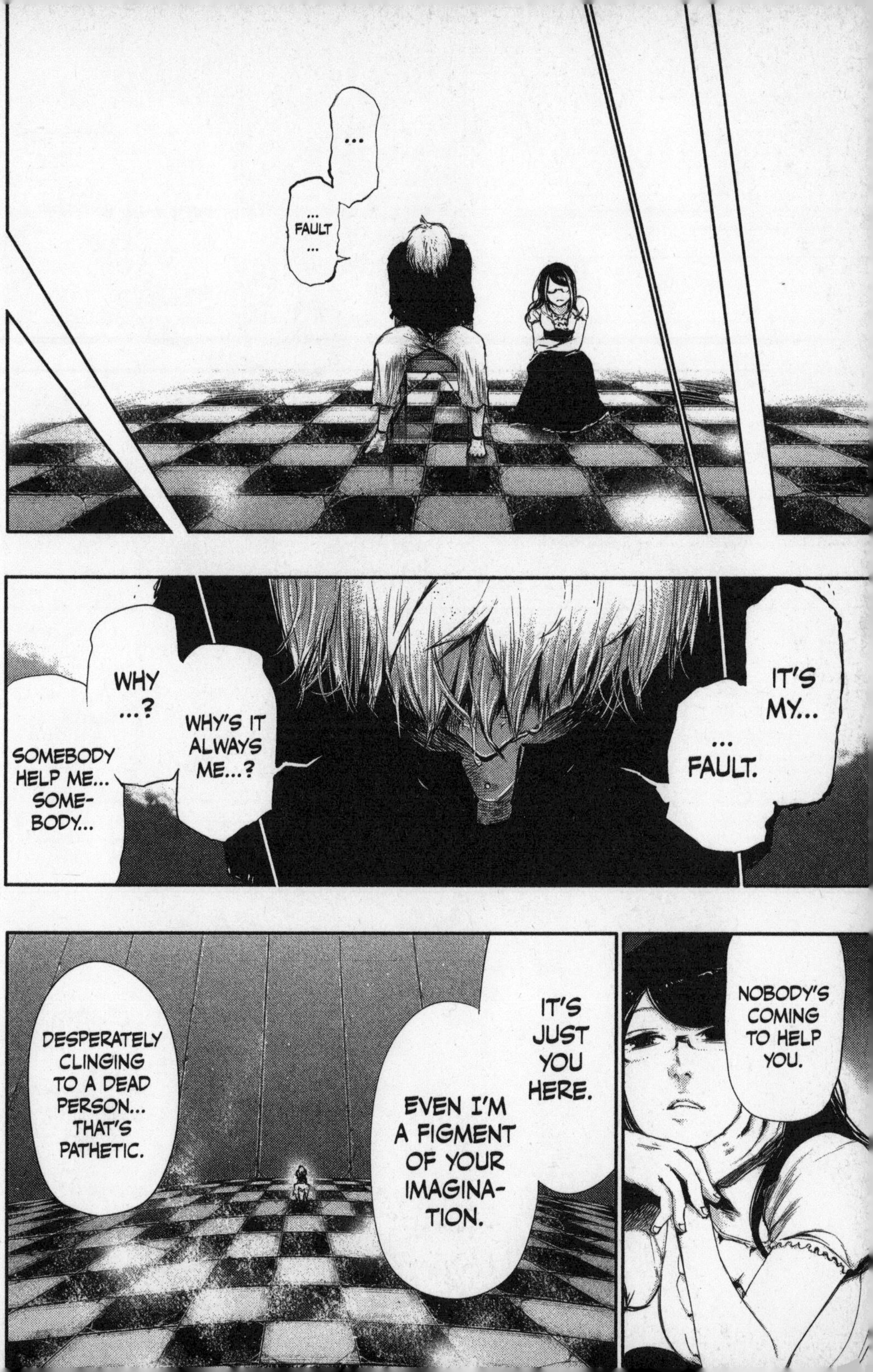
...
... FAULT ...
IT'S MY... ... FAULT.
WHY'S IT ALWAYS ME...?
WHY ...?
SOMEBODY HELP ME... SOME-BODY...
NOBODY'S COMING TO HELP YOU.
IT'S JUST YOU HERE.
EVEN I'M A FIGMENT OF YOUR IMAGINA-TION.
DESPERATELY CLINGING TO A DEAD PERSON... THAT'S PATHETIC.

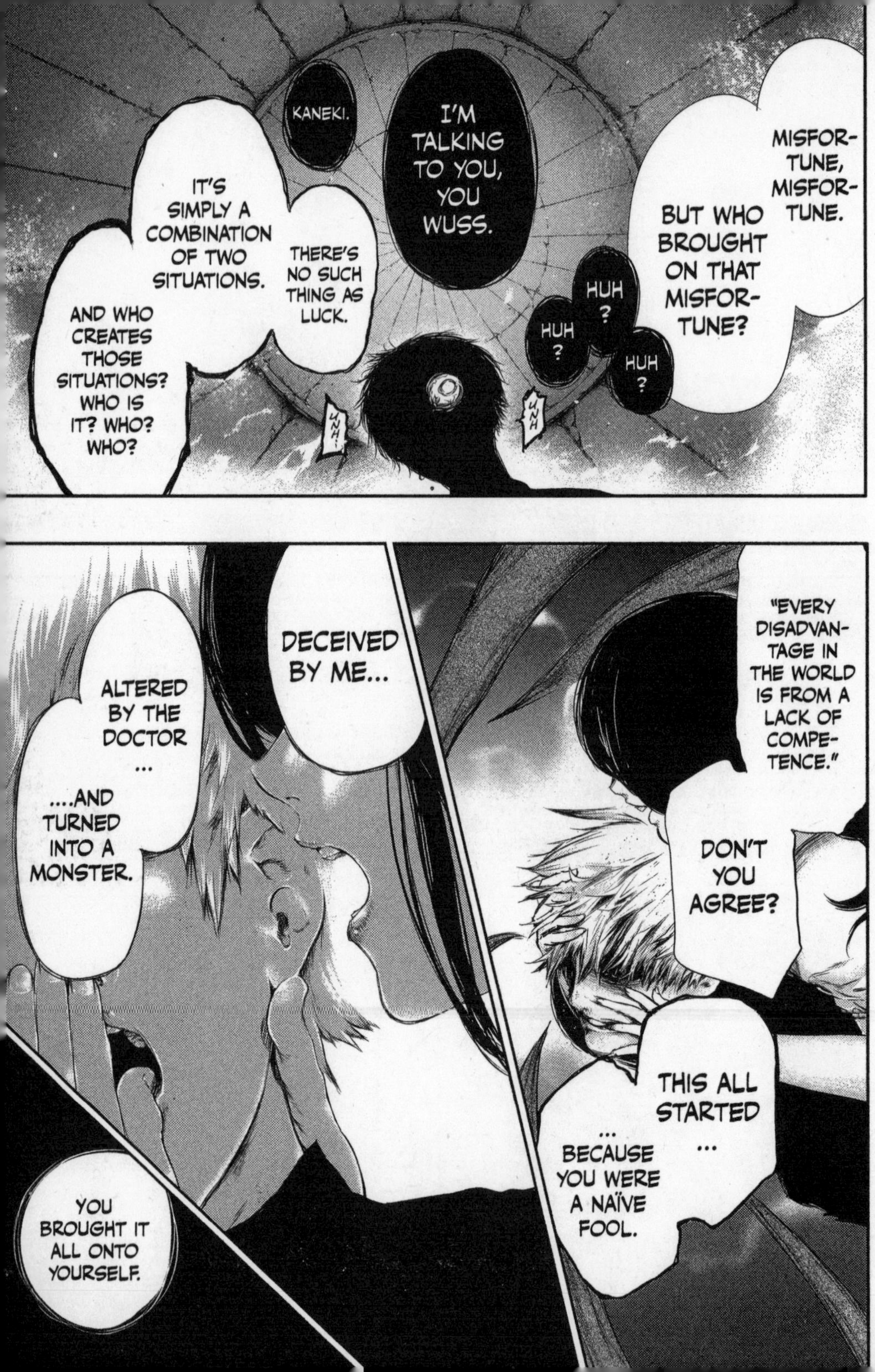
MISFORTUNE, MISFORTUNE.
BUT WHO BROUGHT ON THAT MISFORTUNE?
HUH?
HUH?
HUH?
UNH
I'M TALKING TO YOU, YOU WUSS.
KANEKI.
UNH
THERE'S NO SUCH THING AS LUCK.
IT'S SIMPLY A COMBINATION OF TWO SITUATIONS.
AND WHO CREATES THOSE SITUATIONS? WHO IS IT? WHO? WHO?
"EVERY DISADVANTAGE IN THE WORLD IS FROM A LACK OF COMPETENCE."
DON'T YOU AGREE?
THIS ALL STARTED ...
... BECAUSE YOU WERE A NAÏVE FOOL.
DECEIVED BY ME...
ALTERED BY THE DOCTOR ...
....AND TURNED INTO A MONSTER.
YOU BROUGHT IT ALL ONTO YOURSELF.

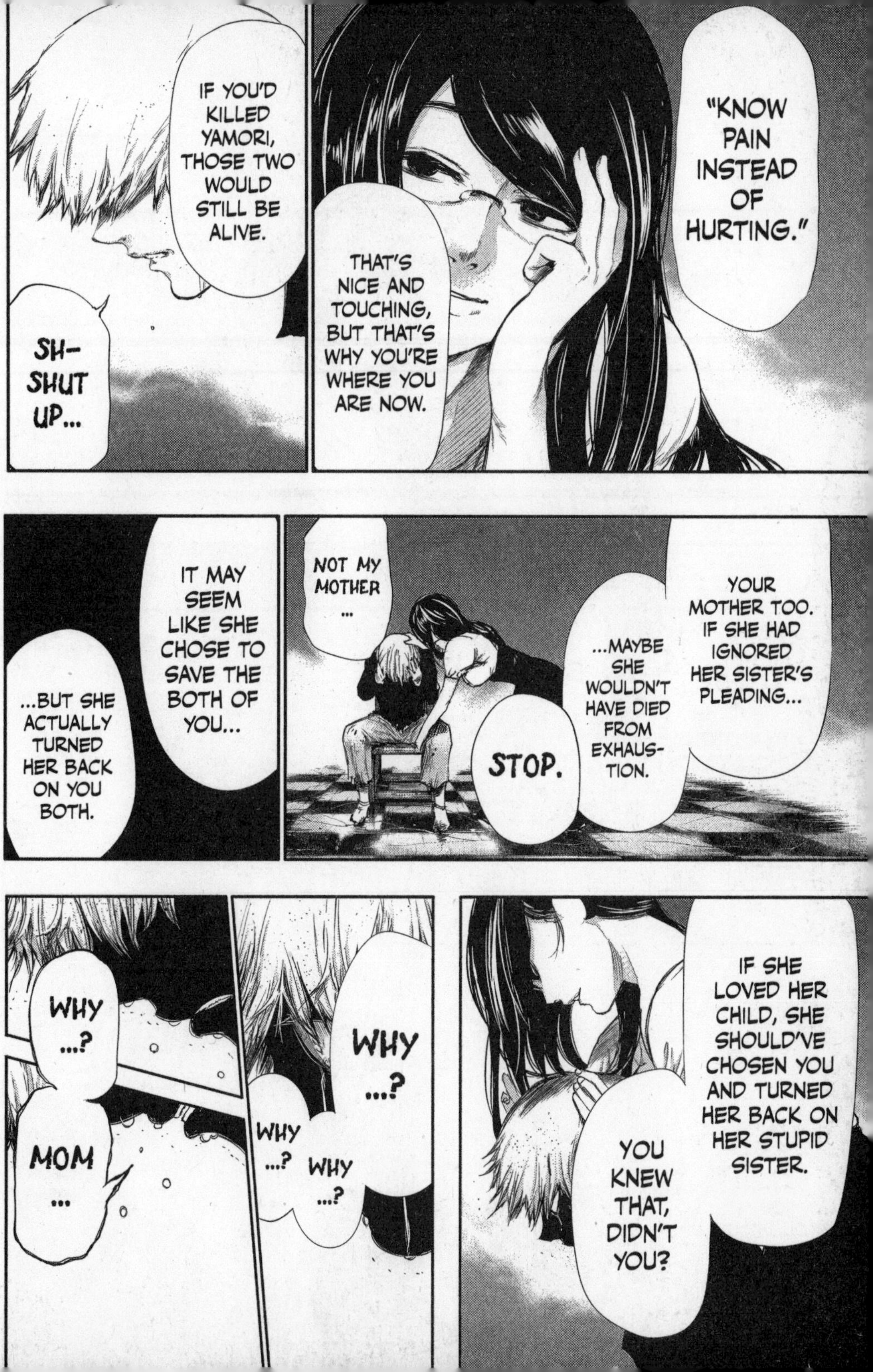
"KNOW PAIN INSTEAD OF HURTING."
THAT'S NICE AND TOUCHING, BUT THAT'S WHY YOU'RE WHERE YOU ARE NOW.
IF YOU'D KILLED YAMORI, THOSE TWO WOULD STILL BE ALIVE.
SH- SHUT UP...
YOUR MOTHER TOO. IF SHE HAD IGNORED HER SISTER'S PLEADING...
...MAYBE SHE WOULDN'T HAVE DIED FROM EXHAUS- TION.
STOP.
NOT MY MOTHER ...
IT MAY SEEM LIKE SHE CHOSE TO SAVE THE BOTH OF YOU...
...BUT SHE ACTUALLY TURNED HER BACK ON YOU BOTH.
IF SHE LOVED HER CHILD, SHE SHOULD'VE CHOSEN YOU AND TURNED HER BACK ON HER STUPID SISTER.
YOU KNEW THAT, DIDN'T YOU?
WHY ...?
WHY ...?
WHY ...?
WHY ...?
MOM ...

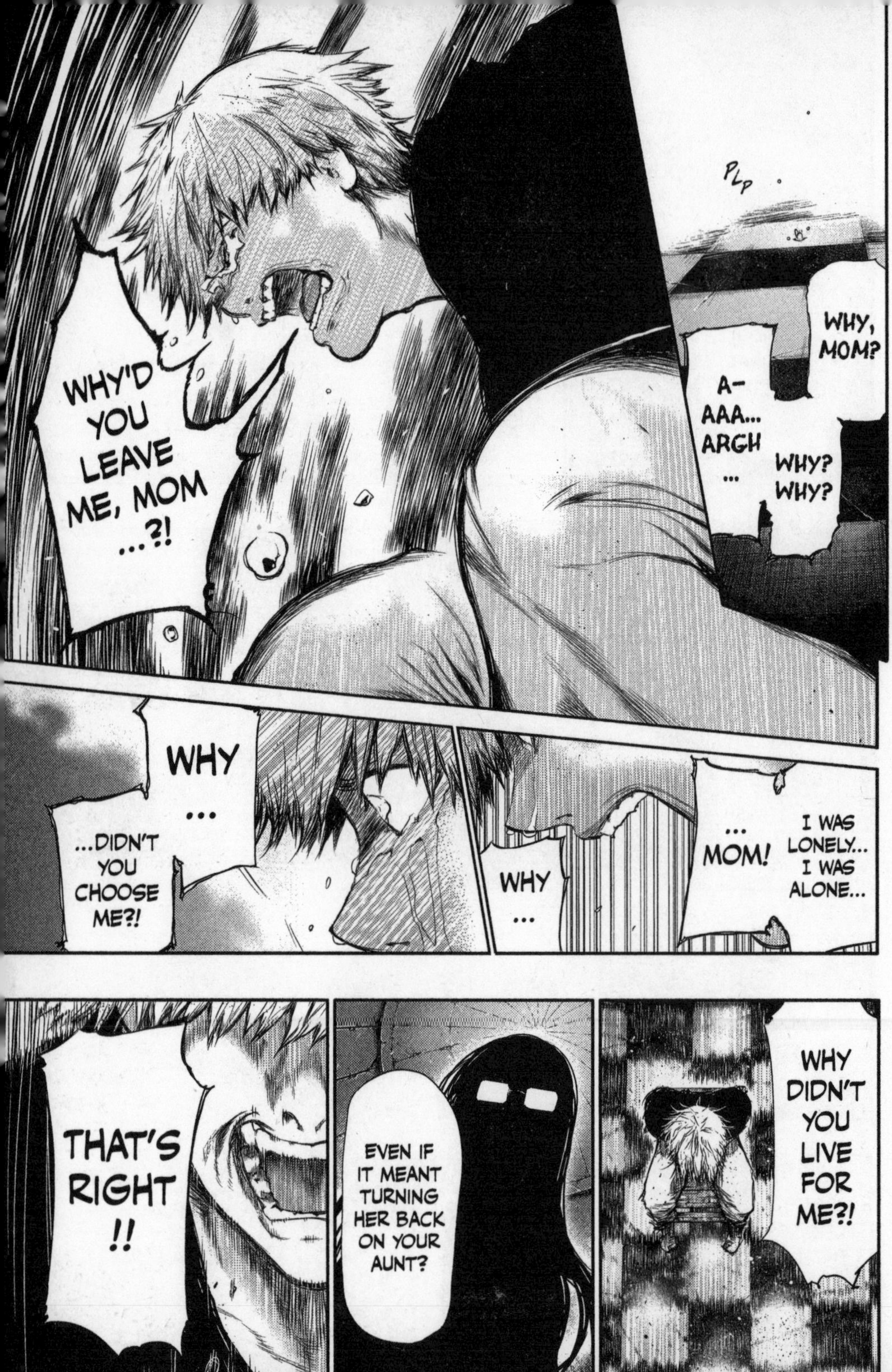
PLP
WHY, MOM?
A-AAA... ARGH...
WHY? WHY?
WHY'D YOU LEAVE ME, MOM...?!
I WAS LONELY... I WAS ALONE...
...MOM!
WHY...
WHY...
...DIDN'T YOU CHOOSE ME?!
WHY DIDN'T YOU LIVE FOR ME?!
EVEN IF IT MEANT TURNING HER BACK ON YOUR AUNT?
THAT'S RIGHT!!

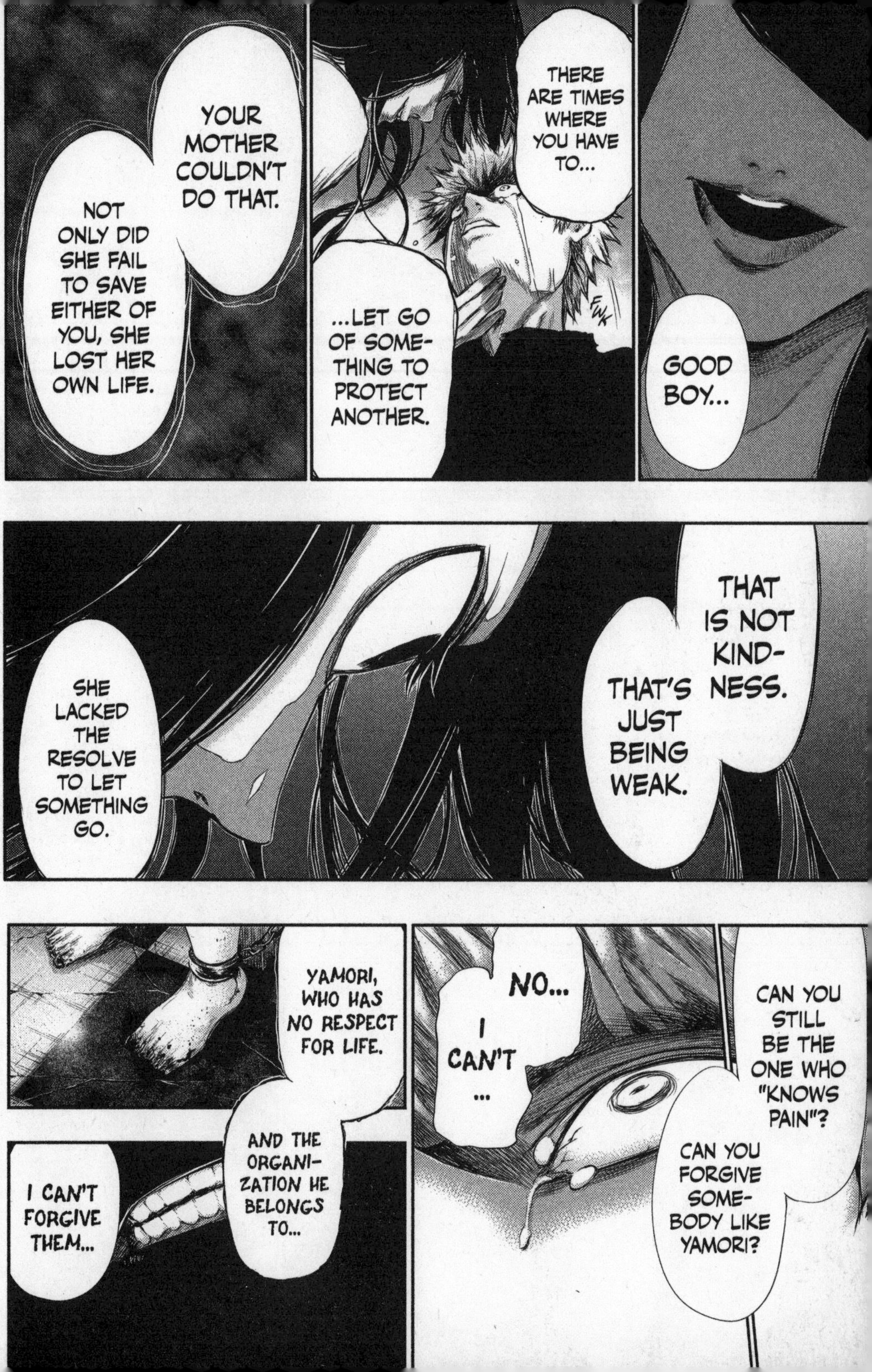
GOOD BOY...
THERE ARE TIMES WHERE YOU HAVE TO...
...LET GO OF SOMETHING TO PROTECT ANOTHER.
FWK
YOUR MOTHER COULDN'T DO THAT.
NOT ONLY DID SHE FAIL TO SAVE EITHER OF YOU, SHE LOST HER OWN LIFE.
THAT IS NOT KINDNESS.
THAT'S JUST BEING WEAK.
SHE LACKED THE RESOLVE TO LET SOMETHING GO.
CAN YOU STILL BE THE ONE WHO "KNOWS PAIN"?
CAN YOU FORGIVE SOMEBODY LIKE YAMORI?
NO...
I CAN'T ...
YAMORI, WHO HAS NO RESPECT FOR LIFE.
AND THE ORGANIZATION HE BELONGS TO...
I CAN'T FORGIVE THEM...

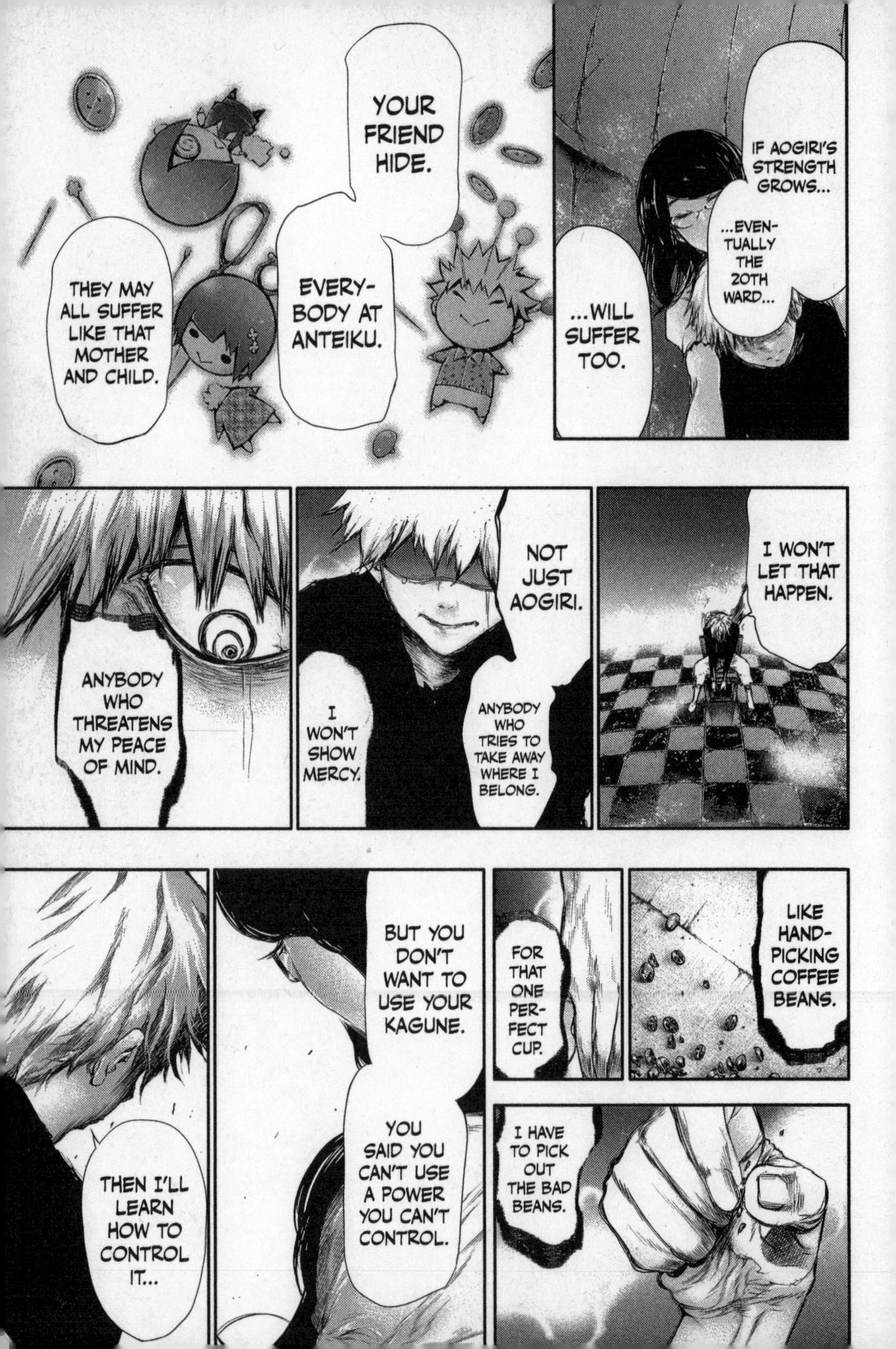
IF AOGIRI'S STRENGTH GROWS...
...EVEN-TUALLY THE 20TH WARD...
...WILL SUFFER TOO.
YOUR FRIEND HIDE.
EVERY-BODY AT ANTEIKU.
THEY MAY ALL SUFFER LIKE THAT MOTHER AND CHILD.
I WON'T LET THAT HAPPEN.
NOT JUST AOGIRI.
ANYBODY WHO TRIES TO TAKE AWAY WHERE I BELONG.
I WON'T SHOW MERCY.
ANYBODY WHO THREATENS MY PEACE OF MIND.
LIKE HAND-PICKING COFFEE BEANS.
FOR THAT ONE PERFECT CUP.
I HAVE TO PICK OUT THE BAD BEANS.
BUT YOU DON'T WANT TO USE YOUR KAGUNE.
YOU SAID YOU CAN'T USE A POWER YOU CAN'T CONTROL.
THEN I'LL LEARN HOW TO CONTROL IT...

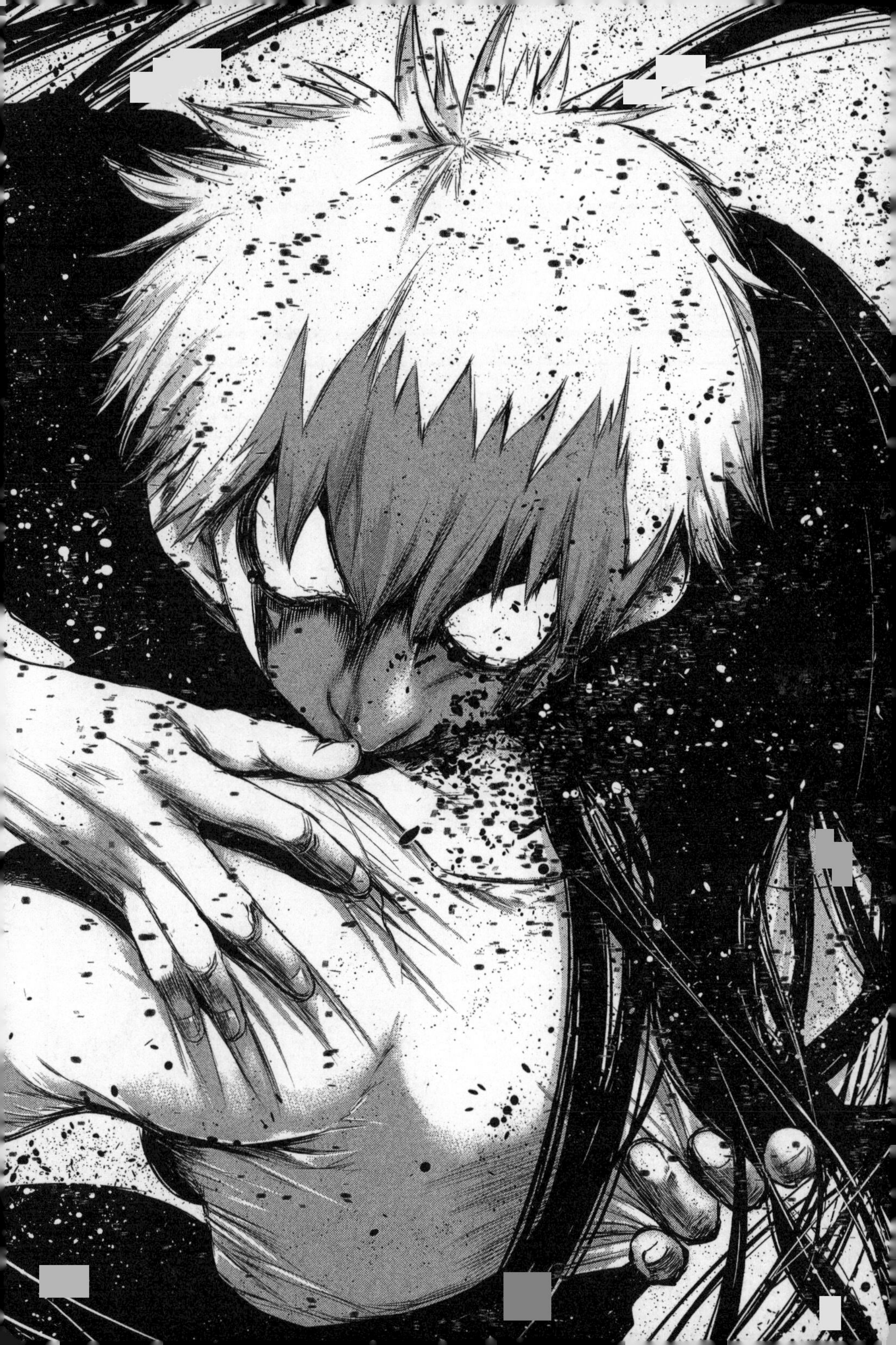

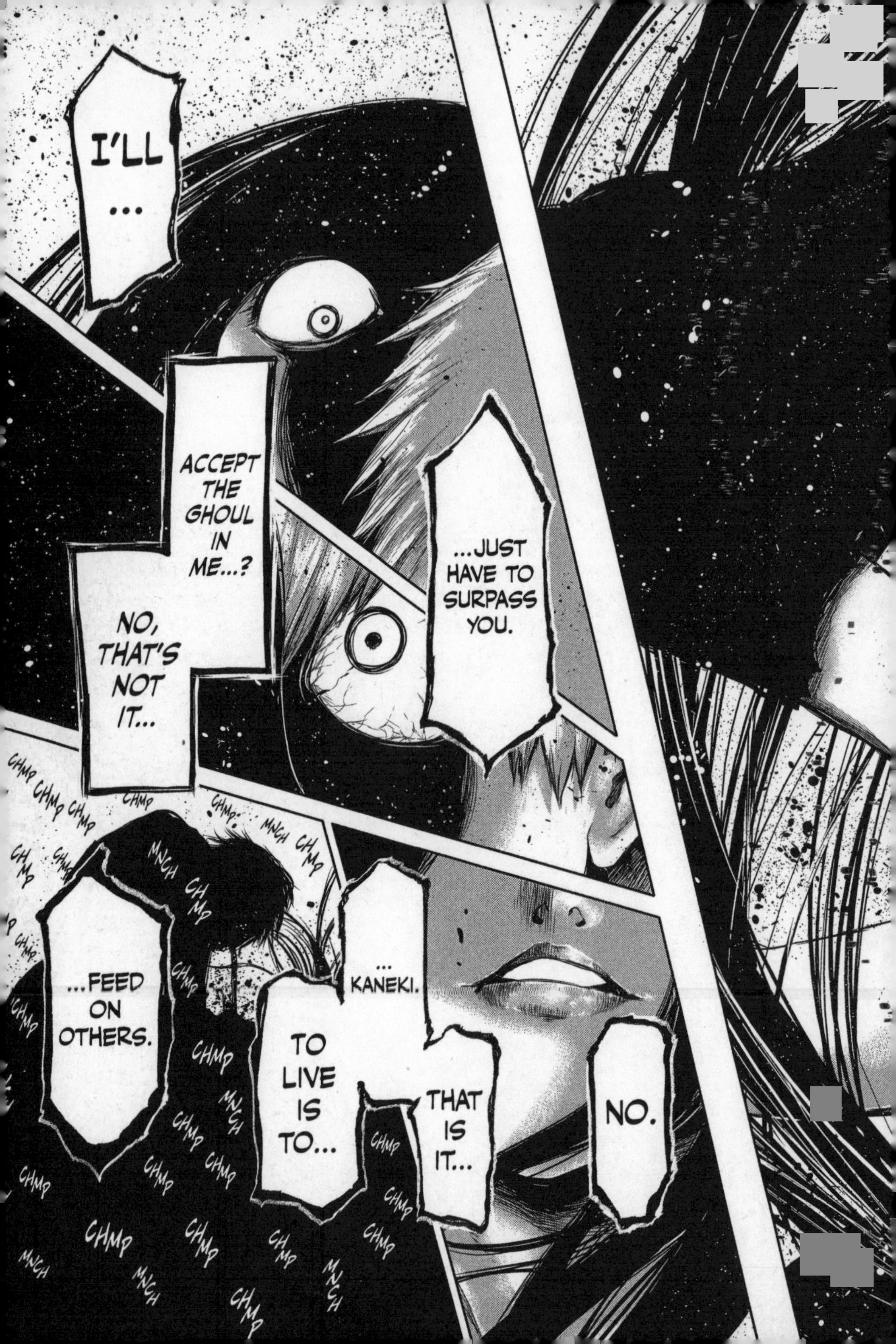
I'LL
...
ACCEPT THE GHOUL IN ME...?
NO, THAT'S NOT IT...
...JUST HAVE TO SURPASS YOU.
NO.
THAT IS IT...
... KANEKI.
TO LIVE IS TO...
...FEED ON OTHERS.
CHMP CHMP CHMP CHMP
CHMP MNCH CHMP
CHMP CHMP MNCH CHMP
CHMP CHMP
CHMP MNCH CHMP CHMP CHMP
CHMP CHMP CHMP CHMP MNCH
CHMP MNCH CHMP CHMP MNCH

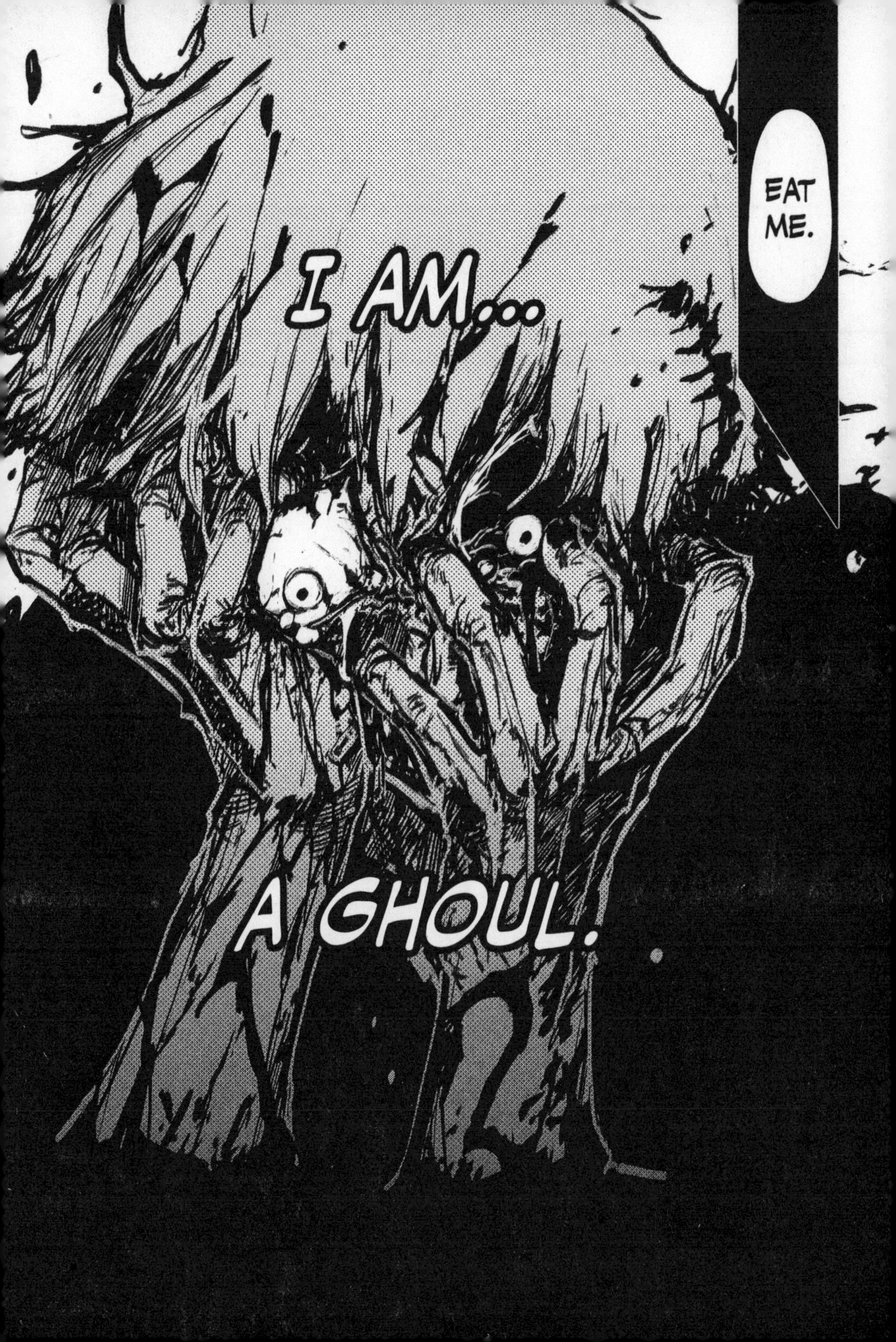
EAT ME.
I AM...
A GHOUL.

東京喰種
トーキョーグール
Tokyo
Ghoul

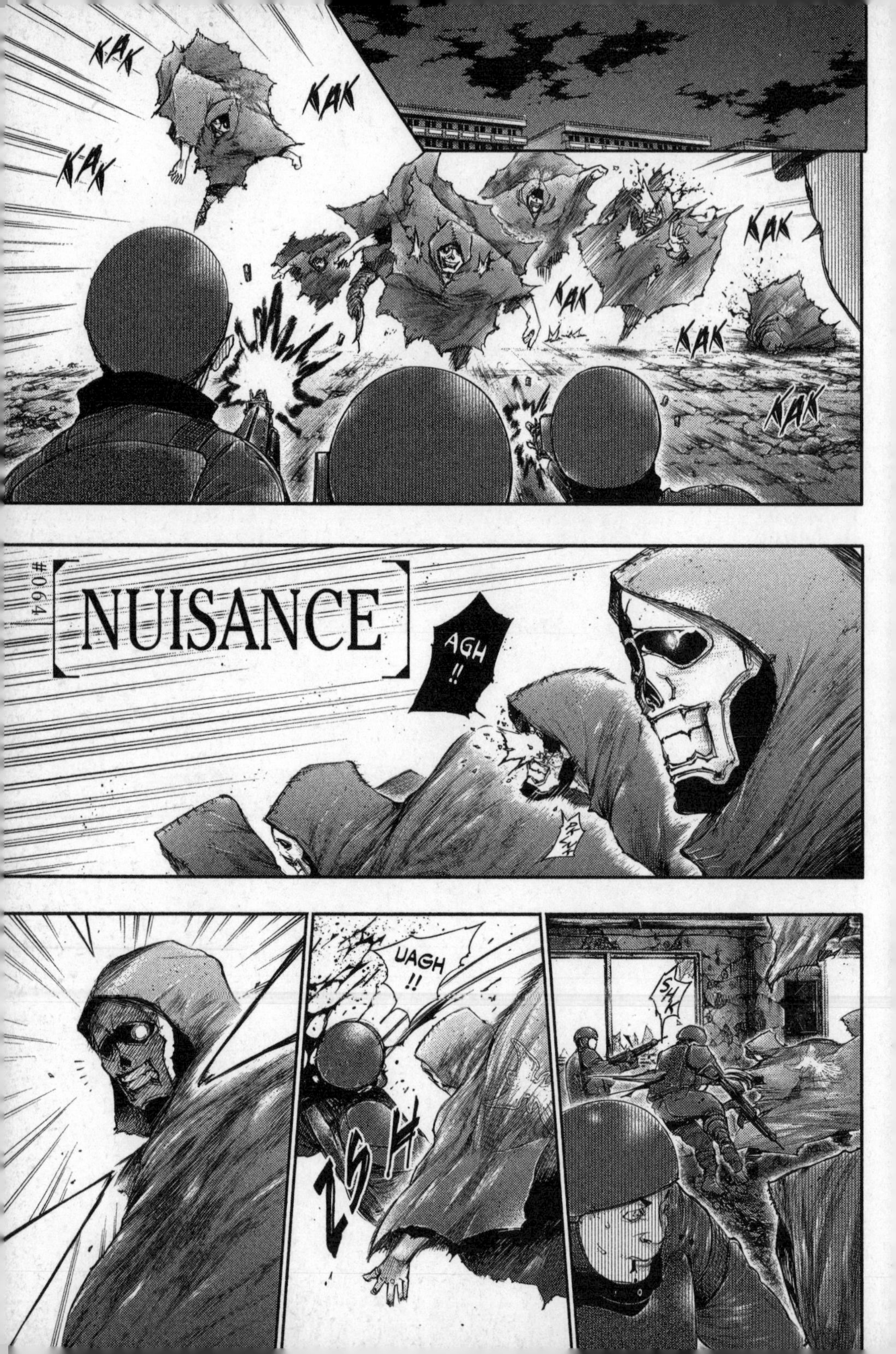
KAK
KAK
KAK
KAK
KAK
KAK
KAK
#064
NUISANCE
AGH !!
SHK
UAGH !!
ZSH

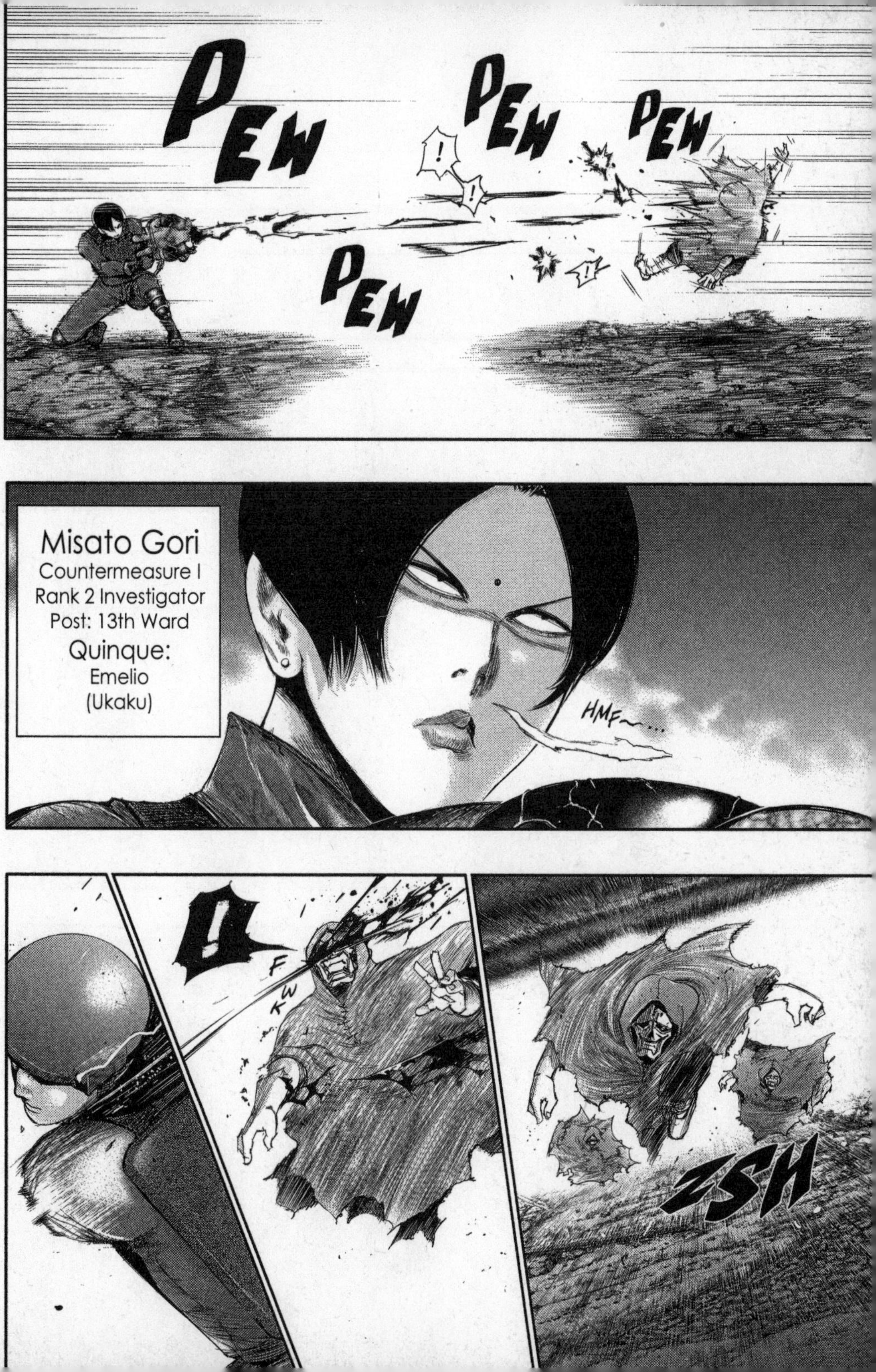
PEW
PEW
!
!
!
PEW
PEW
Misato Gori
Countermeasure I
Rank 2 Investigator
Post: 13th Ward
Quinque:
Emelio
(Ukaku)
HMF~....
ZSH
!
F
KW

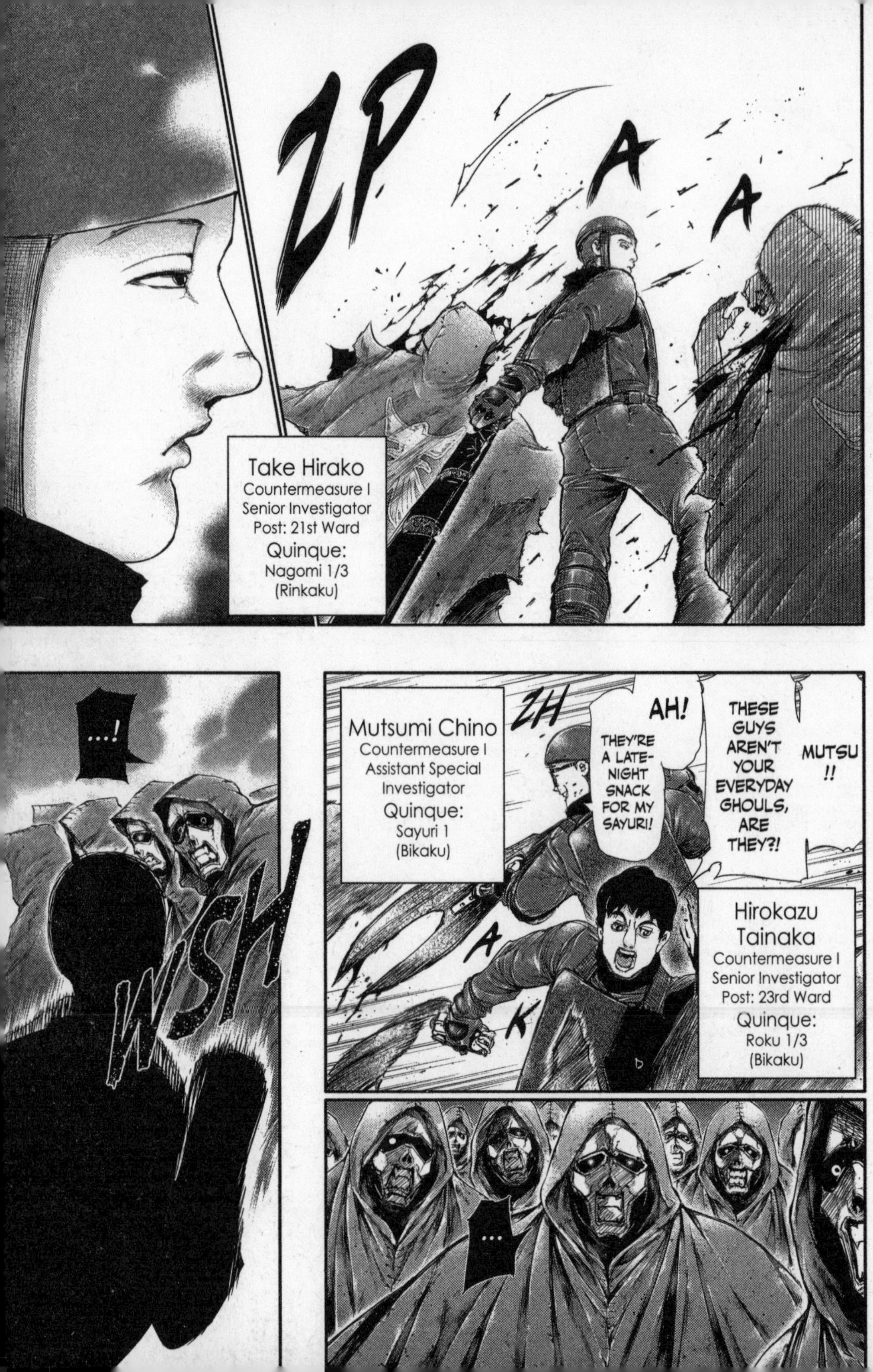
ZP
A
A
Take Hirako
Countermeasure I
Senior Investigator
Post: 21st Ward
Quinque:
Nagomi 1/3
(Rinkaku)
MUTSU !!
THESE GUYS AREN'T YOUR EVERYDAY GHOULS, ARE THEY?!
AH!
THEY'RE A LATE-NIGHT SNACK FOR MY SAYURI!
ZH
Mutsumi Chino
Countermeasure I
Assistant Special Investigator
Quinque:
Sayuri 1
(Bikaku)
Hirokazu Tainaka
Countermeasure I
Senior Investigator
Post: 23rd Ward
Quinque:
Roku 1/3
(Bikaku)
A
K
...
...!
WISH

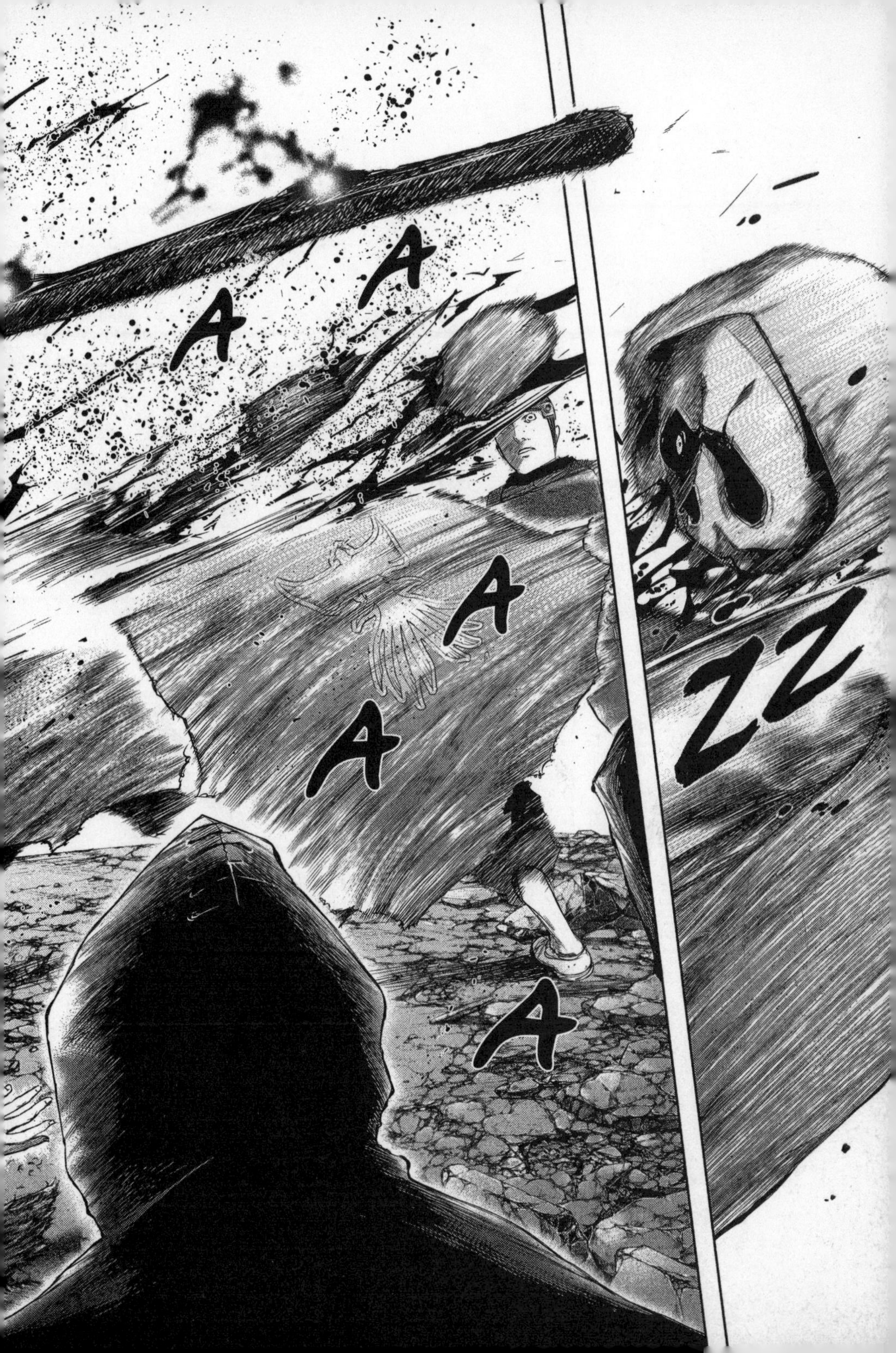
ZZ
AAAAAA

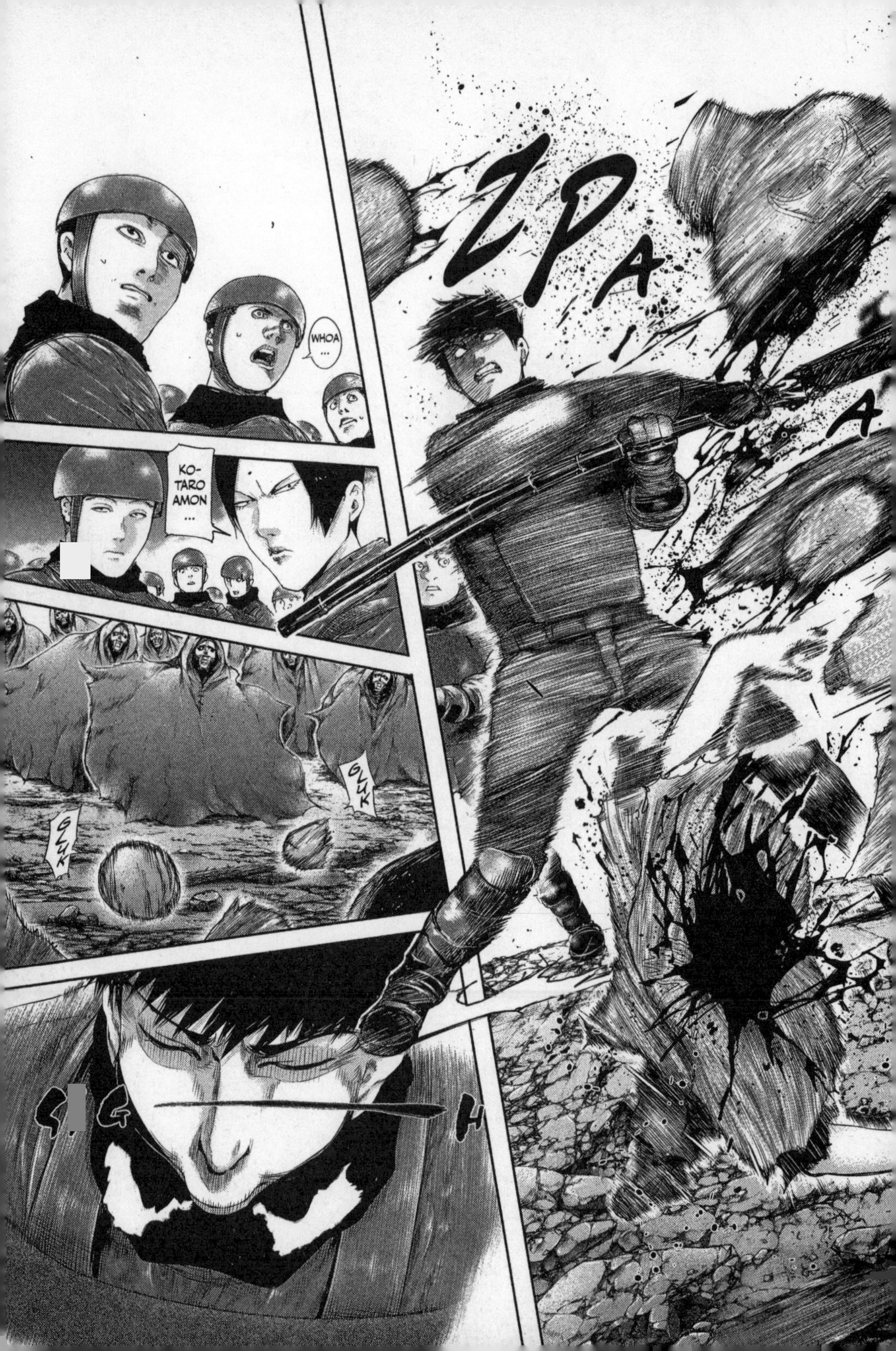

ZPA
A
WHOA ...
KOTARO AMON ...
GLUK
GLUK

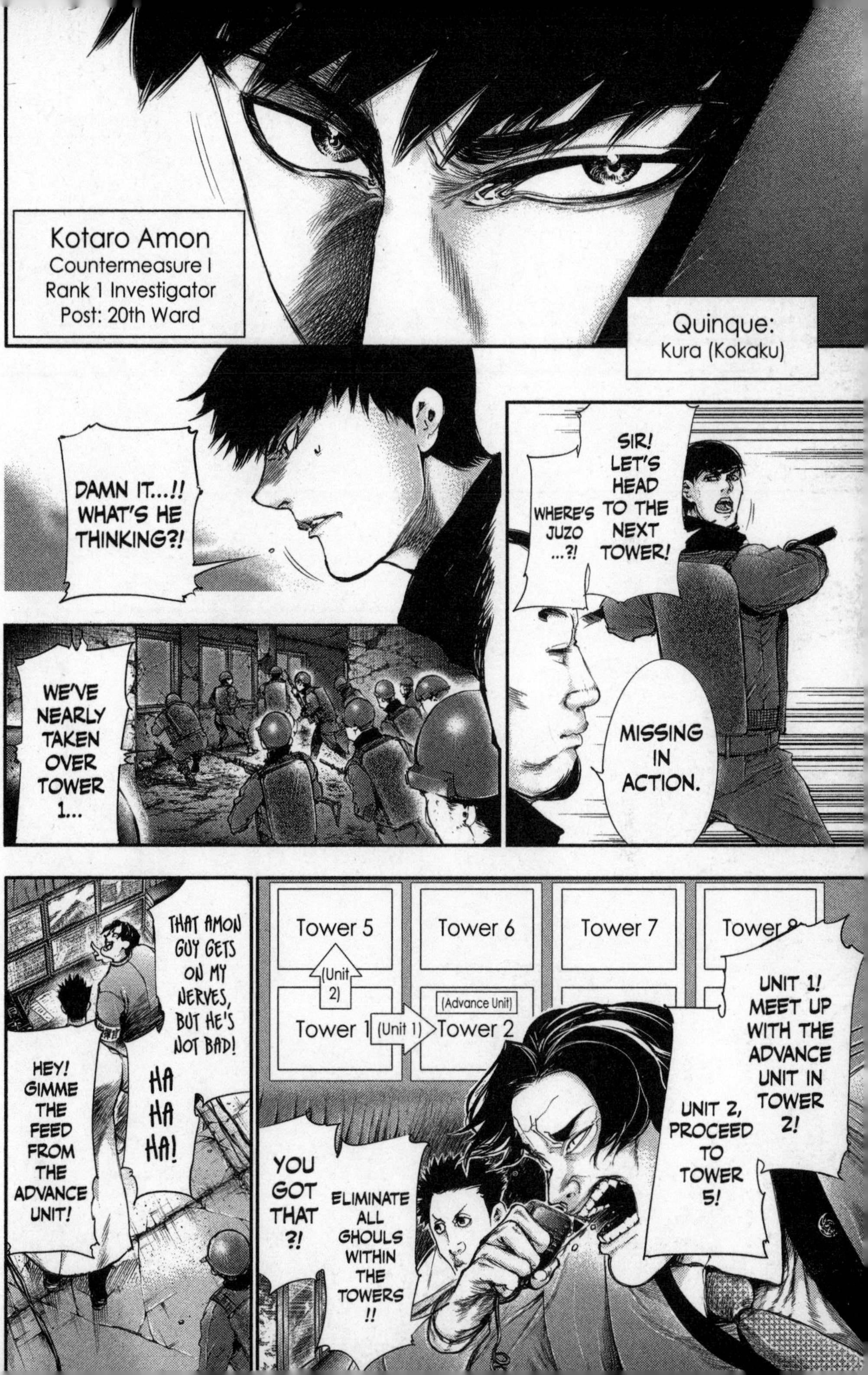
Kotaro Amon
Countermeasure I
Rank 1 Investigator
Post: 20th Ward
Quinque:
Kura (Kokaku)
SIR! LET'S HEAD TO THE NEXT TOWER!
WHERE'S JUZO ...?!
MISSING IN ACTION.
DAMN IT...!! WHAT'S HE THINKING?!
WE'VE NEARLY TAKEN OVER TOWER 1...
Tower 5
Tower 6
Tower 7
Tower
(Unit 2)
(Advance Unit)
Tower 1
(Unit 1)
Tower 2
UNIT 1! MEET UP WITH THE ADVANCE UNIT IN TOWER 2!
UNIT 2, PROCEED TO TOWER 5!
ELIMINATE ALL GHOULS WITHIN THE TOWERS !!
YOU GOT THAT ?!
THAT AMON GUY GETS ON MY NERVES, BUT HE'S NOT BAD!
HA HA HA!
HEY! GIMME THE FEED FROM THE ADVANCE UNIT!

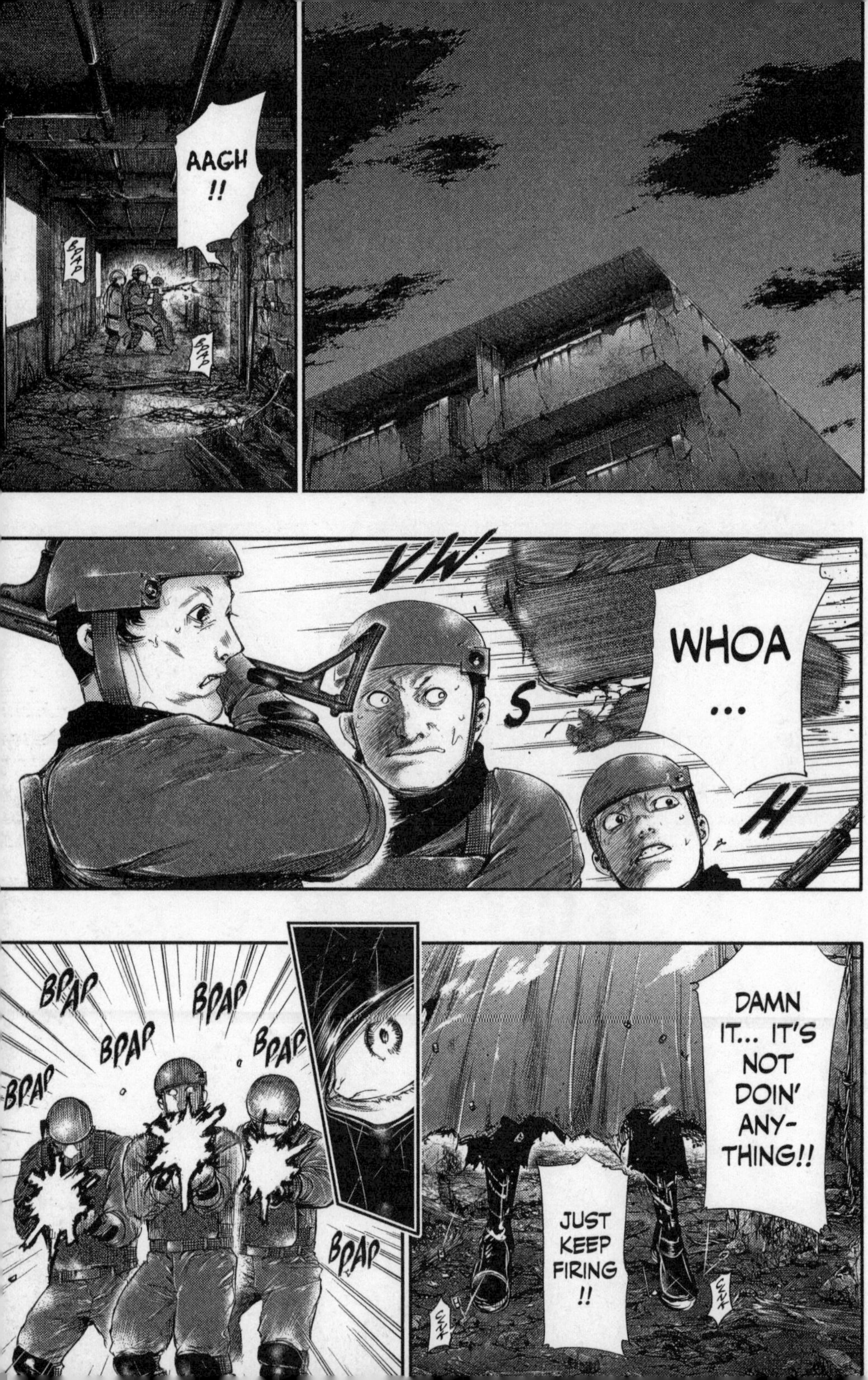
AAGH!!
BDAP
BDAP
WHOA...
VWSH
DAMN IT... IT'S NOT DOIN' ANYTHING!!
JUST KEEP FIRING!!
BDAP
BDAP
BDAP
BDAP
BDAP
BDAP

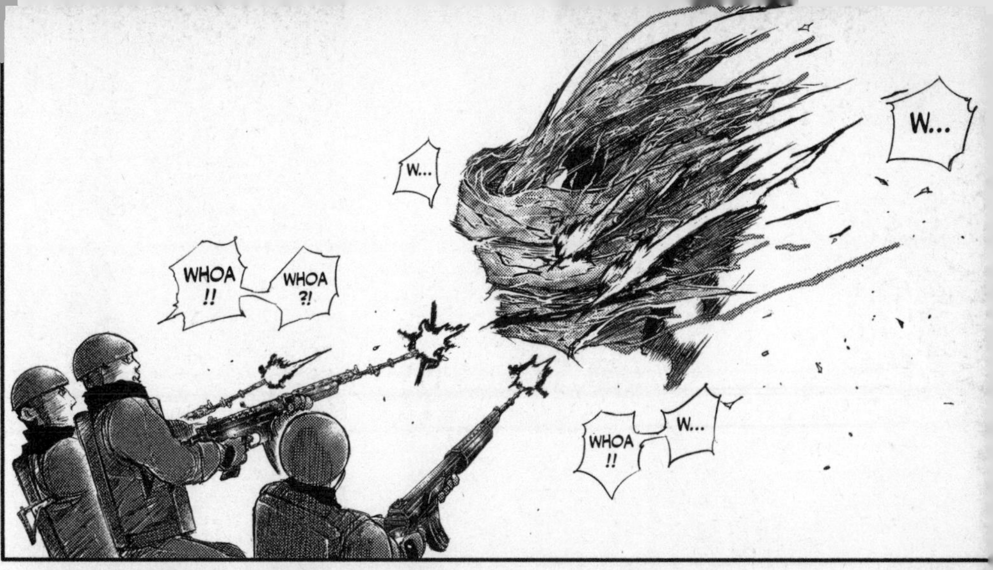
W...
W...
WHOA ?!
WHOA !!
W...
WHOA !!
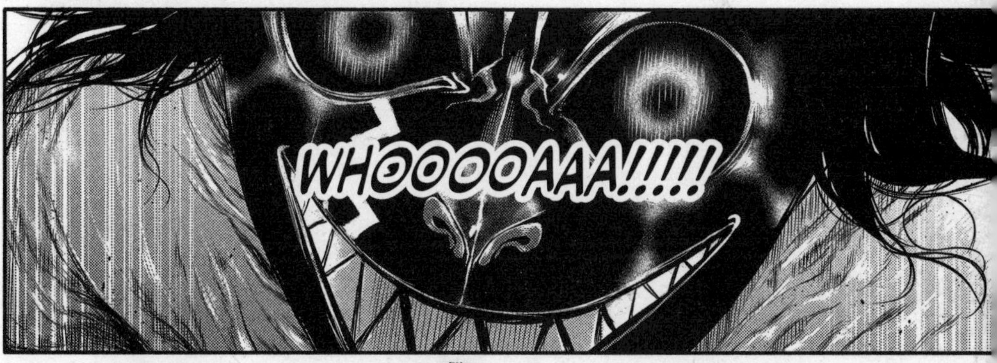
WHOOOOAAA!!!!!!
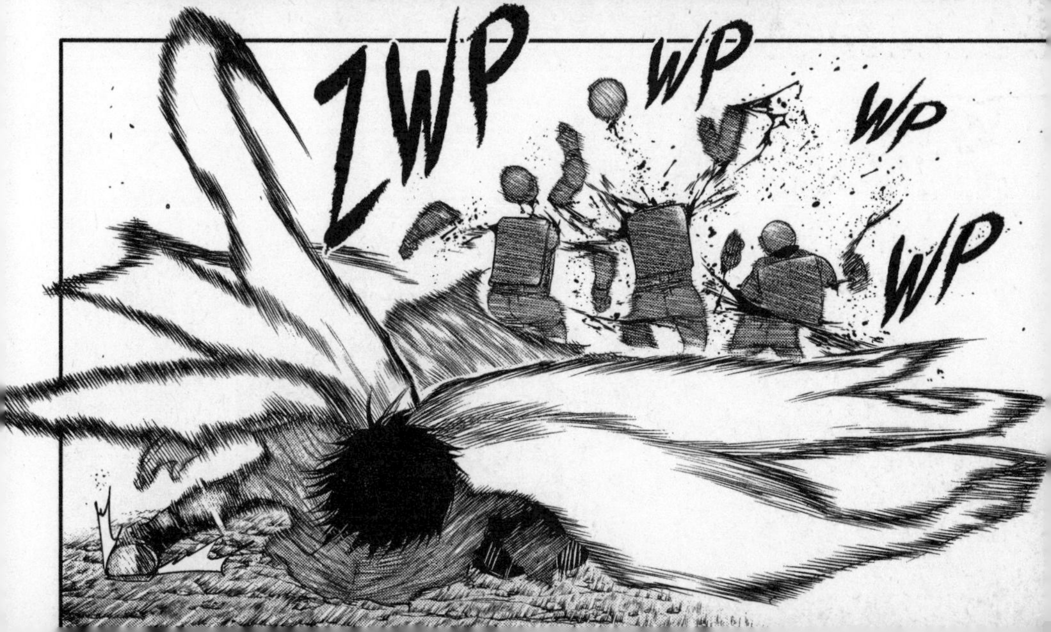
WP
WP
ZWP
WP

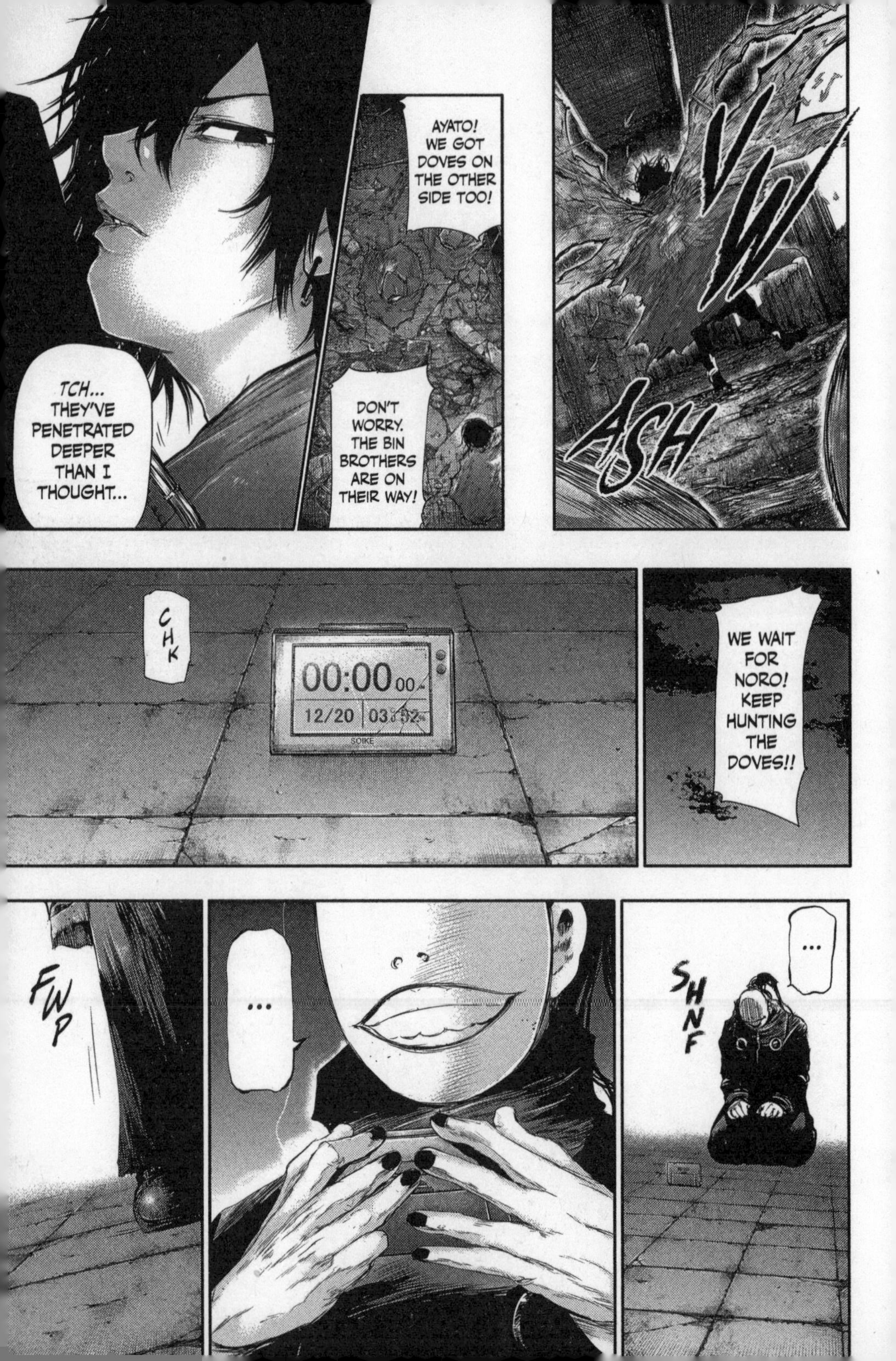
VVW
ASH
AYATO! WE GOT DOVES ON THE OTHER SIDE TOO!
DON'T WORRY. THE BIN BROTHERS ARE ON THEIR WAY!
TCH... THEY'VE PENETRATED DEEPER THAN I THOUGHT...
WE WAIT FOR NORO! KEEP HUNTING THE DOVES!!
CHK
00:00 00
12/20 03:52
SOIKE
...
SHNF
...
FWP

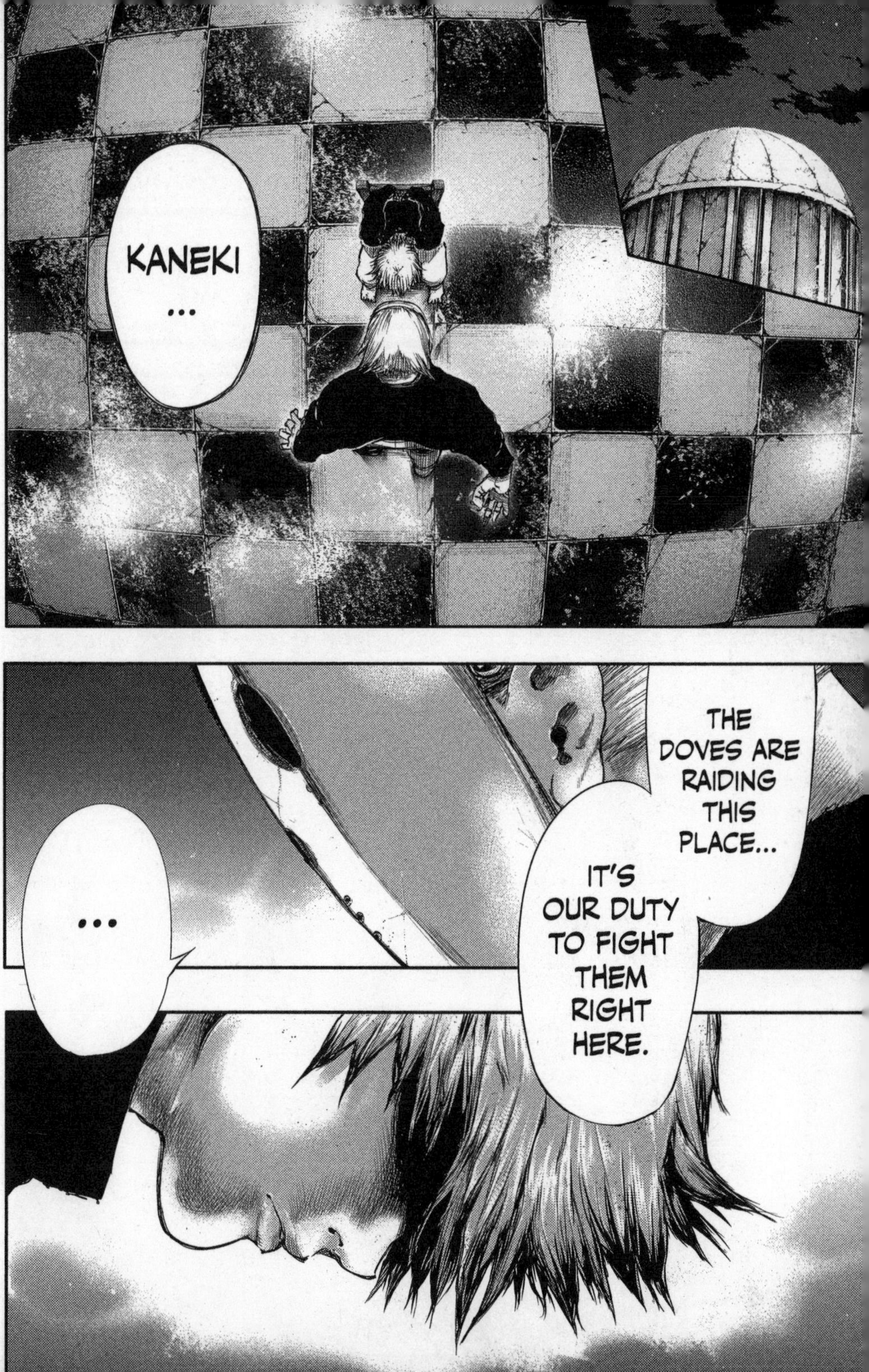
KANEKI ...
THE DOVES ARE RAIDING THIS PLACE...
IT'S OUR DUTY TO FIGHT THEM RIGHT HERE.
...

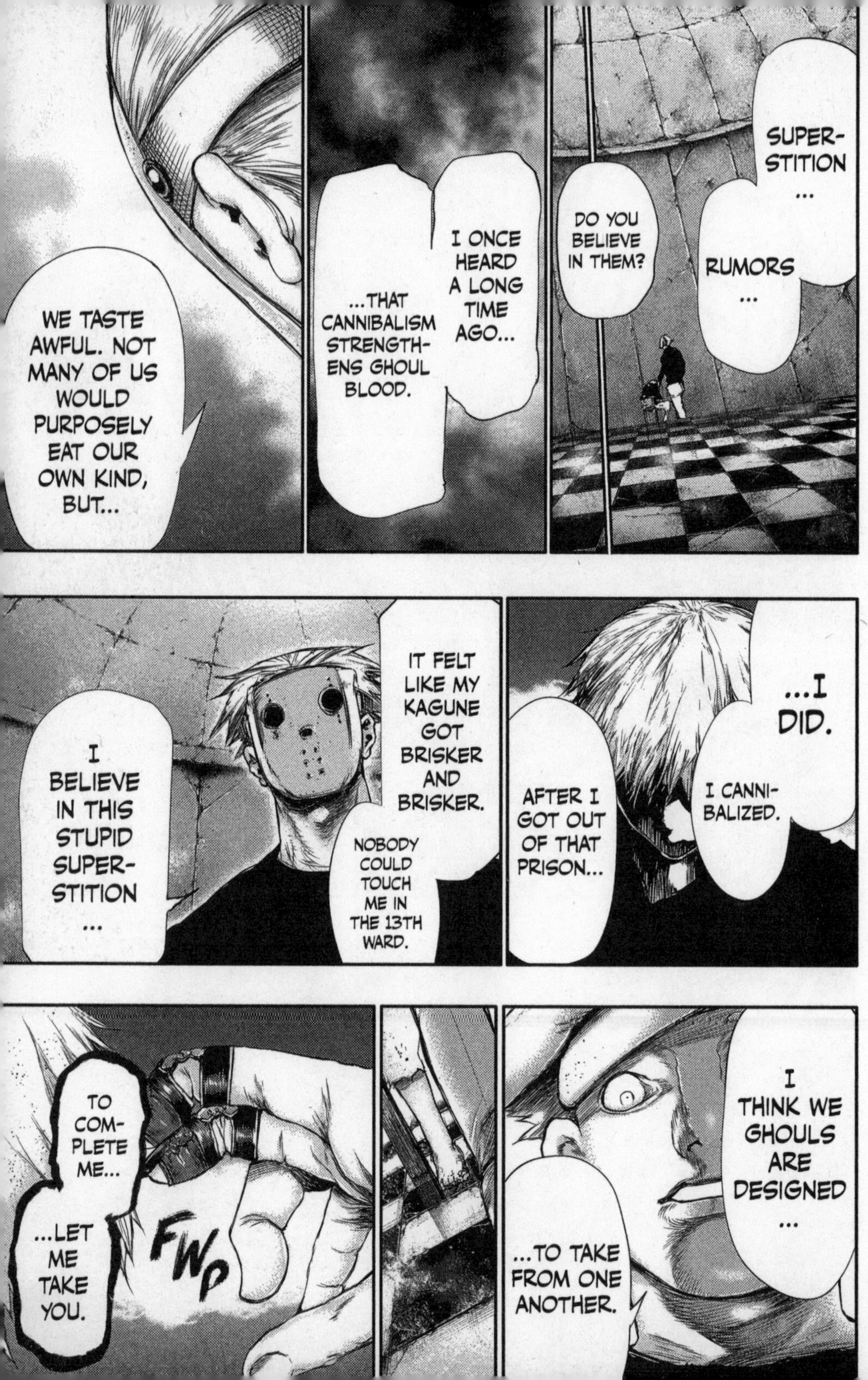
SUPERSTITION ...
RUMORS ...
DO YOU BELIEVE IN THEM?
I ONCE HEARD A LONG TIME AGO...
...THAT CANNIBALISM STRENGTHENS GHOUL BLOOD.
WE TASTE AWFUL. NOT MANY OF US WOULD PURPOSELY EAT OUR OWN KIND, BUT...
...I DID.
I CANNIBALIZED.
AFTER I GOT OUT OF THAT PRISON...
IT FELT LIKE MY KAGUNE GOT BRISKER AND BRISKER.
NOBODY COULD TOUCH ME IN THE 13TH WARD.
I BELIEVE IN THIS STUPID SUPERSTITION ...
I THINK WE GHOULS ARE DESIGNED ...
...TO TAKE FROM ONE ANOTHER.
TO COMPLETE ME...
...LET ME TAKE YOU.
FWP

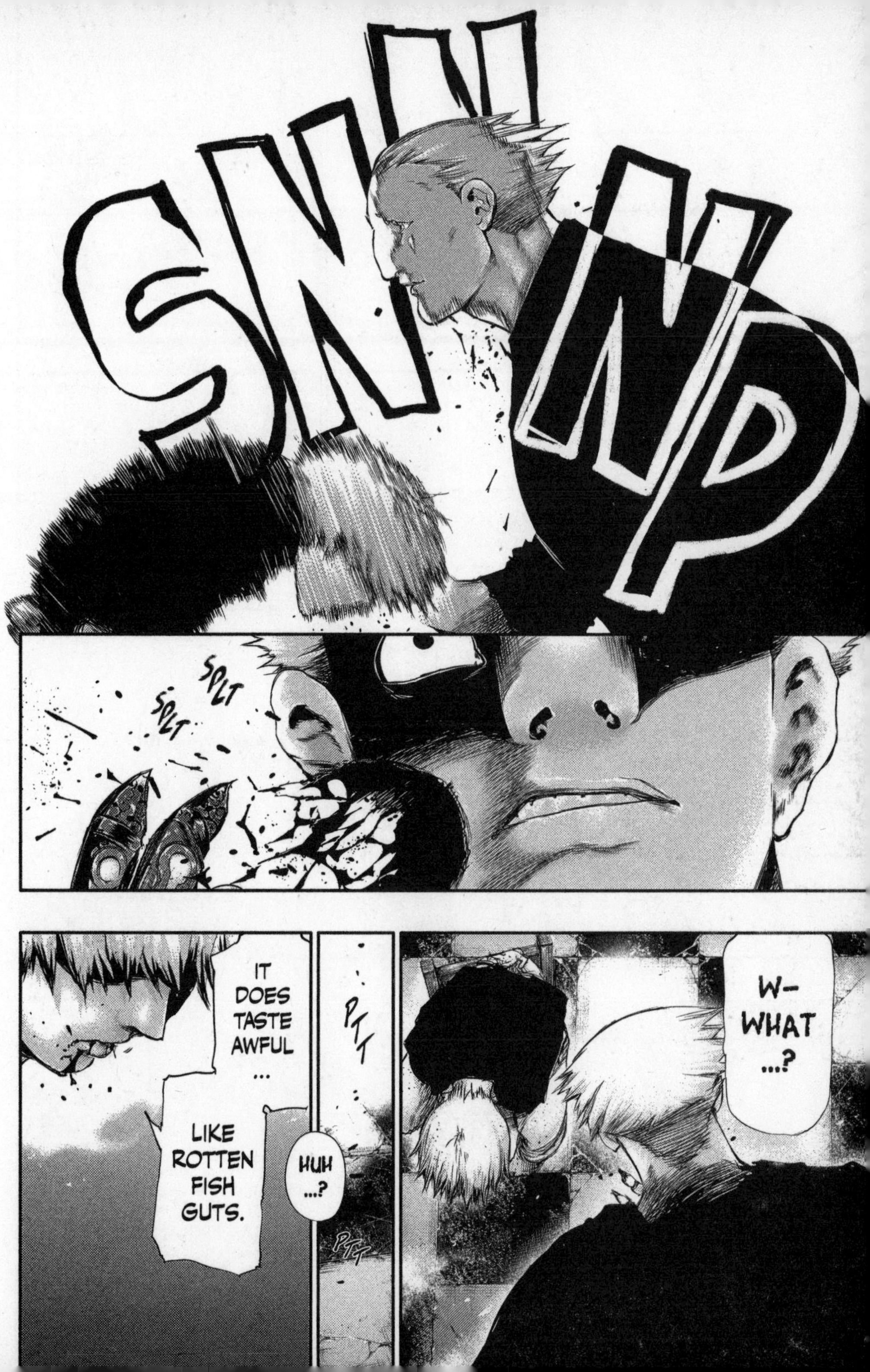
SPLT
SPLT
W-
WHAT
...?
PTT
HUH
...?
PTT
IT
DOES
TASTE
AWFUL
...
LIKE
ROTTEN
FISH
GUTS.

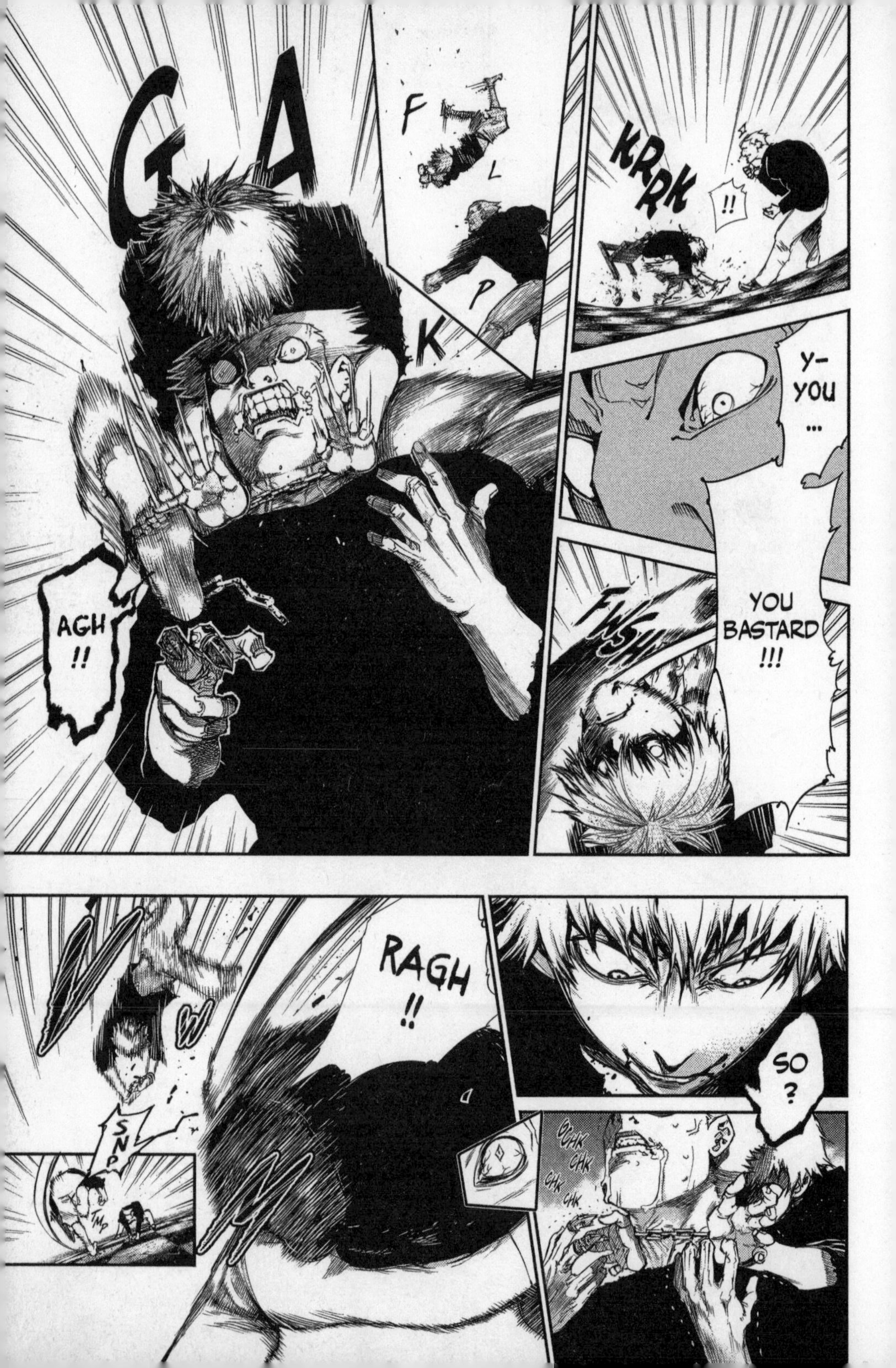
KRRK
!!
Y-YOU ...
YOU BASTARD !!!
FWSH
FLPK
GA
AGH !!
SO ?
GCHK CHK CHK CHK
RAGH !!
!
SNP
TMP

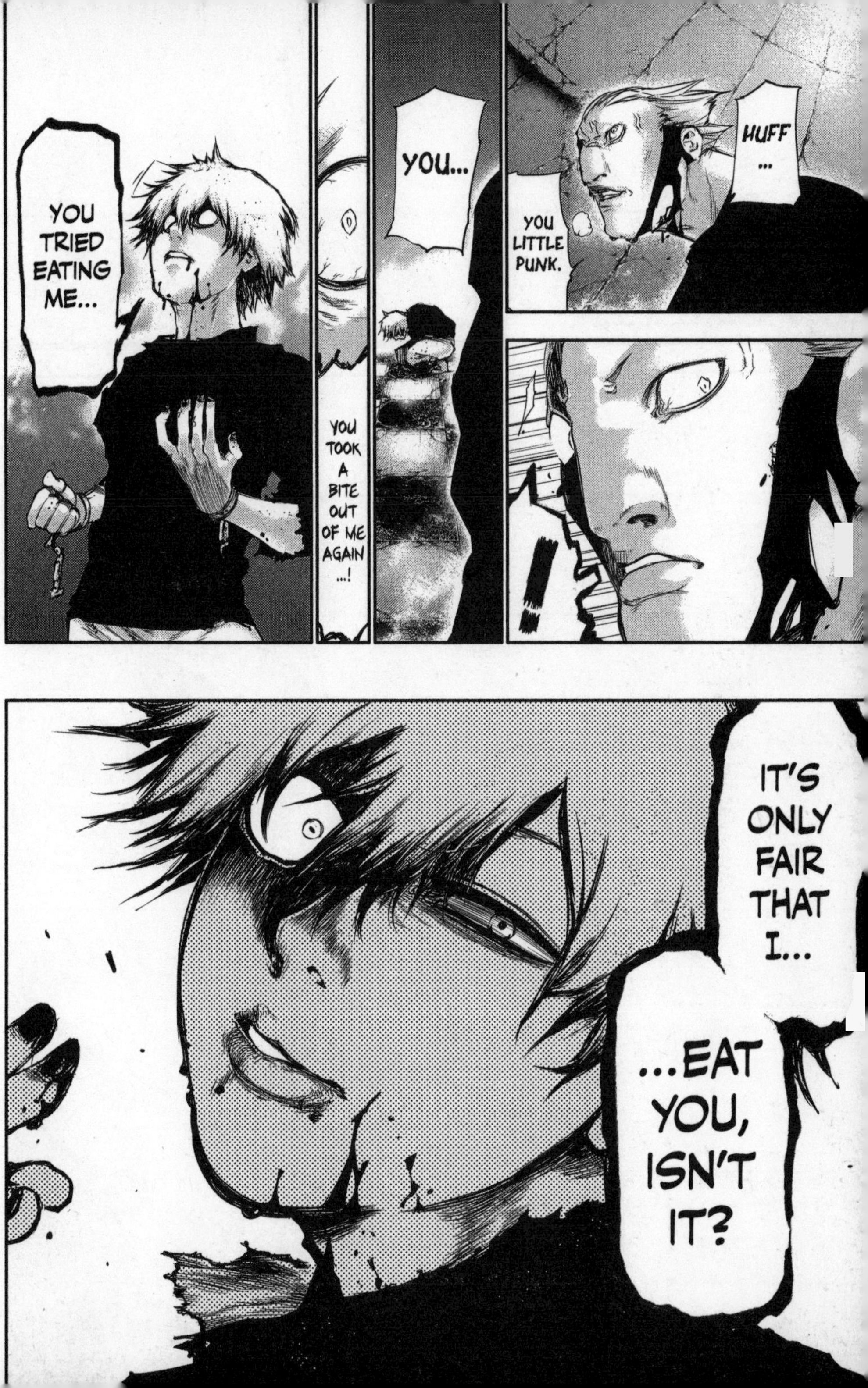
HUFF ...
YOU LITTLE PUNK.
YOU...
YOU TOOK A BITE OUT OF ME AGAIN ...!
YOU TRIED EATING ME...
IT'S ONLY FAIR THAT I...
...EAT YOU, ISN'T IT?

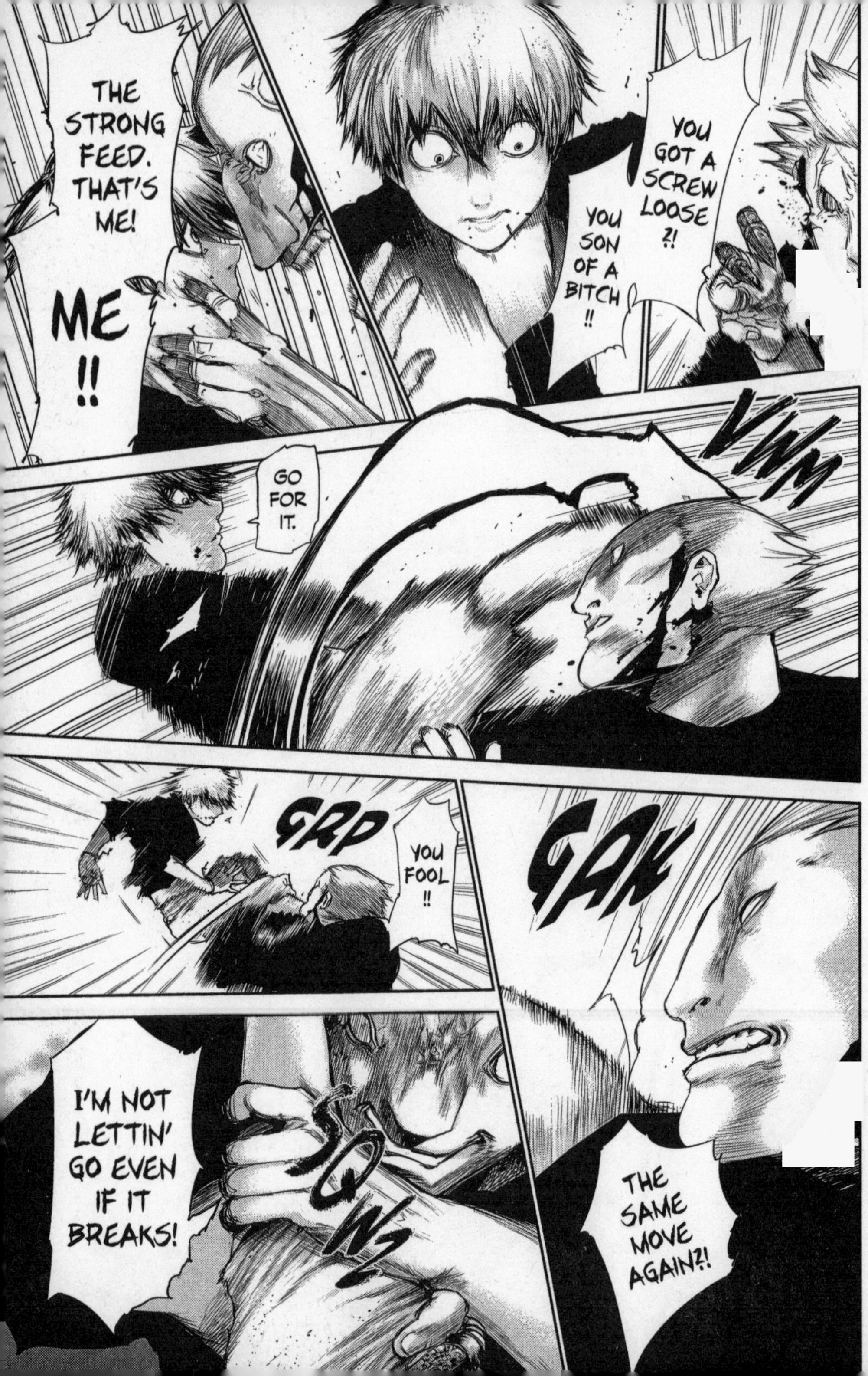
YOU GOT A SCREW LOOSE?!
YOU SON OF A BITCH!!
THE STRONG FEED. THAT'S ME!
ME!!
VWM
GO FOR IT.
GAK
THE SAME MOVE AGAIN?!
GRP
YOU FOOL!!
I'M NOT LETTIN' GO EVEN IF IT BREAKS!

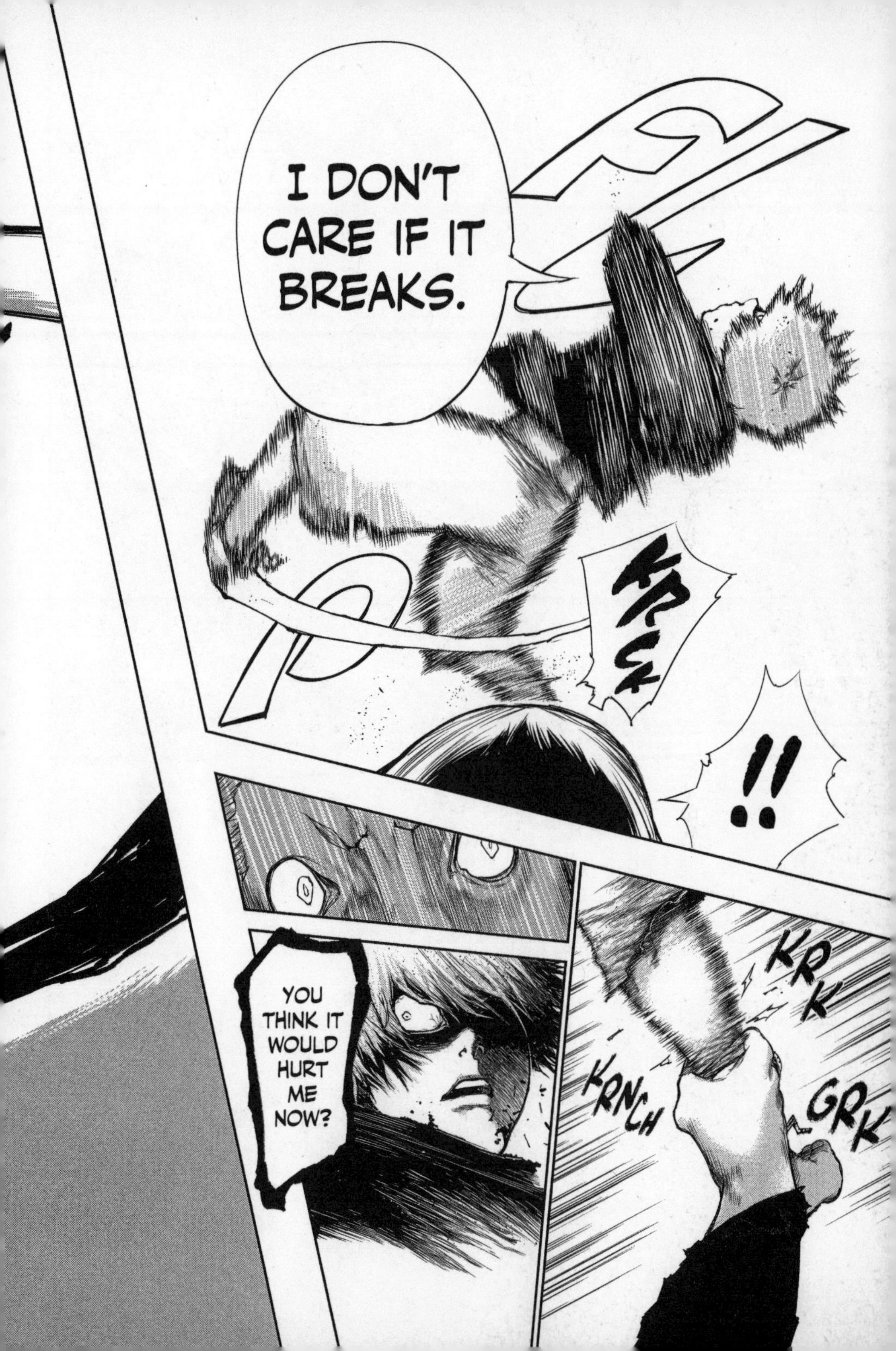
I DON'T CARE IF IT BREAKS.
KRCK
!!
KRK
GRK
KRNCH
YOU THINK IT WOULD HURT ME NOW?

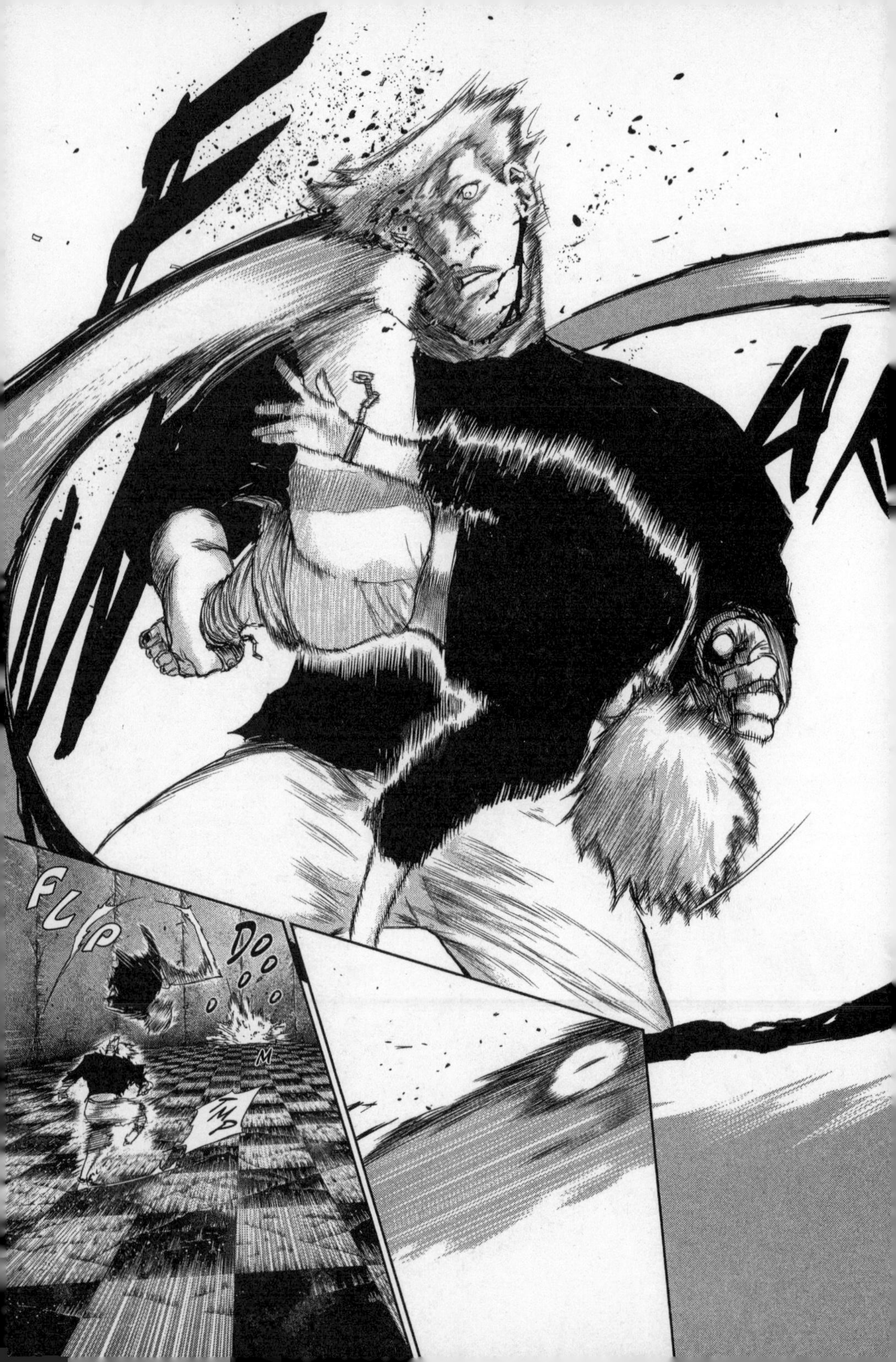
FLIP
TMP

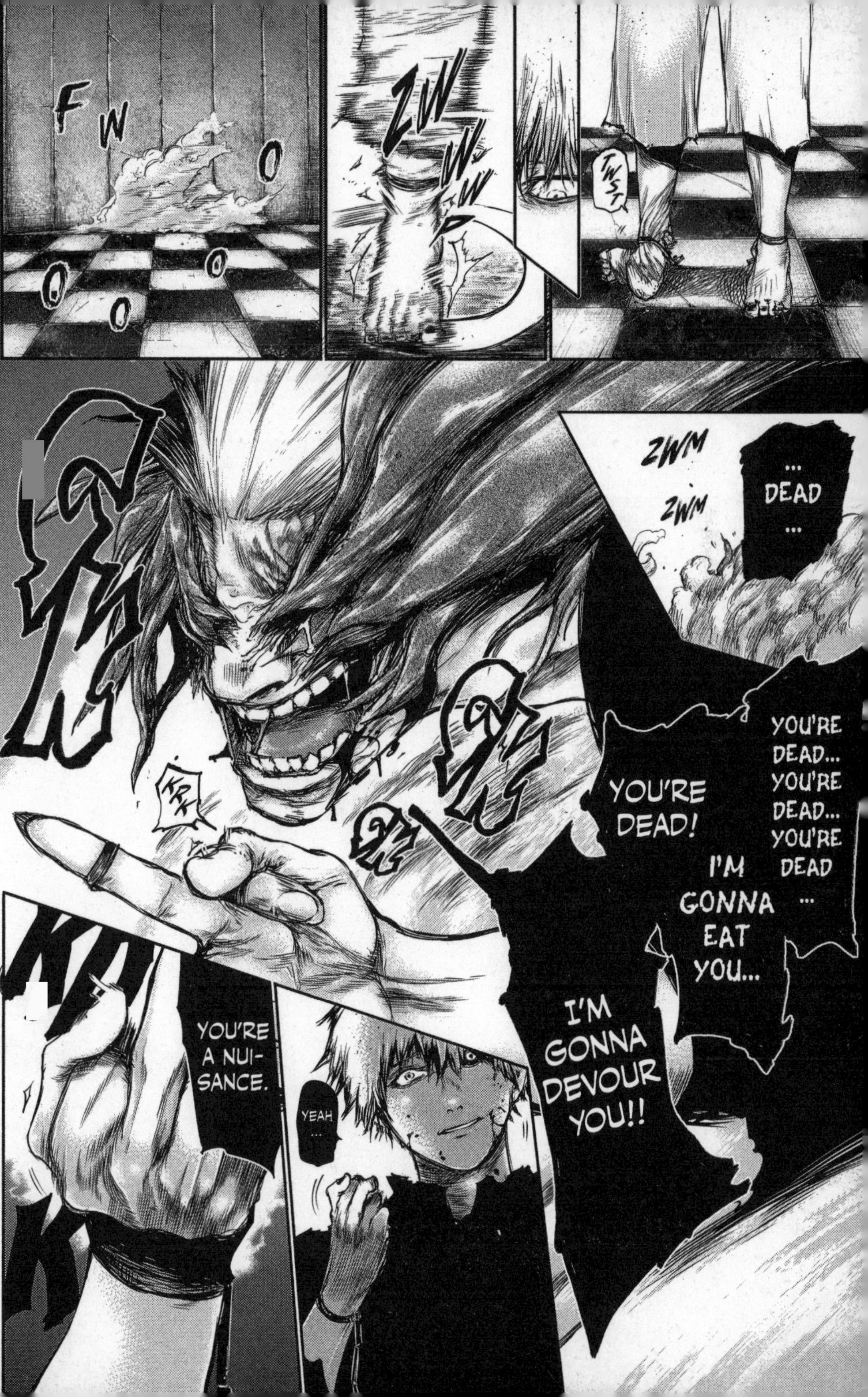

TWST
ZWWWWD
FWOOOOOO
ZWM
ZWM
... DEAD ...
YOU'RE DEAD... YOU'RE DEAD... YOU'RE DEAD ...
YOU'RE DEAD!
I'M GONNA EAT YOU...
I'M GONNA DEVOUR YOU!!
YEAH ...
YOU'RE A NUI-SANCE.

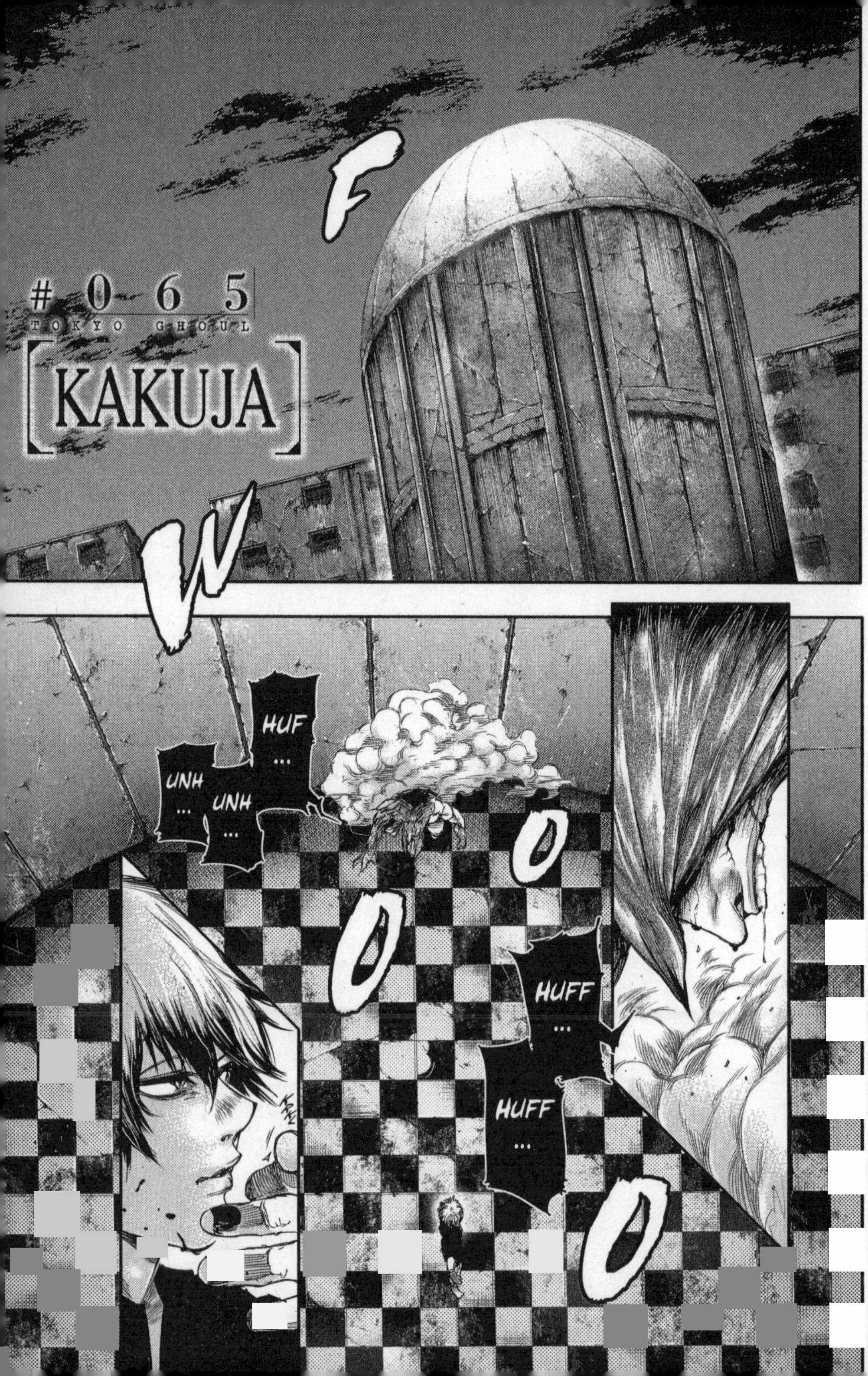
#065
TOKYO GHOUL
KAKUJA
FWOOOO
HUFF...
HUFF...
HUF...
UNH...
UNH...

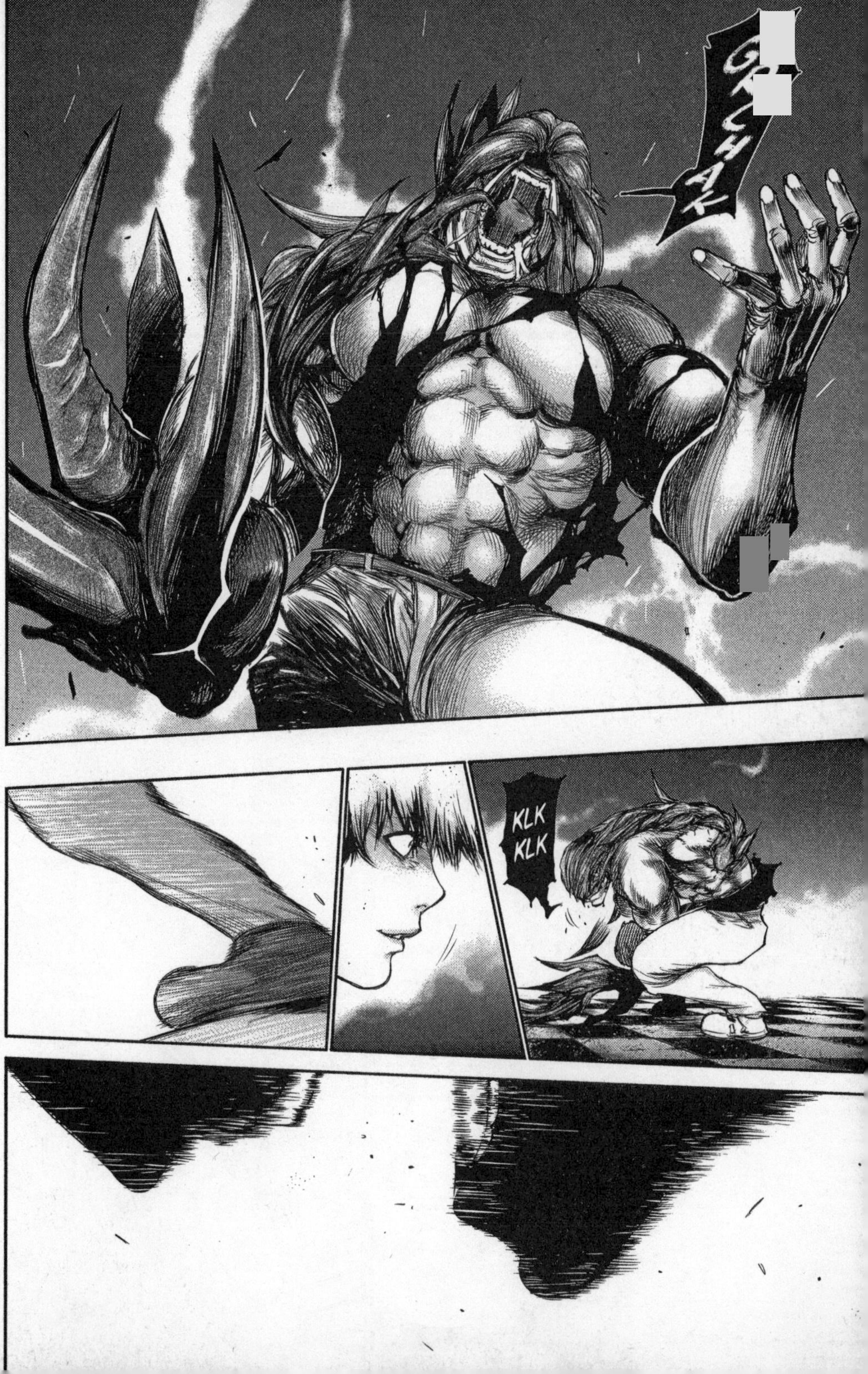
GRCHAK
KLK KLK

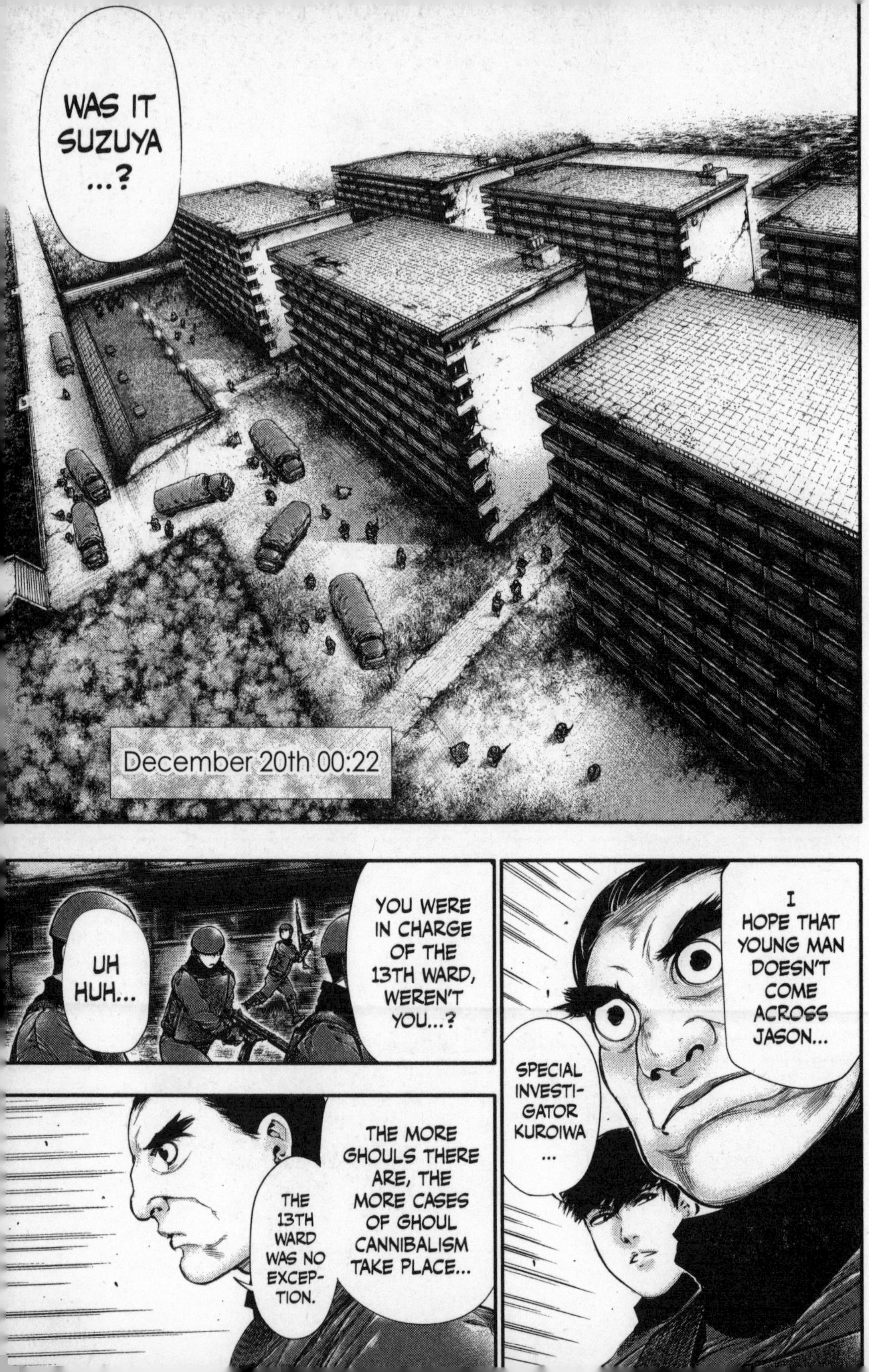
WAS IT SUZUYA ...?
December 20th 00:22
I HOPE THAT YOUNG MAN DOESN'T COME ACROSS JASON...
SPECIAL INVESTI-GATOR KUROIWA ...
YOU WERE IN CHARGE OF THE 13TH WARD, WEREN'T YOU...?
UH HUH...
THE MORE GHOULS THERE ARE, THE MORE CASES OF GHOUL CANNIBALISM TAKE PLACE...
THE 13TH WARD WAS NO EXCEP-TION.

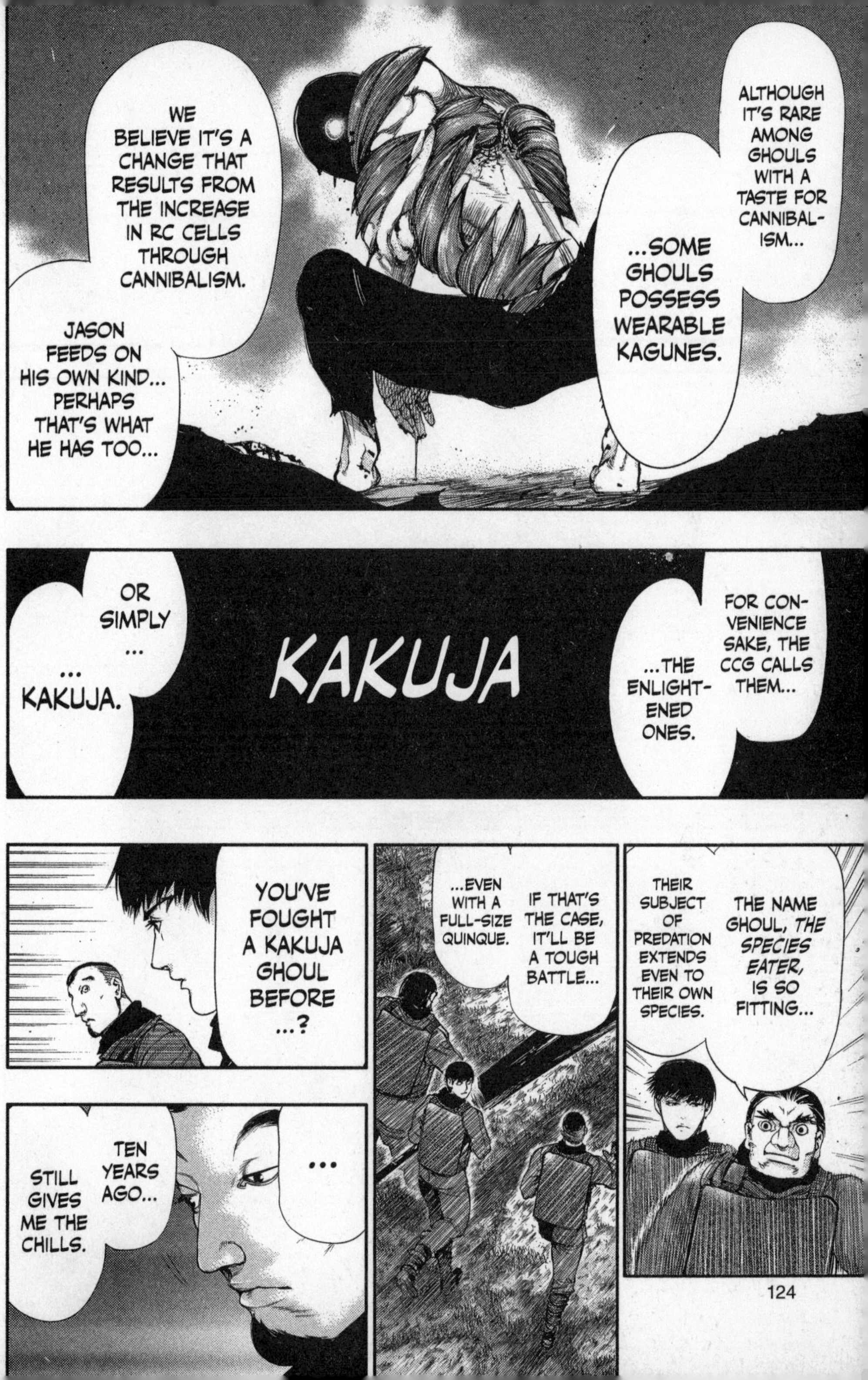
ALTHOUGH IT'S RARE AMONG GHOULS WITH A TASTE FOR CANNIBAL-ISM...
...SOME GHOULS POSSESS WEARABLE KAGUNES.
WE BELIEVE IT'S A CHANGE THAT RESULTS FROM THE INCREASE IN RC CELLS THROUGH CANNIBALISM.
JASON FEEDS ON HIS OWN KIND... PERHAPS THAT'S WHAT HE HAS TOO...
FOR CON-VENIENCE SAKE, THE CCG CALLS THEM...
...THE ENLIGHT-ENED ONES.
KAKUJA
OR SIMPLY ...
... KAKUJA.
THE NAME GHOUL, *THE SPECIES EATER,* IS SO FITTING...
THEIR SUBJECT OF PREDATION EXTENDS EVEN TO THEIR OWN SPECIES.
IF THAT'S THE CASE, IT'LL BE A TOUGH BATTLE...
...EVEN WITH A FULL-SIZE QUINQUE.
YOU'VE FOUGHT A KAKUJA GHOUL BEFORE ...?
...
TEN YEARS AGO...
STILL GIVES ME THE CHILLS.

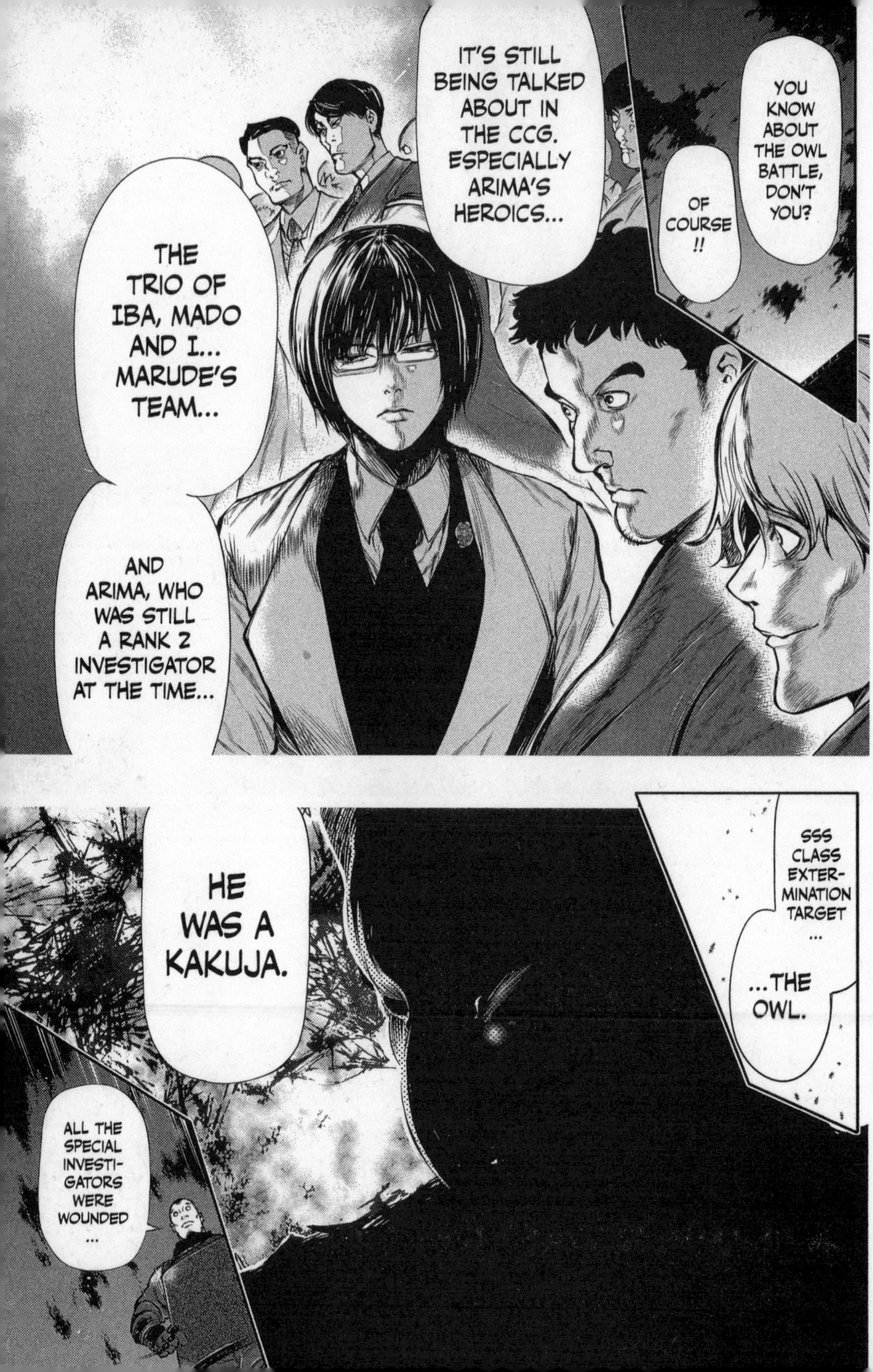
YOU KNOW ABOUT THE OWL BATTLE, DON'T YOU?
OF COURSE!!
IT'S STILL BEING TALKED ABOUT IN THE CCG. ESPECIALLY ARIMA'S HEROICS...
THE TRIO OF IBA, MADO AND I... MARUDE'S TEAM...
AND ARIMA, WHO WAS STILL A RANK 2 INVESTIGATOR AT THE TIME...
SSS CLASS EXTER-MINATION TARGET...
...THE OWL.
HE WAS A KAKUJA.
ALL THE SPECIAL INVESTI-GATORS WERE WOUNDED...

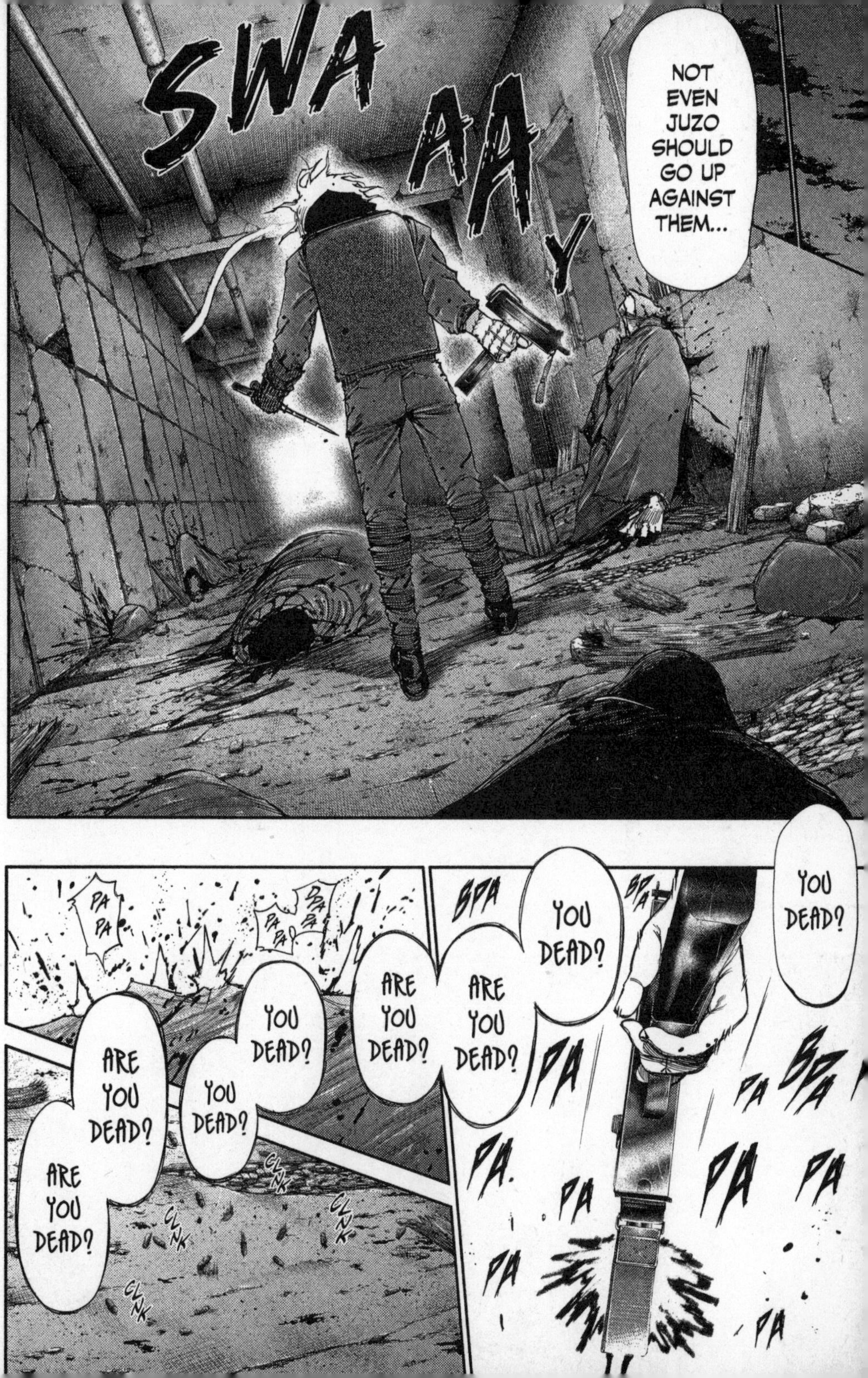
SWAAAY
NOT EVEN JUZO SHOULD GO UP AGAINST THEM...
YOU DEAD?
BPA
YOU DEAD?
ARE YOU DEAD?
ARE YOU DEAD?
BPA
BPA
PA
PA
PA
PA
PA
PA
PA
PA
PA PA
BA PA PA
PA PA
YOU DEAD?
ARE YOU DEAD?
YOU DEAD?
ARE YOU DEAD?
CLNK
CLNK
CLNK
CLNK

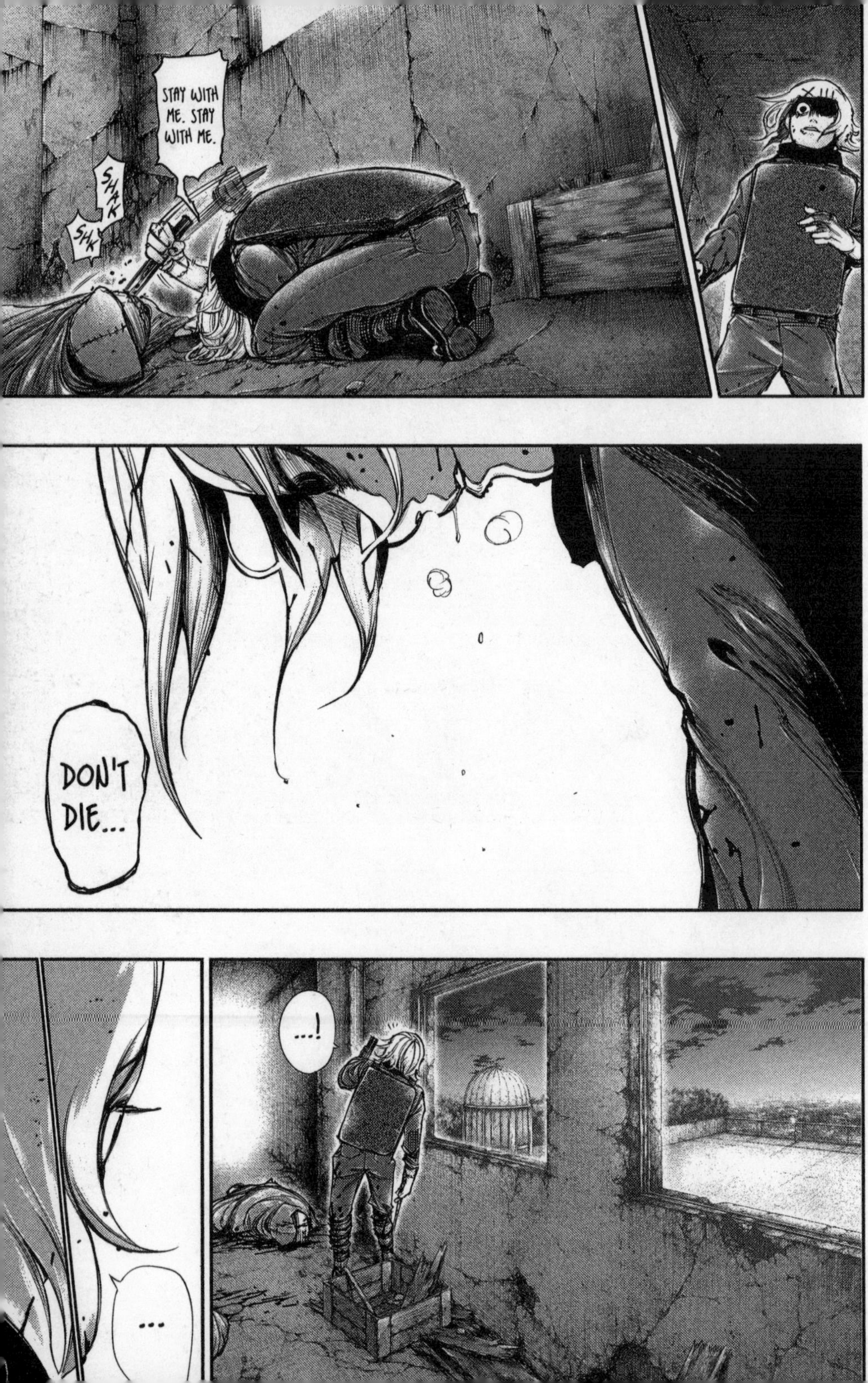
STAY WITH ME. STAY WITH ME.
SHAK
SHK
DON'T DIE...
...!
...

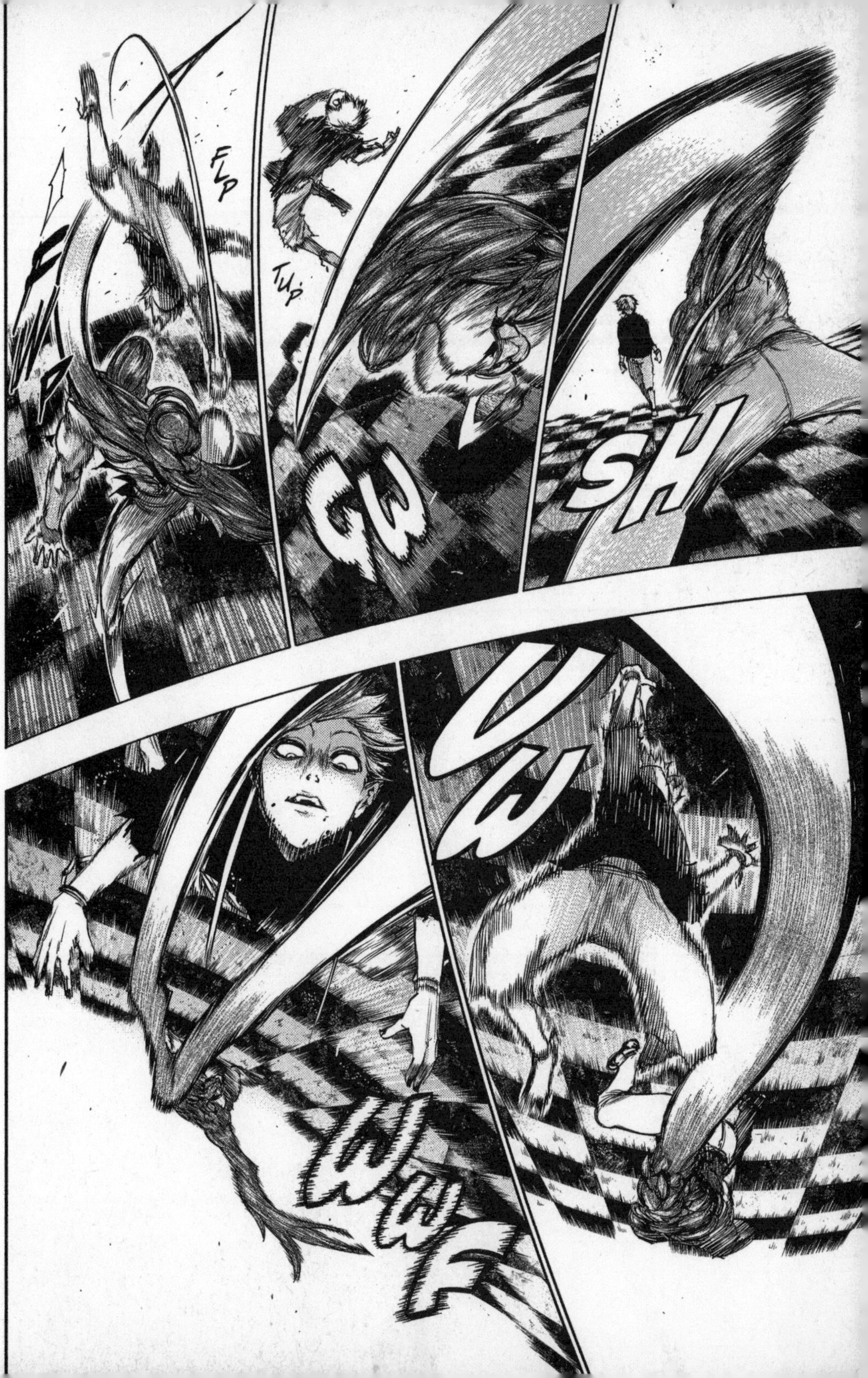
SH
FLP
FWP

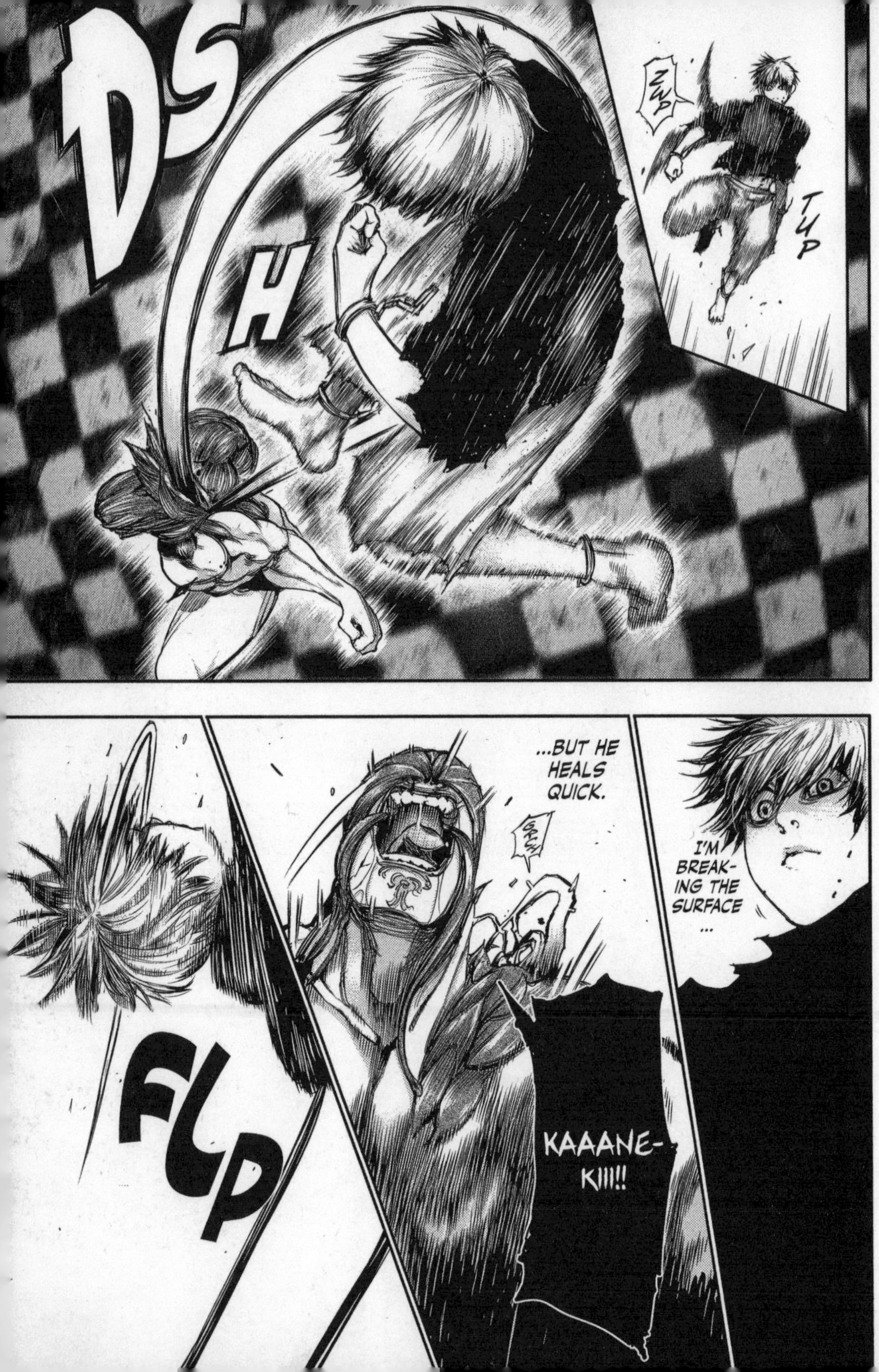
ZWP
TUP
DSH
I'M BREAKING THE SURFACE...
...BUT HE HEALS QUICK.
GRCH
KAAANE-KIII!!
FLP

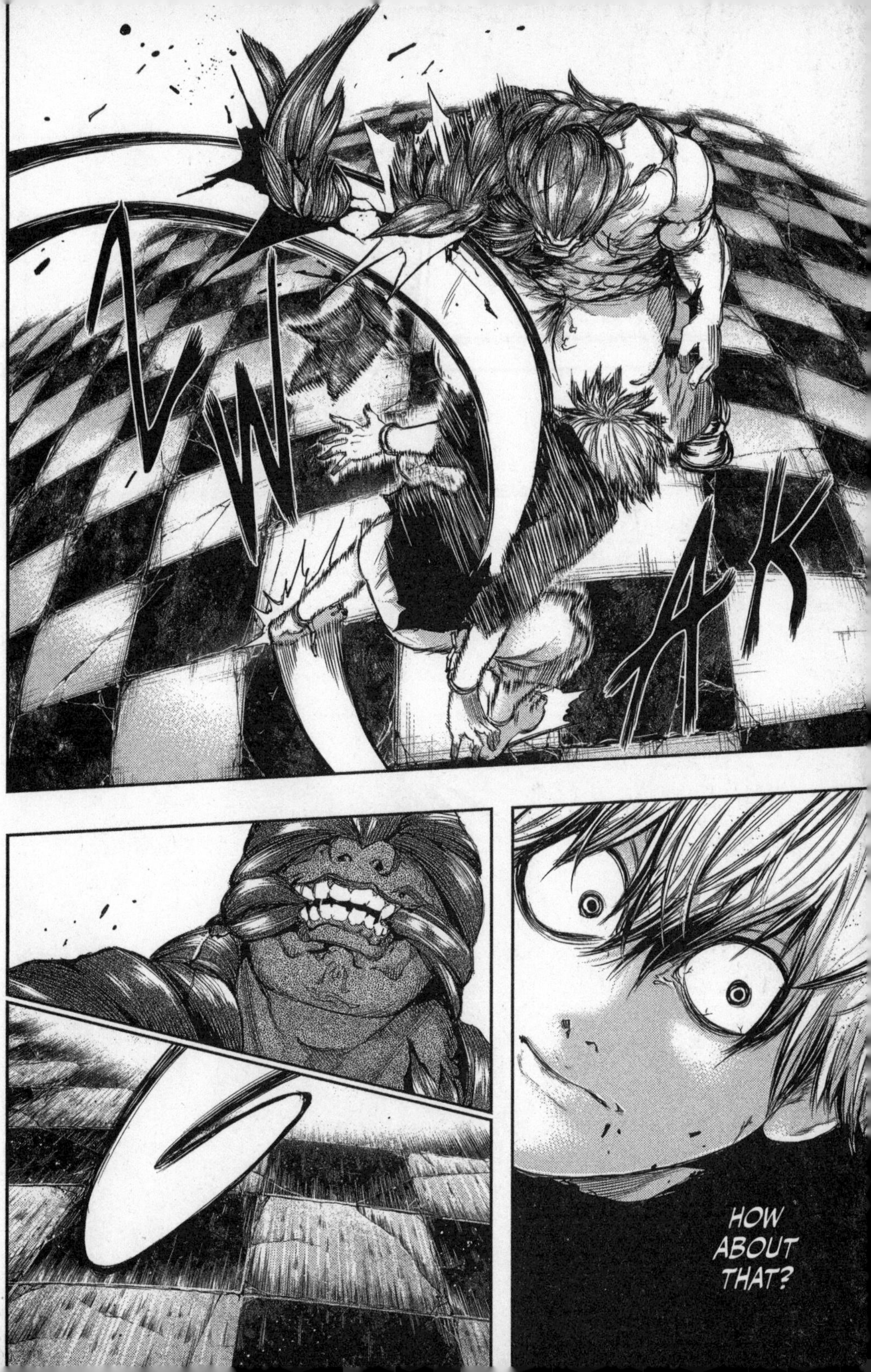
HOW ABOUT THAT?

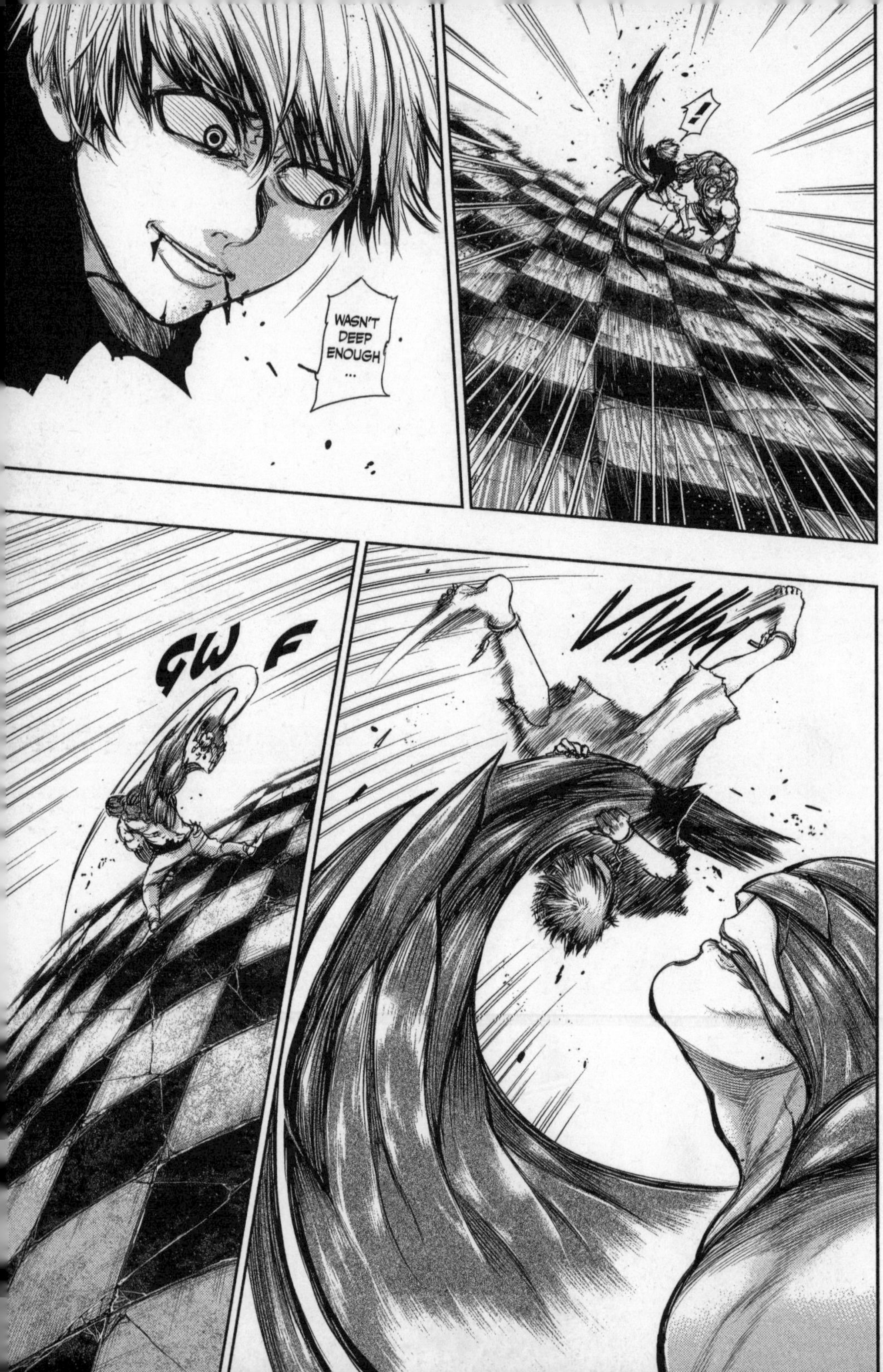
!
WASN'T DEEP ENOUGH ...
GW F

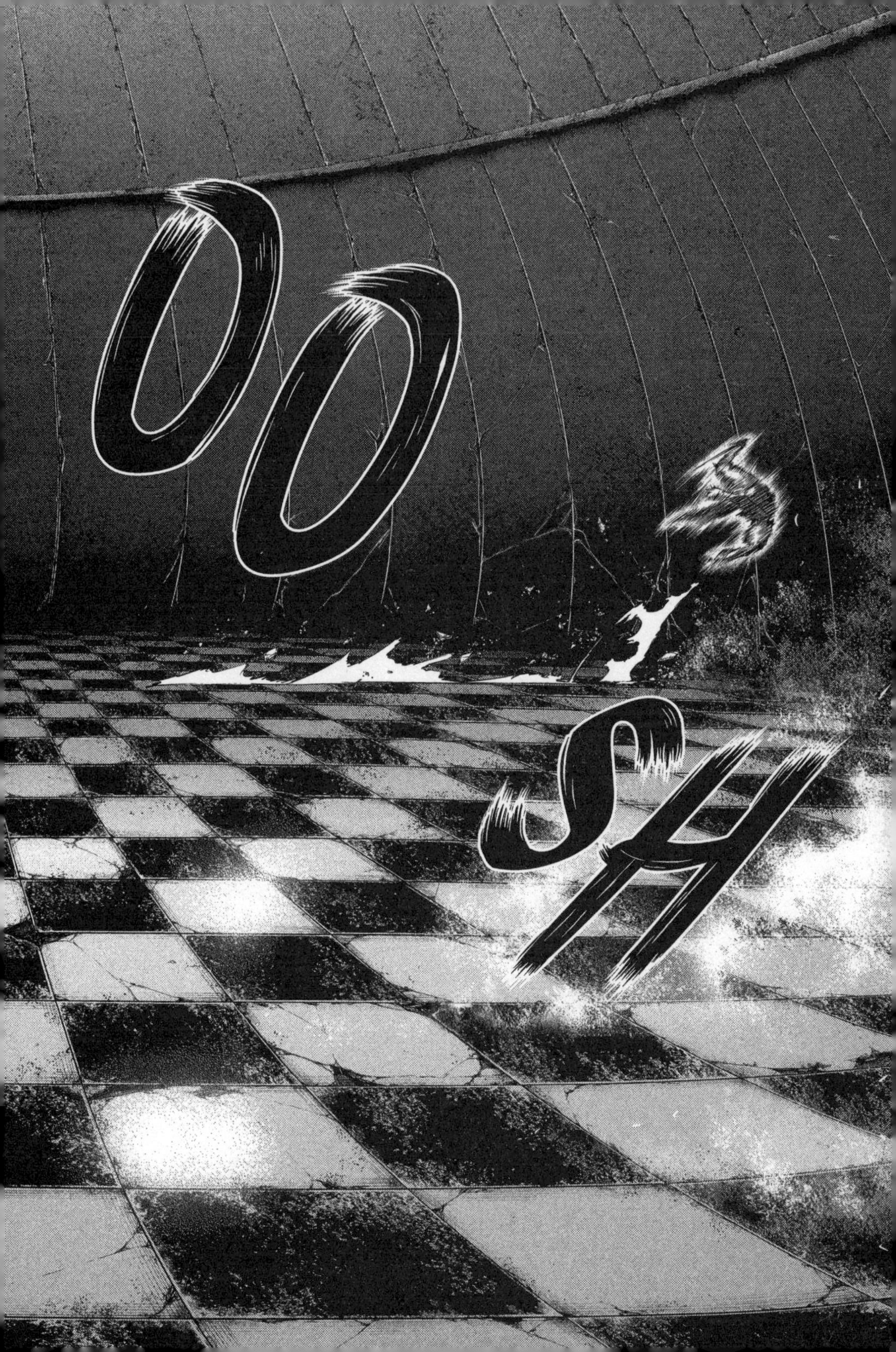
OOSH

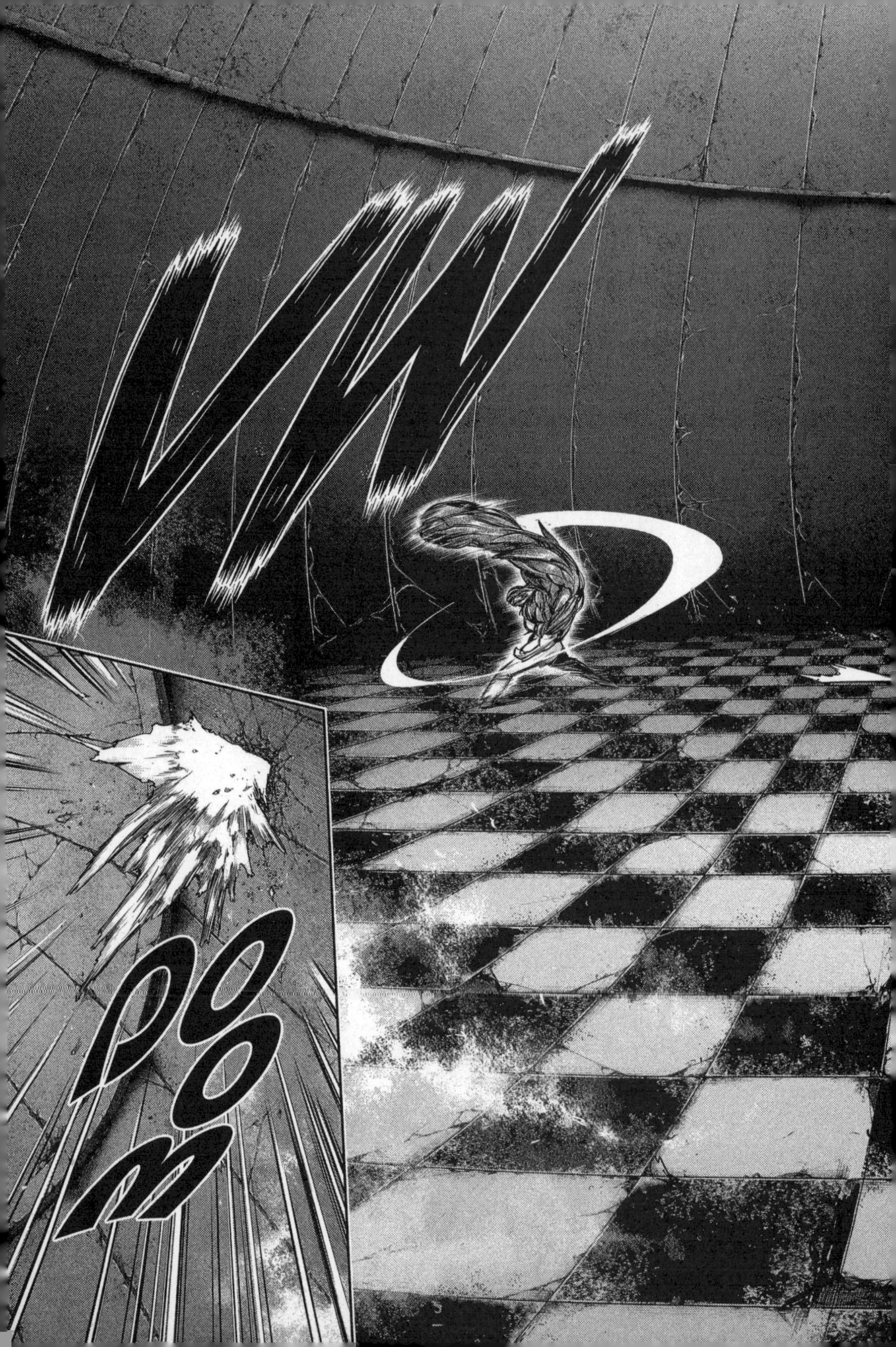
BOOM

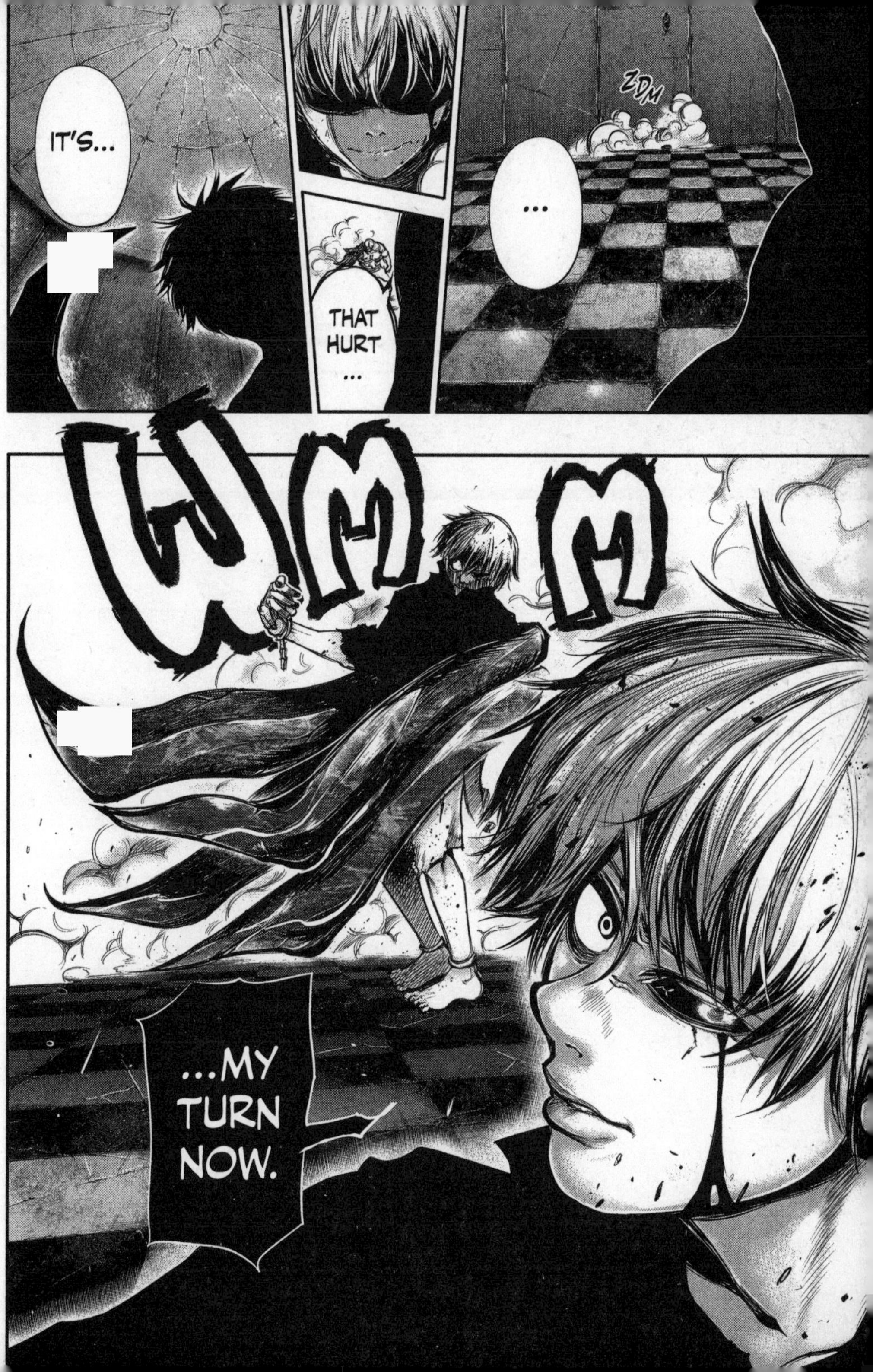
ZDM
...
THAT HURT ...
IT'S...
WMM
...MY TURN NOW.

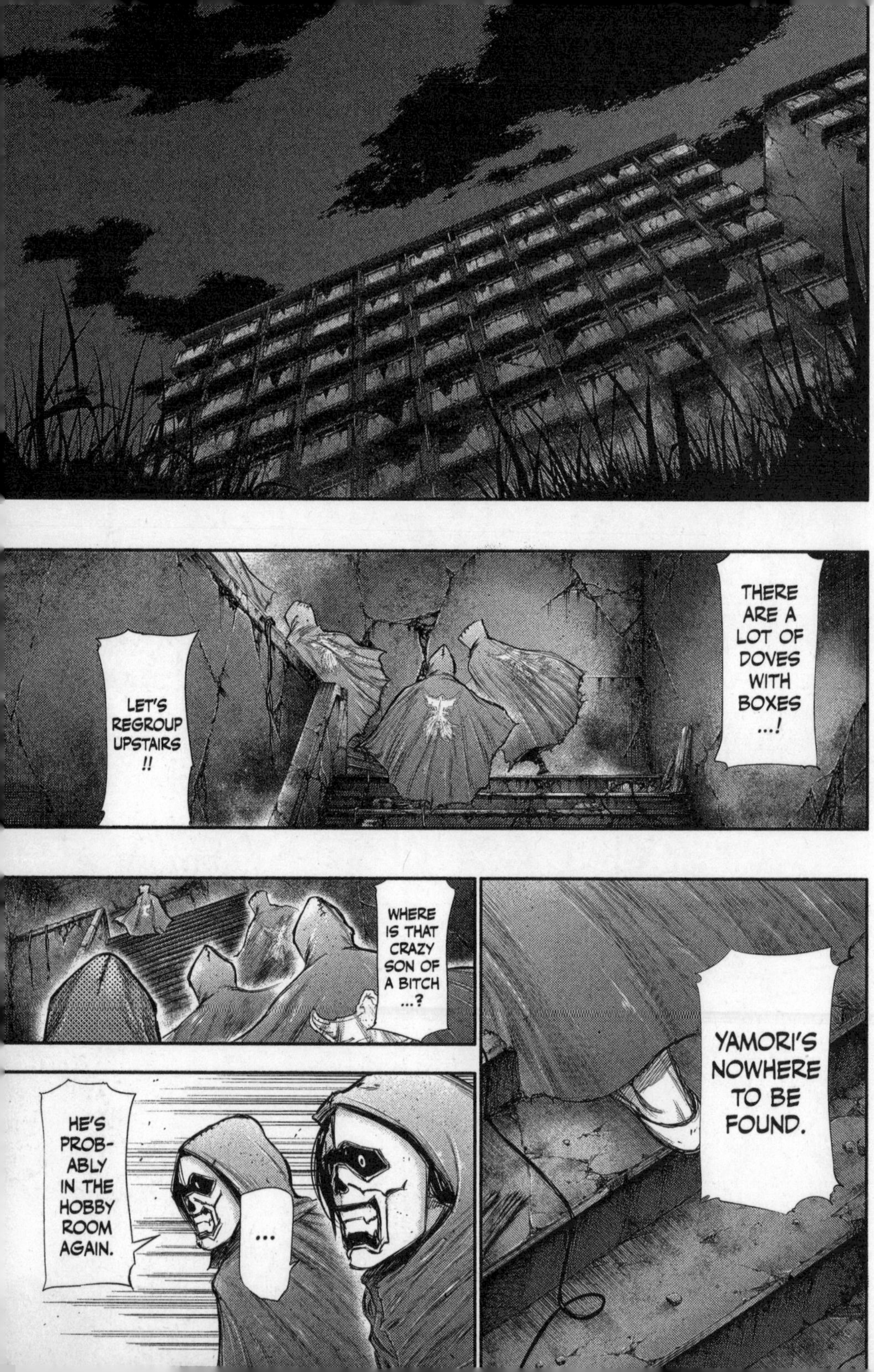
THERE ARE A LOT OF DOVES WITH BOXES ...!
LET'S REGROUP UPSTAIRS !!
YAMORI'S NOWHERE TO BE FOUND.
WHERE IS THAT CRAZY SON OF A BITCH ...?
HE'S PROB-ABLY IN THE HOBBY ROOM AGAIN.
...

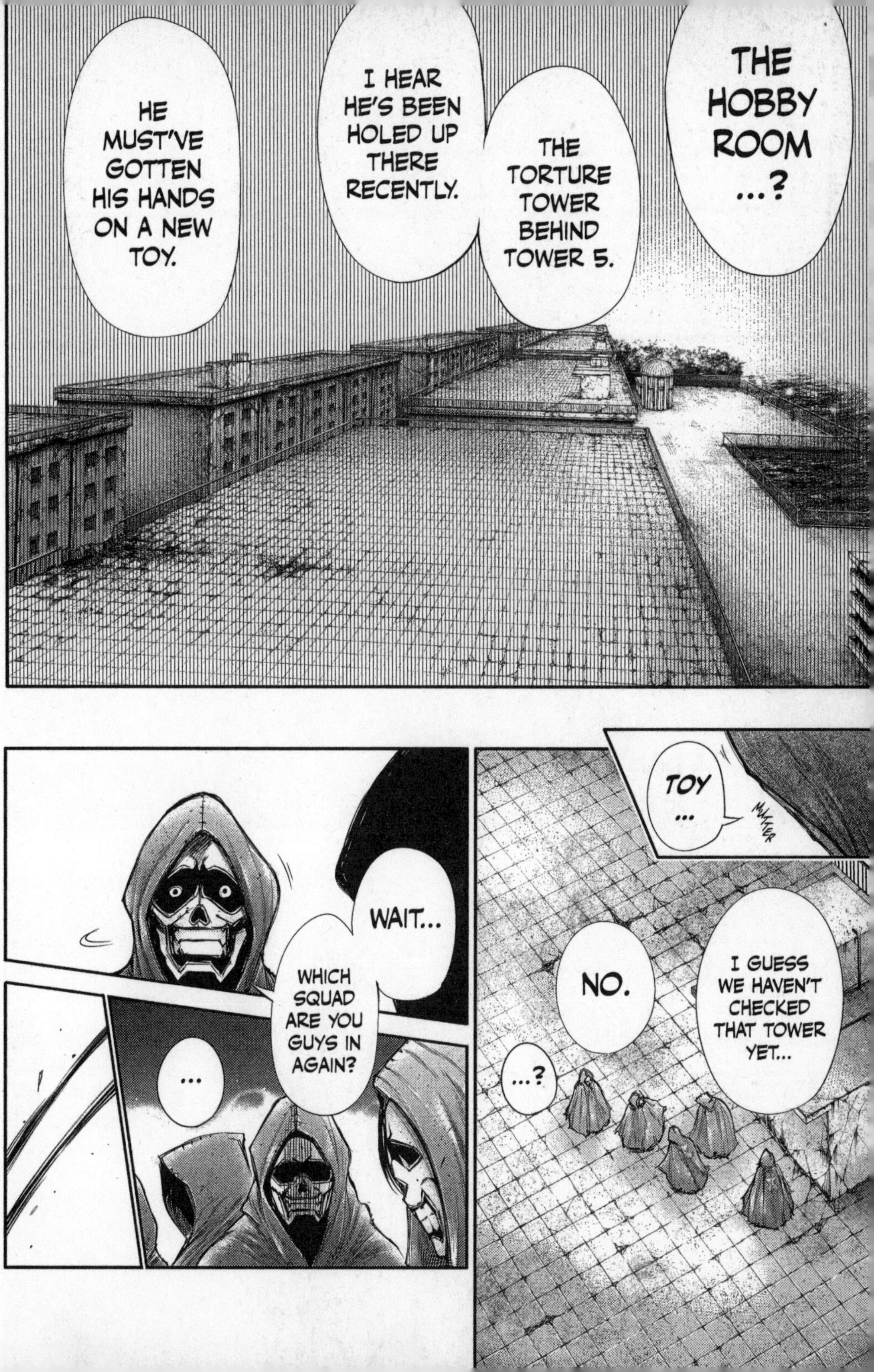
THE HOBBY ROOM ...?
THE TORTURE TOWER BEHIND TOWER 5.
I HEAR HE'S BEEN HOLED UP THERE RECENTLY.
HE MUST'VE GOTTEN HIS HANDS ON A NEW TOY.
TOY ...
MUTTER
I GUESS WE HAVEN'T CHECKED THAT TOWER YET...
NO.
...?
WAIT...
WHICH SQUAD ARE YOU GUYS IN AGAIN?
...

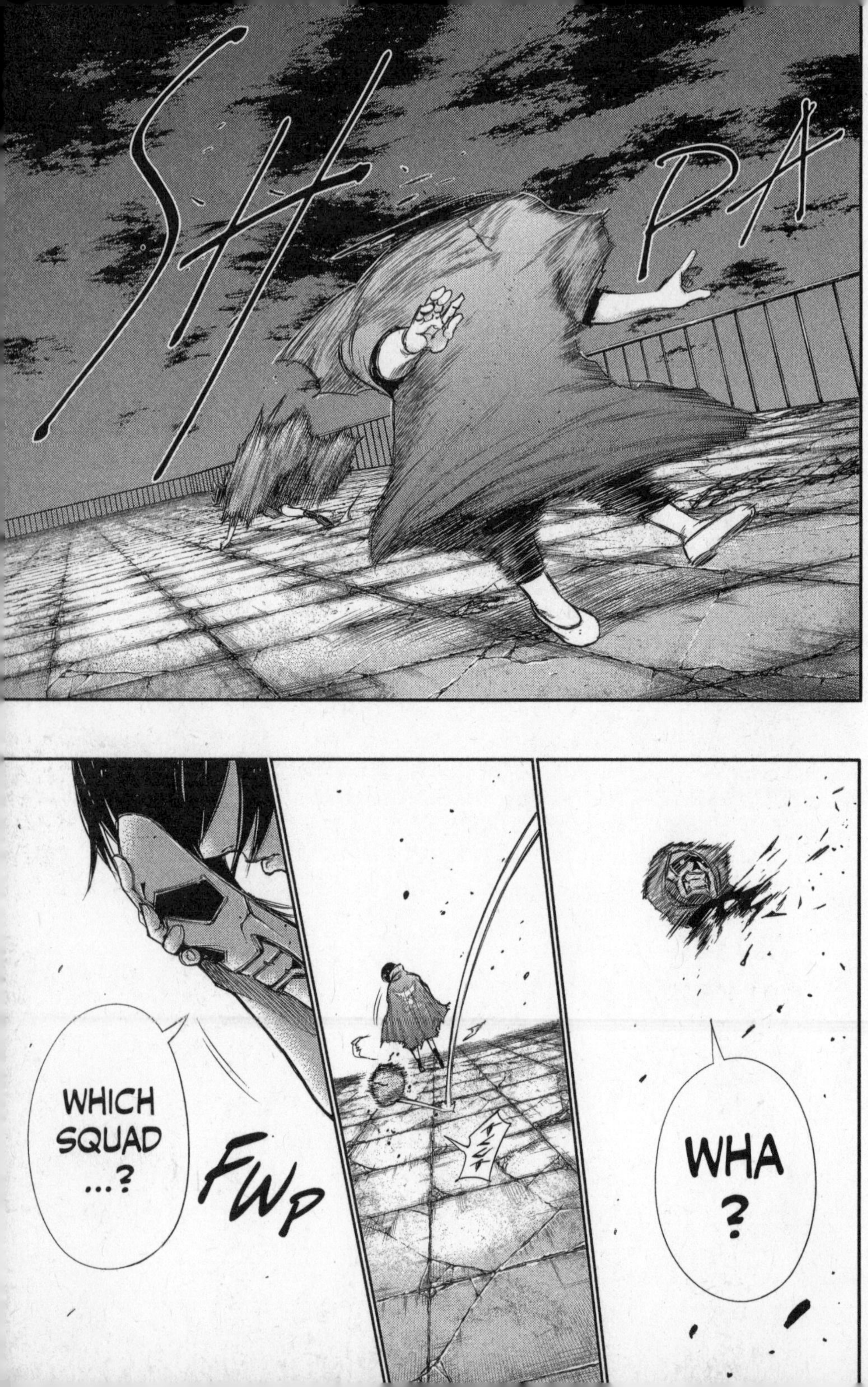
SHPA
WHA?
WHICH SQUAD...?
FWP

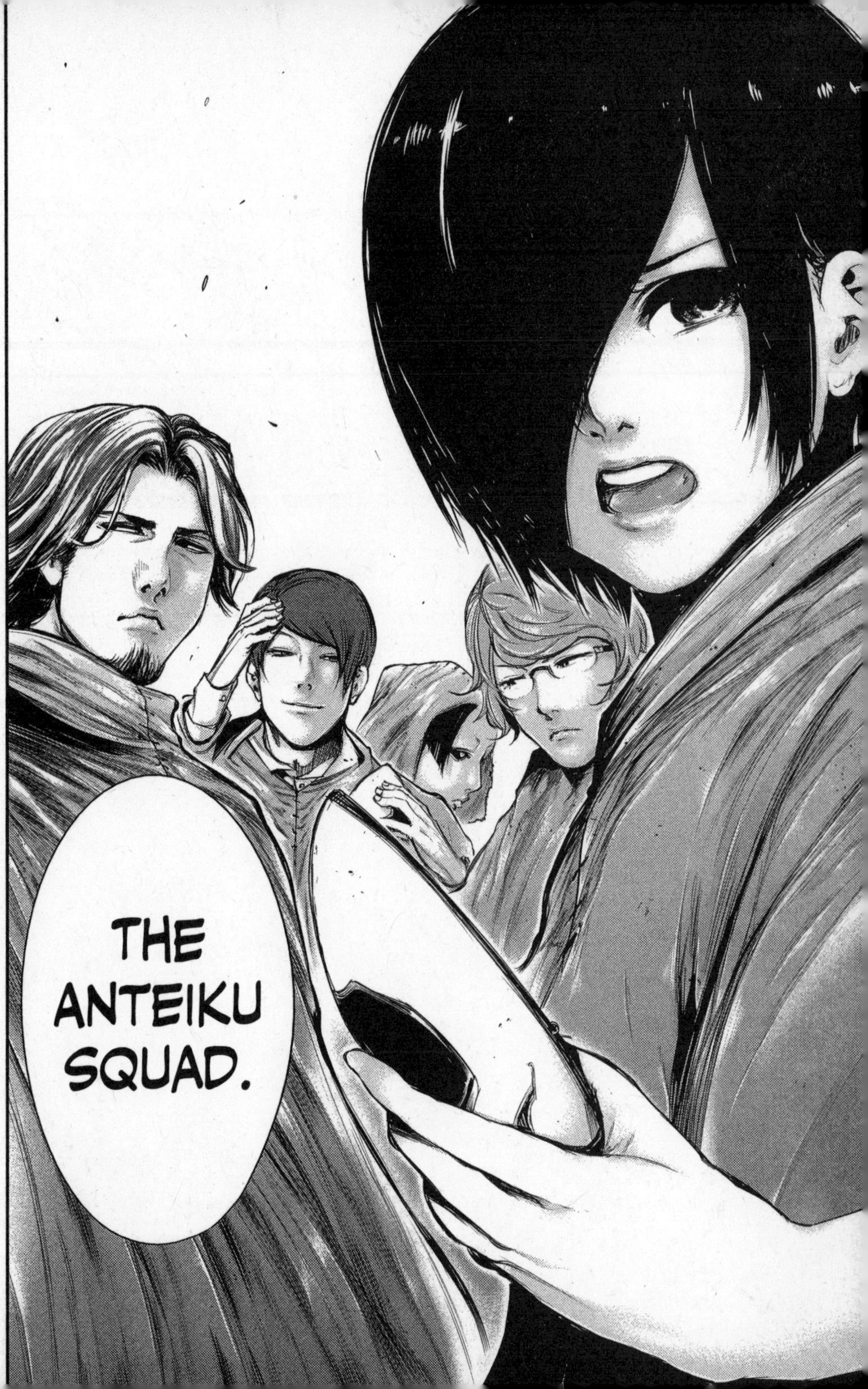
THE ANTEIKU SQUAD.

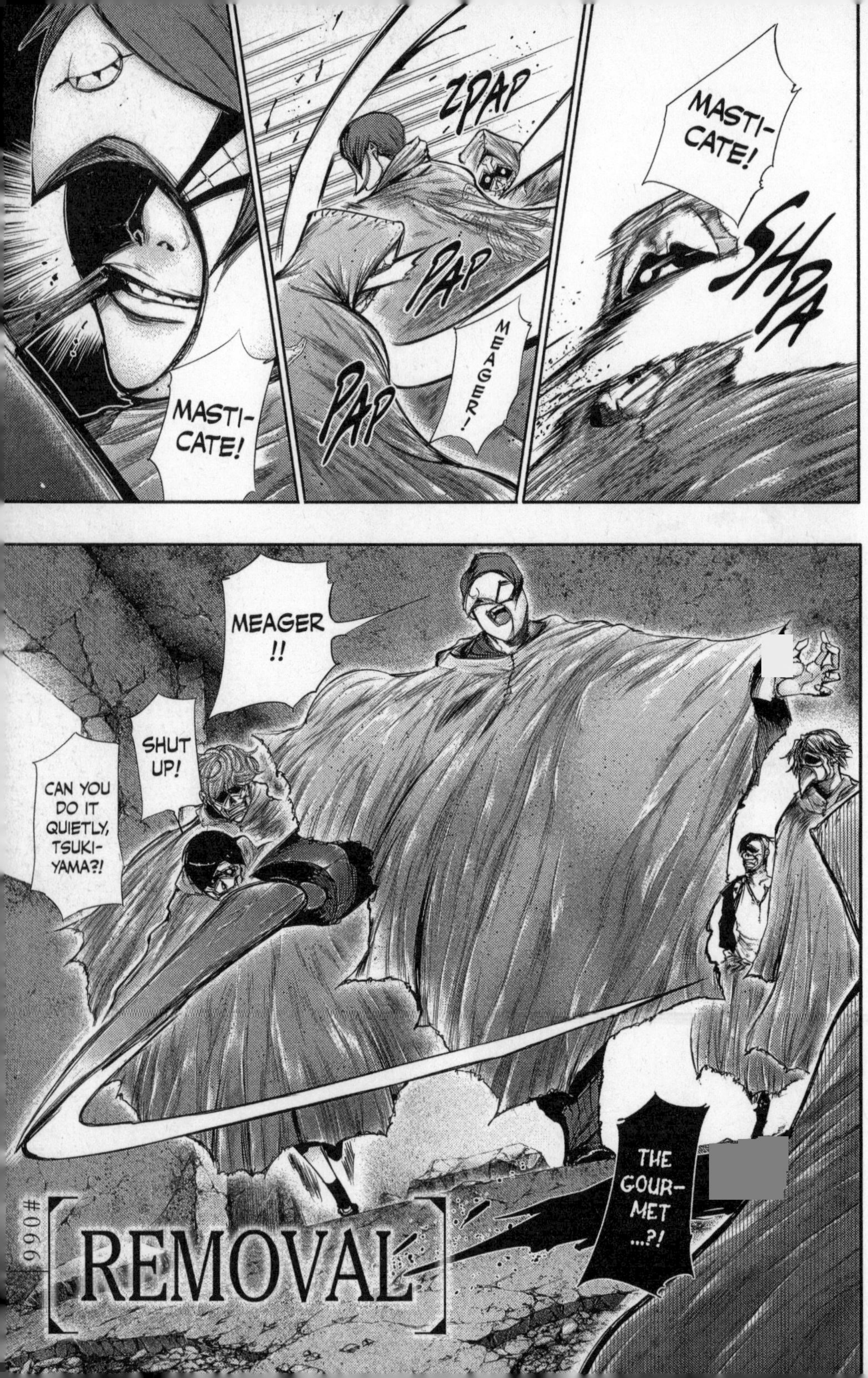
MASTI-CATE!
SHPA
ZPAP
PAP
PAP
MEAGER!
MASTI-CATE!
MEAGER !!
SHUT UP!
CAN YOU DO IT QUIETLY, TSUKI-YAMA?!
THE GOUR-MET ...?!
#066
REMOVAL

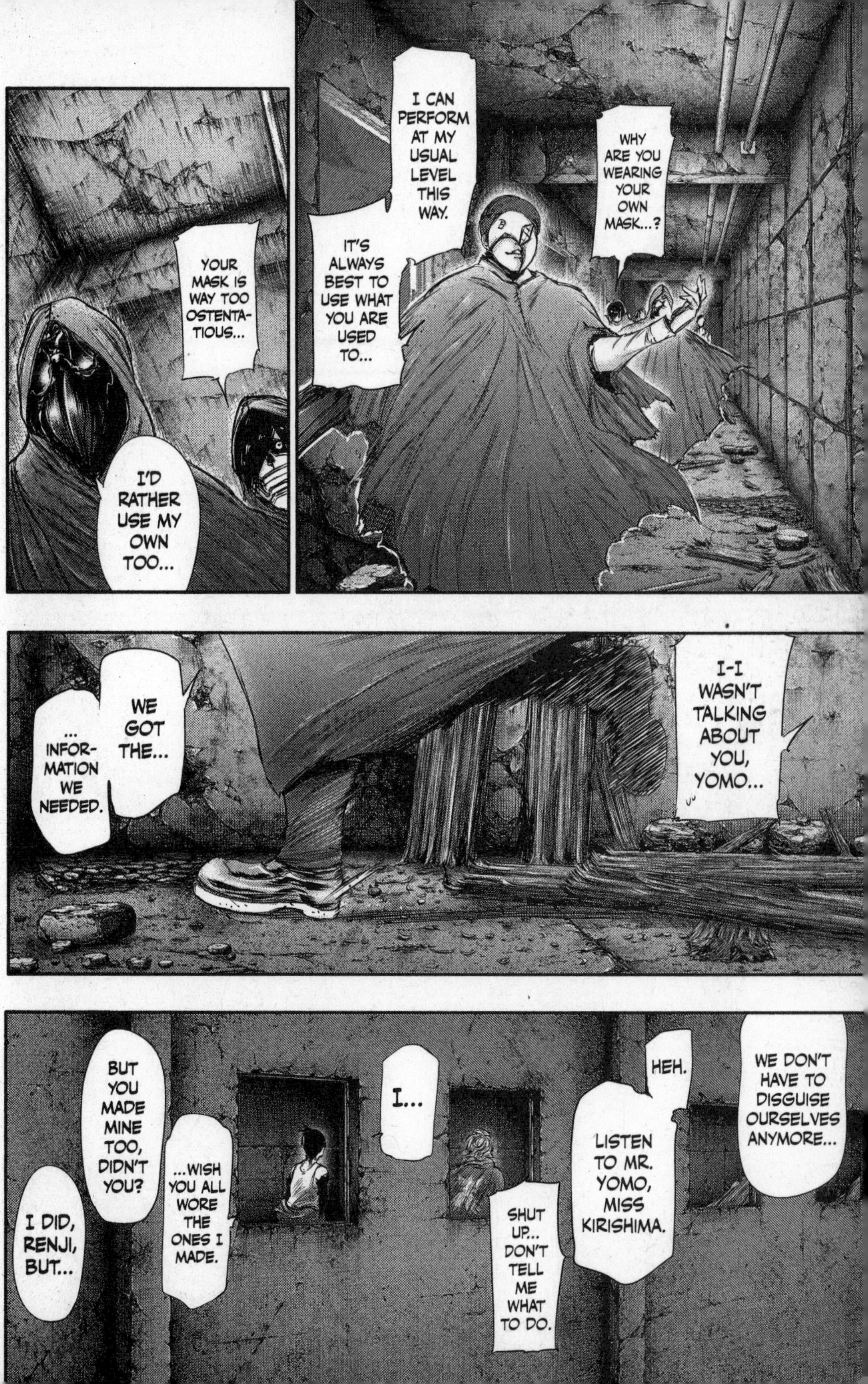
WHY ARE YOU WEARING YOUR OWN MASK...?
I CAN PERFORM AT MY USUAL LEVEL THIS WAY.
IT'S ALWAYS BEST TO USE WHAT YOU ARE USED TO...
YOUR MASK IS WAY TOO OSTENTATIOUS...
I'D RATHER USE MY OWN TOO...
I-I WASN'T TALKING ABOUT YOU, YOMO...
WE GOT THE...
...INFORMATION WE NEEDED.
WE DON'T HAVE TO DISGUISE OURSELVES ANYMORE...
HEH.
LISTEN TO MR. YOMO, MISS KIRISHIMA.
SHUT UP... DON'T TELL ME WHAT TO DO.
I...
...WISH YOU ALL WORE THE ONES I MADE.
BUT YOU MADE MINE TOO, DIDN'T YOU?
I DID, RENJI, BUT...

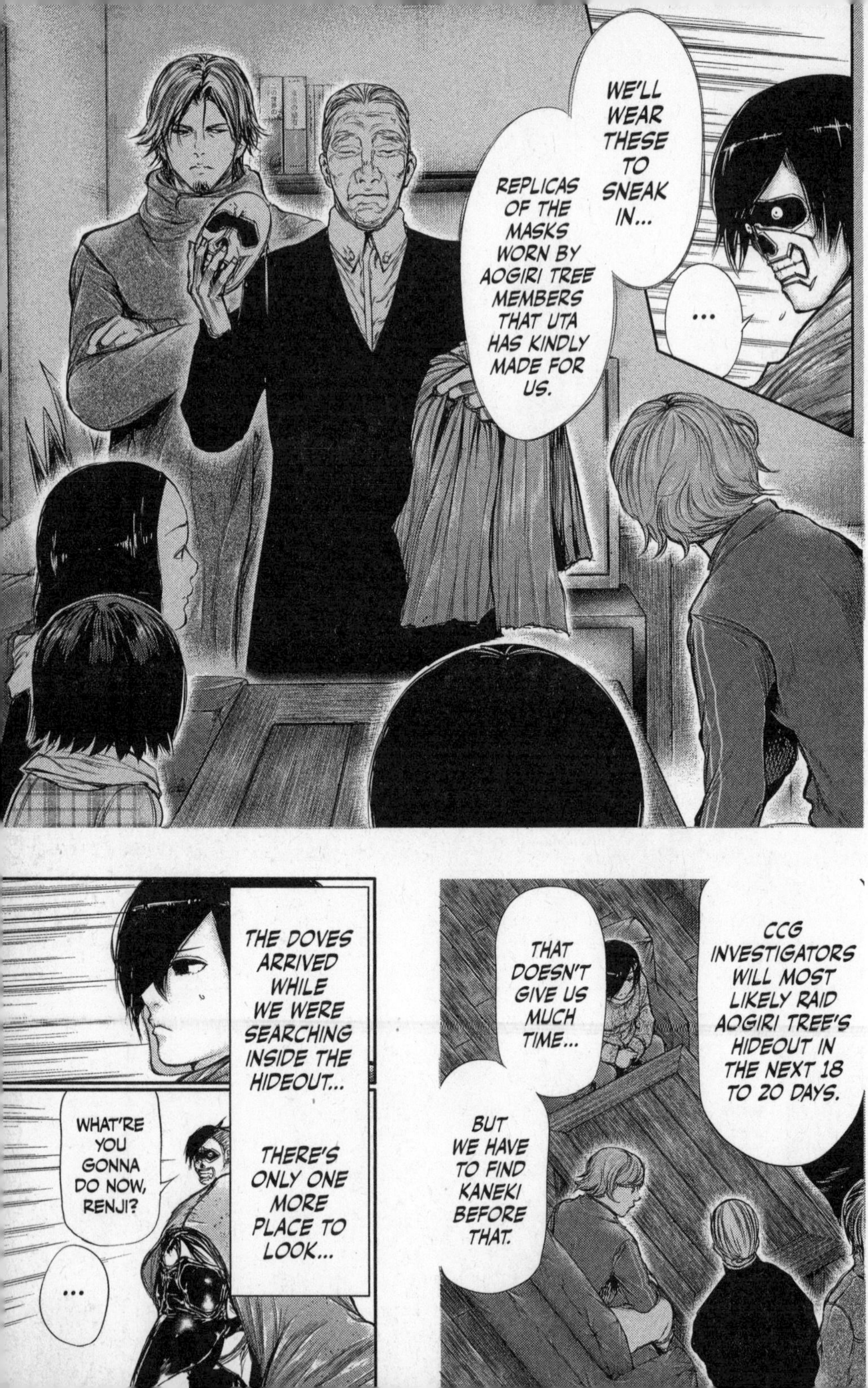
WE'LL WEAR THESE TO SNEAK IN...
REPLICAS OF THE MASKS WORN BY AOGIRI TREE MEMBERS THAT UTA HAS KINDLY MADE FOR US.
...
CCG INVESTIGATORS WILL MOST LIKELY RAID AOGIRI TREE'S HIDEOUT IN THE NEXT 18 TO 20 DAYS.
THAT DOESN'T GIVE US MUCH TIME...
BUT WE HAVE TO FIND KANEKI BEFORE THAT.
THE DOVES ARRIVED WHILE WE WERE SEARCHING INSIDE THE HIDEOUT...
THERE'S ONLY ONE MORE PLACE TO LOOK...
WHAT'RE YOU GONNA DO NOW, RENJI?
...

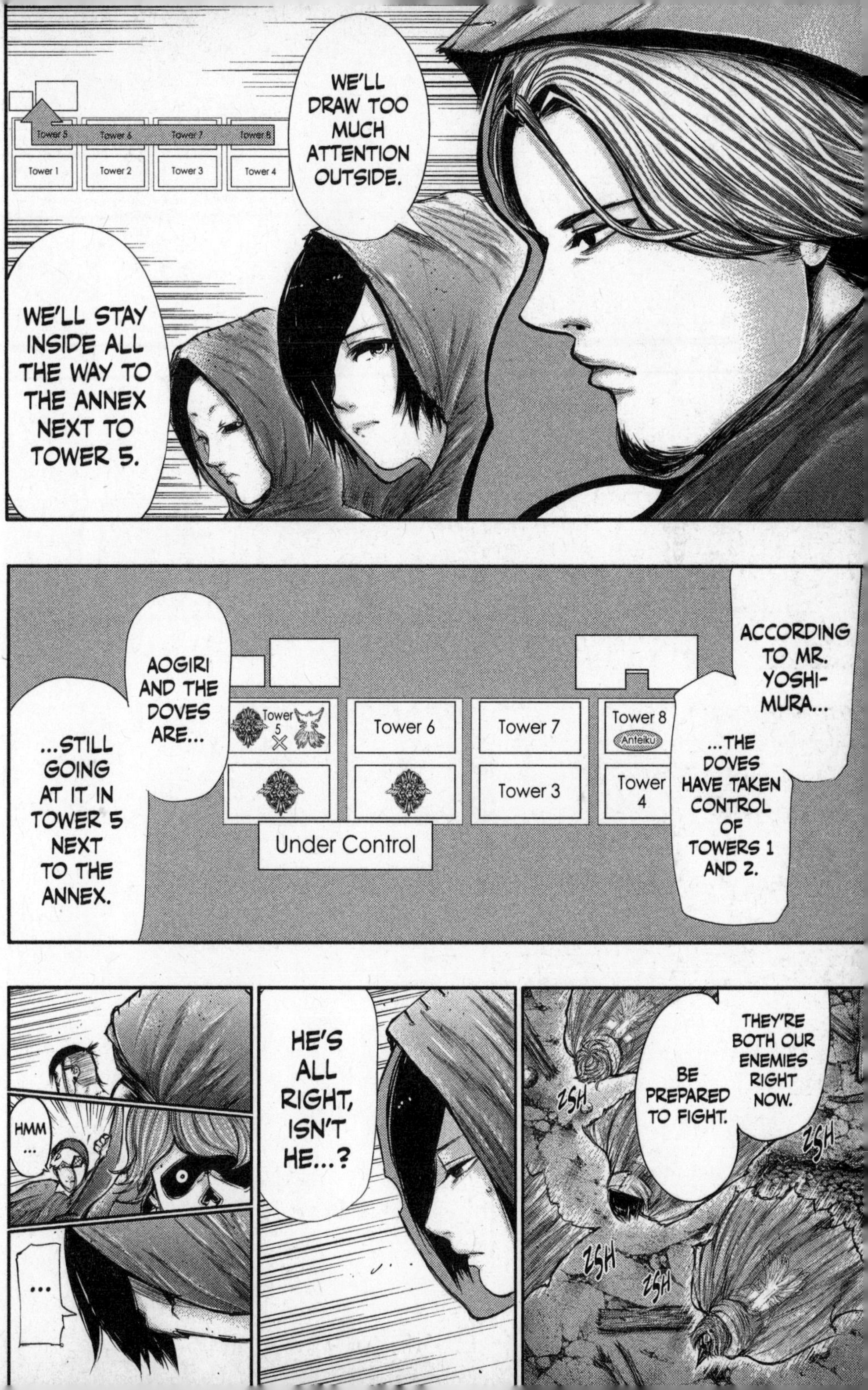
WE'LL DRAW TOO MUCH ATTENTION OUTSIDE.
Tower 5
Tower 6
Tower 7
Tower 8
Tower 1
Tower 2
Tower 3
Tower 4
WE'LL STAY INSIDE ALL THE WAY TO THE ANNEX NEXT TO TOWER 5.
ACCORDING TO MR. YOSHIMURA...
...THE DOVES HAVE TAKEN CONTROL OF TOWERS 1 AND 2.
Tower 8
Anteiku
Tower 4
Tower 7
Tower 3
Tower 6
Tower 5
Under Control
AOGIRI AND THE DOVES ARE...
...STILL GOING AT IT IN TOWER 5 NEXT TO THE ANNEX.
THEY'RE BOTH OUR ENEMIES RIGHT NOW.
BE PREPARED TO FIGHT.
ZSH
ZSH
ZSH
ZSH
HE'S ALL RIGHT, ISN'T HE...?
HMM...
...

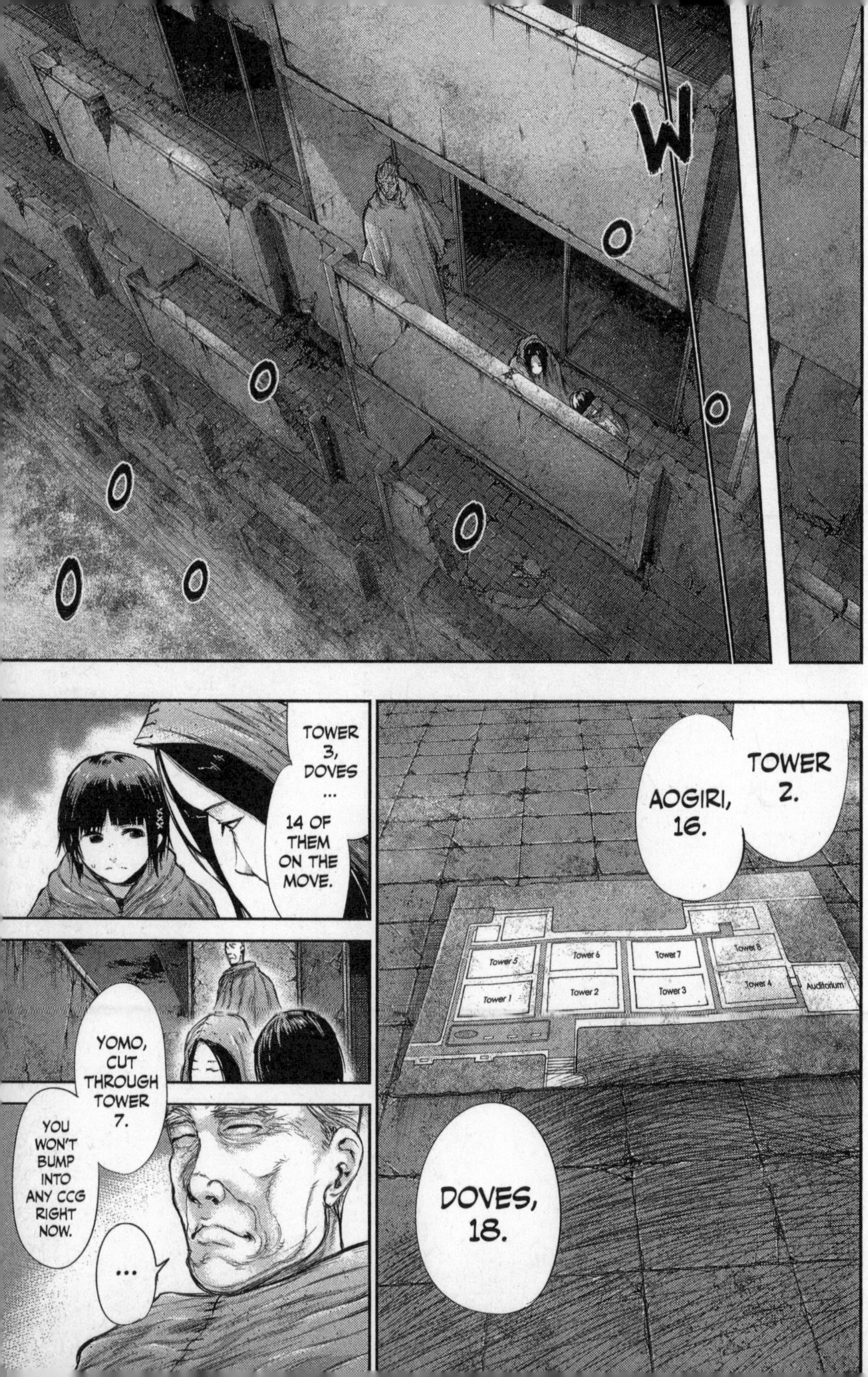
WOOOOOOO
TOWER 2.
AOGIRI, 16.
Tower 5
Tower 6
Tower 7
Tower 8
Tower 1
Tower 2
Tower 3
Tower 4
Auditorium
DOVES, 18.
TOWER 3, DOVES ... 14 OF THEM ON THE MOVE.
YOMO, CUT THROUGH TOWER 7.
YOU WON'T BUMP INTO ANY CCG RIGHT NOW.
...

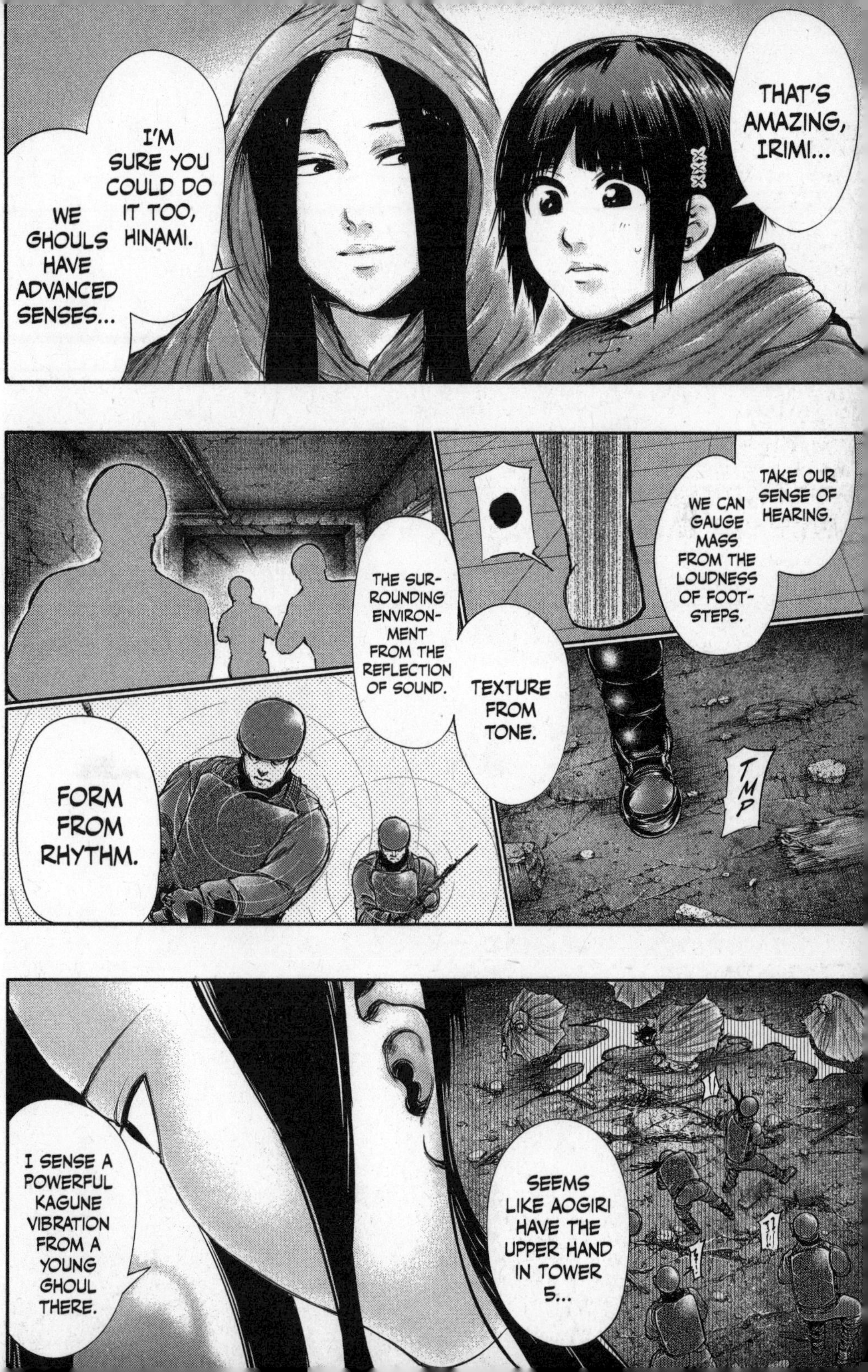
THAT'S AMAZING, IRIMI...
I'M SURE YOU COULD DO IT TOO, HINAMI.
WE GHOULS HAVE ADVANCED SENSES...
TAKE OUR SENSE OF HEARING.
WE CAN GAUGE MASS FROM THE LOUDNESS OF FOOT-STEPS.
TMP
THE SUR-ROUNDING ENVIRON-MENT FROM THE REFLECTION OF SOUND.
TEXTURE FROM TONE.
FORM FROM RHYTHM.
SEEMS LIKE AOGIRI HAVE THE UPPER HAND IN TOWER 5...
I SENSE A POWERFUL KAGUNE VIBRATION FROM A YOUNG GHOUL THERE.

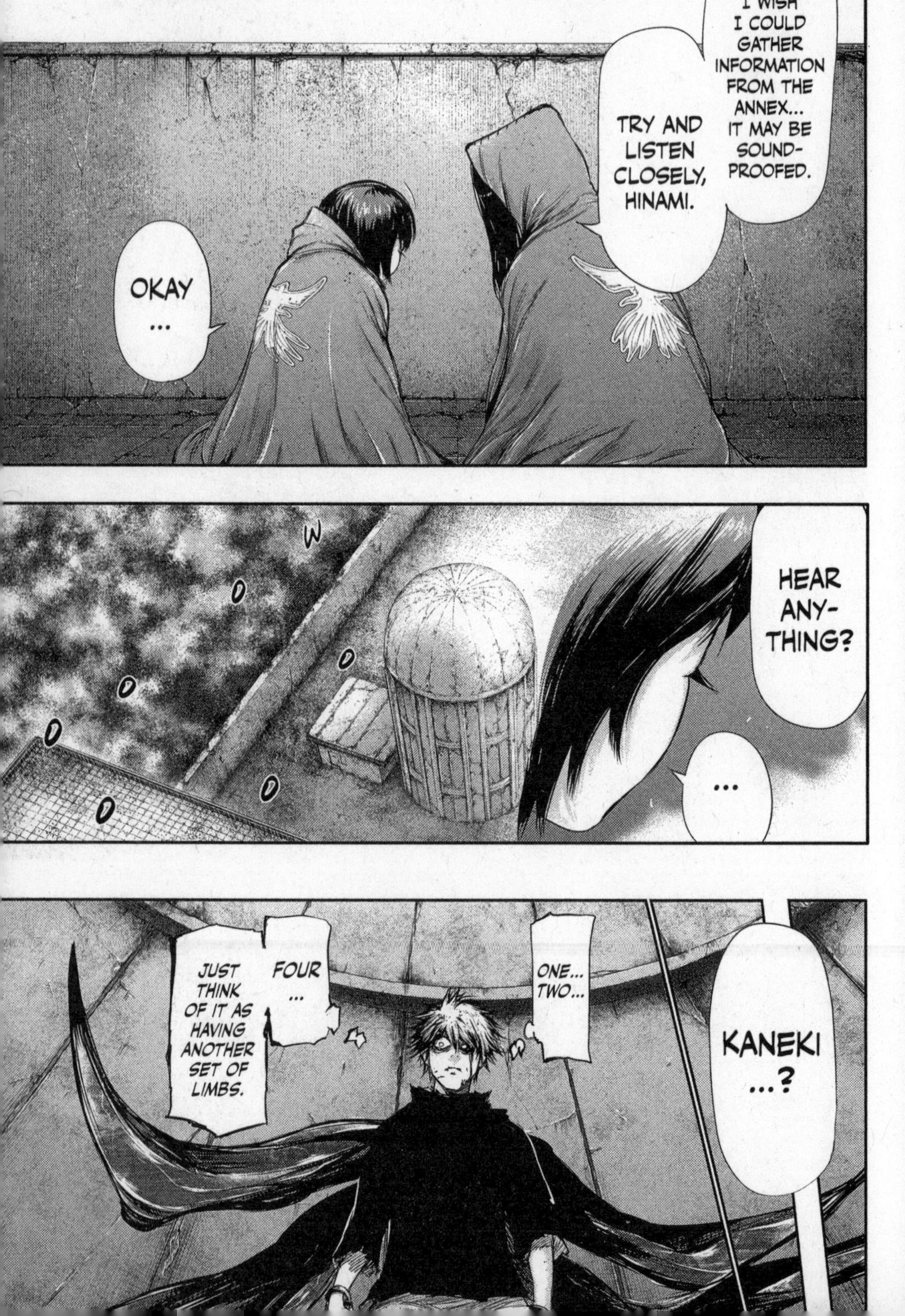
I WISH I COULD GATHER INFORMATION FROM THE ANNEX... IT MAY BE SOUND-PROOFED.
TRY AND LISTEN CLOSELY, HINAMI.
OKAY ...
HEAR ANY-THING?
...
KANEKI ...?
ONE... TWO...
FOUR ...
JUST THINK OF IT AS HAVING ANOTHER SET OF LIMBS.

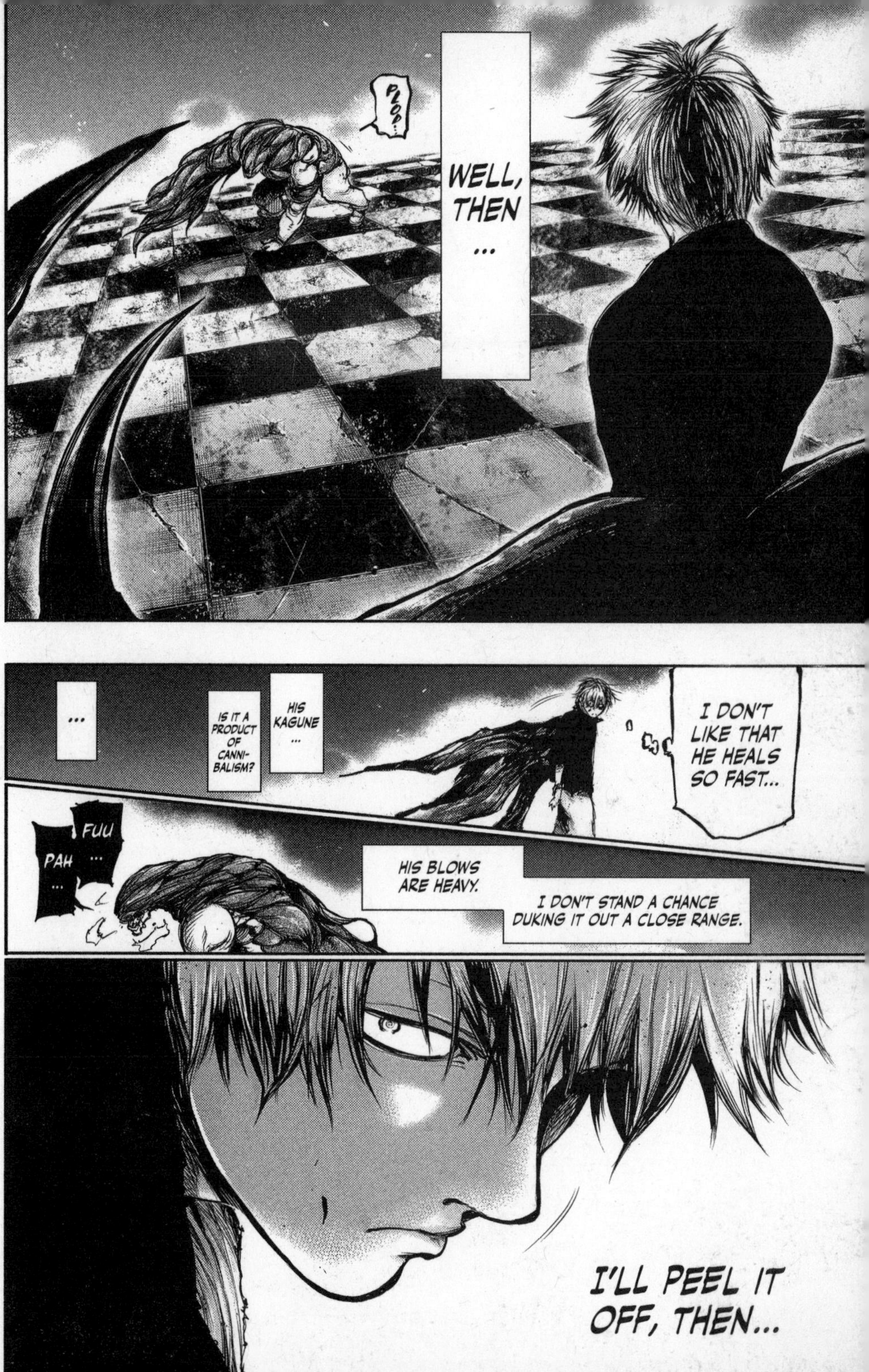
WELL, THEN ...
PLOP...
I DON'T LIKE THAT HE HEALS SO FAST...
HIS KAGUNE ...
IS IT A PRODUCT OF CANNI-BALISM?
...
HIS BLOWS ARE HEAVY.
I DON'T STAND A CHANCE DUKING IT OUT A CLOSE RANGE.
FUU ...
PAH ...
I'LL PEEL IT OFF, THEN...

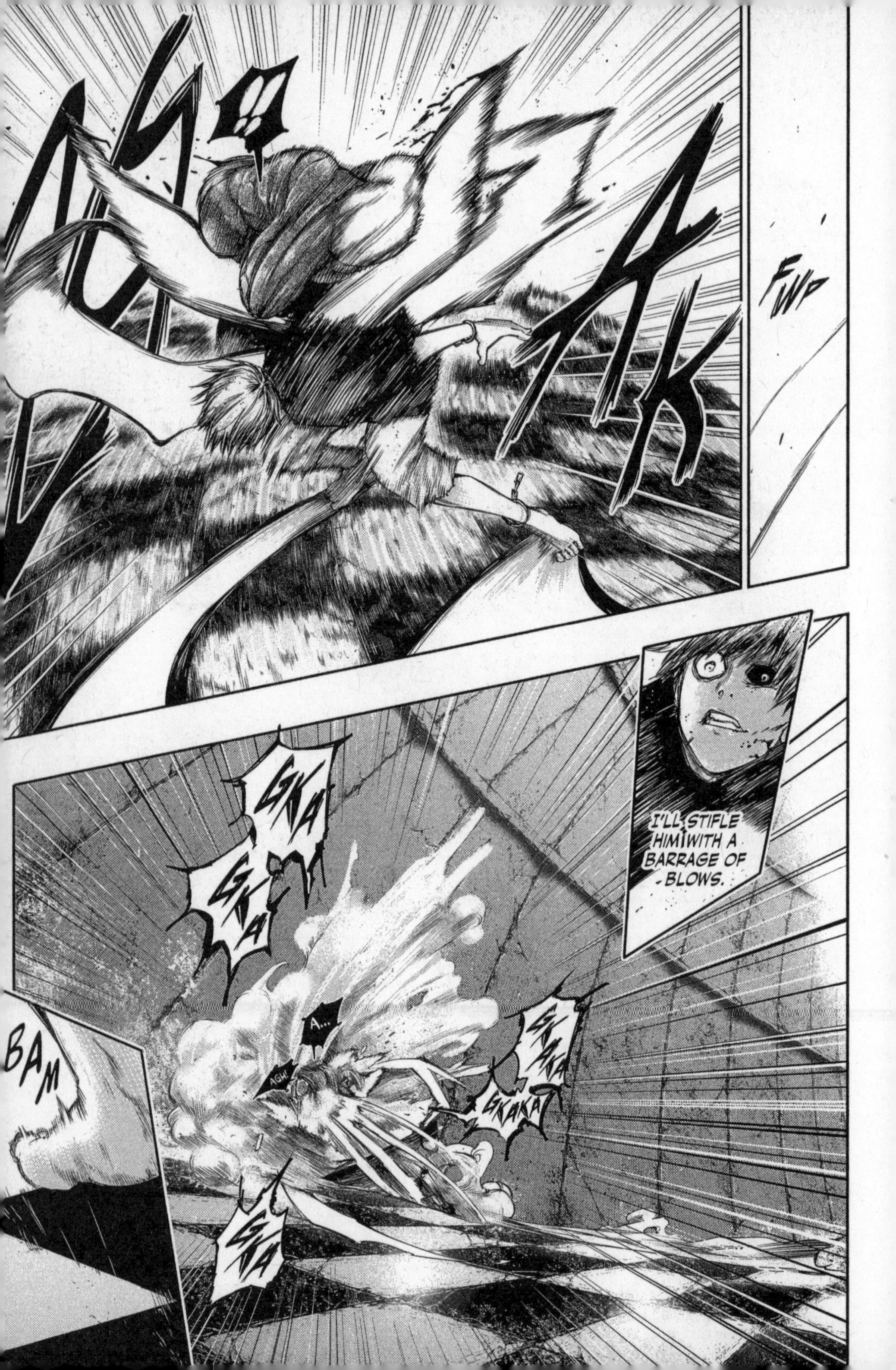
FWP
I'LL STIFLE HIM WITH A BARRAGE OF BLOWS.
GKAKA
GKAKA
A...
AGH!
GKA
GKA
GKA
BAM
GKA

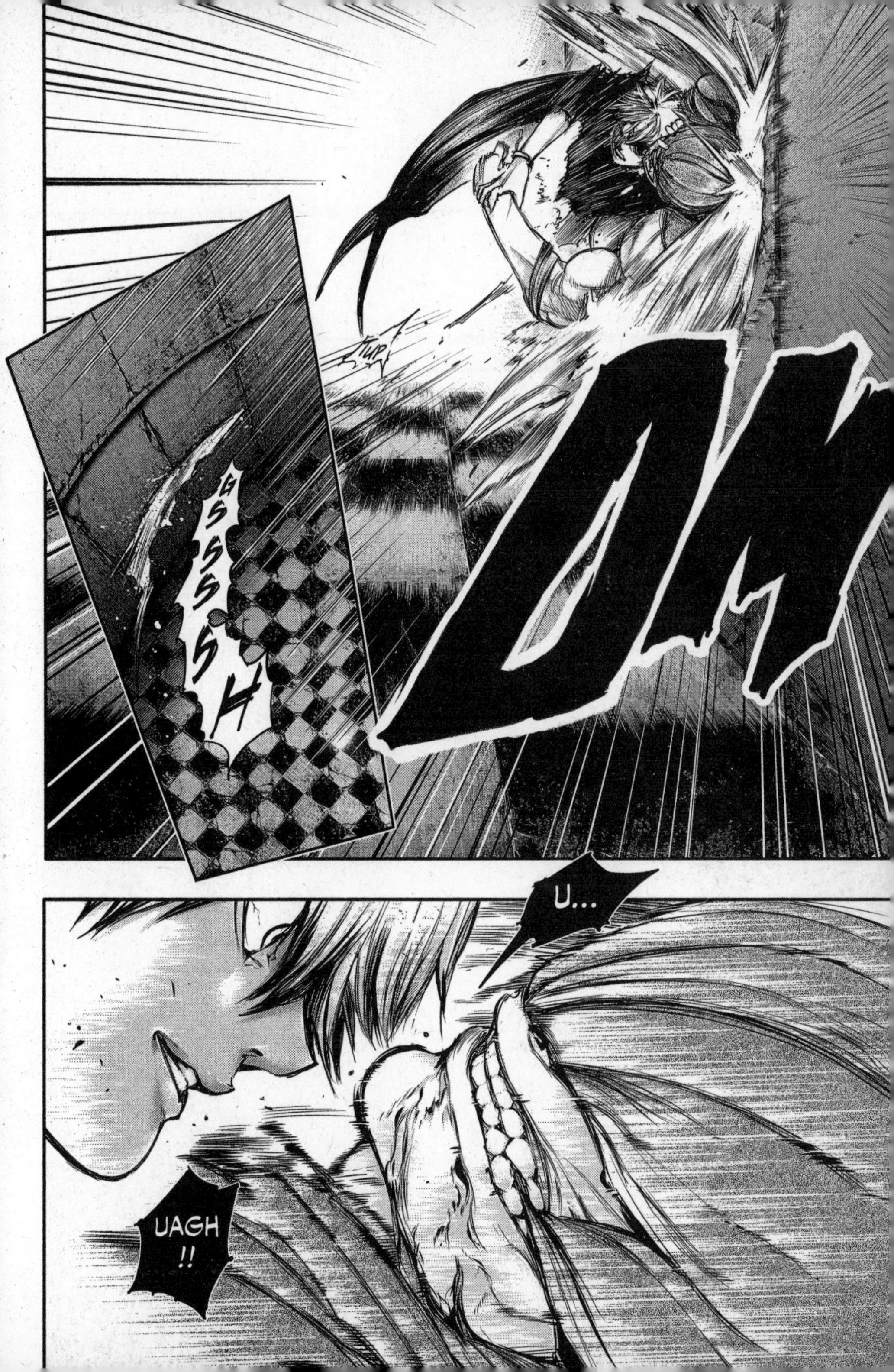
FUP
GSSSSSH
U...
UAGH !!

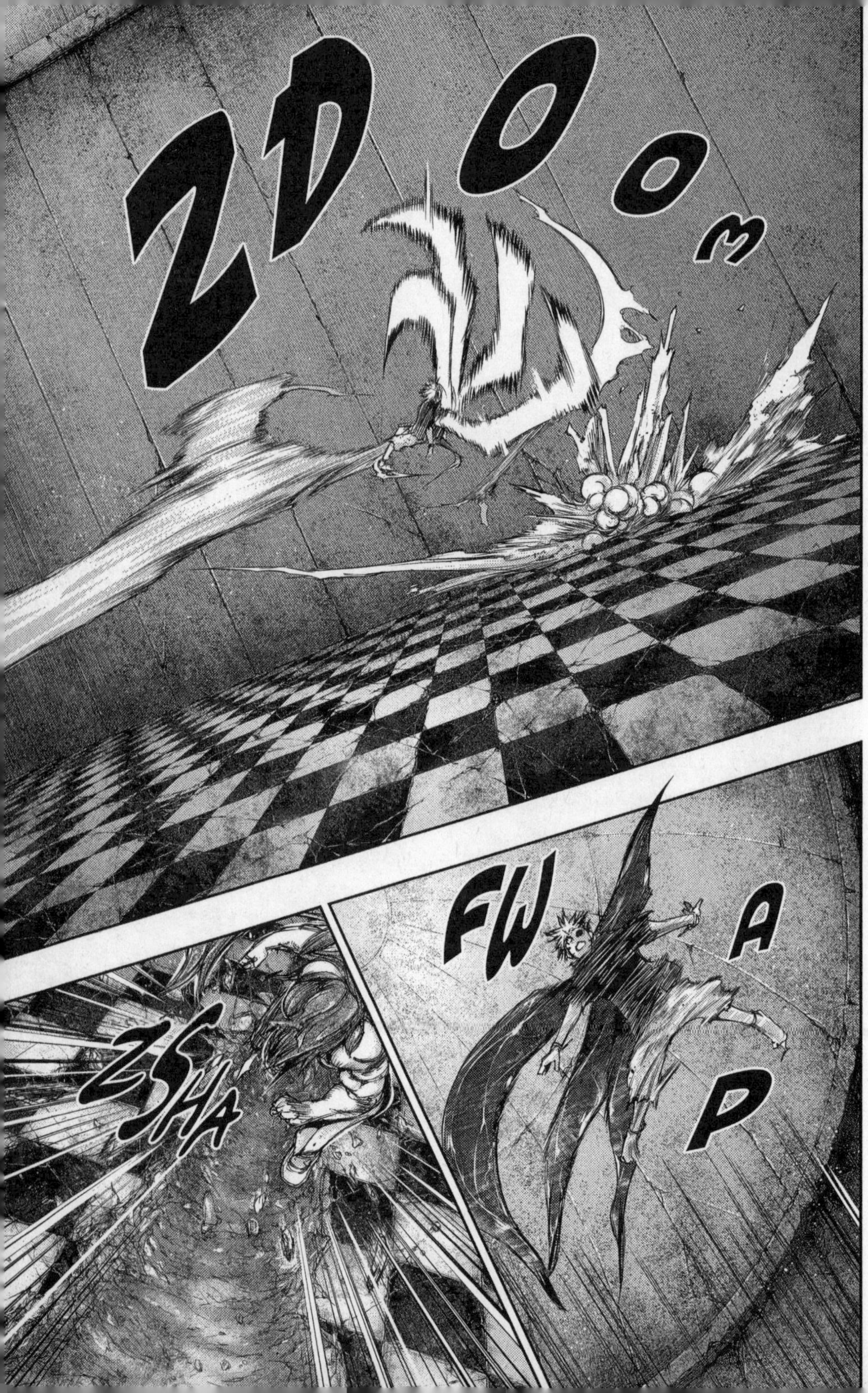
ZDOom
FWAP
ZSHA

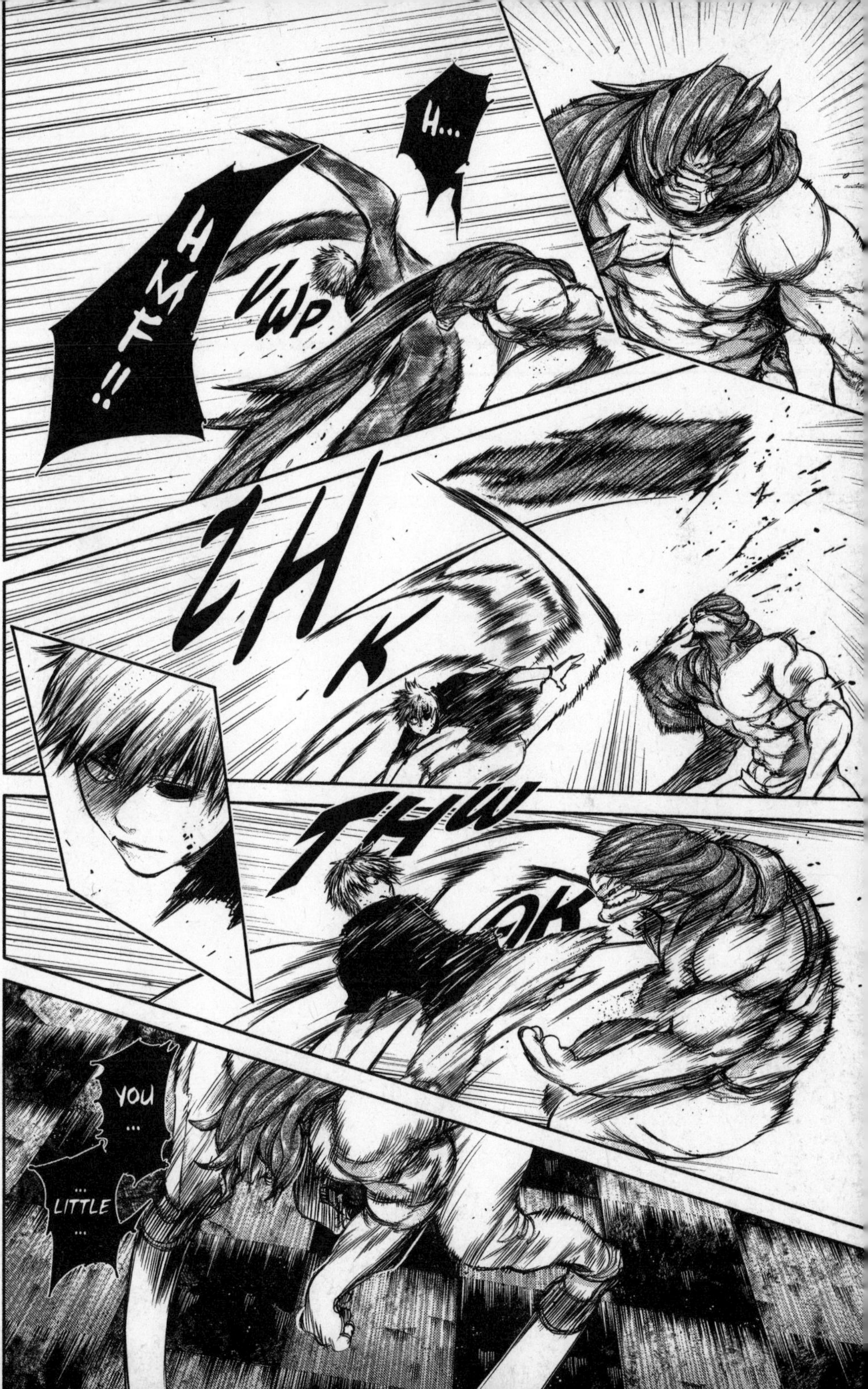
H...
UWP
HMF!!
ZHK
THW
OK
YOU ...
... LITTLE ...

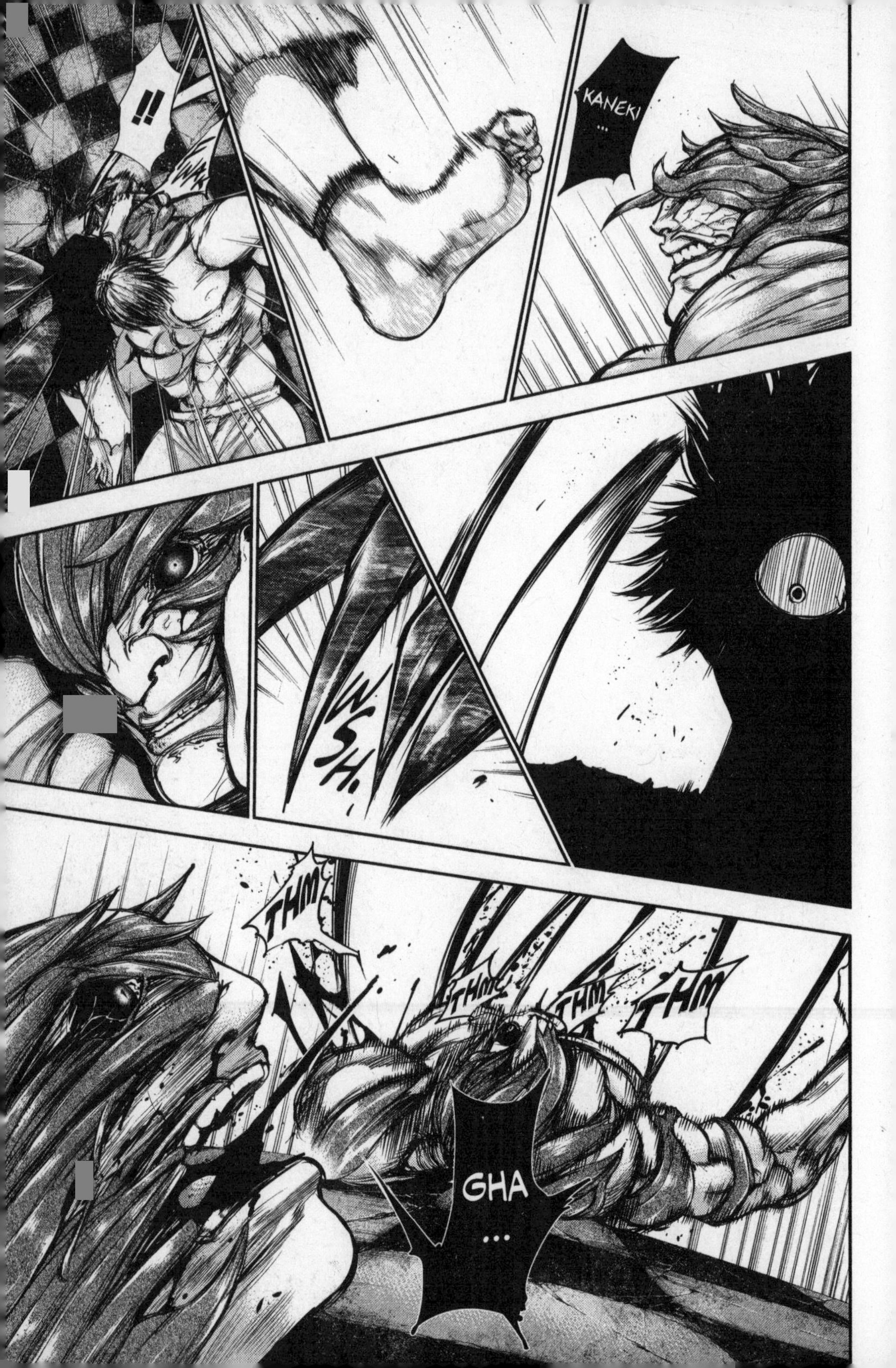
KANEKI ...
!!
WAK
WSH!
THM
THM
THM
THM
GHA ...

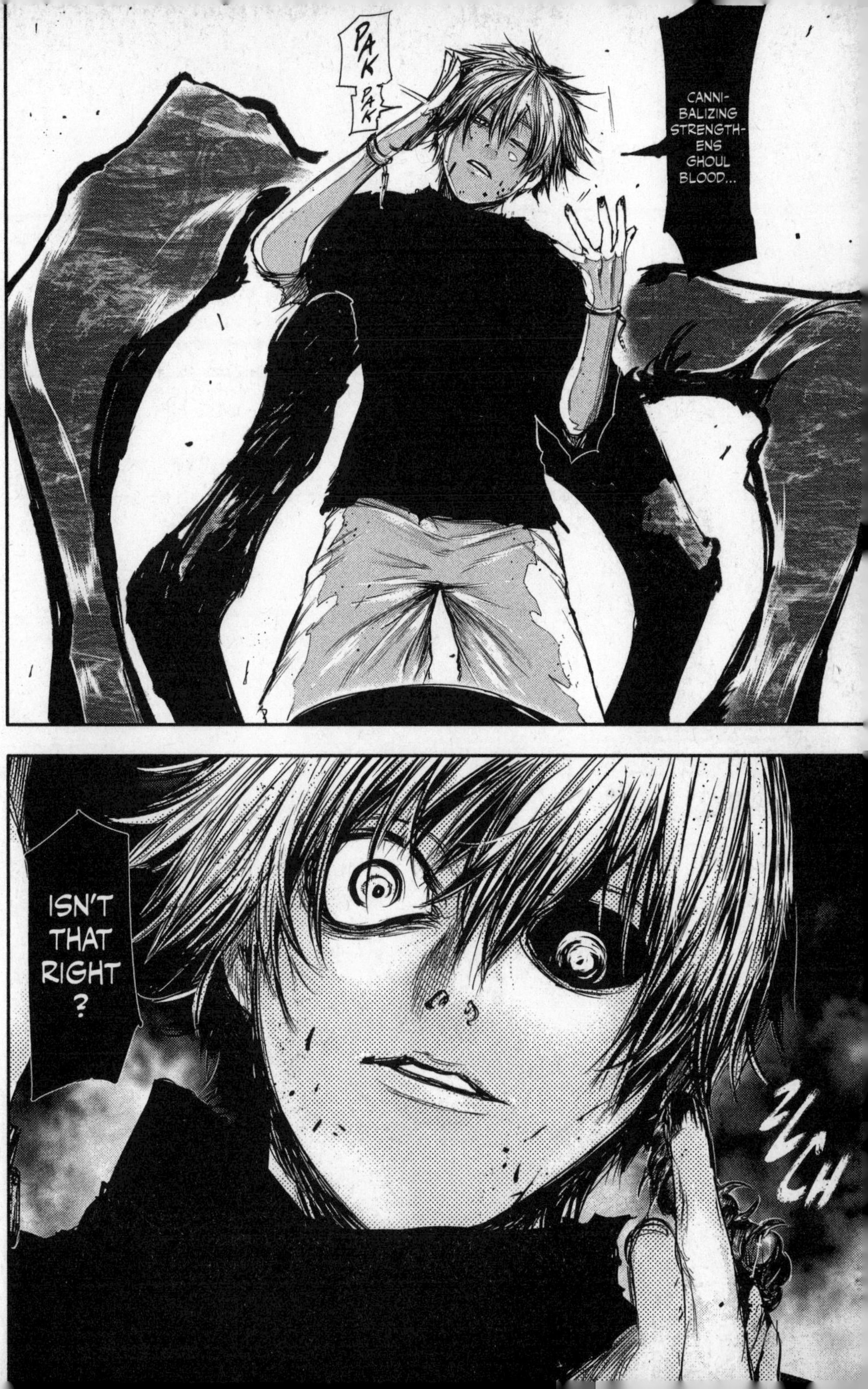
CANNI-BALIZING STRENGTH-ENS GHOUL BLOOD...
PAK PAK PAK
ISN'T THAT RIGHT?
ZLCH

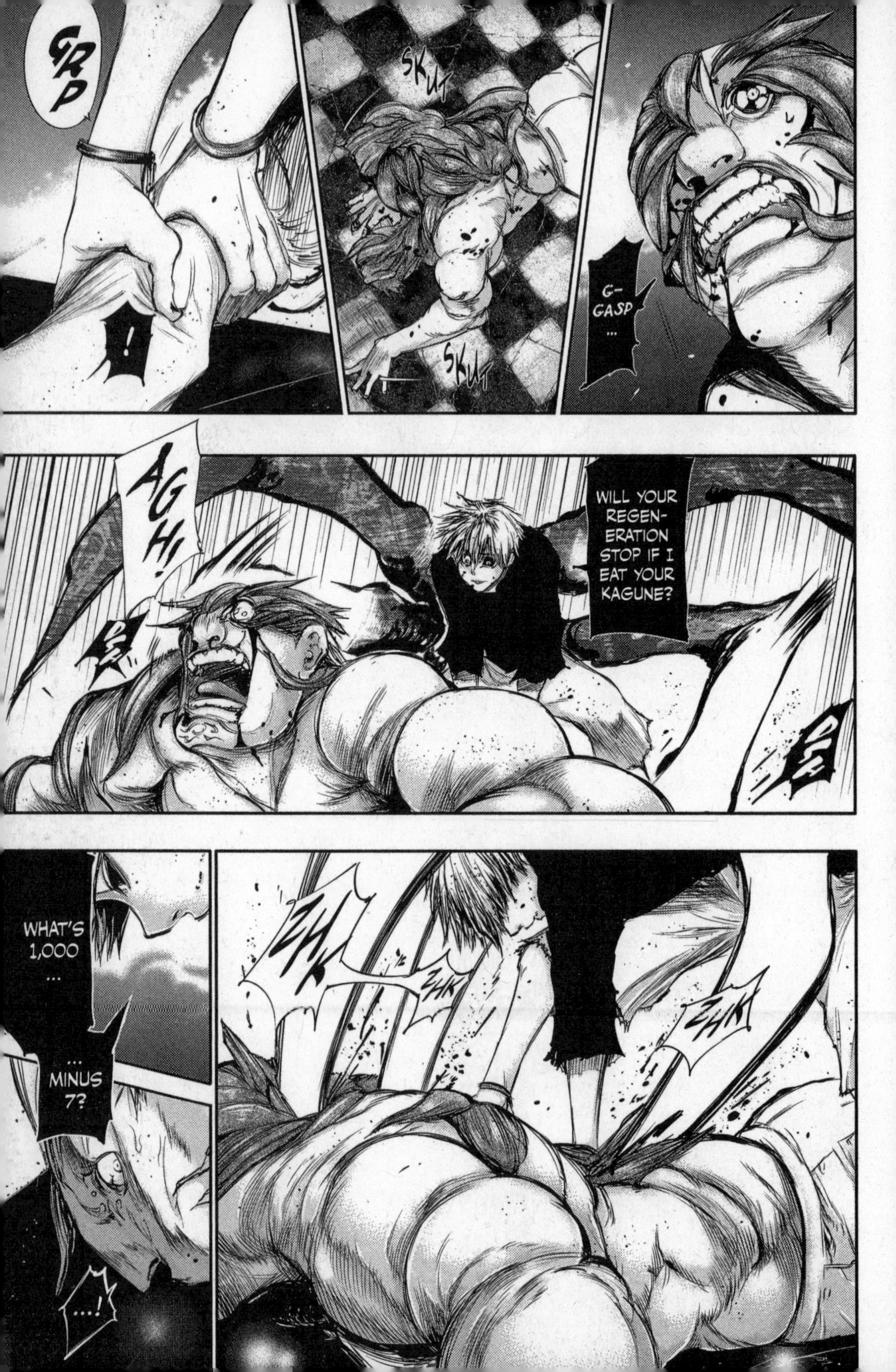
G-GASP ...
SKUT
SKUT
GRP
!
WILL YOUR REGEN-ERATION STOP IF I EAT YOUR KAGUNE?
AGH!
ZHK
ZHK
ZHK
WHAT'S 1,000 ...
... MINUS 7?
...!

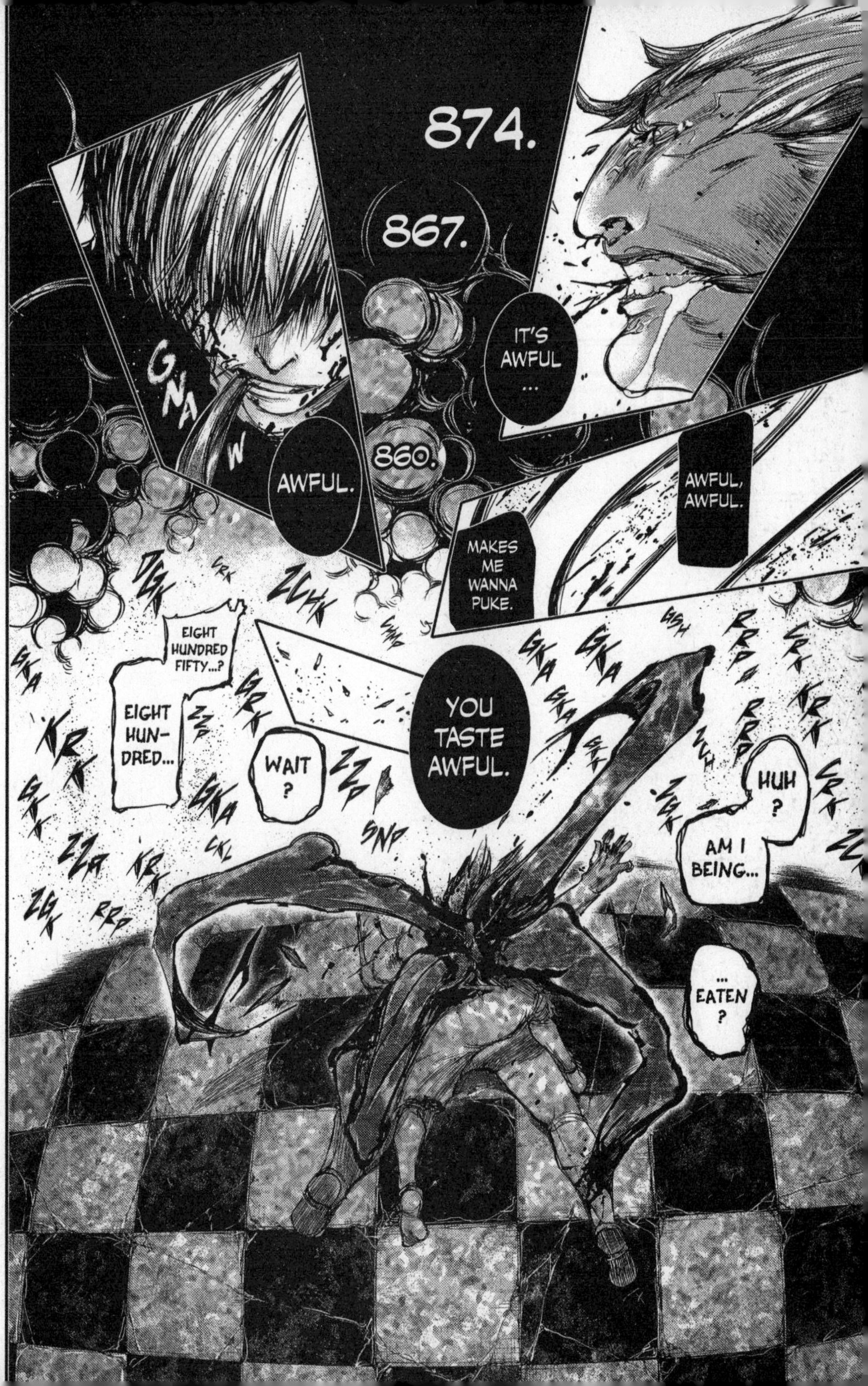
874.
867.
IT'S AWFUL ...
GNAW
AWFUL.
860.
AWFUL, AWFUL.
MAKES ME WANNA PUKE.
YOU TASTE AWFUL.
HUH?
AM I BEING...
... EATEN?
WAIT?
EIGHT HUNDRED FIFTY...?
EIGHT HUN-DRED...

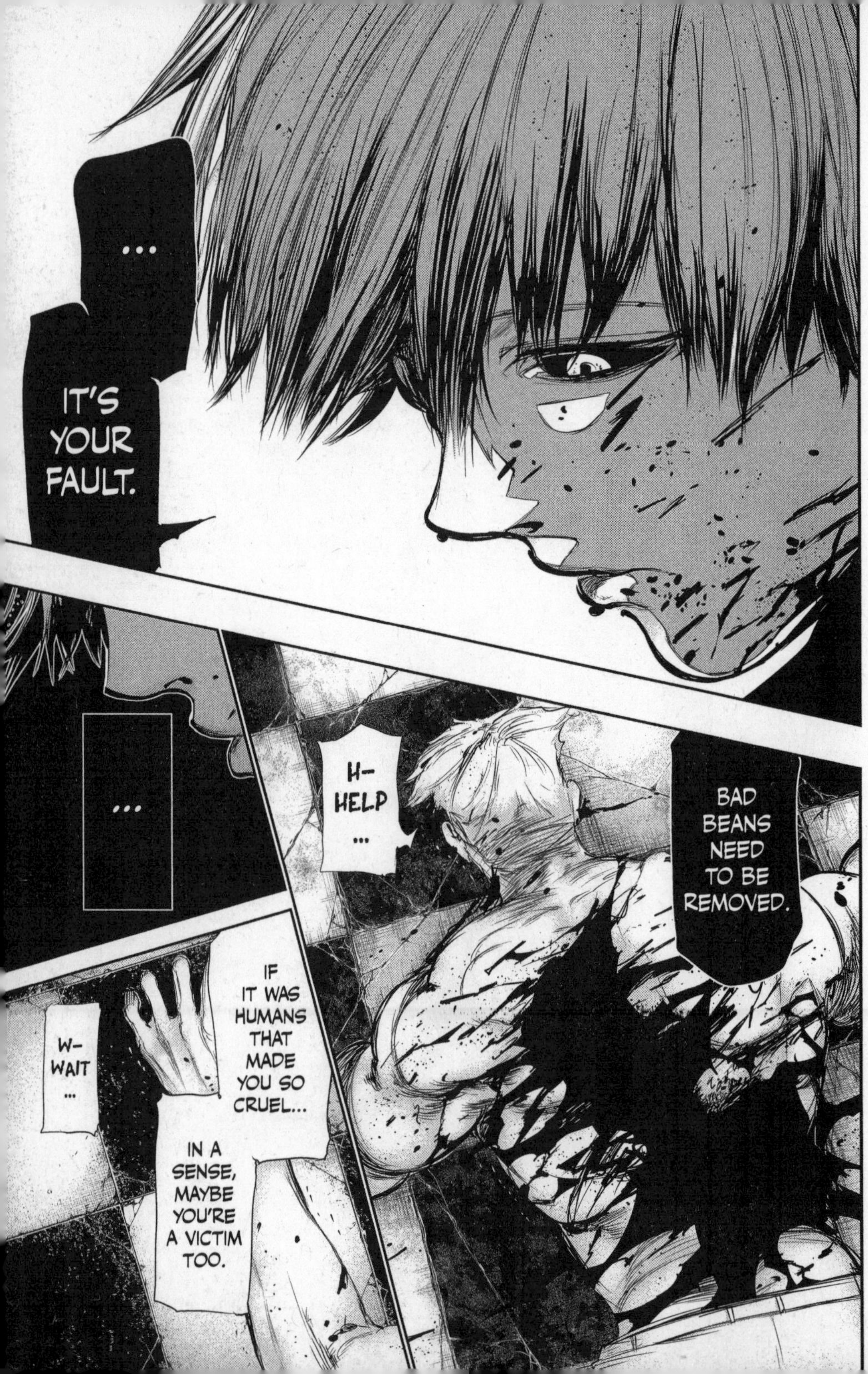
...
IT'S YOUR FAULT.
BAD BEANS NEED TO BE REMOVED.
H-HELP ...
...
IF IT WAS HUMANS THAT MADE YOU SO CRUEL...
IN A SENSE, MAYBE YOU'RE A VICTIM TOO.
W-WAIT ...

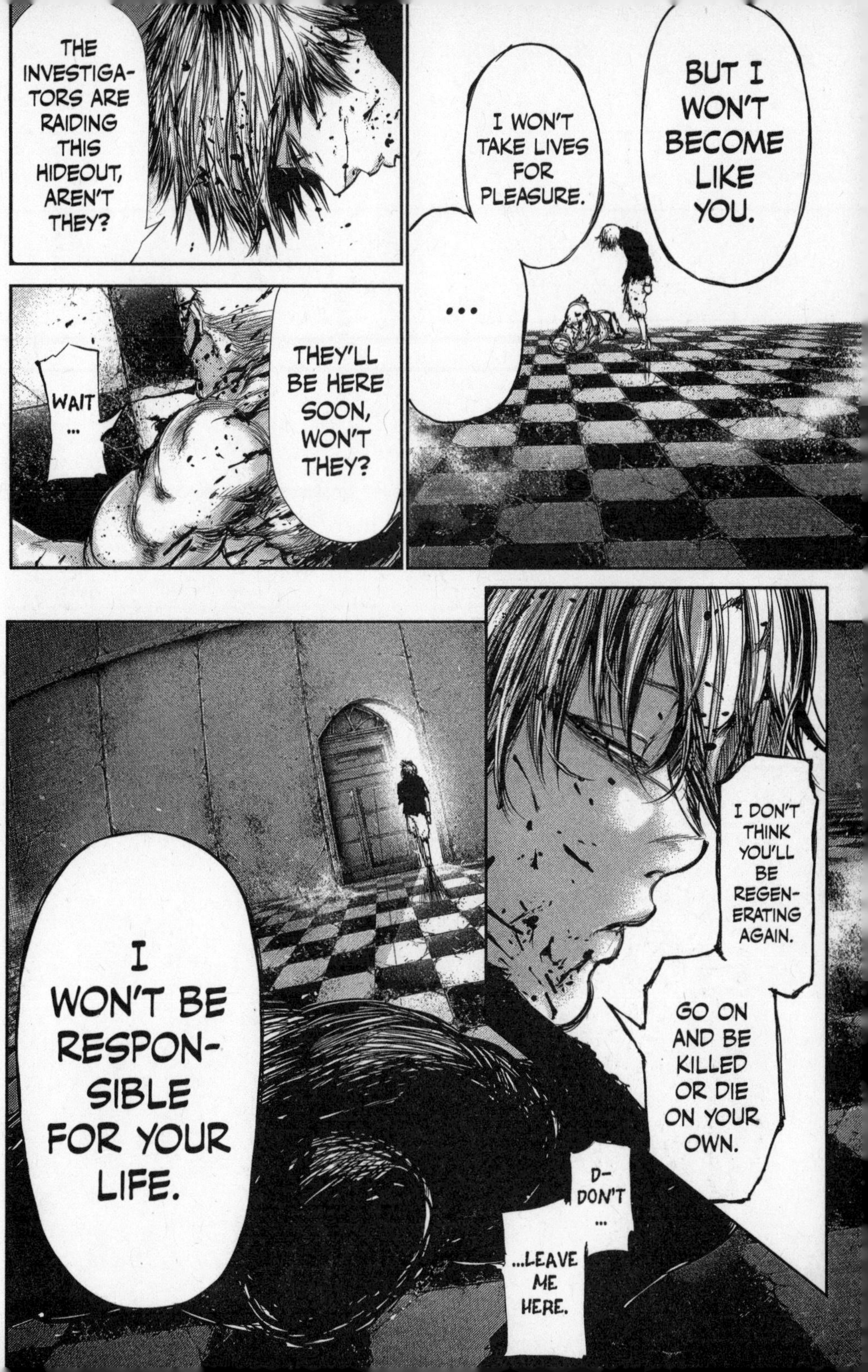

BUT I WON'T BECOME LIKE YOU.
I WON'T TAKE LIVES FOR PLEASURE.
...
THE INVESTIGATORS ARE RAIDING THIS HIDEOUT, AREN'T THEY?
THEY'LL BE HERE SOON, WON'T THEY?
WAIT ...
I DON'T THINK YOU'LL BE REGENERATING AGAIN.
GO ON AND BE KILLED OR DIE ON YOUR OWN.
D-DON'T ...
...LEAVE ME HERE.
I WON'T BE RESPONSIBLE FOR YOUR LIFE.

東京喰種
トーキョーグール
喰種
Tokyo
Ghoul

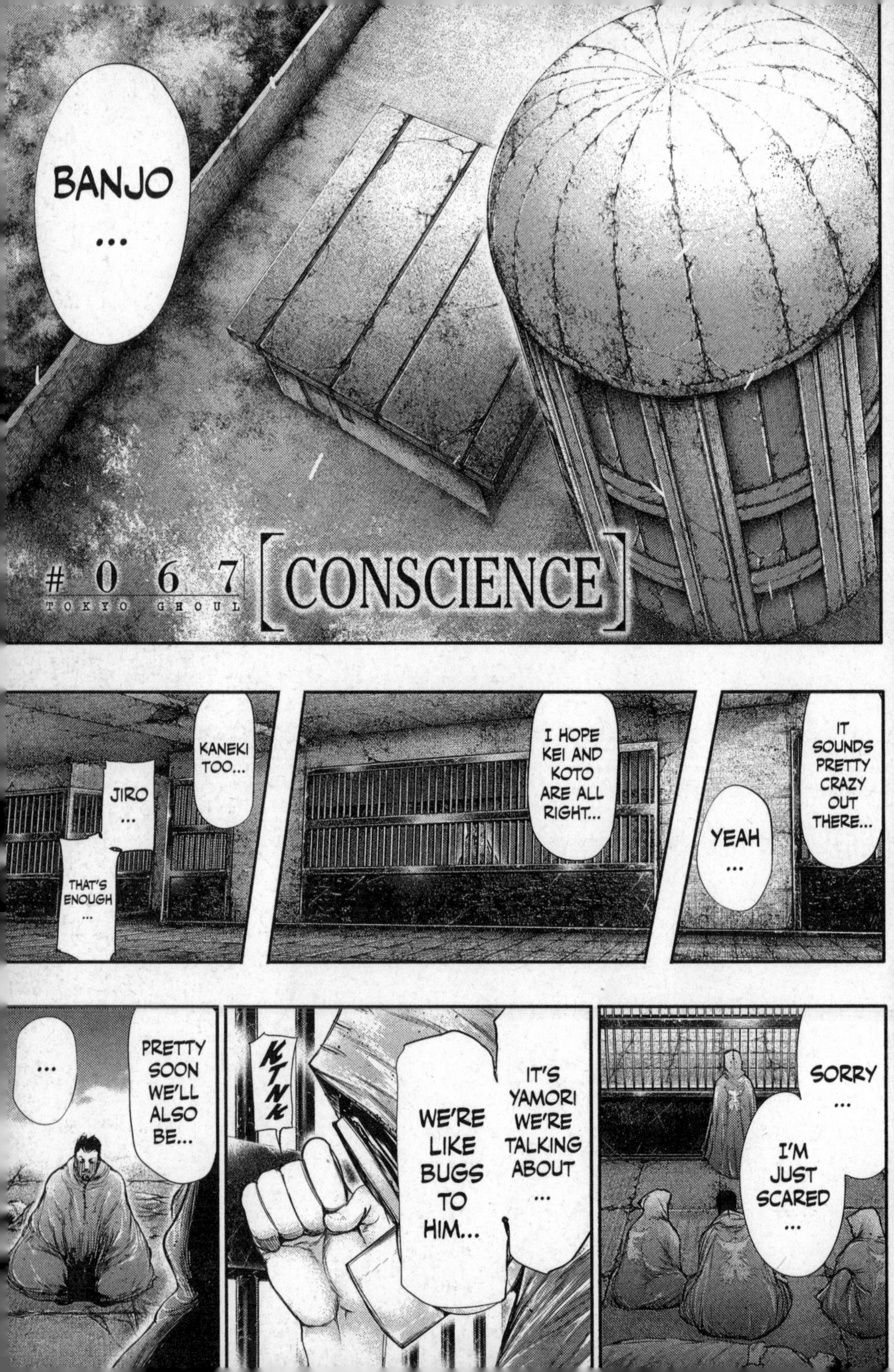
BANJO ...
#067 CONSCIENCE
TOKYO GHOUL
IT SOUNDS PRETTY CRAZY OUT THERE...
YEAH ...
I HOPE KEI AND KOTO ARE ALL RIGHT...
KANEKI TOO...
JIRO ...
THAT'S ENOUGH ...
SORRY ...
I'M JUST SCARED ...
IT'S YAMORI WE'RE TALKING ABOUT ...
WE'RE LIKE BUGS TO HIM...
KTNK
PRETTY SOON WE'LL ALSO BE...
...

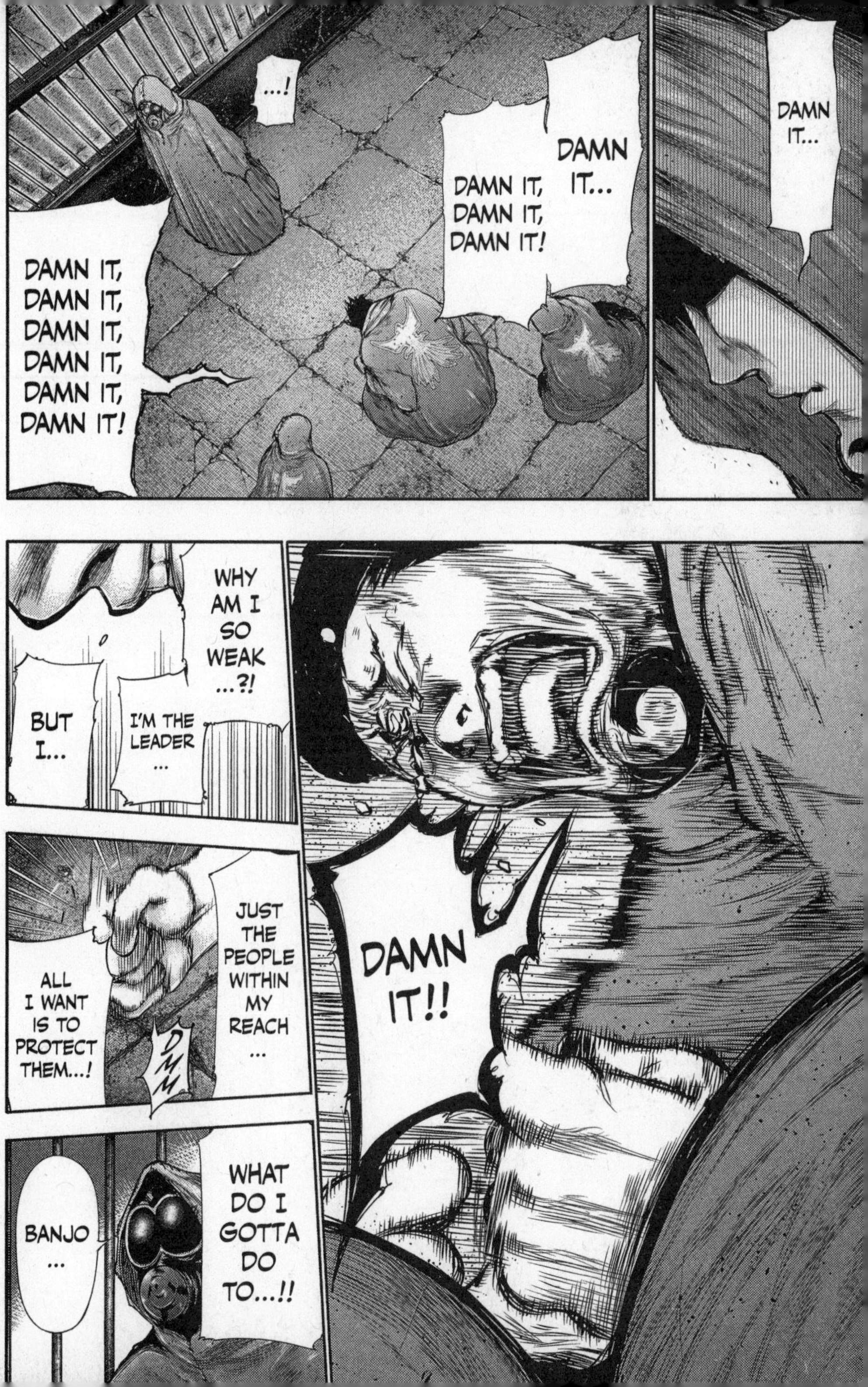

DAMN IT...
DAMN IT...
DAMN IT, DAMN IT, DAMN IT!
...!
DAMN IT, DAMN IT, DAMN IT, DAMN IT, DAMN IT, DAMN IT!
DAMN IT!!
WHY AM I SO WEAK...?!
I'M THE LEADER...
BUT I...
JUST THE PEOPLE WITHIN MY REACH...
DMM
ALL I WANT IS TO PROTECT THEM...!
WHAT DO I GOTTA DO TO...!!
BANJO...

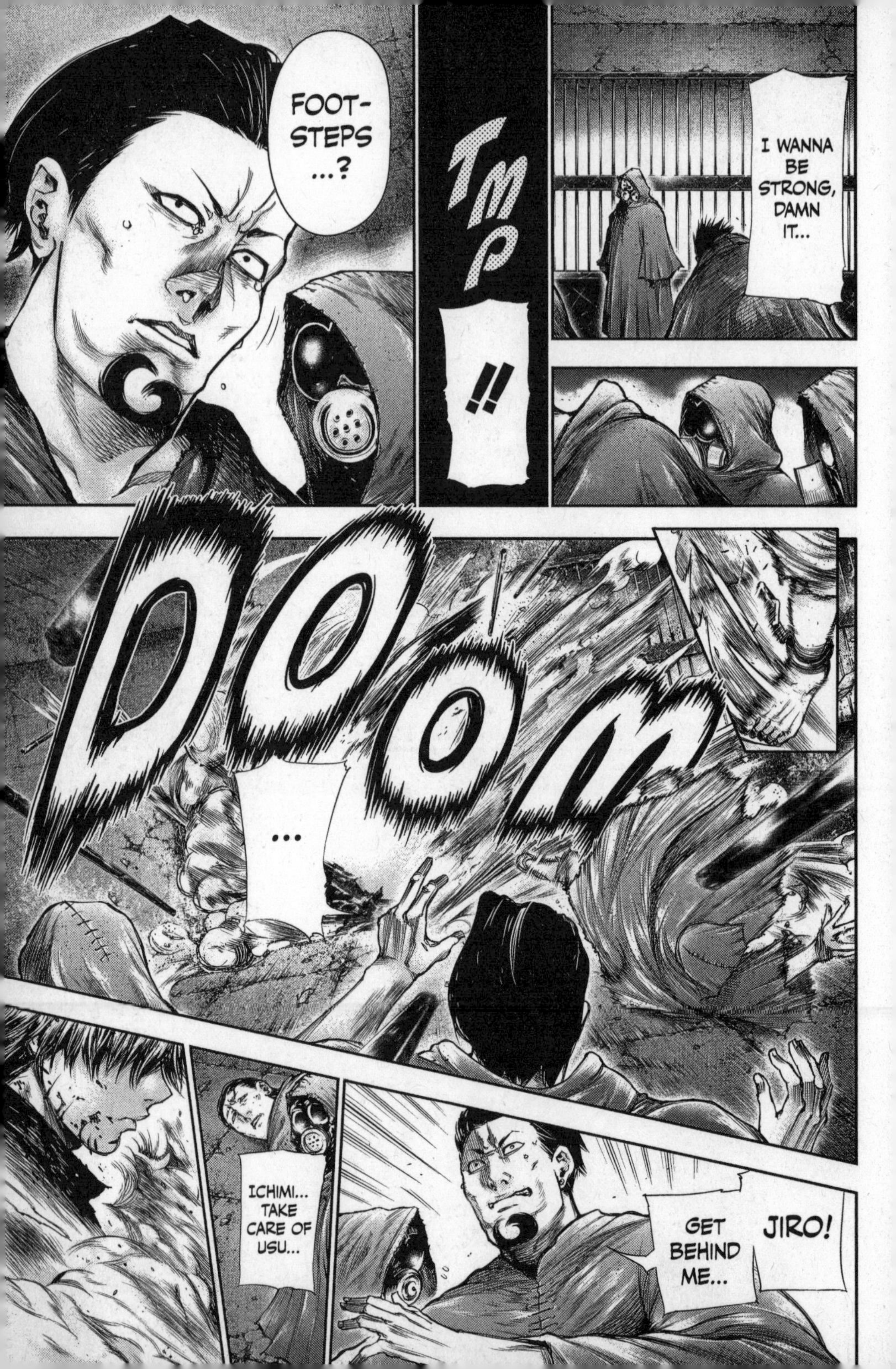
I WANNA BE STRONG, DAMN IT...
TMP!!
FOOT-STEPS...?
DOOM
...
JIRO!
GET BEHIND ME...
ICHIMI... TAKE CARE OF USU...

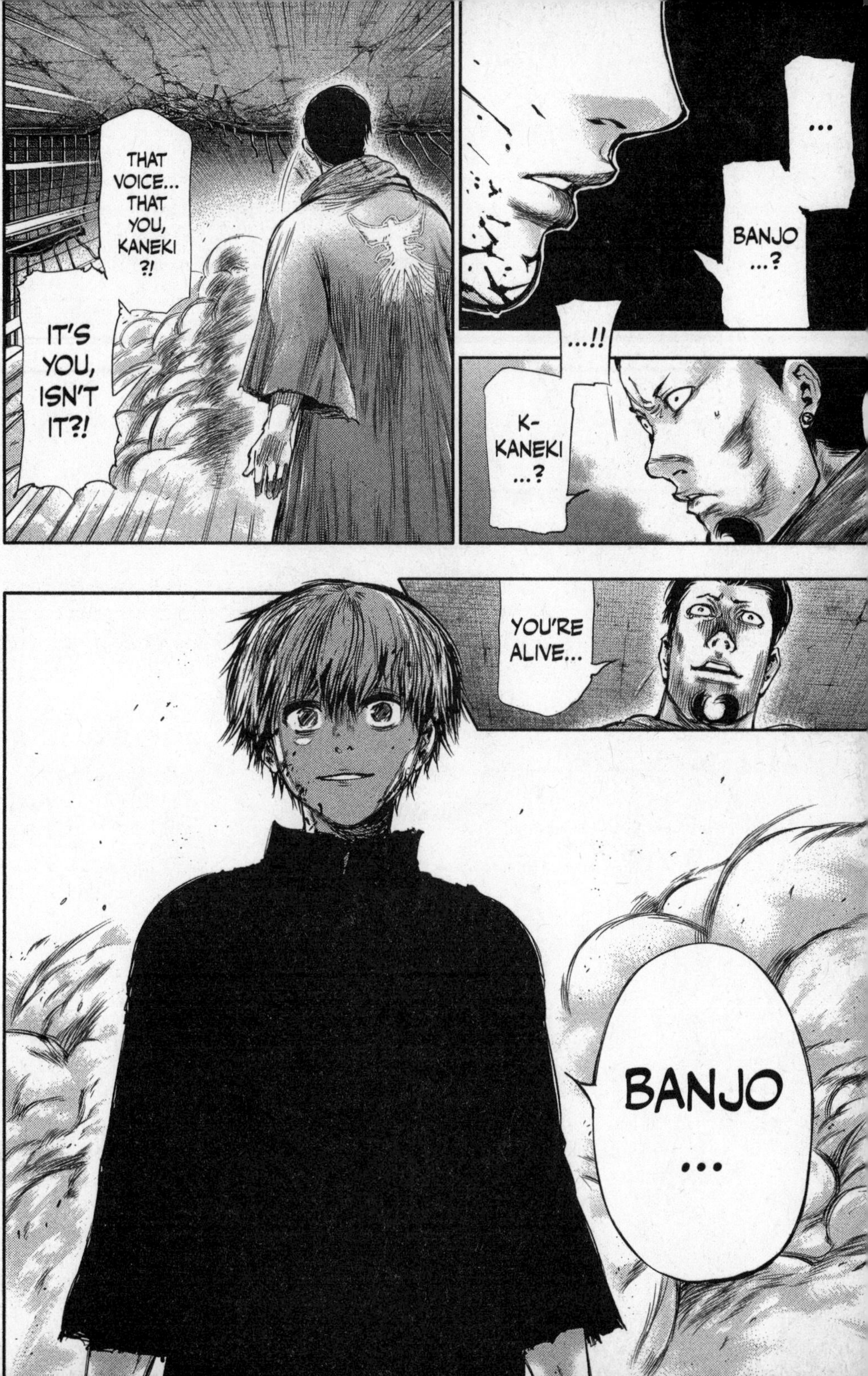
...
BANJO ...?
...!!
K-KANEKI ...?
THAT VOICE... THAT YOU, KANEKI ?!
IT'S YOU, ISN'T IT?!
YOU'RE ALIVE...
BANJO ...

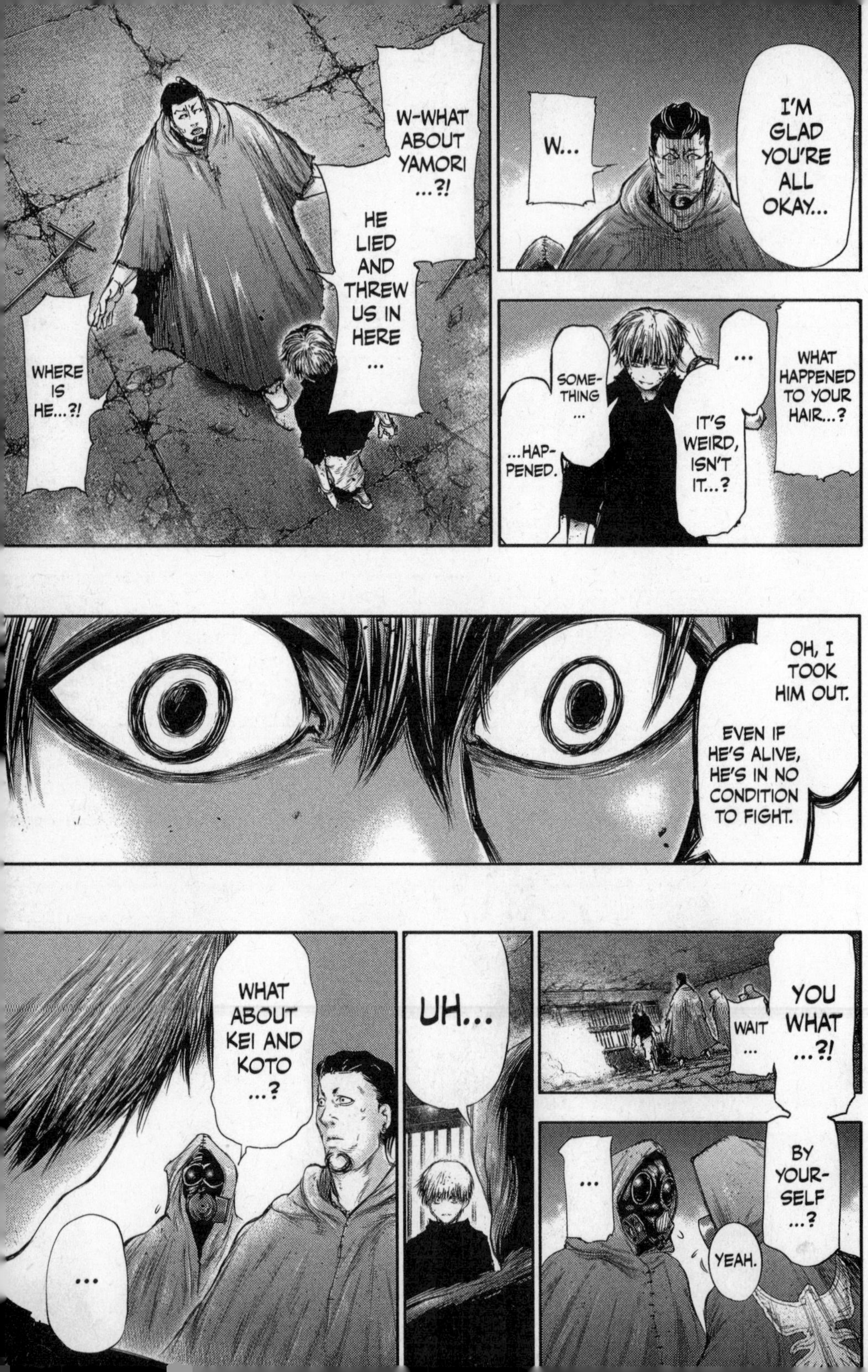
I'M GLAD YOU'RE ALL OKAY...
W...
WHAT HAPPENED TO YOUR HAIR...?
...
IT'S WEIRD, ISN'T IT...?
SOME-THING ...
...HAP-PENED.
W-WHAT ABOUT YAMORI ...?!
HE LIED AND THREW US IN HERE ...
WHERE IS HE...?!
OH, I TOOK HIM OUT.
EVEN IF HE'S ALIVE, HE'S IN NO CONDITION TO FIGHT.
YOU WHAT ...?!
WAIT ...
BY YOUR-SELF ...?
...
YEAH.
UH...
WHAT ABOUT KEI AND KOTO ...?
...

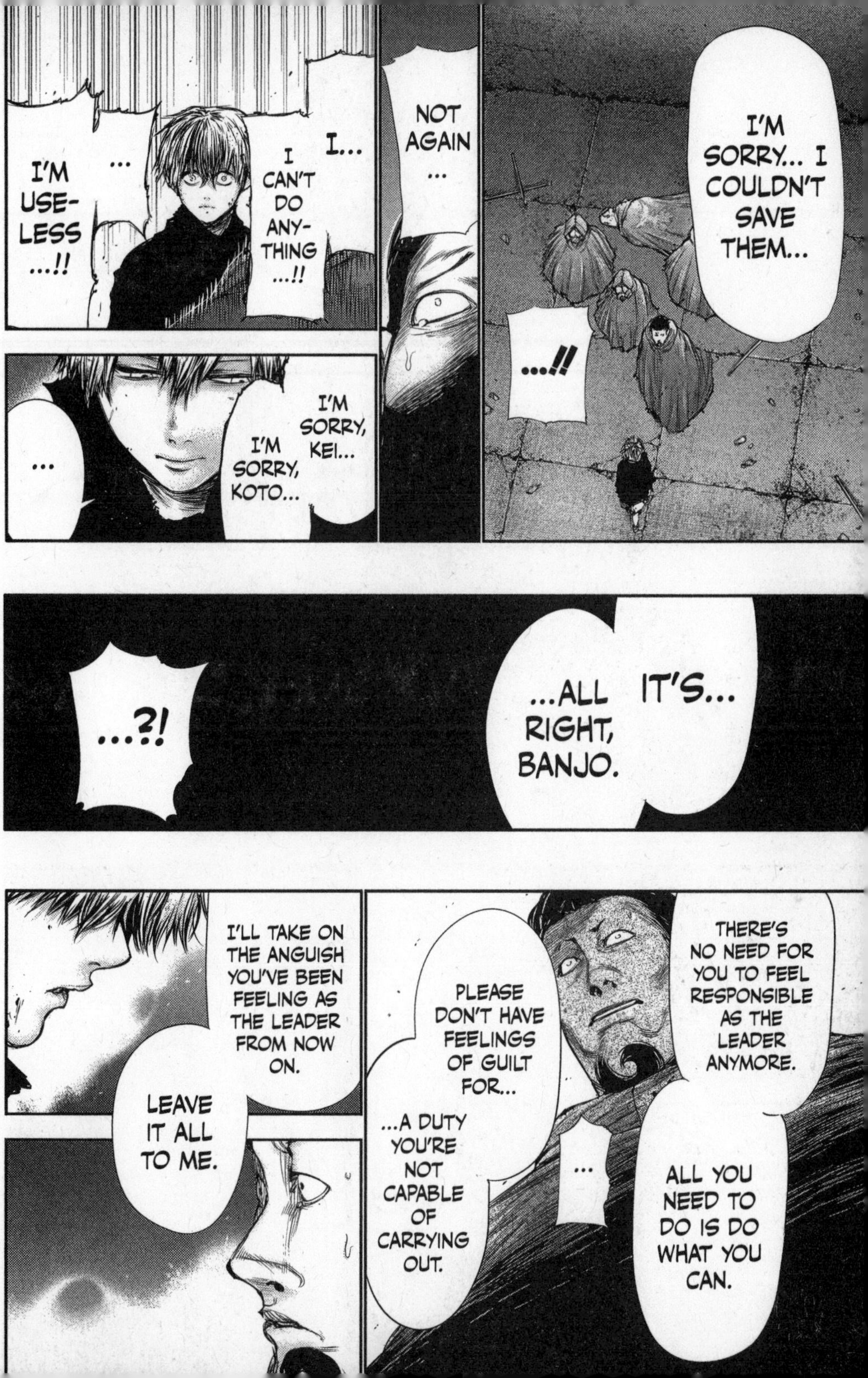
I'M SORRY... I COULDN'T SAVE THEM...
...!!
NOT AGAIN ...
I...
I CAN'T DO ANYTHING ...!!
...
I'M USELESS ...!!
I'M SORRY, KEI...
I'M SORRY, KOTO...
...
IT'S...
...ALL RIGHT, BANJO.
...?!
THERE'S NO NEED FOR YOU TO FEEL RESPONSIBLE AS THE LEADER ANYMORE.
PLEASE DON'T HAVE FEELINGS OF GUILT FOR...
...A DUTY YOU'RE NOT CAPABLE OF CARRYING OUT.
...
ALL YOU NEED TO DO IS DO WHAT YOU CAN.
I'LL TAKE ON THE ANGUISH YOU'VE BEEN FEELING AS THE LEADER FROM NOW ON.
LEAVE IT ALL TO ME.

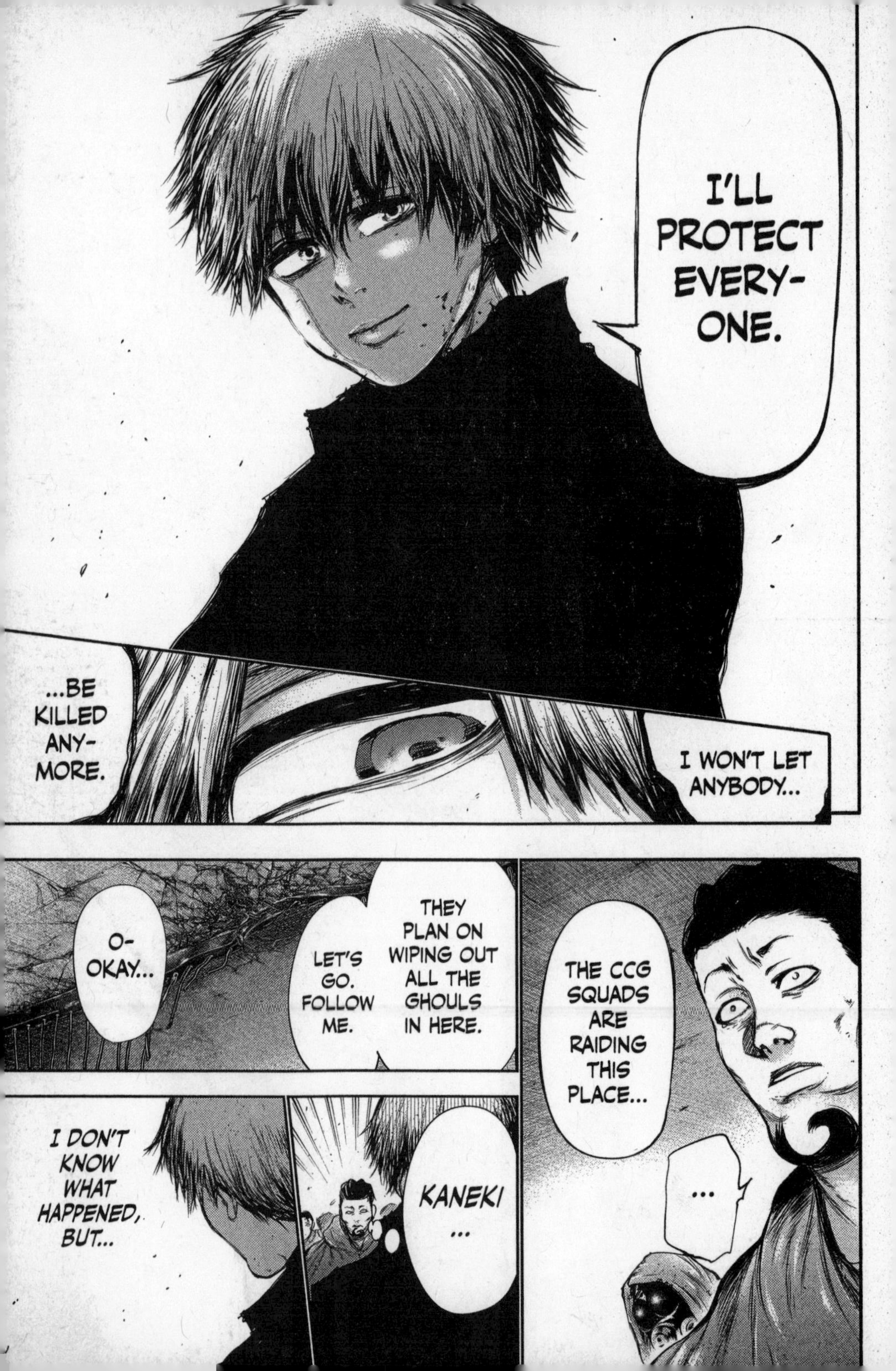

I'LL PROTECT EVERY-ONE.
I WON'T LET ANYBODY...
...BE KILLED ANY-MORE.
THE CCG SQUADS ARE RAIDING THIS PLACE...
...
THEY PLAN ON WIPING OUT ALL THE GHOULS IN HERE.
LET'S GO. FOLLOW ME.
O-OKAY...
KANEKI ...
I DON'T KNOW WHAT HAPPENED, BUT...

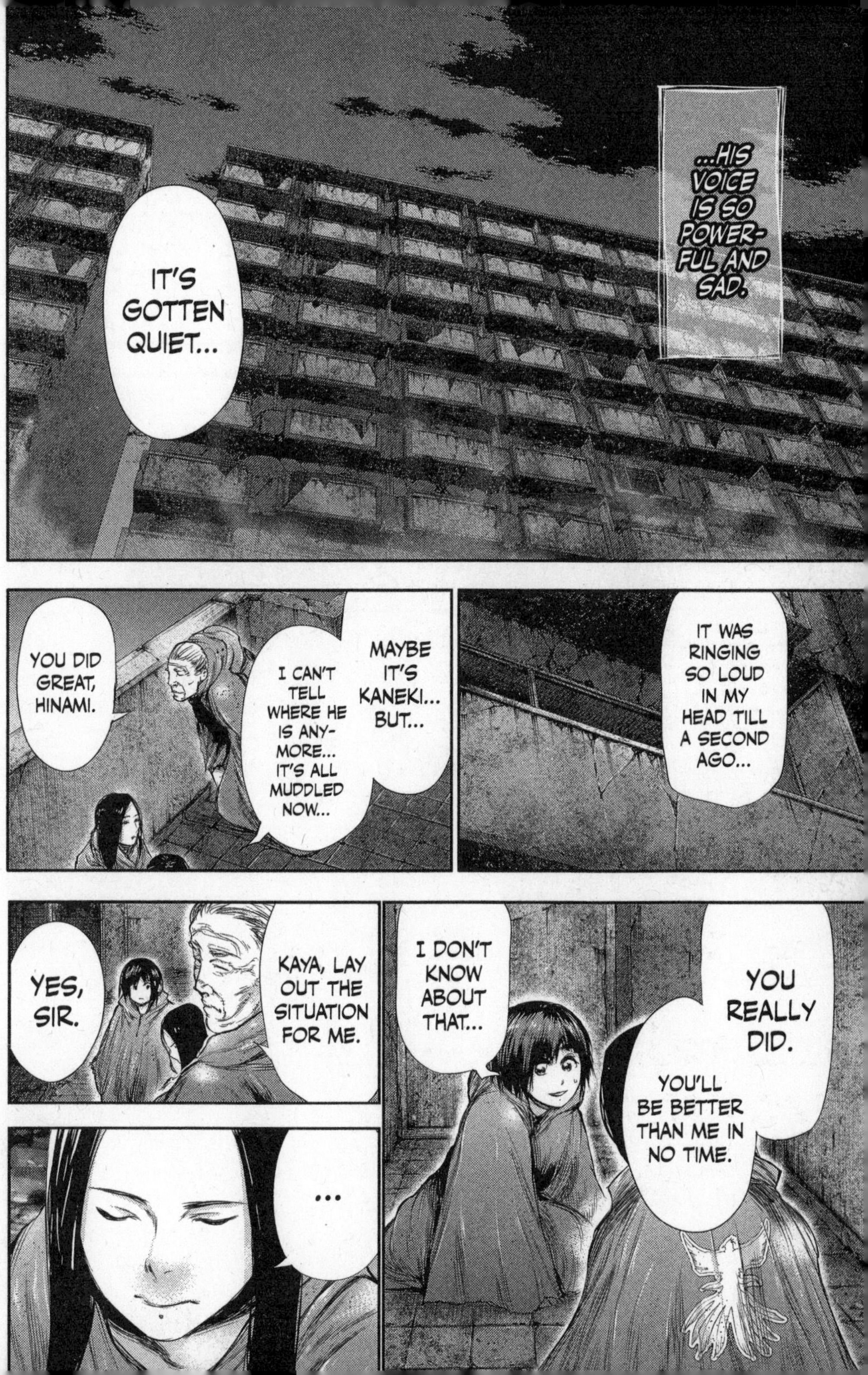
...HIS VOICE IS SO POWERFUL AND SAD.
IT'S GOTTEN QUIET...
IT WAS RINGING SO LOUD IN MY HEAD TILL A SECOND AGO...
MAYBE IT'S KANEKI... BUT...
I CAN'T TELL WHERE HE IS ANYMORE... IT'S ALL MUDDLED NOW...
YOU DID GREAT, HINAMI.
YOU REALLY DID.
YOU'LL BE BETTER THAN ME IN NO TIME.
I DON'T KNOW ABOUT THAT...
KAYA, LAY OUT THE SITUATION FOR ME.
YES, SIR.
...

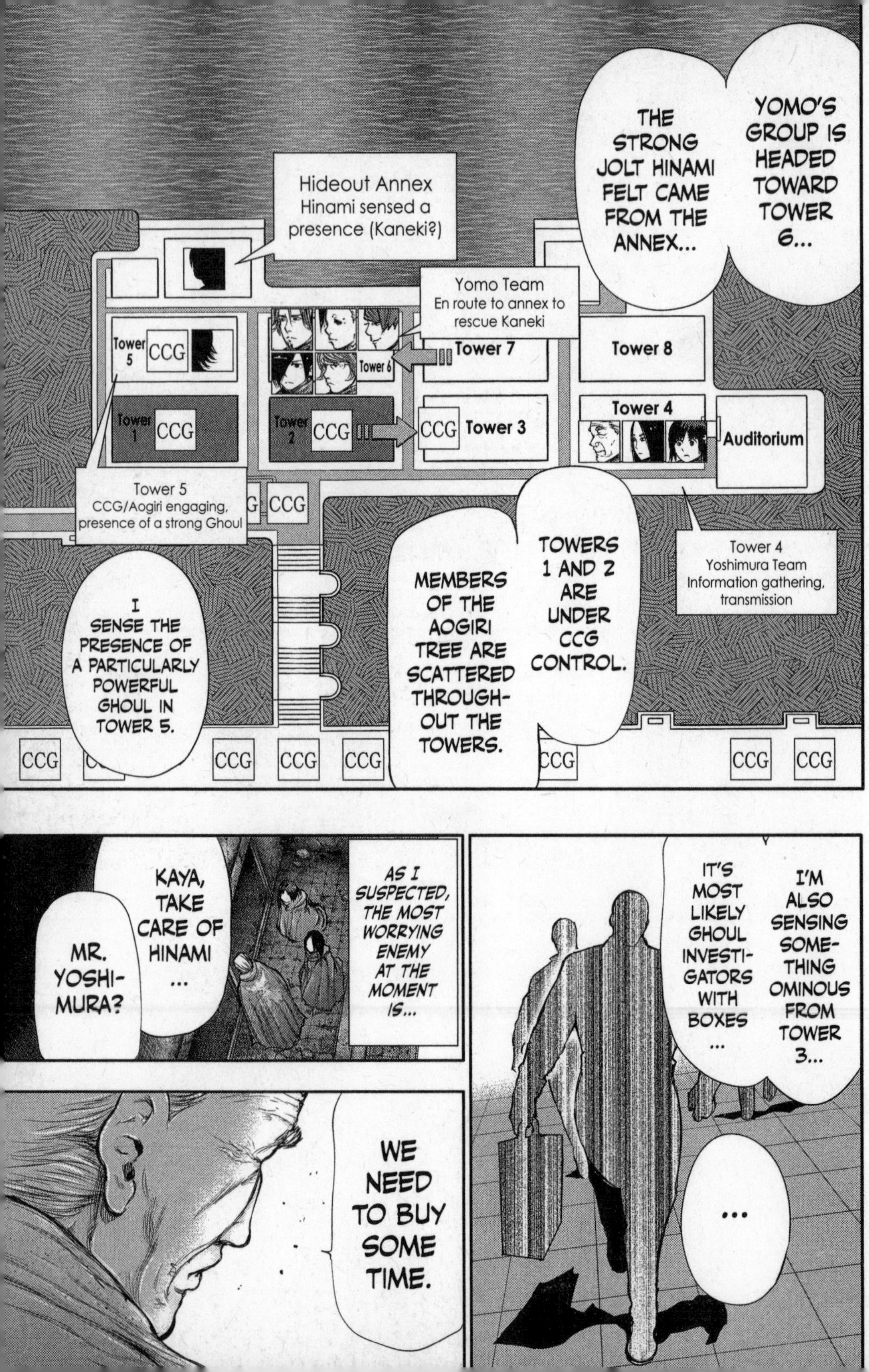
YOMO'S GROUP IS HEADED TOWARD TOWER 6...
THE STRONG JOLT HINAMI FELT CAME FROM THE ANNEX...
Hideout Annex Hinami sensed a presence (Kaneki?)
Yomo Team En route to annex to rescue Kaneki
Tower 8
Tower 7
Tower 6
Tower 5
CCG
Tower 4
Auditorium
Tower 3
Tower 2
Tower 1
Tower 4 Yoshimura Team Information gathering, transmission
Tower 5 CCG/Aogiri engaging, presence of a strong Ghoul
TOWERS 1 AND 2 ARE UNDER CCG CONTROL.
MEMBERS OF THE AOGIRI TREE ARE SCATTERED THROUGH-OUT THE TOWERS.
I SENSE THE PRESENCE OF A PARTICULARLY POWERFUL GHOUL IN TOWER 5.
I'M ALSO SENSING SOME-THING OMINOUS FROM TOWER 3...
IT'S MOST LIKELY GHOUL INVESTI-GATORS WITH BOXES ...
...
AS I SUSPECTED, THE MOST WORRYING ENEMY AT THE MOMENT IS...
KAYA, TAKE CARE OF HINAMI ...
MR. YOSHI-MURA?
WE NEED TO BUY SOME TIME.

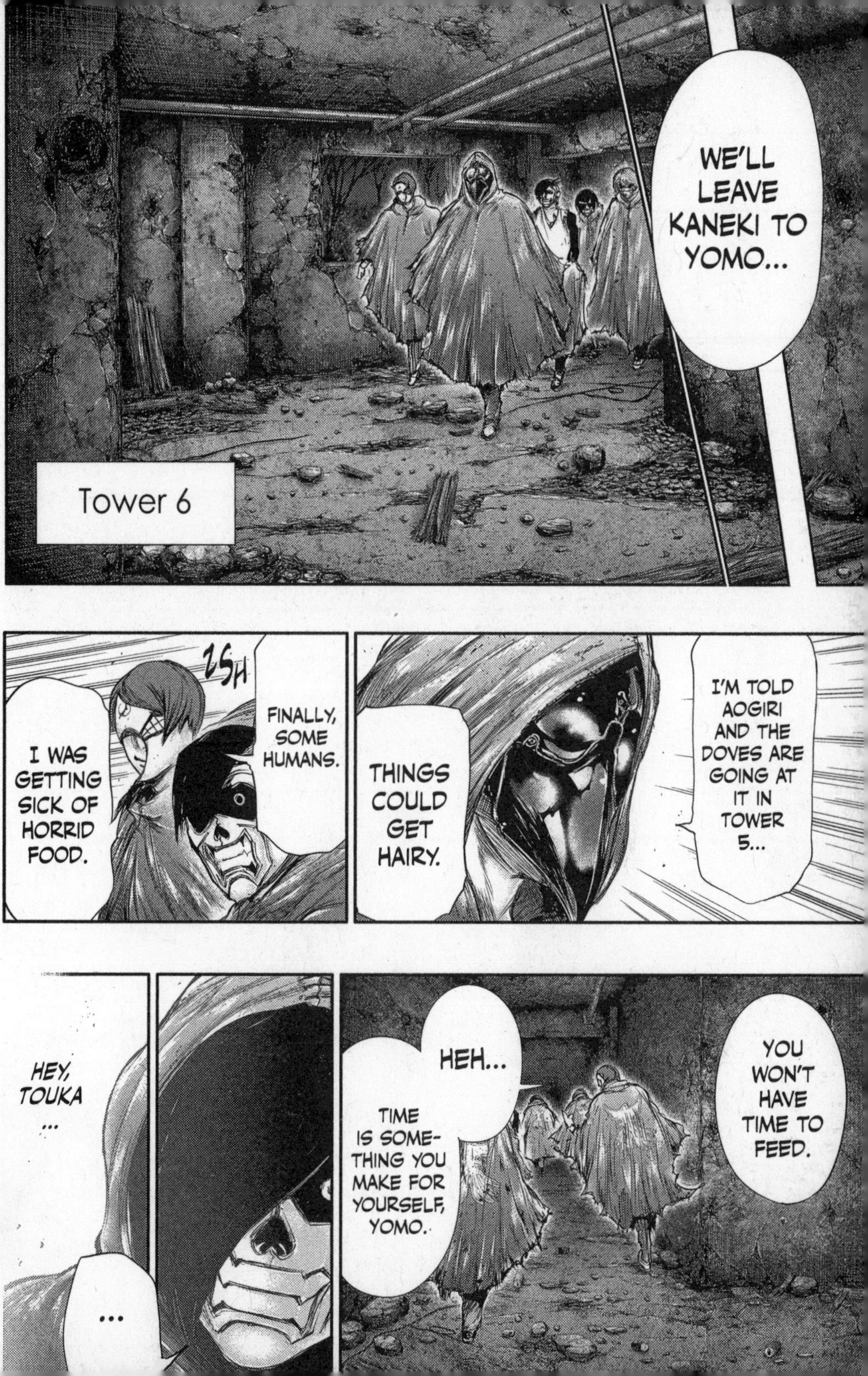
WE'LL LEAVE KANEKI TO YOMO...
Tower 6
I'M TOLD AOGIRI AND THE DOVES ARE GOING AT IT IN TOWER 5...
THINGS COULD GET HAIRY.
ZSH
FINALLY, SOME HUMANS.
I WAS GETTING SICK OF HORRID FOOD.
YOU WON'T HAVE TIME TO FEED.
HEH...
TIME IS SOME-THING YOU MAKE FOR YOURSELF, YOMO.
HEY, TOUKA ...
...

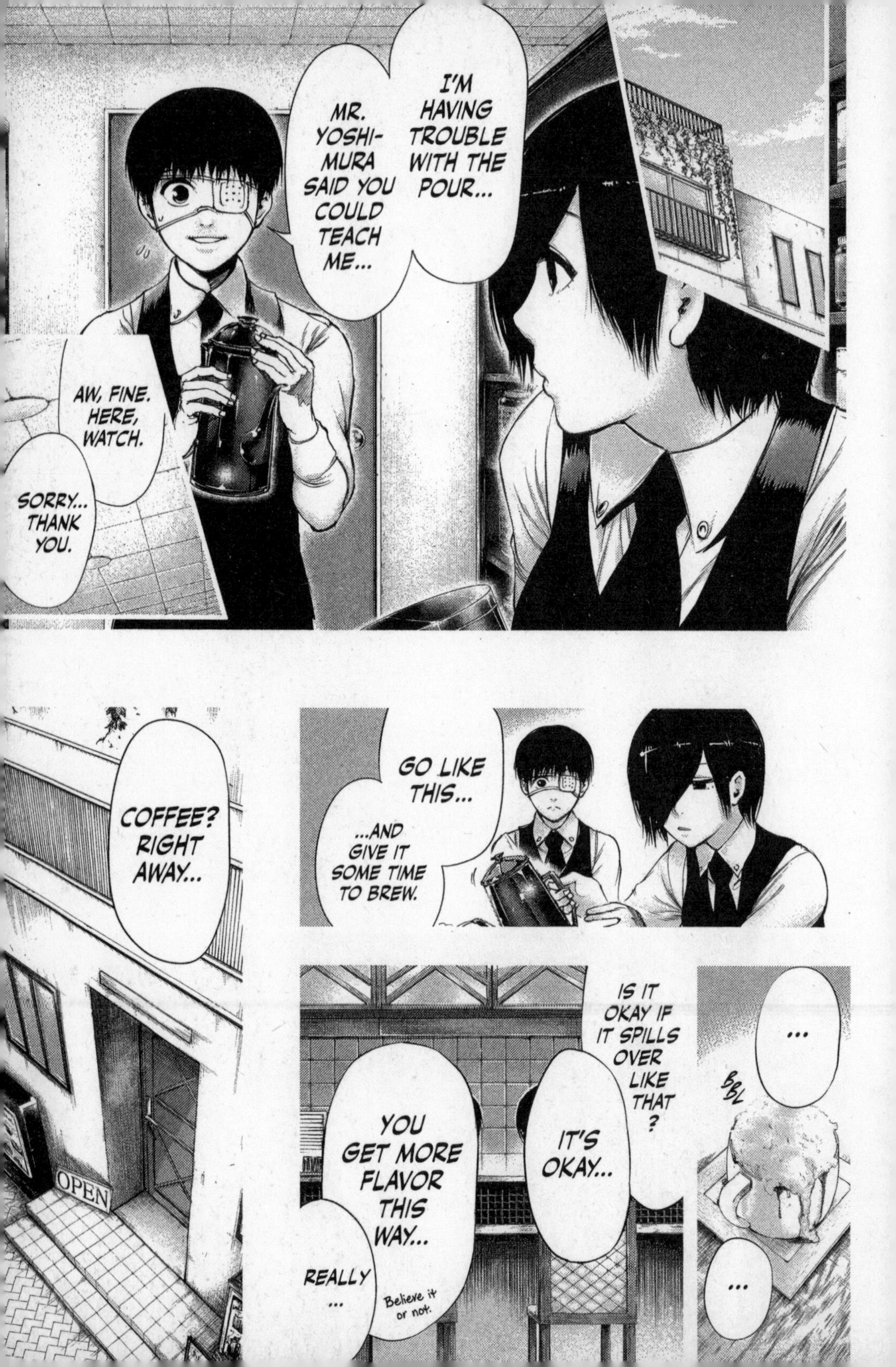
I'M HAVING TROUBLE WITH THE POUR...
MR. YOSHIMURA SAID YOU COULD TEACH ME...
AW, FINE. HERE, WATCH.
SORRY... THANK YOU.
GO LIKE THIS...
...AND GIVE IT SOME TIME TO BREW.
...
BBL
...
IS IT OKAY IF IT SPILLS OVER LIKE THAT?
IT'S OKAY...
YOU GET MORE FLAVOR THIS WAY...
REALLY...
Believe it or not.
COFFEE? RIGHT AWAY...
OPEN

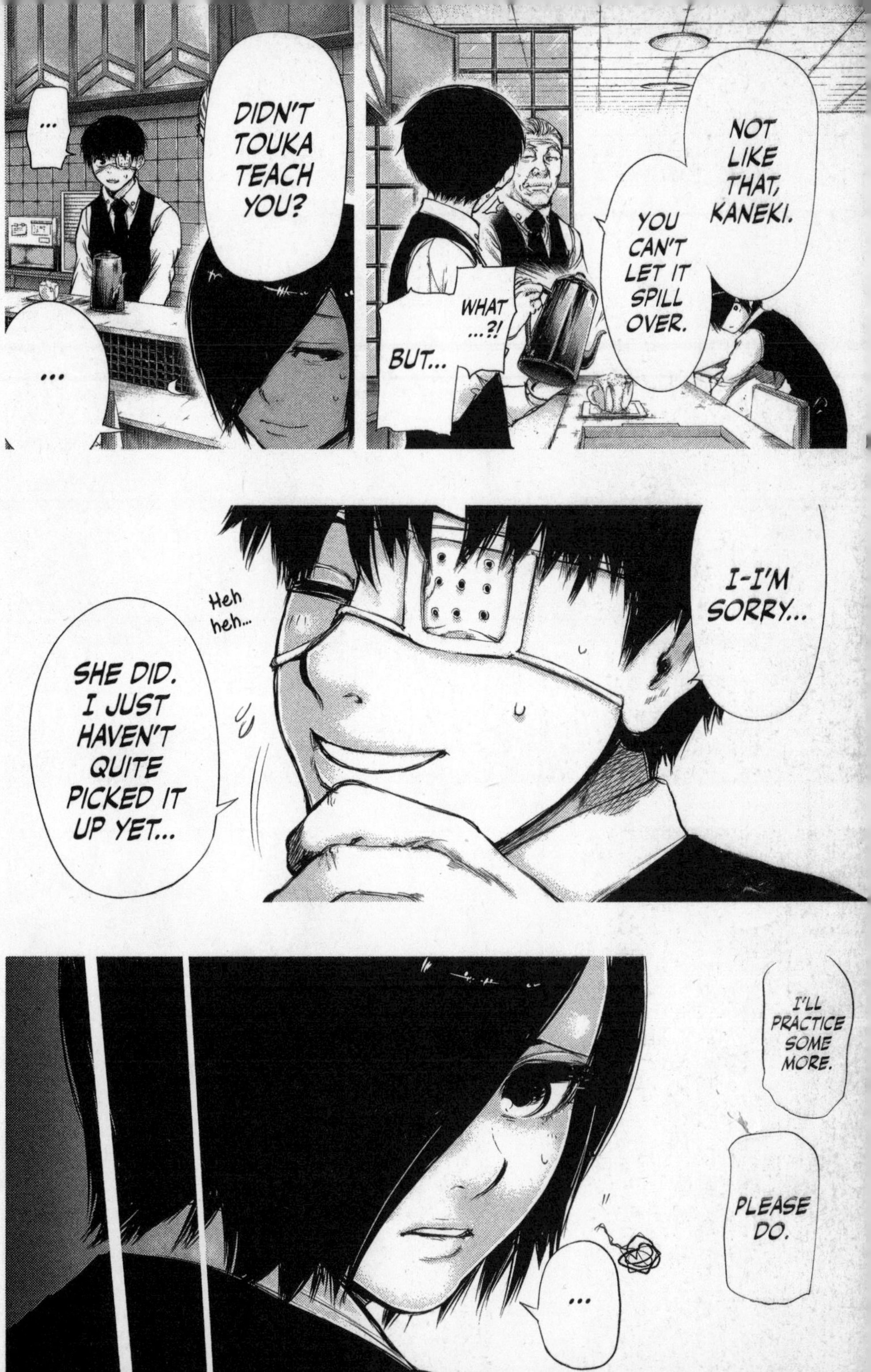
NOT LIKE THAT, KANEKI.
YOU CAN'T LET IT SPILL OVER.
WHAT ...?!
BUT...
DIDN'T TOUKA TEACH YOU?
...
...
I-I'M SORRY...
Heh heh...
SHE DID. I JUST HAVEN'T QUITE PICKED IT UP YET...
I'LL PRACTICE SOME MORE.
PLEASE DO.
...

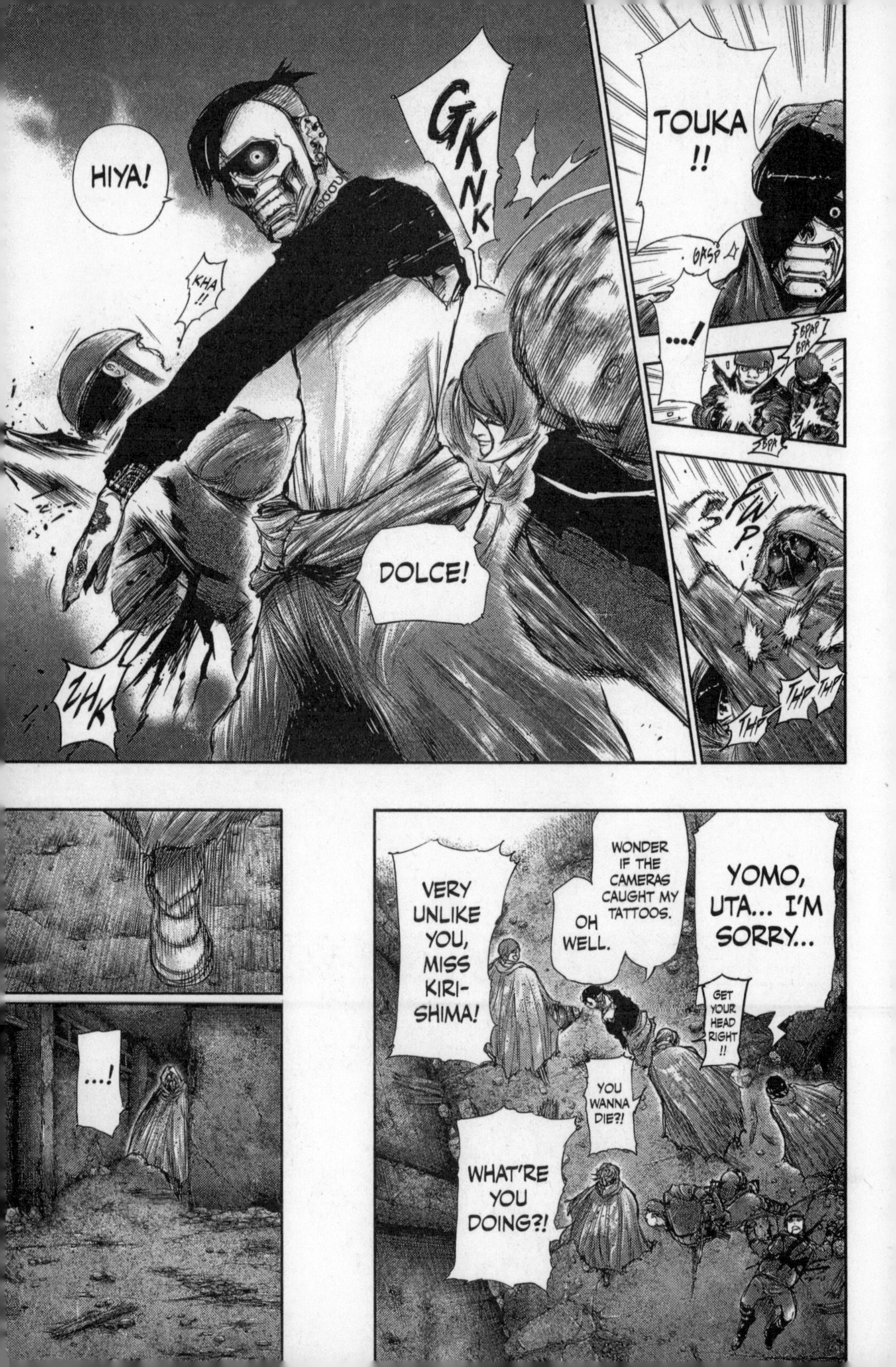
TOUKA !!
GASP
...!
BPAP BPA
BPA
FWP
THP THP THP
GKNK
HIYA!
KHA !!
DOLCE!
ZHK
YOMO, UTA... I'M SORRY...
GET YOUR HEAD RIGHT !!
WONDER IF THE CAMERAS CAUGHT MY TATTOOS.
OH WELL.
VERY UNLIKE YOU, MISS KIRI-SHIMA!
YOU WANNA DIE?!
WHAT'RE YOU DOING?!
...!

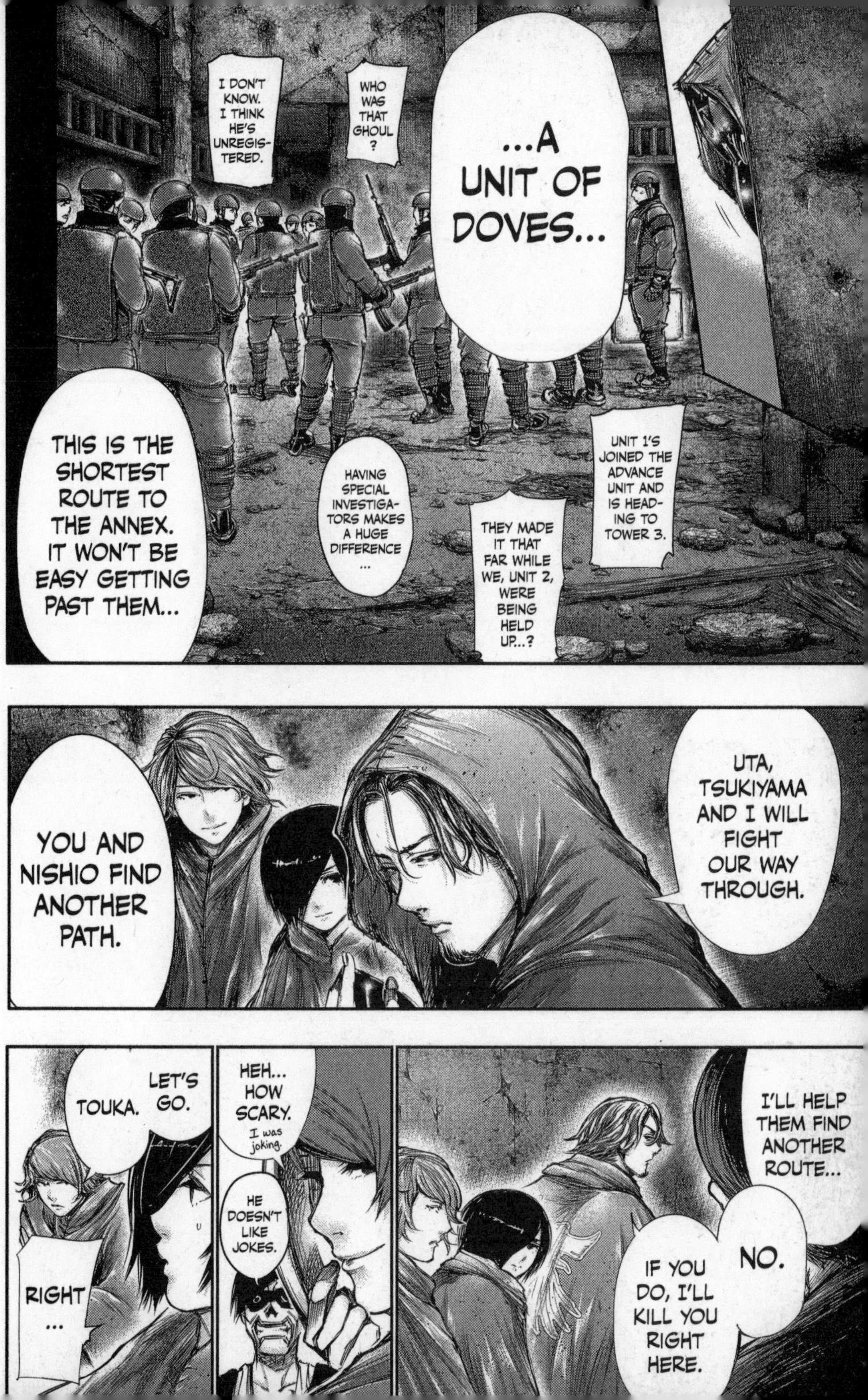
...A UNIT OF DOVES...
WHO WAS THAT GHOUL?
I DON'T KNOW. I THINK HE'S UNREGISTERED.
UNIT 1'S JOINED THE ADVANCE UNIT AND IS HEADING TO TOWER 3.
THEY MADE IT THAT FAR WHILE WE, UNIT 2, WERE BEING HELD UP...?
HAVING SPECIAL INVESTIGATORS MAKES A HUGE DIFFERENCE...
THIS IS THE SHORTEST ROUTE TO THE ANNEX. IT WON'T BE EASY GETTING PAST THEM...
UTA, TSUKIYAMA AND I WILL FIGHT OUR WAY THROUGH.
YOU AND NISHIO FIND ANOTHER PATH.
I'LL HELP THEM FIND ANOTHER ROUTE...
NO.
IF YOU DO, I'LL KILL YOU RIGHT HERE.
HEH... HOW SCARY.
I was joking.
HE DOESN'T LIKE JOKES.
TOUKA. LET'S GO.
RIGHT...

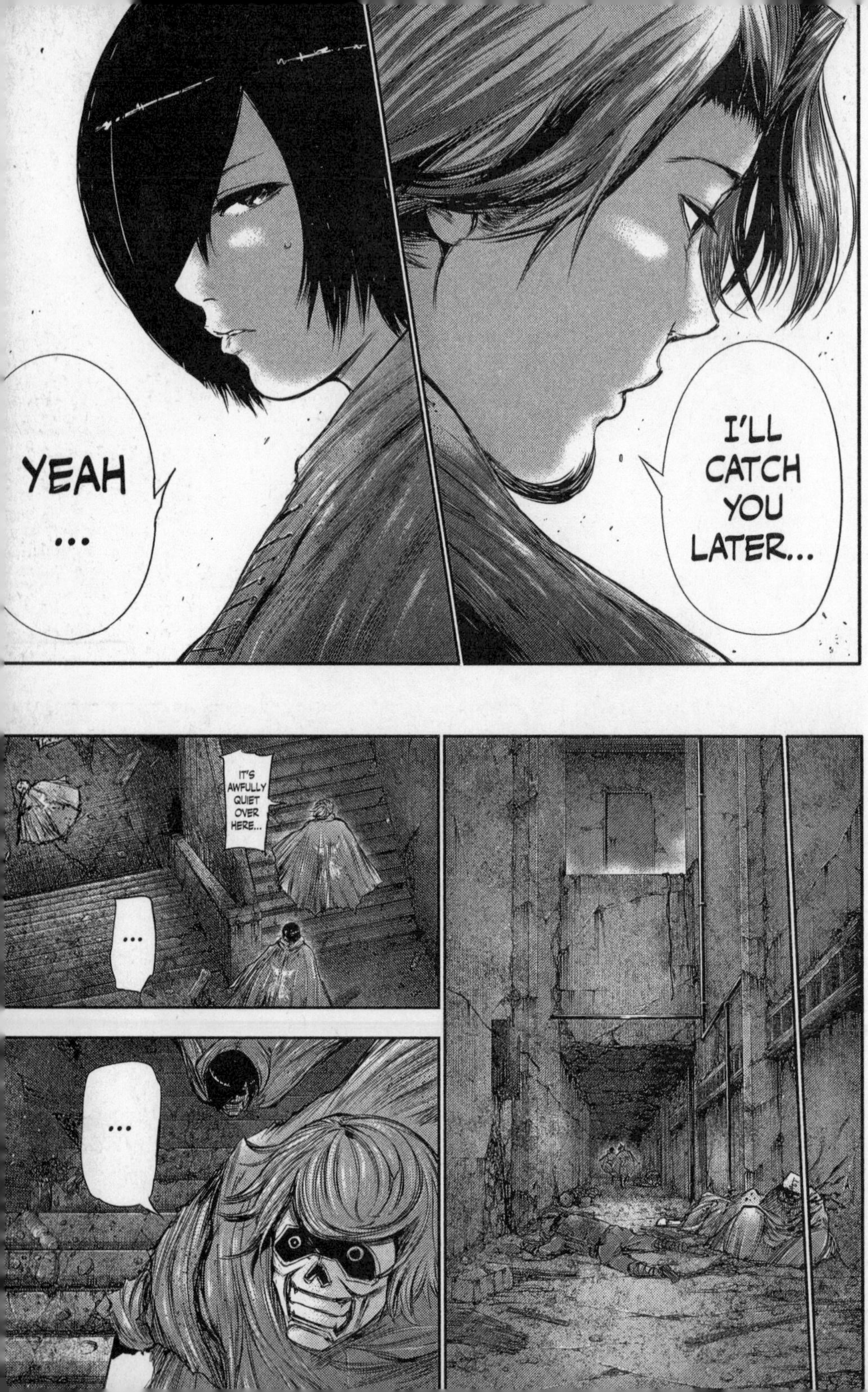
I'LL CATCH YOU LATER...
YEAH ...
IT'S AWFULLY QUIET OVER HERE...
...
...

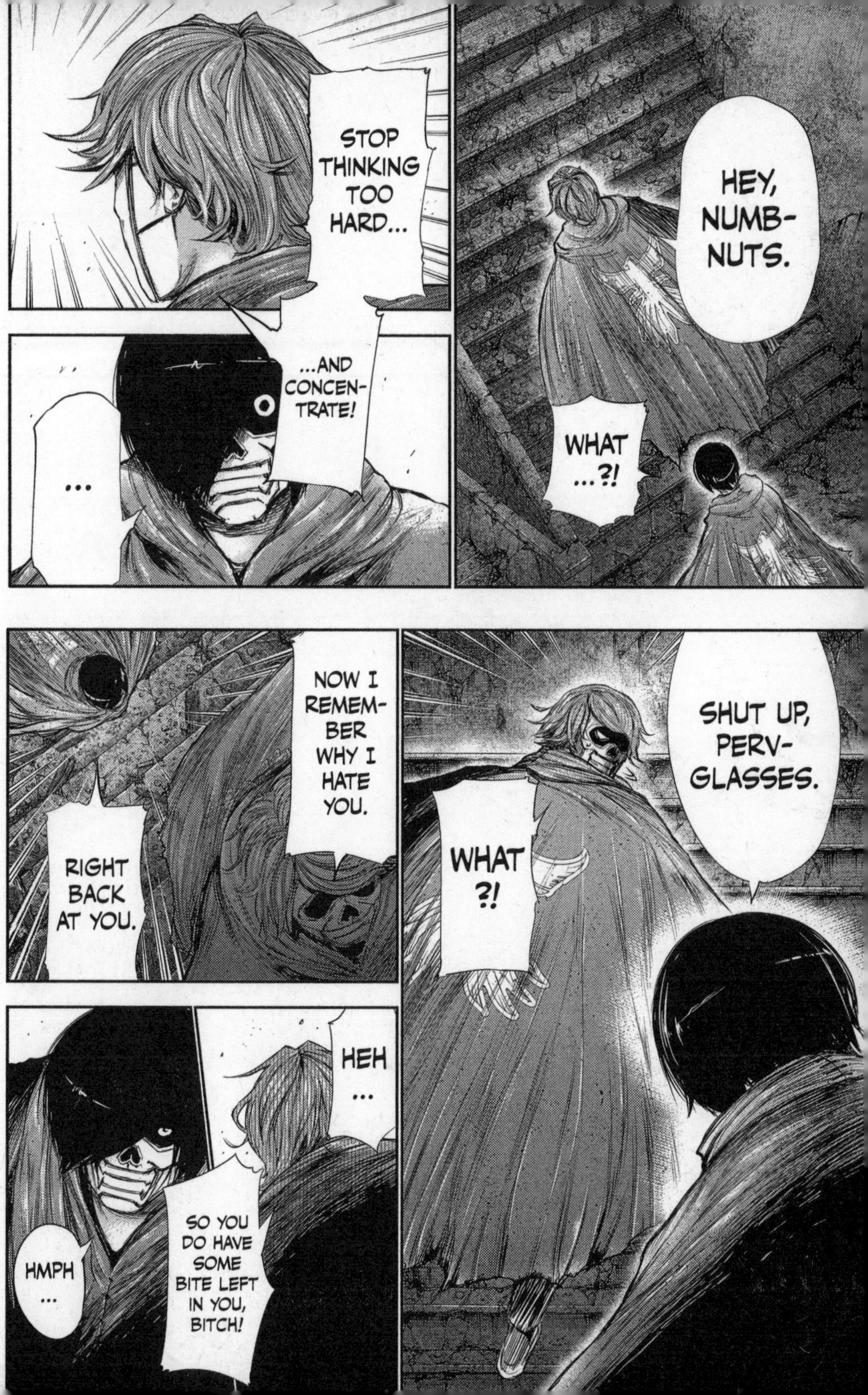
HEY, NUMB-NUTS.
WHAT ...?!
STOP THINKING TOO HARD...
...AND CONCENTRATE!
...
SHUT UP, PERV-GLASSES.
WHAT ?!
NOW I REMEMBER WHY I HATE YOU.
RIGHT BACK AT YOU.
HEH ...
SO YOU DO HAVE SOME BITE LEFT IN YOU, BITCH!
HMPH ...

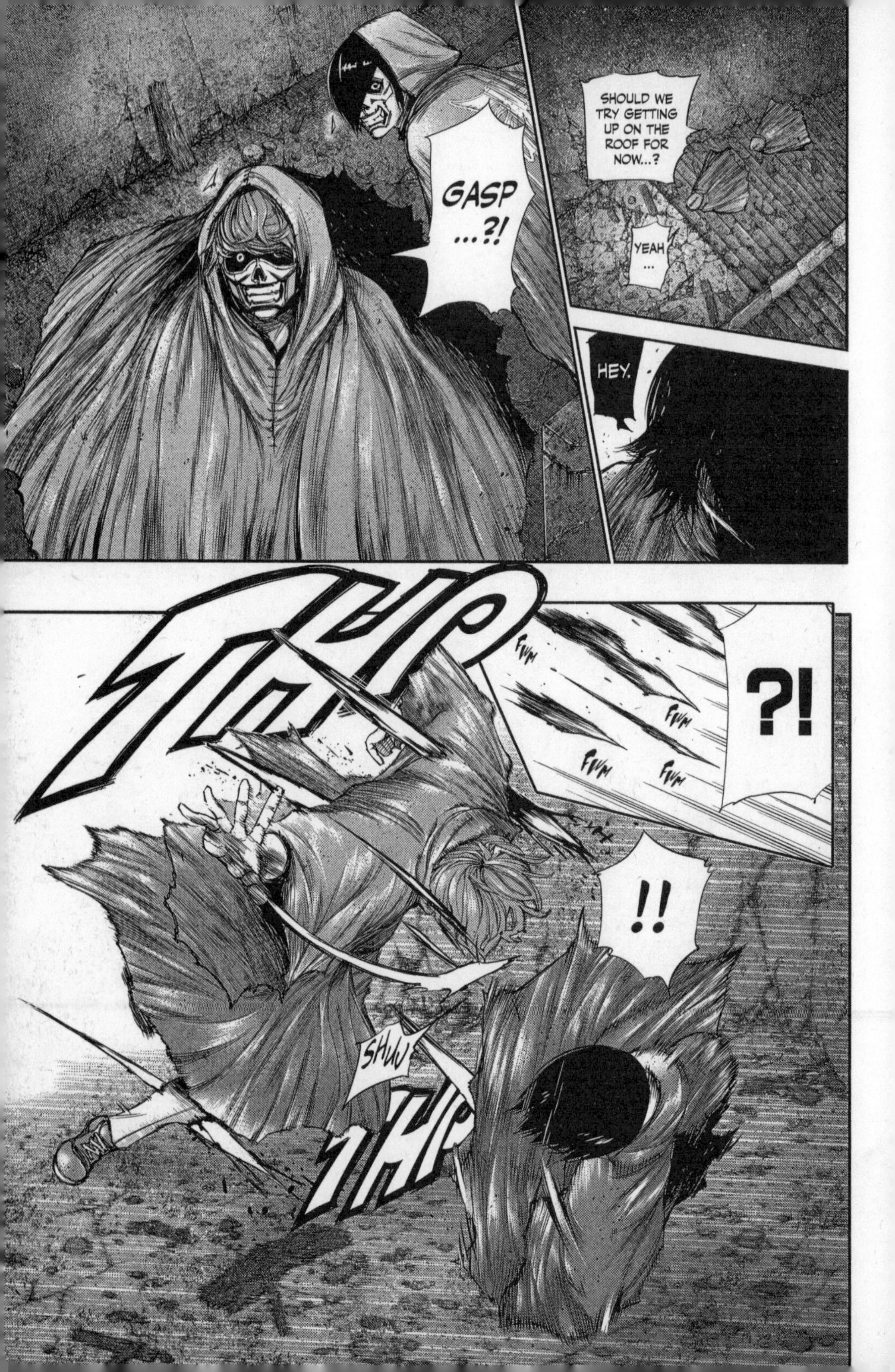
SHOULD WE TRY GETTING UP ON THE ROOF FOR NOW...?
YEAH ...
HEY.
GASP ...?!
?!
FWUM
FWUM
FWUM
FWUM
FWUM
!!
SHUU

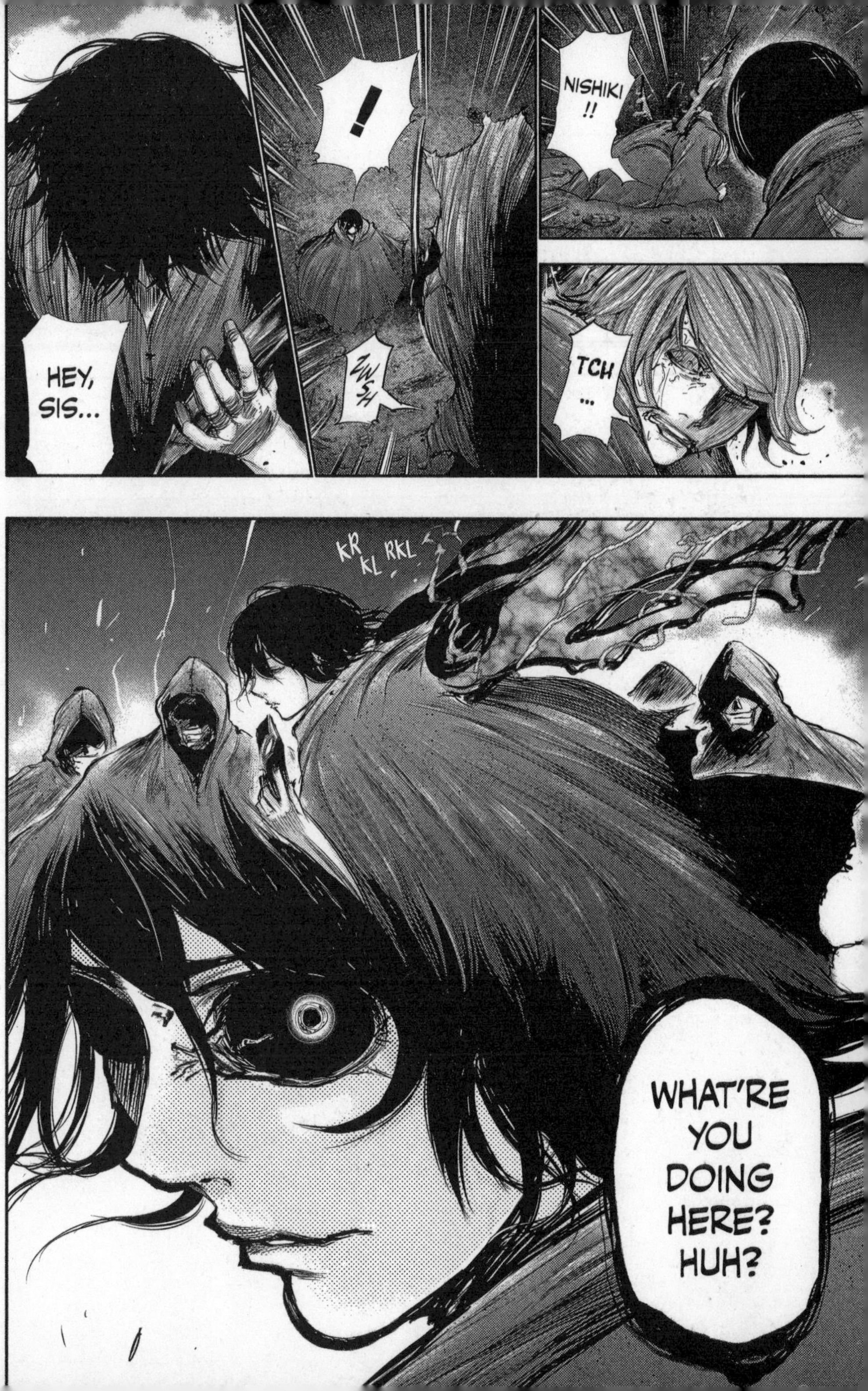
NISHIKI !!
TCH ...
!
ZWSH
HEY, SIS...
KR KL RKL
WHAT'RE YOU DOING HERE? HUH?

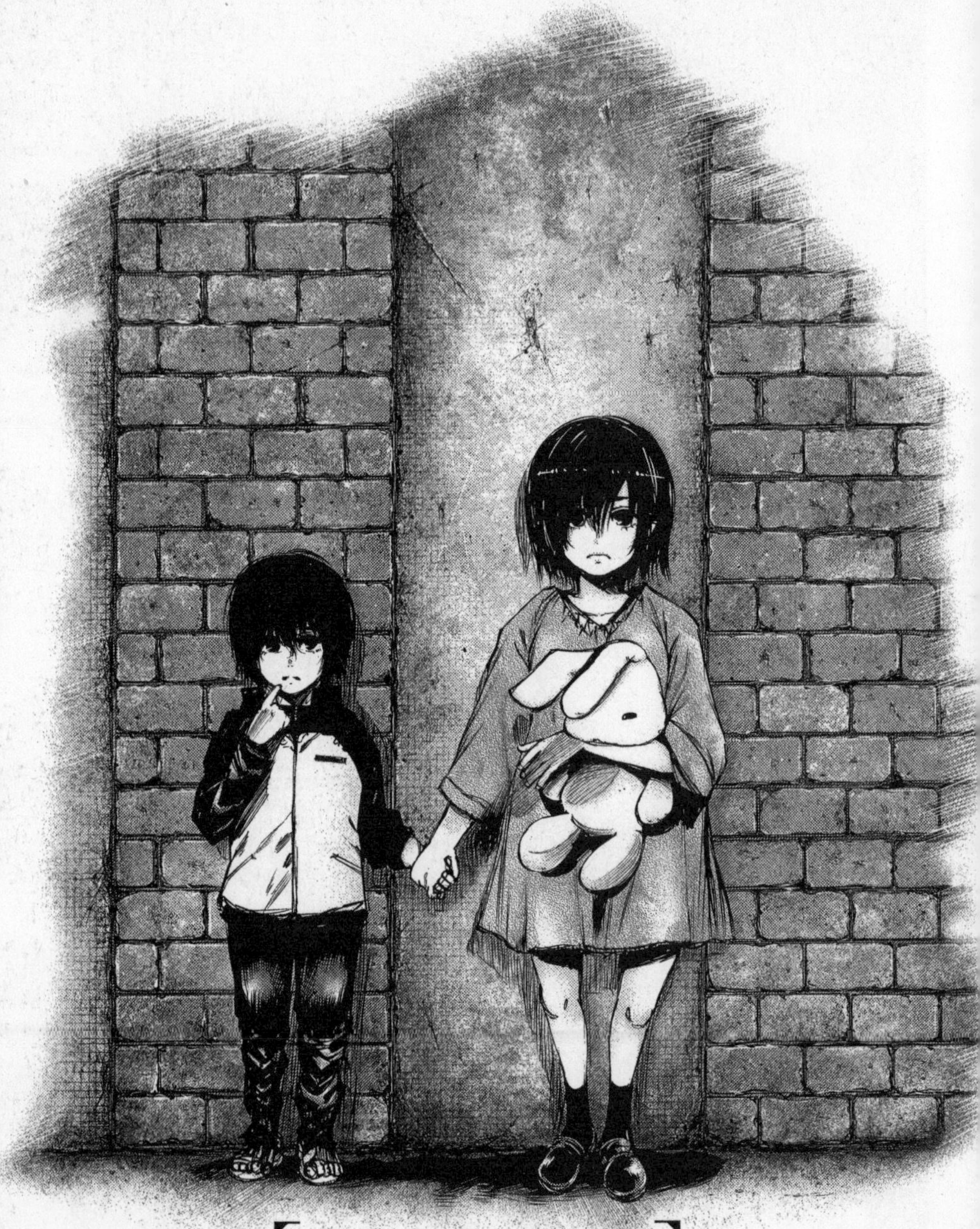

#068 [ENCOUNTER]

TOKYO GHOUL

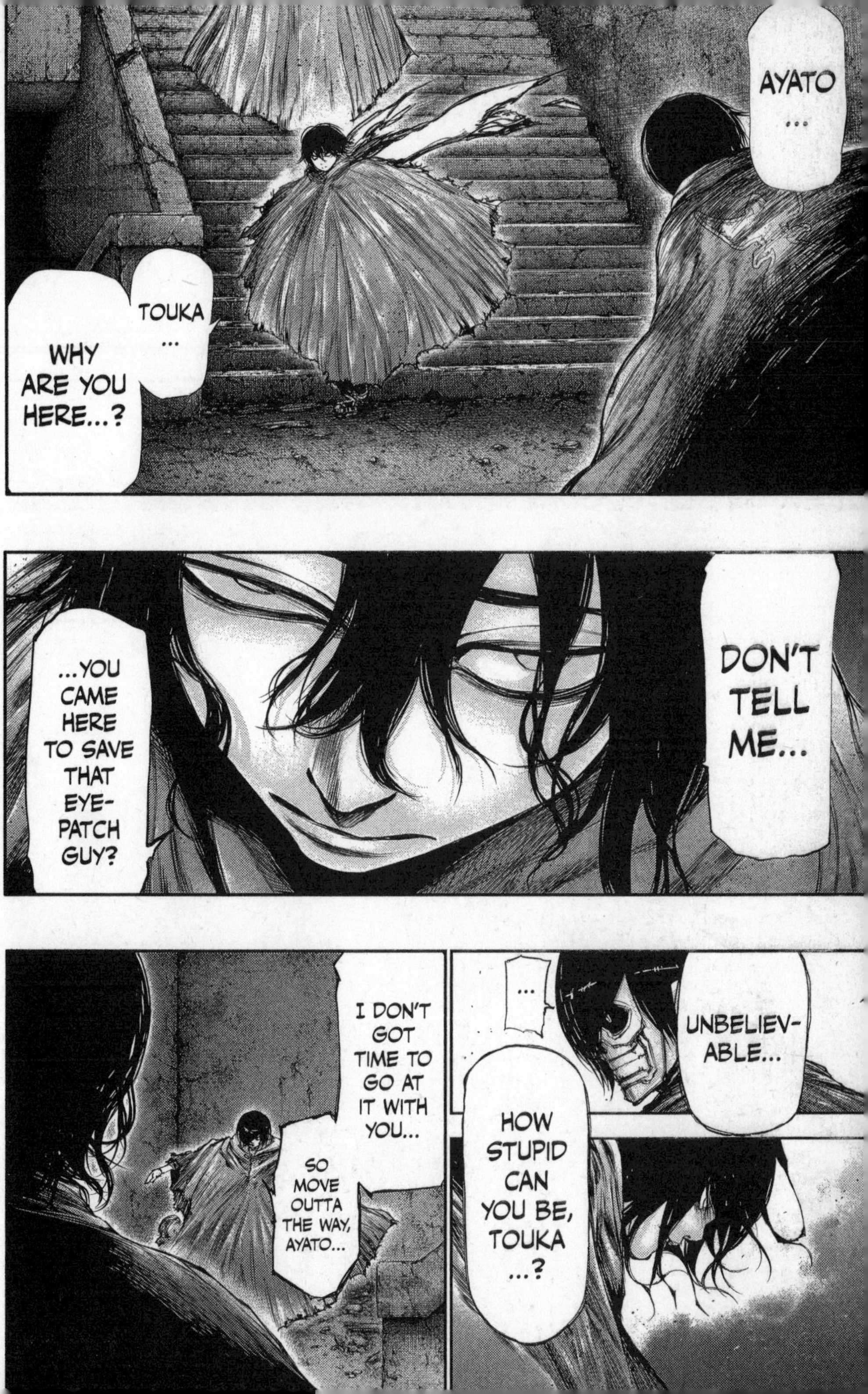
AYATO ...
TOUKA ...
WHY ARE YOU HERE...?
DON'T TELL ME...
...YOU CAME HERE TO SAVE THAT EYE-PATCH GUY?
UNBELIEV-ABLE...
...
HOW STUPID CAN YOU BE, TOUKA ...?
I DON'T GOT TIME TO GO AT IT WITH YOU...
SO MOVE OUTTA THE WAY, AYATO...

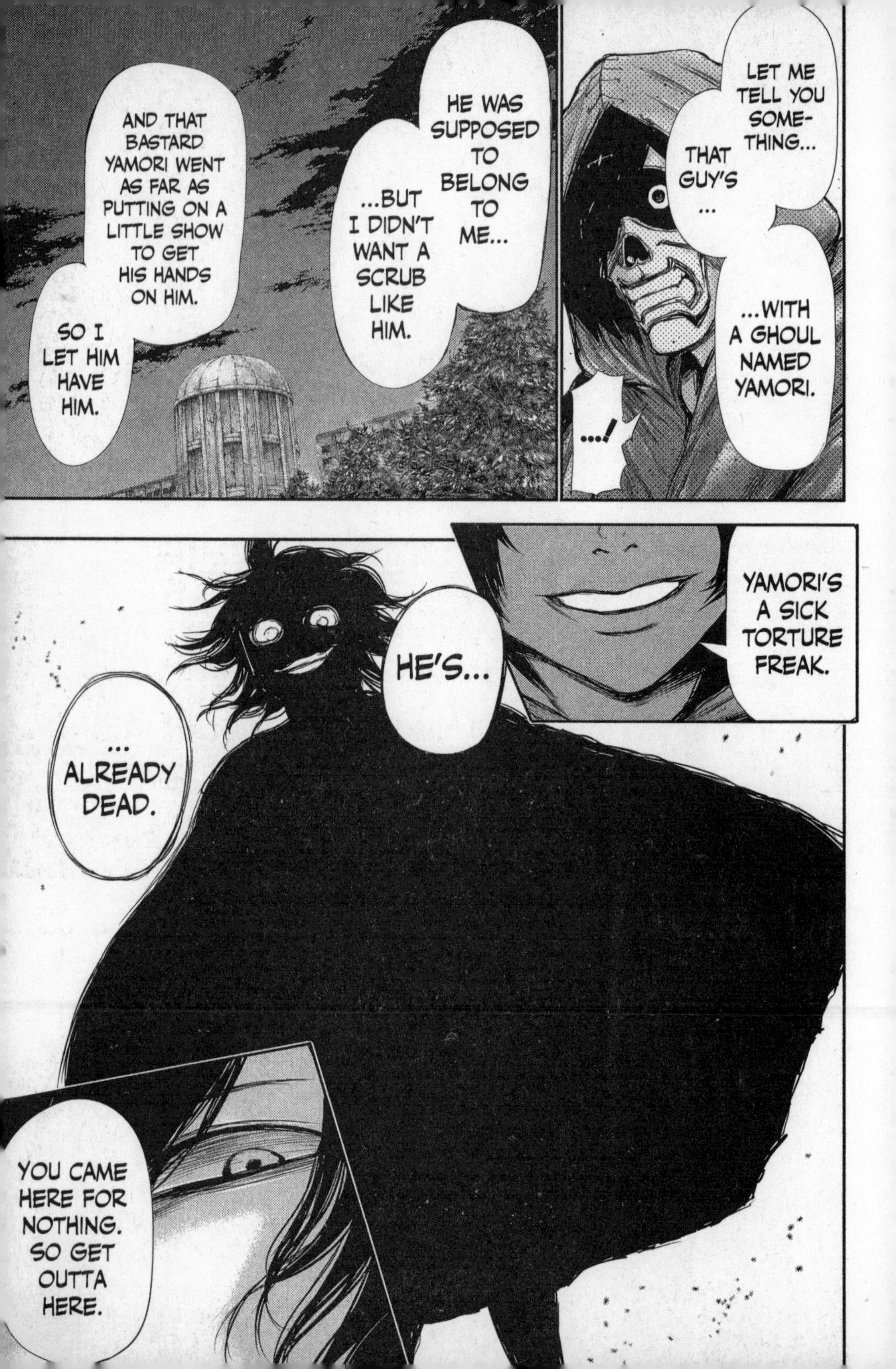

LET ME TELL YOU SOME-THING...
THAT GUY'S ...
...WITH A GHOUL NAMED YAMORI.
...!
HE WAS SUPPOSED TO BELONG TO ME...
...BUT I DIDN'T WANT A SCRUB LIKE HIM.
AND THAT BASTARD YAMORI WENT AS FAR AS PUTTING ON A LITTLE SHOW TO GET HIS HANDS ON HIM.
SO I LET HIM HAVE HIM.
YAMORI'S A SICK TORTURE FREAK.
HE'S...
... ALREADY DEAD.
YOU CAME HERE FOR NOTHING. SO GET OUTTA HERE.

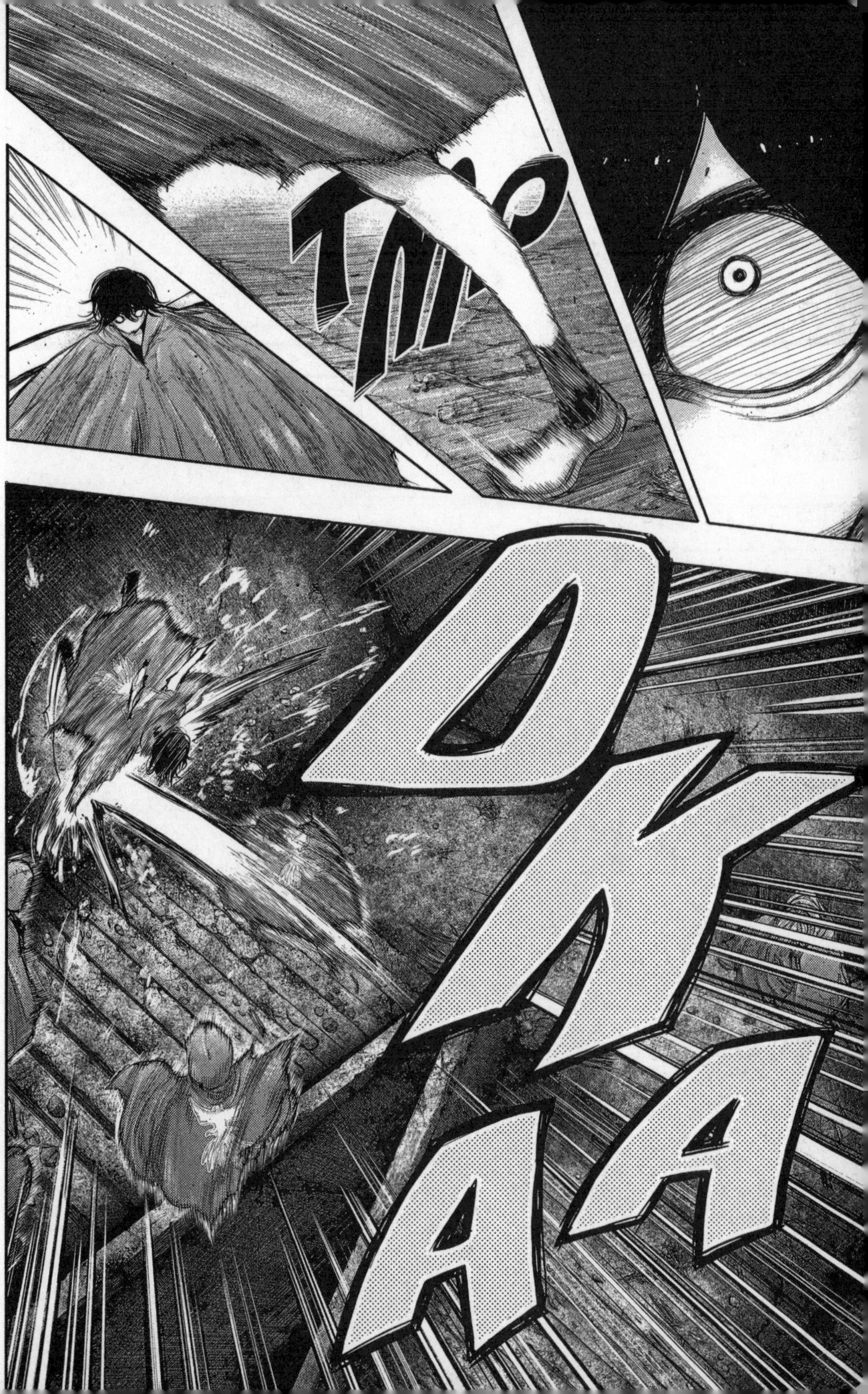
THP
DKAA

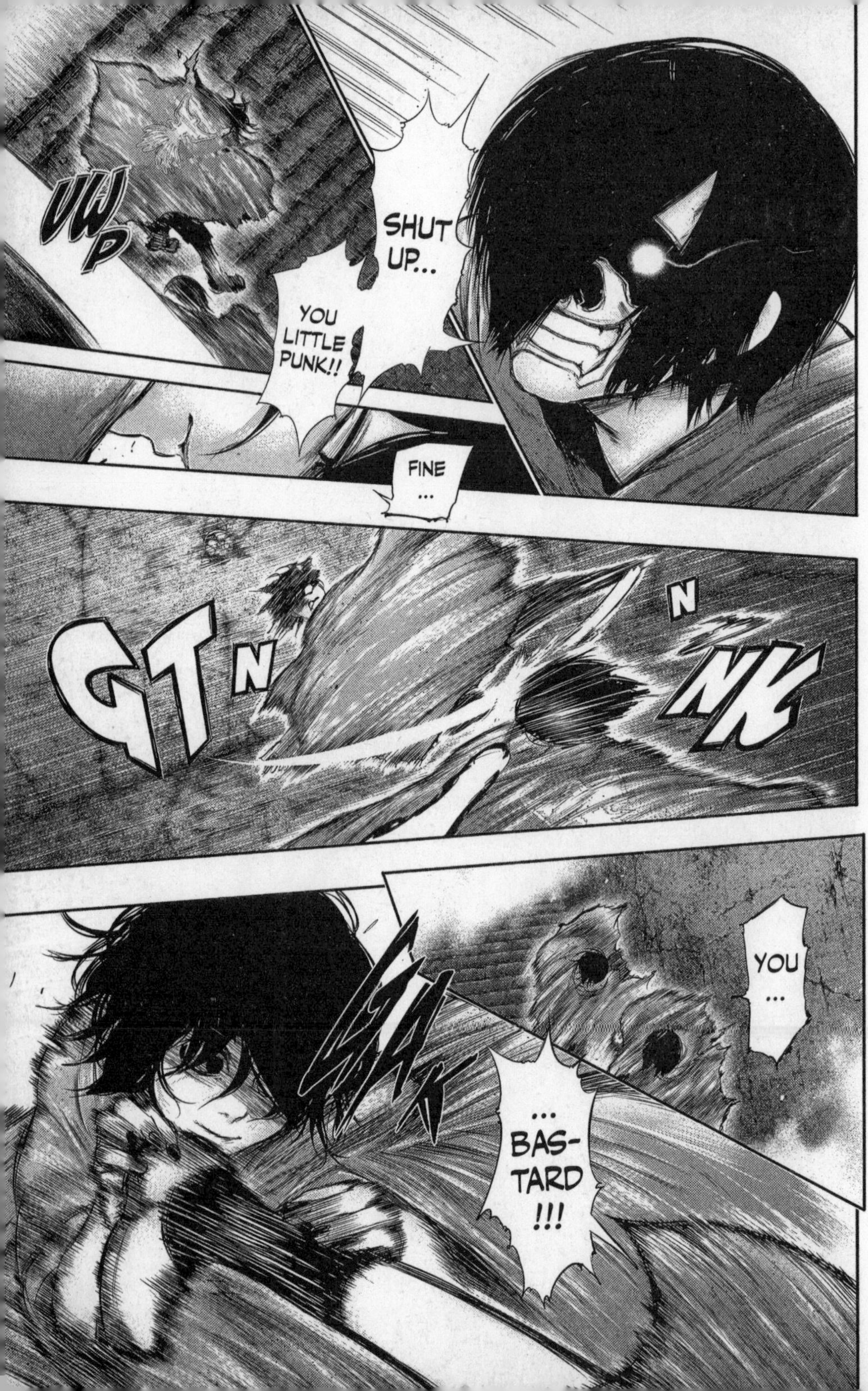
SHUT UP...
YOU LITTLE PUNK!!
FINE ...
GTNNNK
YOU ...
... BAS-TARD !!!

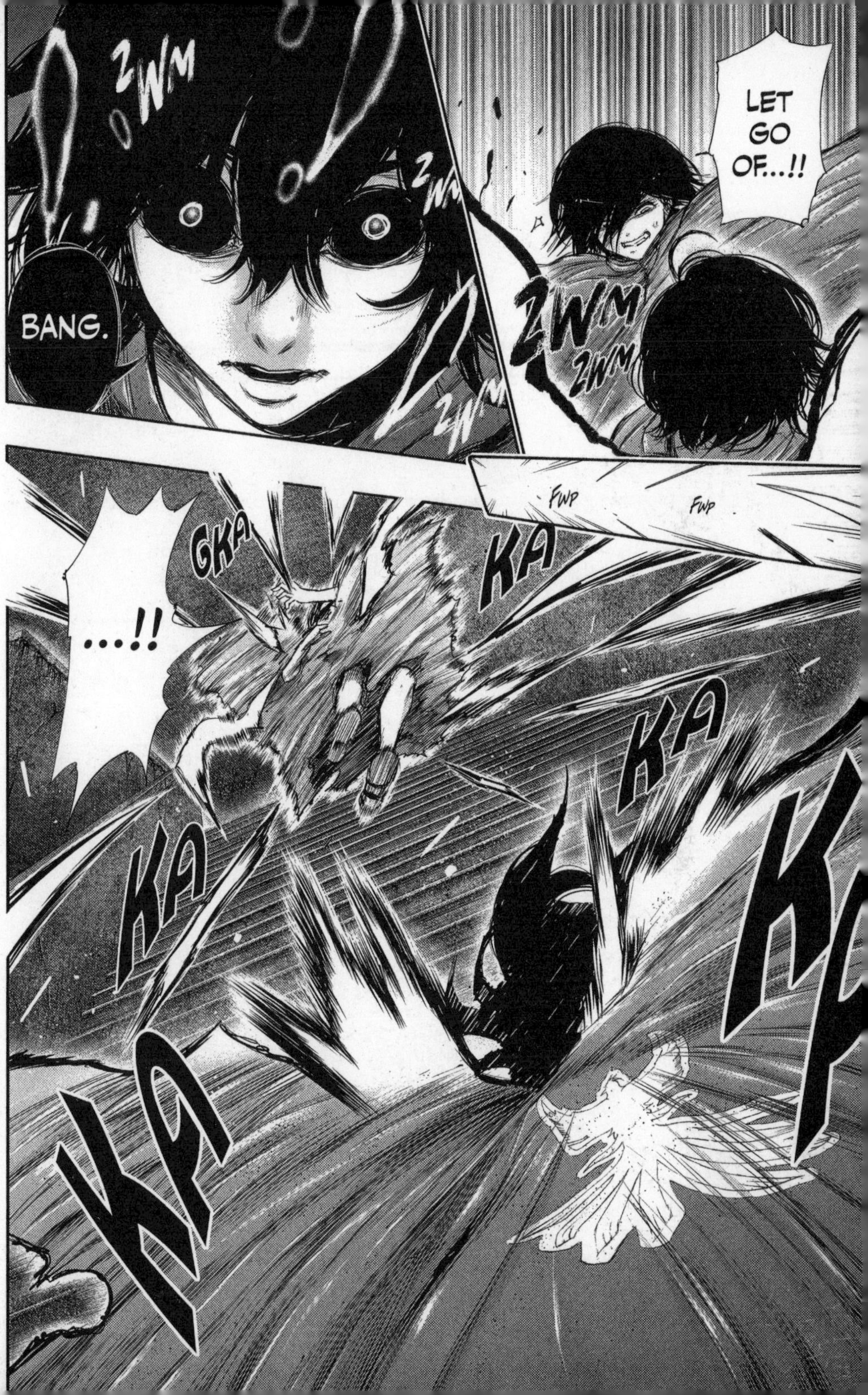
LET GO OF...!!
ZWM
ZWM
ZWM
ZWM
BANG.
ZWM
FWP
FWP
KA
GKA
...!!
KA
KA
KA
KA

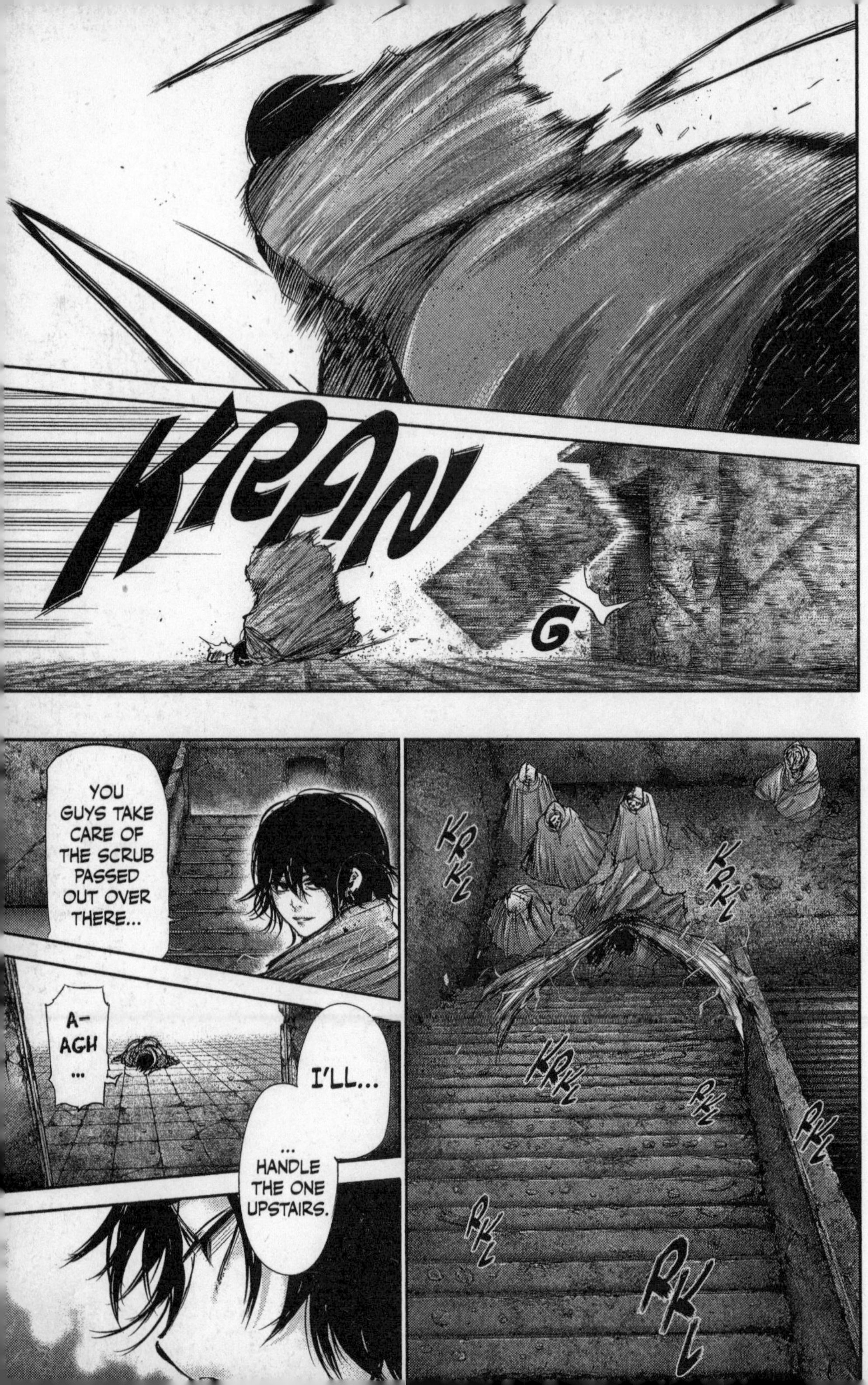
G
KRKL
KRKL
KRKL
RKL
RKL
RKL
RKL
YOU GUYS TAKE CARE OF THE SCRUB PASSED OUT OVER THERE...
A-AGH...
I'LL...
...HANDLE THE ONE UPSTAIRS.

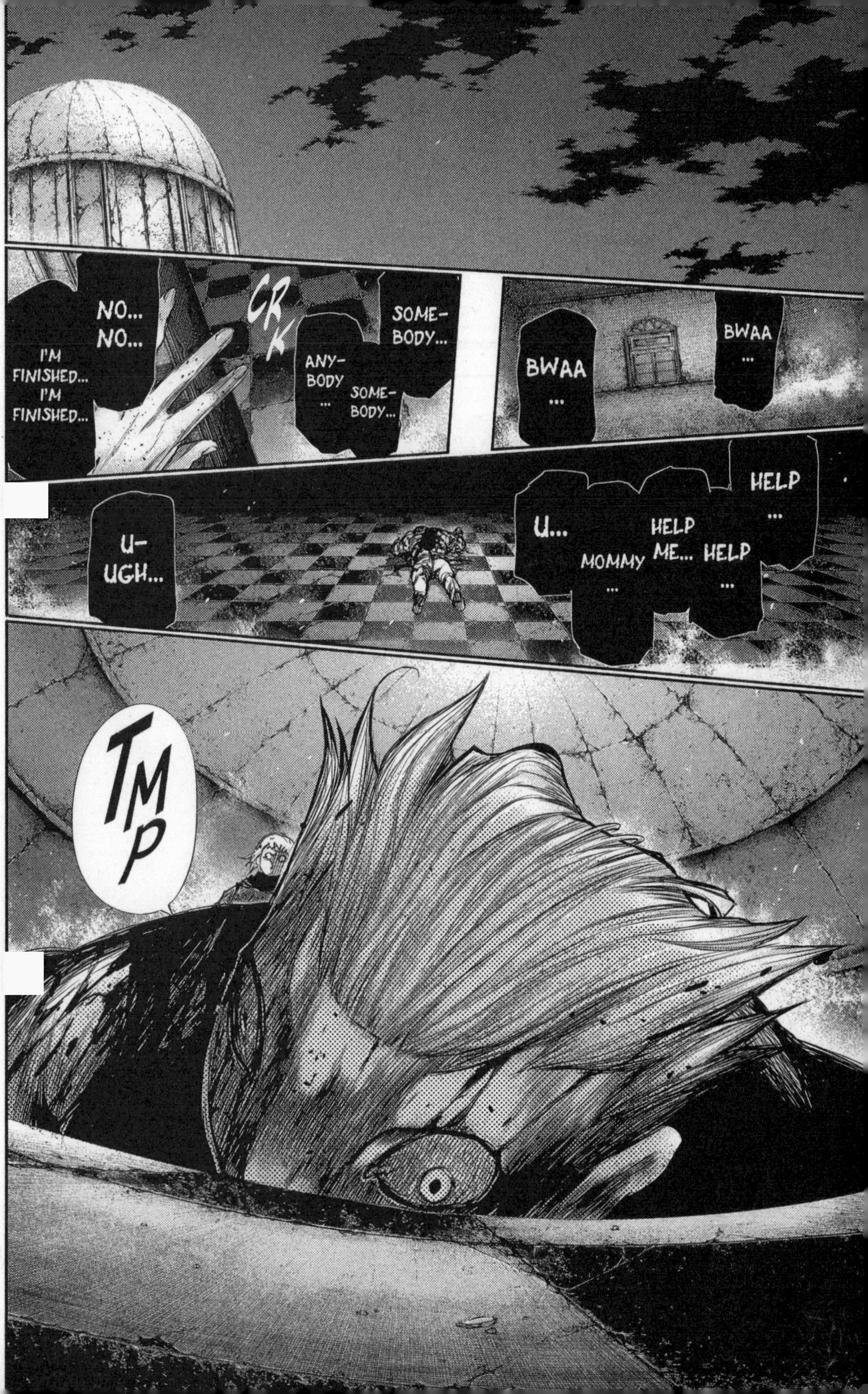
BWAA...
BWAA...
SOME-BODY...
ANY-BODY...
SOME-BODY...
CRK
NO... NO...
I'M FINISHED... I'M FINISHED...
HELP...
HELP ME... HELP...
U...
MOMMY...
U-UGH...
TMP

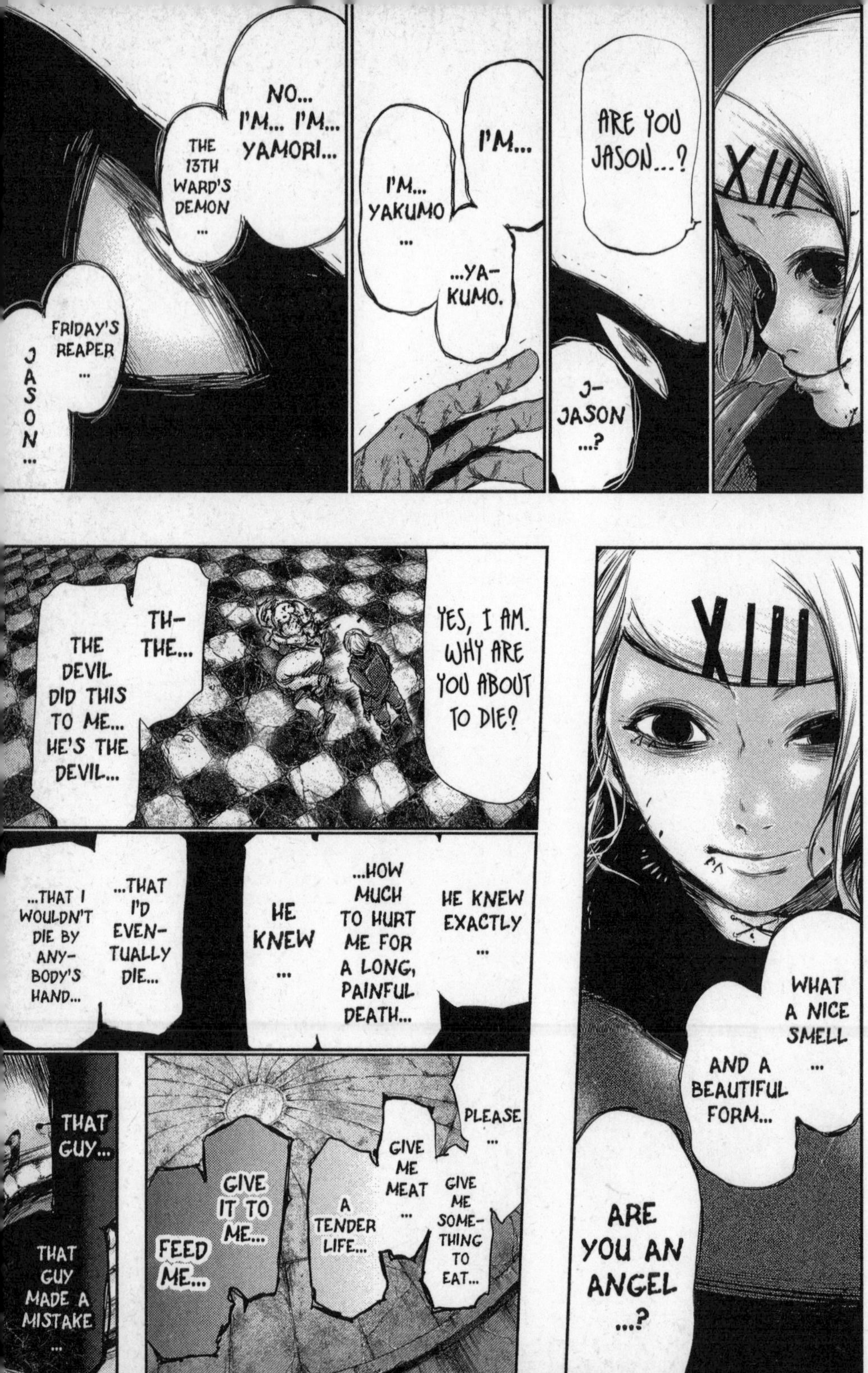
ARE YOU JASON...?
J-JASON...?
I'M...
I'M... YAKUMO...
...YA-KUMO.
NO... I'M... I'M... YAMORI...
THE 13TH WARD'S DEMON...
FRIDAY'S REAPER...
JASON...
WHAT A NICE SMELL...
AND A BEAUTIFUL FORM...
ARE YOU AN ANGEL...?
YES, I AM. WHY ARE YOU ABOUT TO DIE?
TH-THE...
THE DEVIL DID THIS TO ME... HE'S THE DEVIL...
HE KNEW EXACTLY...
...HOW MUCH TO HURT ME FOR A LONG, PAINFUL DEATH...
HE KNEW...
...THAT I'D EVENTUALLY DIE...
...THAT I WOULDN'T DIE BY ANYBODY'S HAND...
PLEASE...
GIVE ME MEAT...
GIVE ME SOMETHING TO EAT...
A TENDER LIFE...
GIVE IT TO ME...
FEED ME...
THAT GUY...
THAT GUY MADE A MISTAKE...

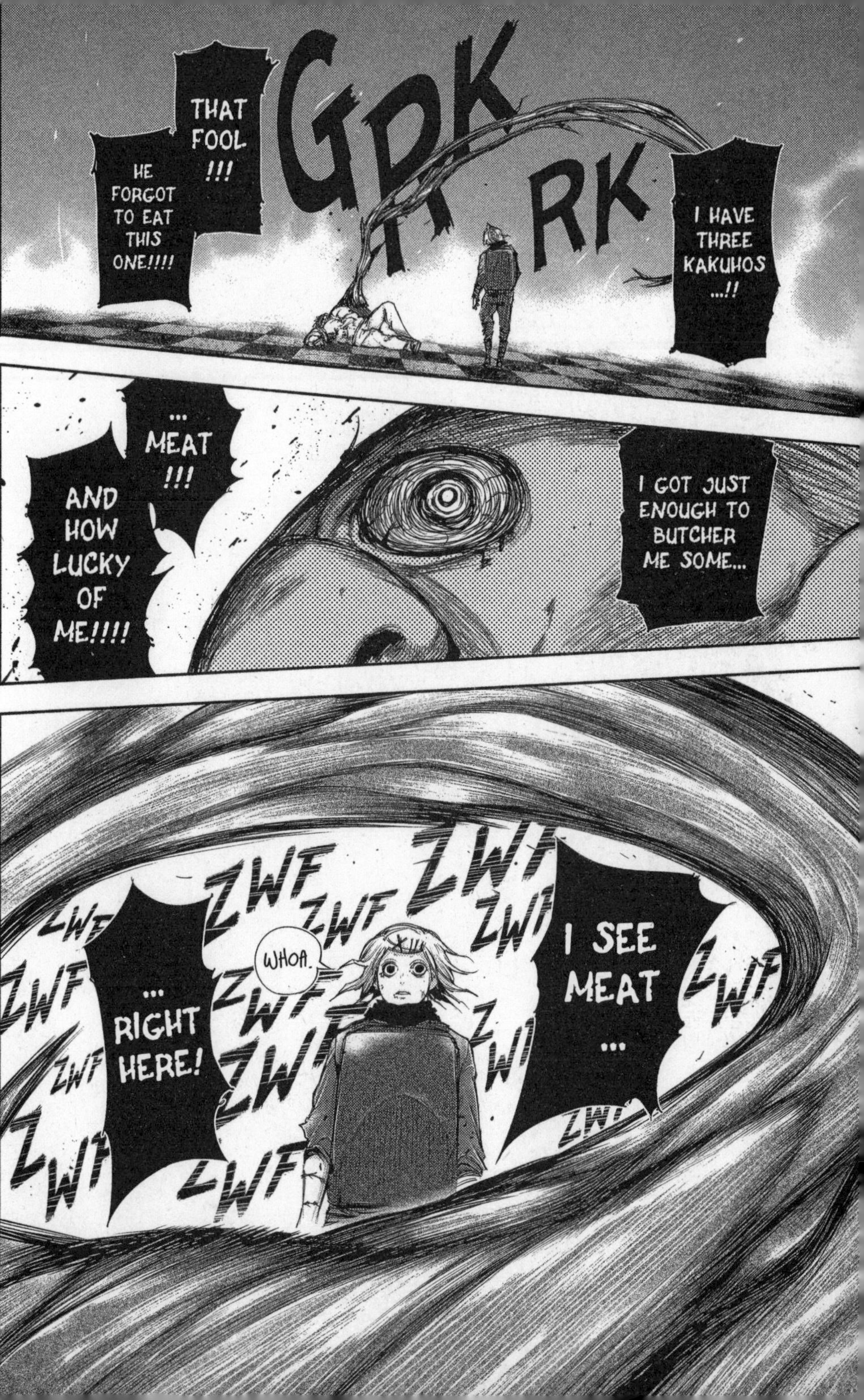
I HAVE THREE KAKUHOS ...!!
GPK RK
THAT FOOL!!!
HE FORGOT TO EAT THIS ONE!!!!
I GOT JUST ENOUGH TO BUTCHER ME SOME...
...MEAT!!!
AND HOW LUCKY OF ME!!!!
ZWF ZWF ZWF ZWF ZWF
I SEE MEAT...
WHOA.
...RIGHT HERE!
ZWF ZWF ZWF ZWF ZWF

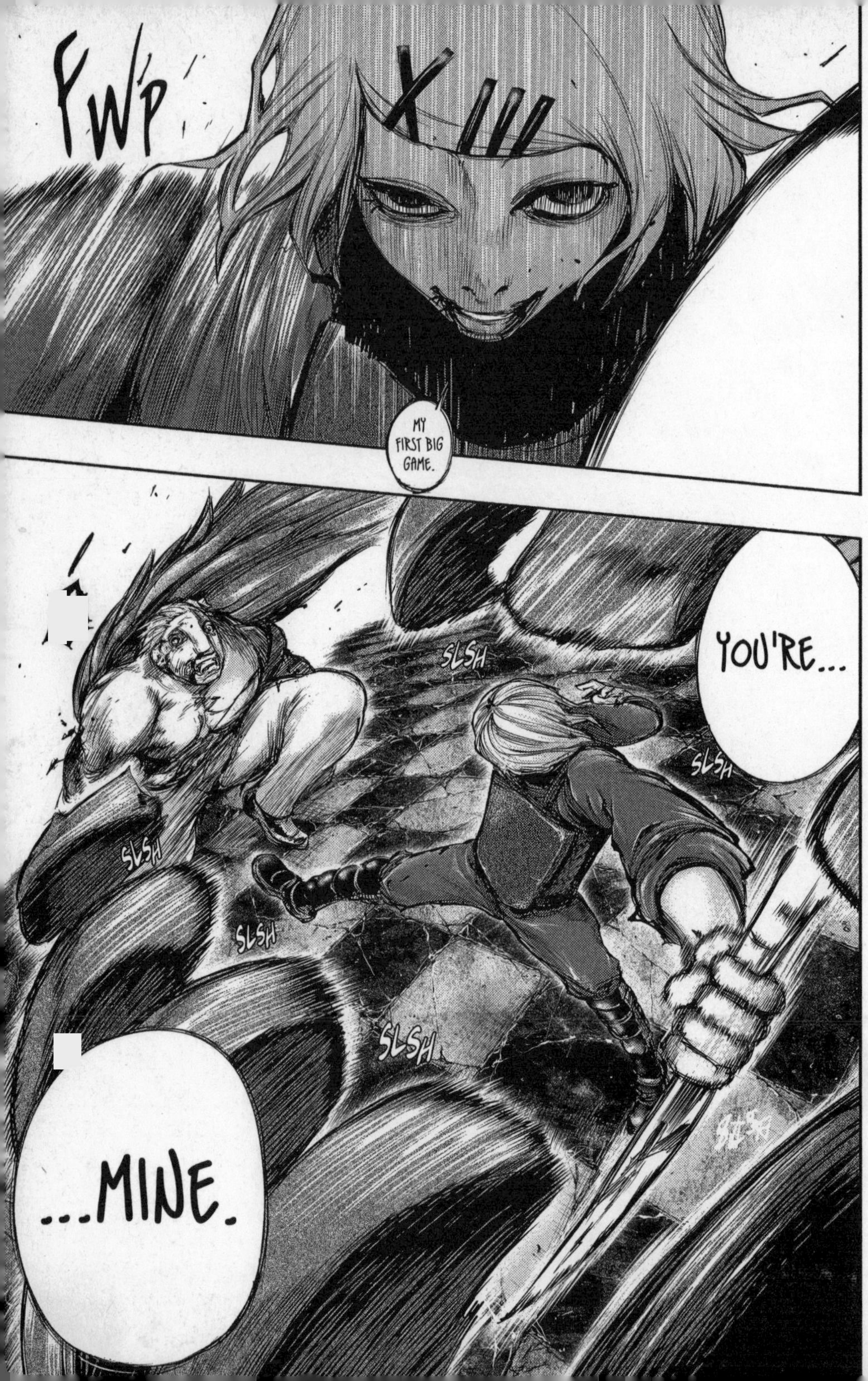
FWP
MY FIRST BIG GAME.
YOU'RE...
SLSH
SLSH
SLSH
SLSH
SLSH
...MINE.

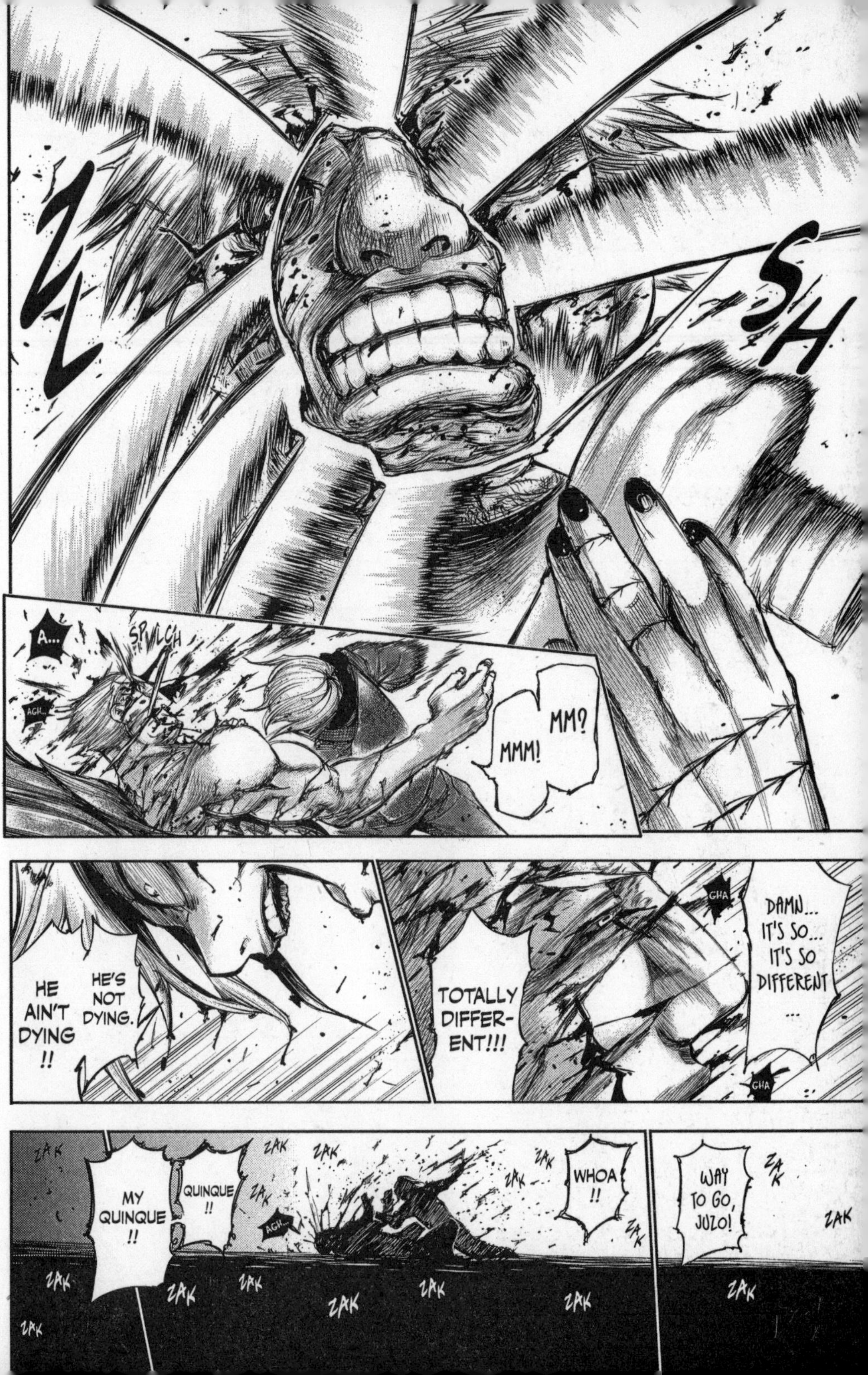
SH
ZZ
MM?
MMM!
A...
SPLLCH
AGH...
DAMN... IT'S SO... IT'S SO DIFFERENT ...
GHA
GHA
TOTALLY DIFFER-ENT!!!
HE'S NOT DYING.
HE AIN'T DYING !!
ZAK
WAY TO GO, JUZO!
ZAK
ZAK
WHOA !!
ZAK
QUINQUE !!
MY QUINQUE !!
AGH...
ZAK
ZAK
ZAK
ZAK
ZAK
ZAK
ZAK

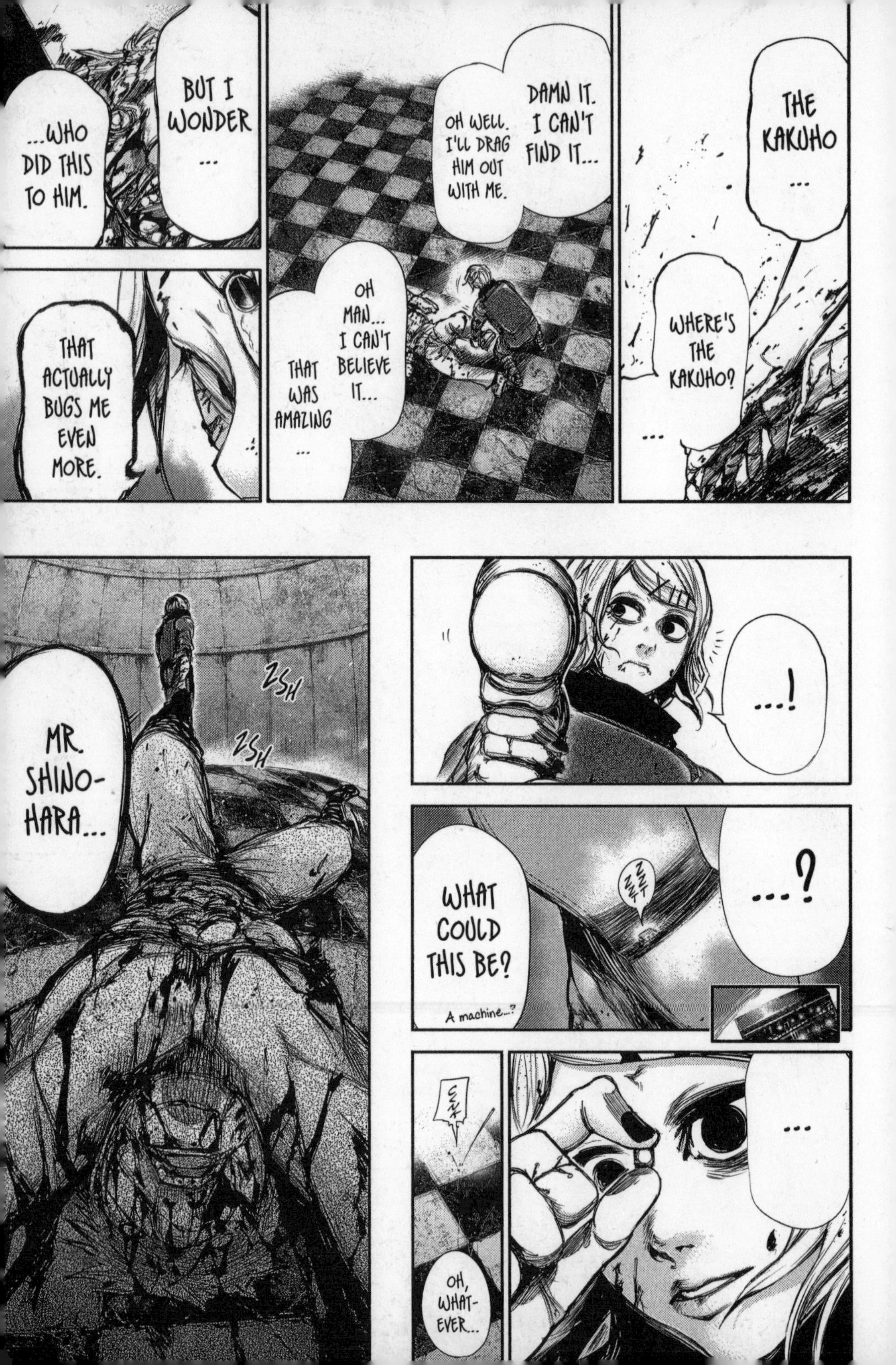
THE KAKUHO ...
WHERE'S THE KAKUHO?
...
DAMN IT. I CAN'T FIND IT...
OH WELL. I'LL DRAG HIM OUT WITH ME.
OH MAN... I CAN'T BELIEVE IT...
THAT WAS AMAZING ...
BUT I WONDER ...
...WHO DID THIS TO HIM.
THAT ACTUALLY BUGS ME EVEN MORE.
...!
...?
WHAT COULD THIS BE?
A machine...?
...
OH, WHAT-EVER...
ZSH
ZSH
MR. SHINO-HARA...

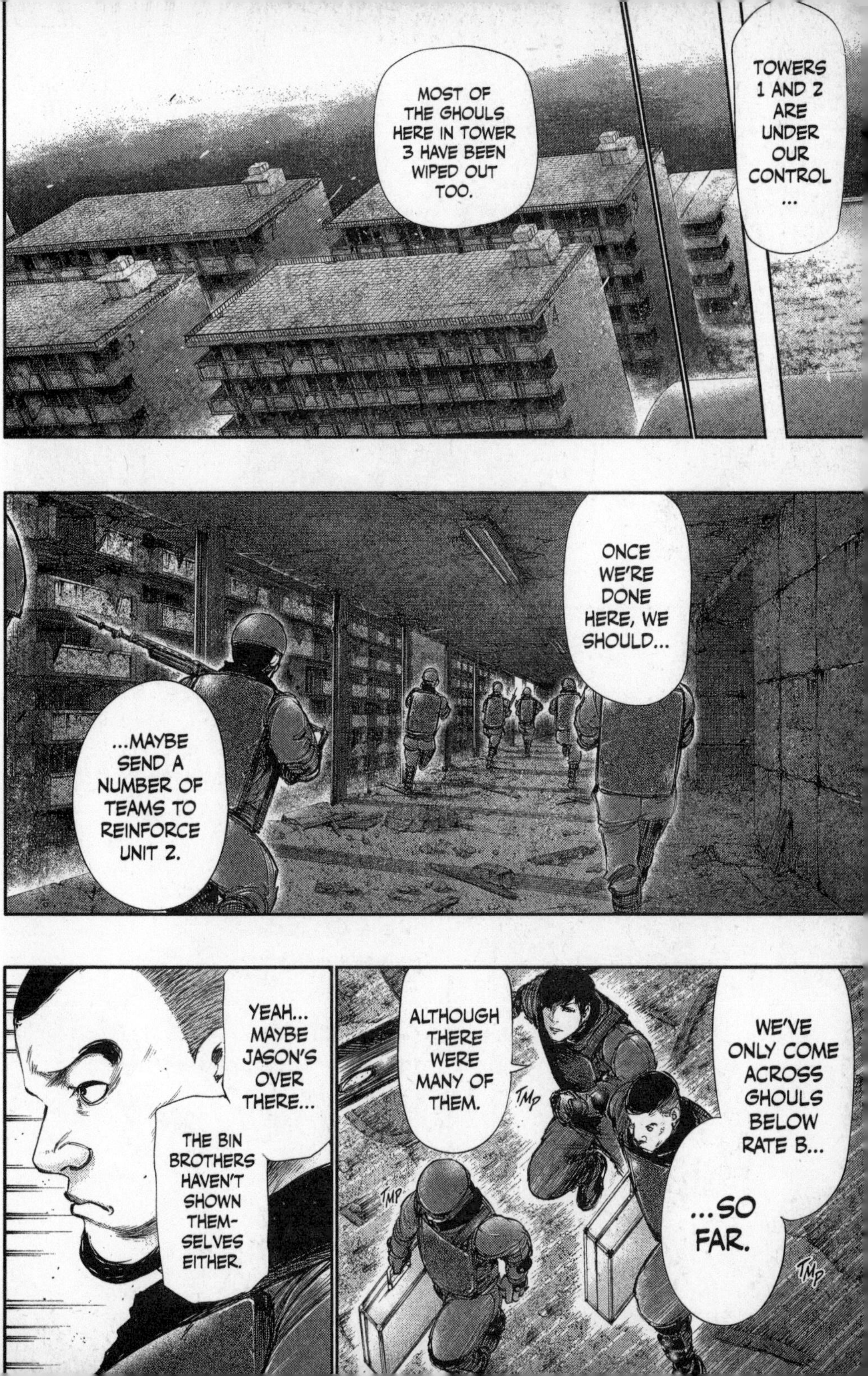
TOWERS 1 AND 2 ARE UNDER OUR CONTROL ...
MOST OF THE GHOULS HERE IN TOWER 3 HAVE BEEN WIPED OUT TOO.
ONCE WE'RE DONE HERE, WE SHOULD...
...MAYBE SEND A NUMBER OF TEAMS TO REINFORCE UNIT 2.
WE'VE ONLY COME ACROSS GHOULS BELOW RATE B...
...SO FAR.
TMP
ALTHOUGH THERE WERE MANY OF THEM.
TMP
TMP
YEAH... MAYBE JASON'S OVER THERE...
THE BIN BROTHERS HAVEN'T SHOWN THEM-SELVES EITHER.

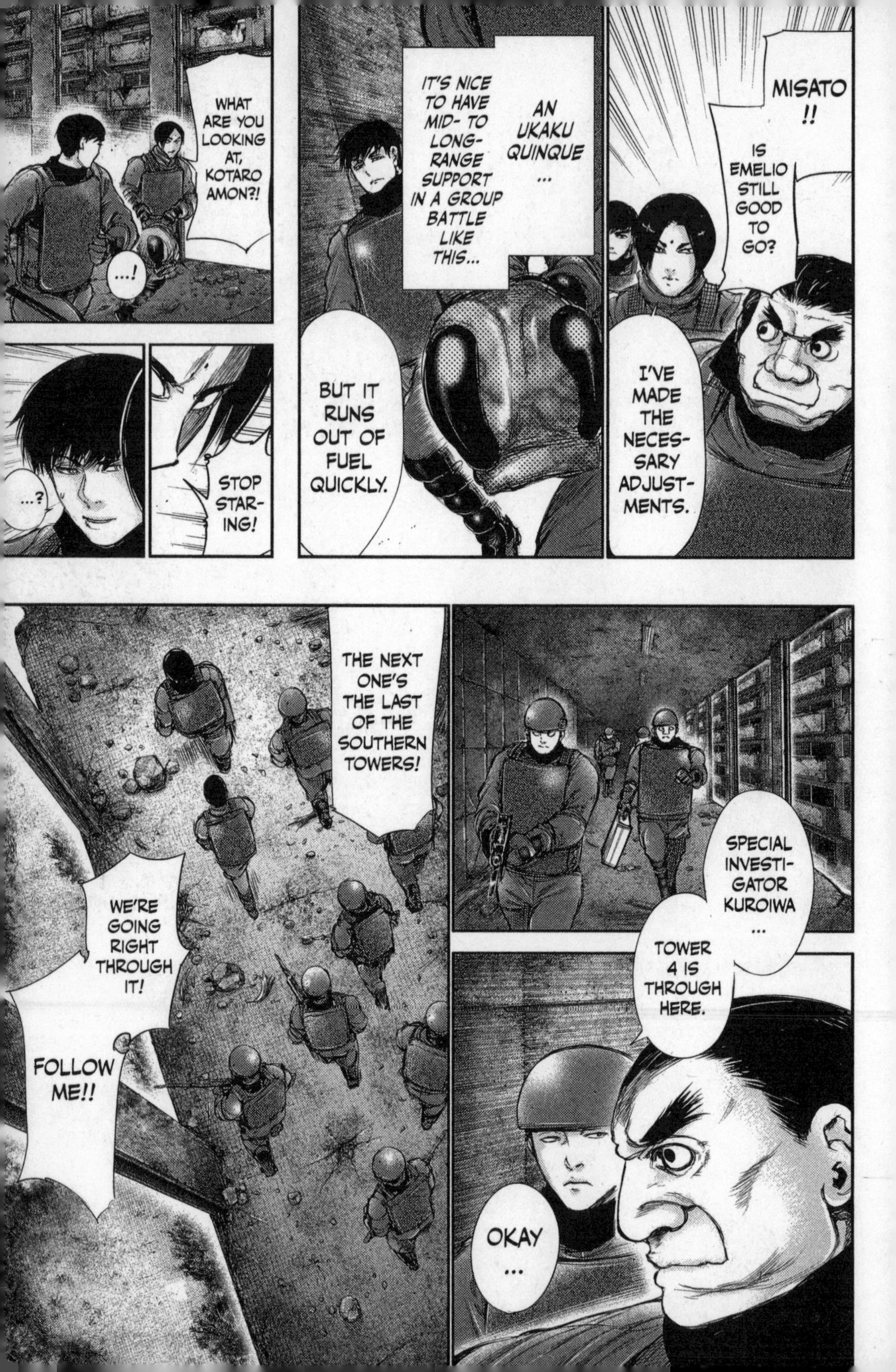
MISATO !!
IS EMELIO STILL GOOD TO GO?
I'VE MADE THE NECESSARY ADJUSTMENTS.
AN UKAKU QUINQUE ...
IT'S NICE TO HAVE MID- TO LONG-RANGE SUPPORT IN A GROUP BATTLE LIKE THIS...
BUT IT RUNS OUT OF FUEL QUICKLY.
WHAT ARE YOU LOOKING AT, KOTARO AMON?!
...!
STOP STARING!
...?
SPECIAL INVESTIGATOR KUROIWA ...
TOWER 4 IS THROUGH HERE.
OKAY ...
THE NEXT ONE'S THE LAST OF THE SOUTHERN TOWERS!
WE'RE GOING RIGHT THROUGH IT!
FOLLOW ME!!

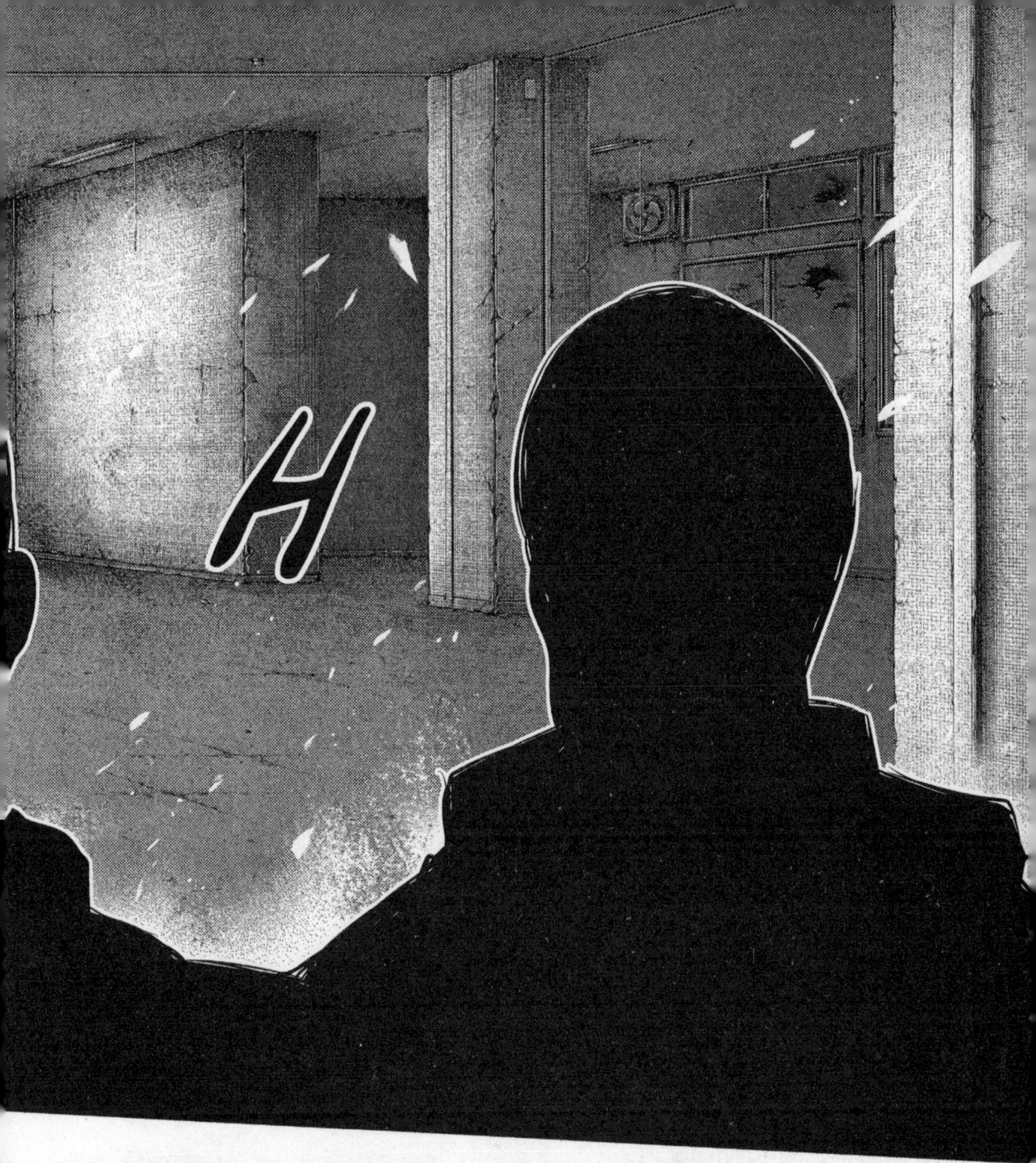
H
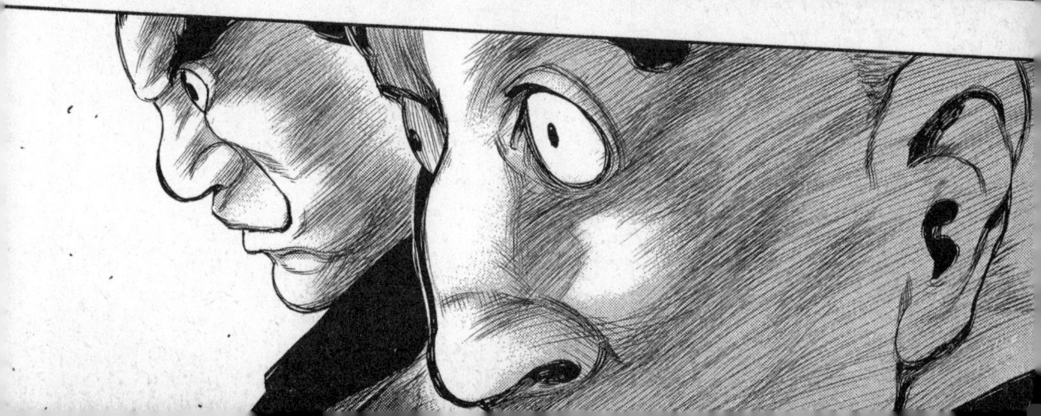

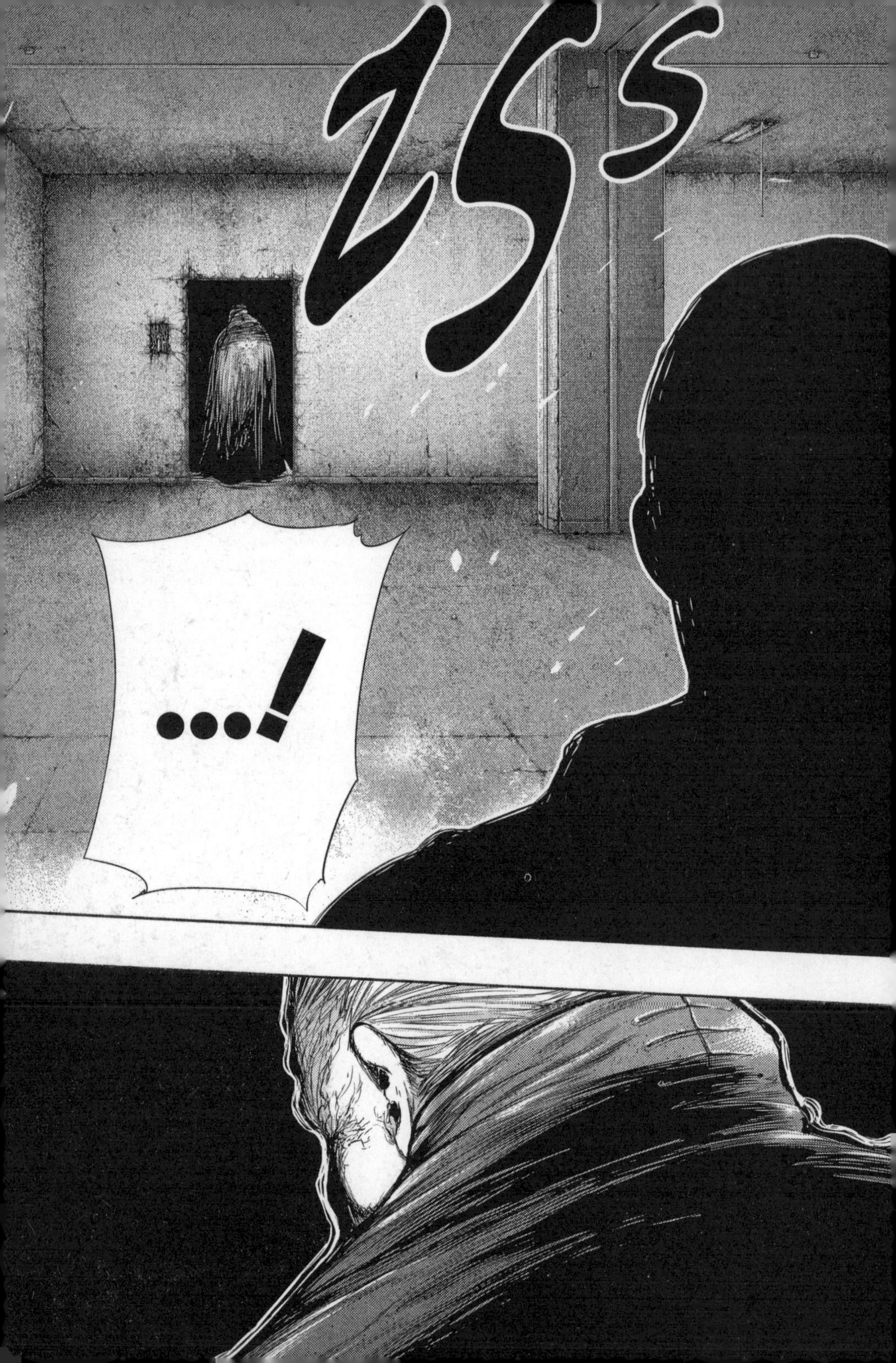
ZSS
...!

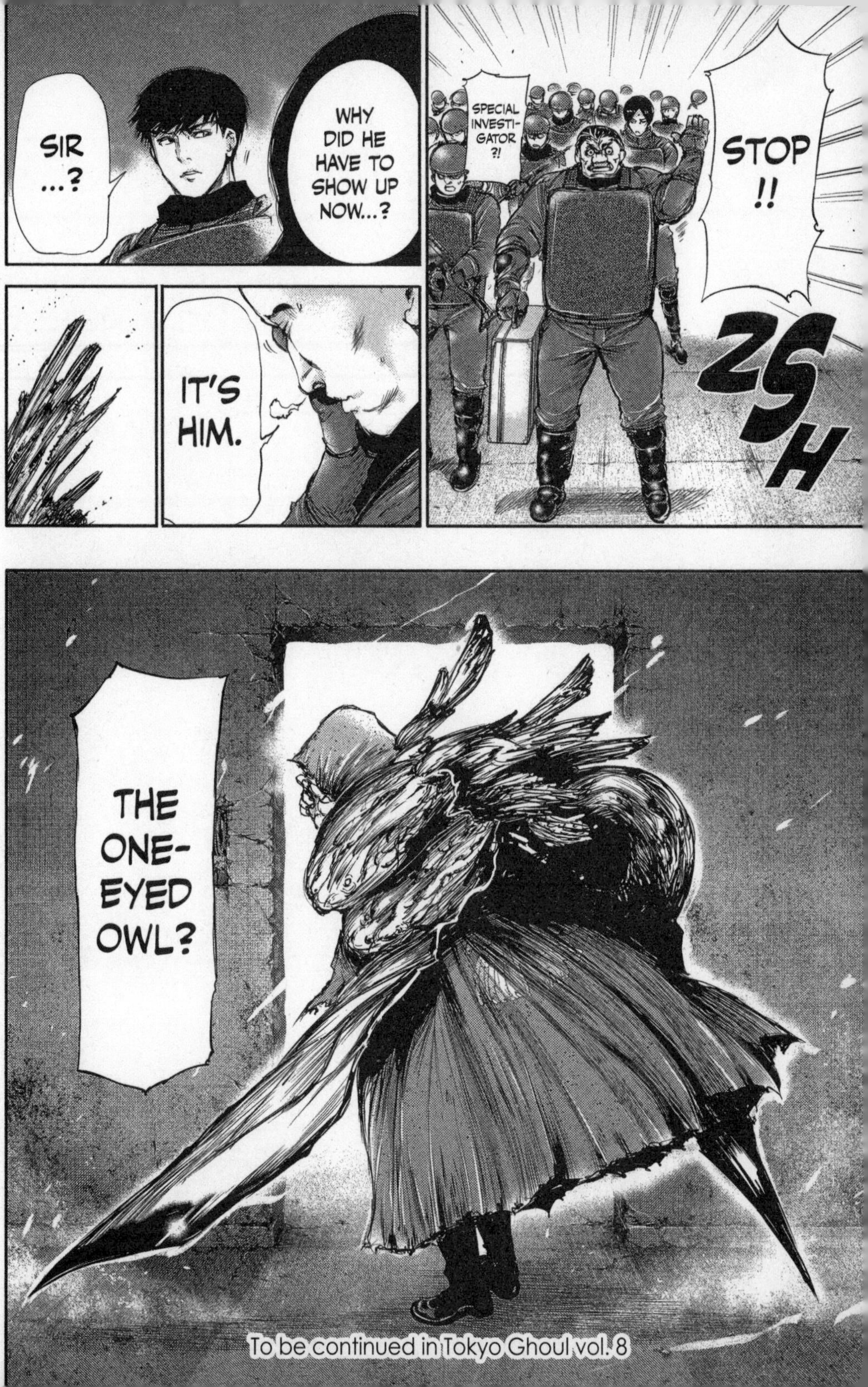
STOP!!
SPECIAL INVESTI-GATOR?!
ZSH
WHY DID HE HAVE TO SHOW UP NOW...?
SIR...?
IT'S HIM.
THE ONE-EYED OWL?
To be continued in Tokyo Ghoul vol. 8

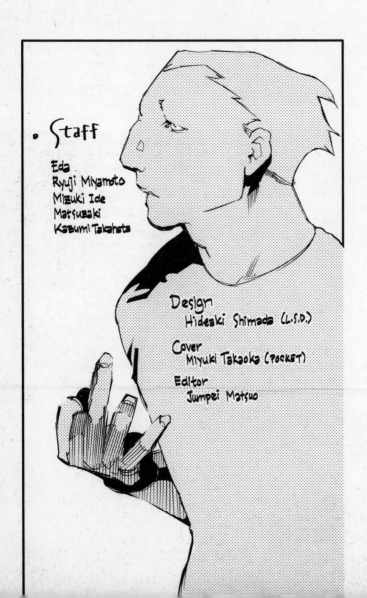

° Staff

Eda
Ryuji Miyamoto
Mizuki Ide
Matsuzaki
Kazumi Takahata

Design
Hideaki Shimada (L.S.D.)

Cover
Miyuki Takaoka (POCKET)

Editor
Jumpei Matsuo

Stay at Home Ghoul

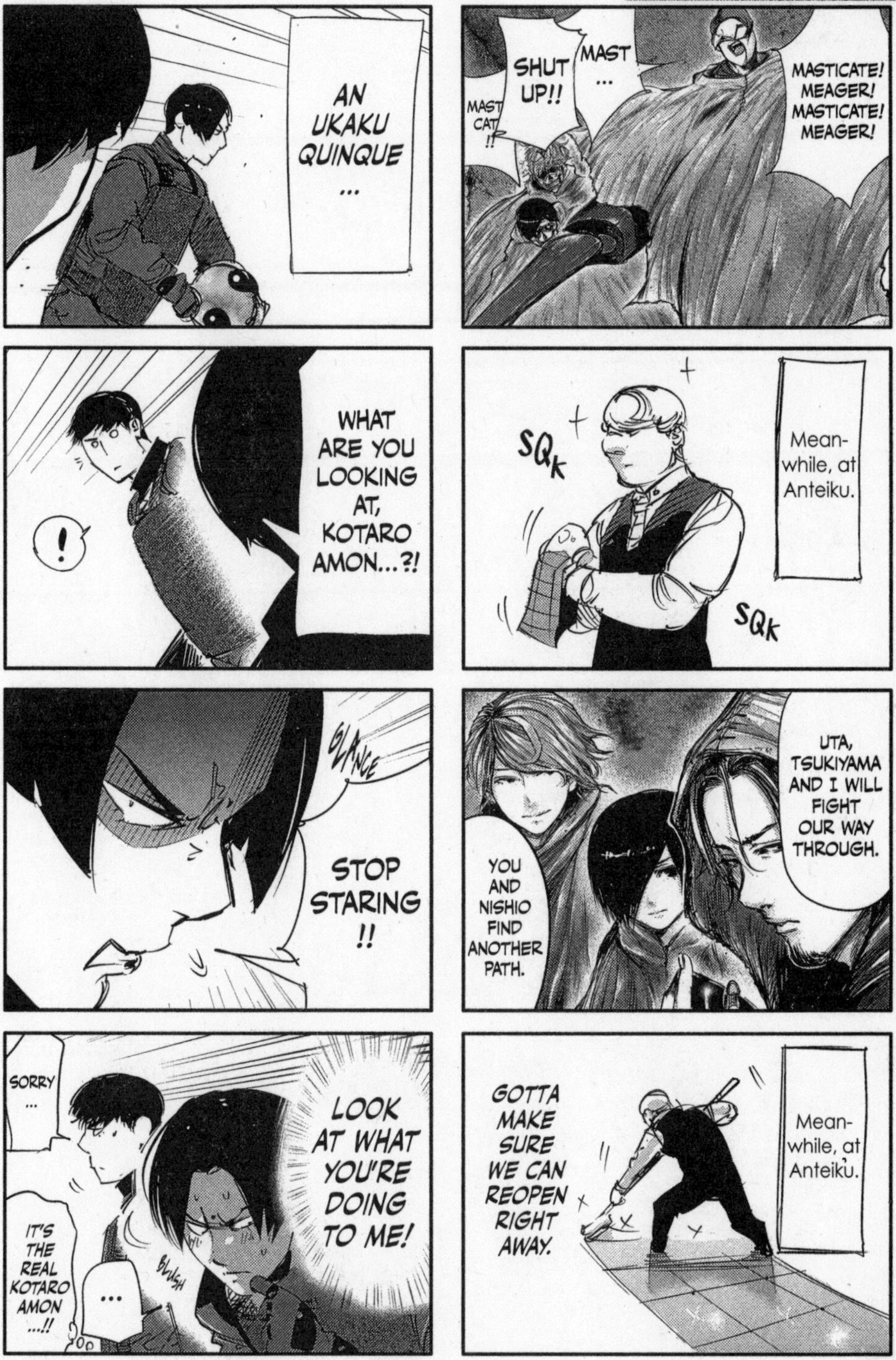

MASTICATE! MEAGER! MASTICATE! MEAGER!
MAST...
SHUT UP!!
MAST CAT!!
Meanwhile, at Anteiku.
SQK
SQK
UTA, TSUKIYAMA AND I WILL FIGHT OUR WAY THROUGH.
YOU AND NISHIO FIND ANOTHER PATH.
Meanwhile, at Anteiku.
GOTTA MAKE SURE WE CAN REOPEN RIGHT AWAY.
AN UKAKU QUINQUE...
WHAT ARE YOU LOOKING AT, KOTARO AMON...?!
!
GLANCE
STOP STARING!!
LOOK AT WHAT YOU'RE DOING TO ME!
SORRY...
BLUSH
...
IT'S THE REAL KOTARO AMON...!!

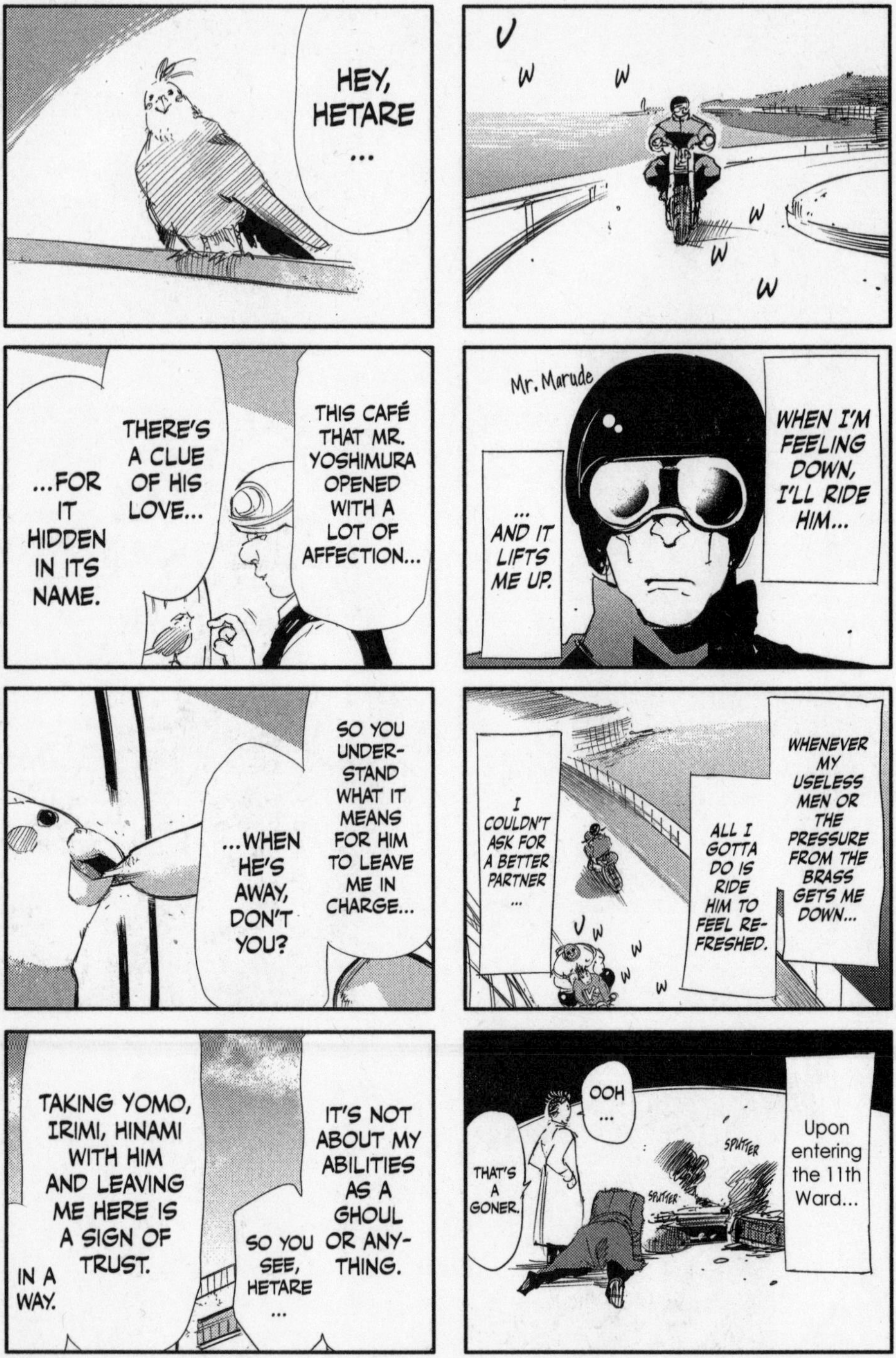
V W W W W W
HEY, HETARE ...
Mr. Marude
WHEN I'M FEELING DOWN, I'LL RIDE HIM...
... AND IT LIFTS ME UP.
THIS CAFÉ THAT MR. YOSHIMURA OPENED WITH A LOT OF AFFECTION...
THERE'S A CLUE OF HIS LOVE...
...FOR IT HIDDEN IN ITS NAME.
WHENEVER MY USELESS MEN OR THE PRESSURE FROM THE BRASS GETS ME DOWN...
ALL I GOTTA DO IS RIDE HIM TO FEEL RE-FRESHED.
I COULDN'T ASK FOR A BETTER PARTNER ...
V W W W W W
SO YOU UNDER-STAND WHAT IT MEANS FOR HIM TO LEAVE ME IN CHARGE...
...WHEN HE'S AWAY, DON'T YOU?
Upon entering the 11th Ward...
OOH ...
SPUTTER
SPUTTER
THAT'S A GONER.
IT'S NOT ABOUT MY ABILITIES AS A GHOUL OR ANY-THING.
SO YOU SEE, HETARE ...
TAKING YOMO, IRIMI, HINAMI WITH HIM AND LEAVING ME HERE IS A SIGN OF TRUST.
IN A WAY.

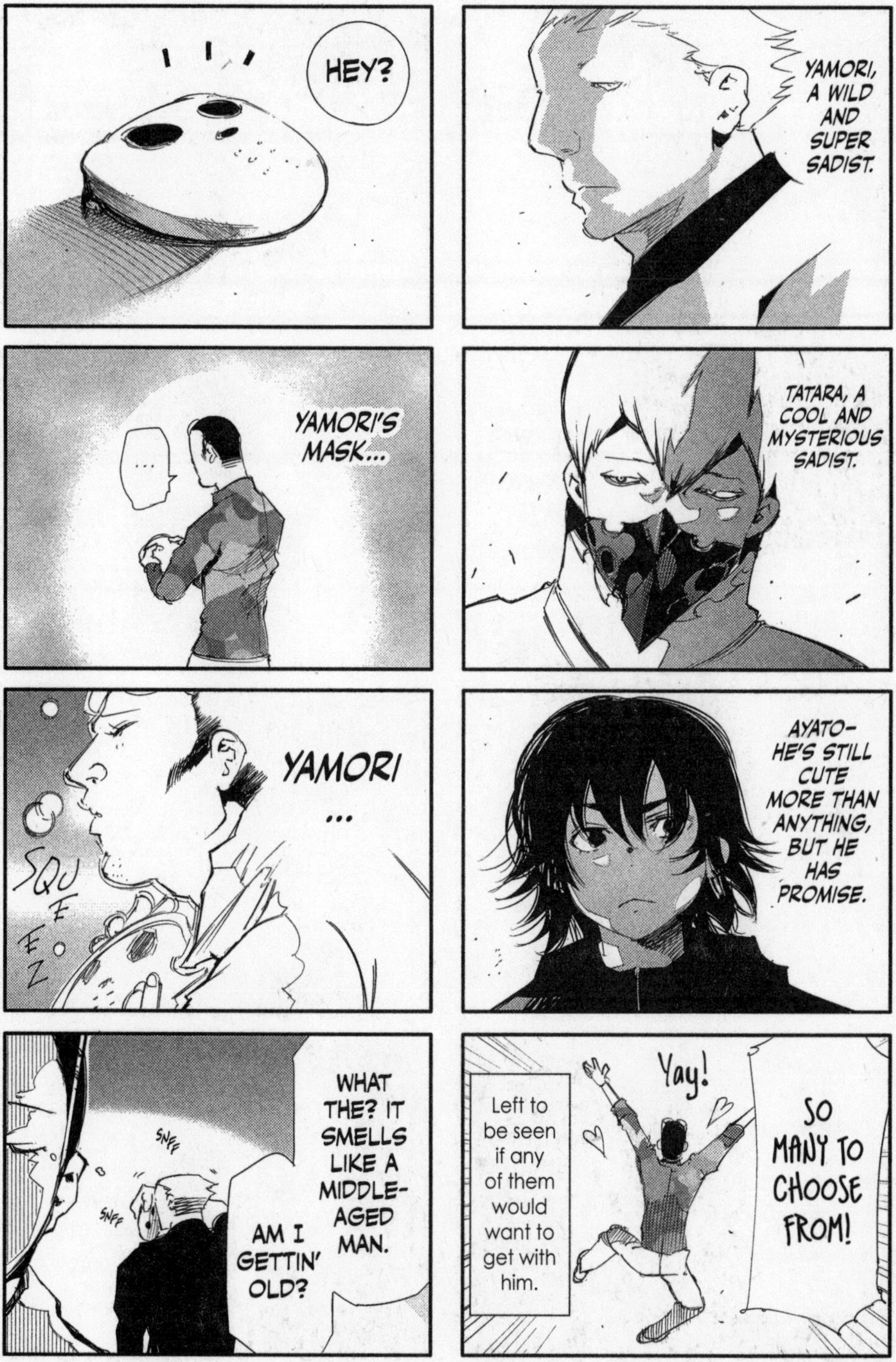
YAMORI, A WILD AND SUPER SADIST.
HEY?
TATARA, A COOL AND MYSTERIOUS SADIST.
YAMORI'S MASK...
...
AYATO-HE'S STILL CUTE MORE THAN ANYTHING, BUT HE HAS PROMISE.
YAMORI ...
SQUEEZE
SO MANY TO CHOOSE FROM!
Yay!
Left to be seen if any of them would want to get with him.
WHAT THE? IT SMELLS LIKE A MIDDLE-AGED MAN.
SNFF
SNFF
AM I GETTIN' OLD?

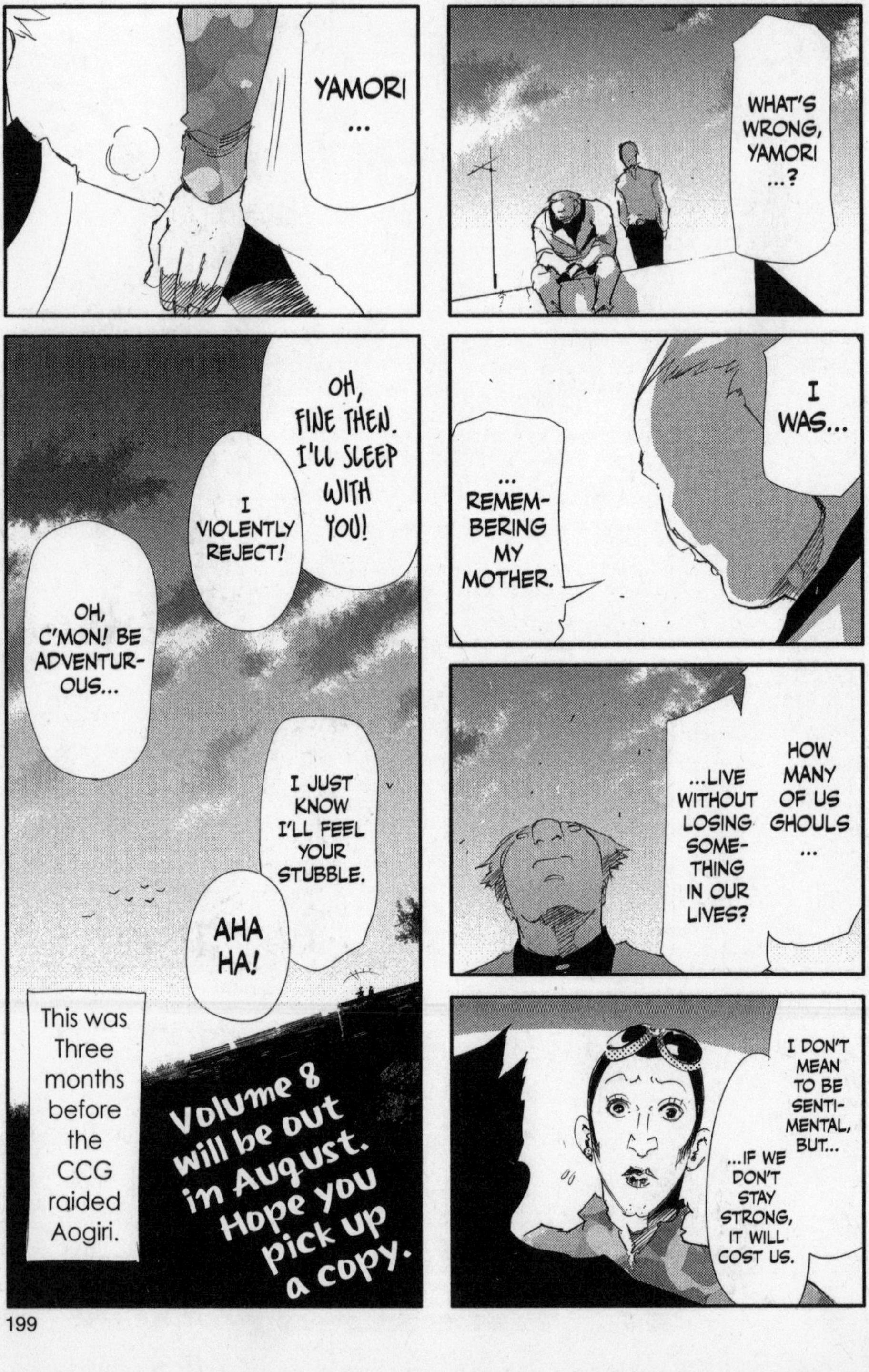
WHAT'S WRONG, YAMORI ...?
YAMORI ...
I WAS...
... REMEMBERING MY MOTHER.
HOW MANY OF US GHOULS ...
...LIVE WITHOUT LOSING SOMETHING IN OUR LIVES?
I DON'T MEAN TO BE SENTIMENTAL, BUT...
...IF WE DON'T STAY STRONG, IT WILL COST US.
OH, FINE THEN. I'LL SLEEP WITH YOU!
I VIOLENTLY REJECT!
OH, C'MON! BE ADVENTUROUS...
I JUST KNOW I'LL FEEL YOUR STUBBLE.
AHA HA!
This was Three months before the CCG raided Aogiri.
Volume 8 will be out in August. Hope you pick up a copy.

TOKYO GHOUL

THIS IS THE LAST PAGE

TOKYO GHOUL READS RIGHT TO LEFT

TOKYO GHOUL
東京喰種

VOLUME 7
VIZ Signature Edition

Story and art by
SUI ISHIDA

First published in Japan in 2011 by SHUEISHA Inc., Tokyo.
English translation rights arranged by SHUEISHA Inc.

TRANSLATION. Joe Yamazaki

TOUCH-UP ART AND LETTERING. Vanessa Satone

DESIGN. Fawn Lau

EDITOR. Joel Enos

Printed in the U.S.A.

Published by VIZ Media, LLC
P.O. Box 77010
San Francisco, CA 94107

10 9 8 7 6 5 4 3 2 1
First printing, June 2016

VIZ media
www.viz.com

VIZ SIGNATURE